SECOND EDITION

Multicultural Counseling in Schools

A Practical Handbook

Paul B. Pedersen
Professor Emeritus, Syracuse University
Visiting Professor, University of Hawaii

John C. Carey
Associate Professor of School Counseling,
University of Massachusetts, Amherst

Boston   New York   San Francisco
Mexico City   Montreal   Toronto   London   Madrid   Munich   Paris
Hong Kong   Singapore   Tokyo   Cape Town   Sydney

Executive Editor: *Virginia Lanigan*
Series Editorial Assistant: *Erin Liedel*
Marketing Manager: *Taryn Wahlquist*
Production Editor: *Annette Pagliaro*
Editorial Production: *Modern Graphics, Inc.*
Composition Buyer: *Linda Cox*
Manufacturing Buyer: *JoAnne Sweeney*
Cover Administrator: *Kristina Mose-Libon*
Electronic Composition: *Modern Graphics, Inc.*

Between the time Website information is gathered and then published, it is not unusual for some sites to have closed. Also, the transcription of URLs can result in unintended typographical errors. The publisher would appreciate notification where these errors occur so that they may be corrected in subsequent editions.

Library of Congress Cataloging-in-Publication Data

Multicultural counseling in schools: a practical handbook / [edited by] Paul Pedersen and John Carey.—2nd ed.
    p.   cm.
  Includes bibliographical references (p.) and index.
  ISBN 0-205-32197-6 (alk. paper)
    1. Educational counseling—United States. 2. Multiculturalism. 3. Minority students—Counseling of—United States. I. Pedersen, Paul, 1936– II. Carey, John C.

LB1027.5 M75 2003
370.117—dc21

2001056197

Printed in the United States of America

10 9 8 7 6 5 4 3 2 1   07 06 05 04 03 02

TABLE OF CONTENTS

PREFACE

In the ten years since the publication of the first edition of *Multicultural Counseling in Schools*, the landscape of public education has changed dramatically catalyzing the on-going changes we now see in the profession and practice of school counseling. Public acknowledgment of the failure of public education systems to adequately serve all students has generalized to a public distrust of all public educational systems. This distrust has led to the imposition of external accountability measures by state legislators in an attempt to drive public education reform through state standards and legislated consequences. This distrust has also led to efforts to privatize K–12 education under the assumption that competition between schools will result in school improvement.

School counseling has been seen as a villain—more concerned with children feeling good about themselves than actually achieving in school. Increasingly, multi-cultural education has been seen as a negative force potentially undermining academic ___ ___ diverting public education from the transmission of American myths, ___ ___tates have passed or are considering leg-___ ___t in brief transitional formats) because of ___ ___imited English proficient children to lan-

___ ___n evident that the academic achievement ___ ___ildren has worsened and that the societal ___ ___e of underfunded, inner-city schools has ___ ___t rates soar, the casualties of the War on ___ ___e, lives are lost, and the flame of hope is

___ ___ulticultural Counseling in Schools* at a time ___ ___hat the problems with public education ___ ___ngual education, or school counselors' ___ ___er, we believe that these problems result ___ ___ nation's inability to come to grips with ___ ___lity to commit to the types and levels of ___ ___nd public education that will "level the playing field.

This second edition documents the tremendous change and improvement that is evident in the theory and practice of multicultural school counseling. Consistent with the new directions of the American School Counselor Association and the pioneering work of the Education Trust, this second edition reflects cutting-edge thinking about the proper role and function of school counselors in a pluralistic society. Out of criticism and adversity, the profession of school counseling is developing a stronger commitment to promoting the academic achievement and psychosocial development of all children. *Multicultural Counseling in Schools* presents many of the tools that are needed for effective practice.

Multicultural Counseling in Schools: Second Edition represents the ideas of multicultural counseling in a variety of other contexts as they relate to the school situation.
There are probably more counselors being trained to work in school settings than in
any other particular social context. However, there are fewer than a handful of books
that focus on the very specialized multicultural problems that counselors face in
school settings. This second edition attempts to meet the special needs of counselors
being trained to work in K–12 settings among our increasingly multicultural schools.
We would like to thank the following reviewers of the text: Christine Yeh, Teachers
College, Columbia University and Connie M. Kane, California State University,
Stanislaus.

To accomplish this goal, MCS2 has added new chapters and refined the focus of
previous chapters to create an even more practical resource book for school counselors. These chapters were guided by specific considerations:

1. The level of writing for each chapter is appropriate for advanced undergraduate
   students as well as graduate students preparing for a career in school counseling.
2. Each chapter has a special and separate focus highlighting one of the major cultural issues confronting school counselors.
3. Each chapter addresses the practical applications of multicultural theory and
   practice.
4. Each chapter begins with a Primary Objective and several Secondary Objectives.

The chapter authors were given a list of general "Alerts" to address in
their chapters: (1) cross-references with other chapters where appropriate; (2) case
examples, where possible, to give a practical application to otherwise abstract theories and principles; (3) an emphasis throughout on practical and applied skills that
can be used in schools; (4) demonstration of how school counseling is both similar
to and different from conventional individual and group counseling; (5) the functions of "organizational culture" in schools along with other cultural examples;
(6) the effect of developmental age levels for school-age youth; (7) specific applications of different ethnic minority groups; (8) an update on the violence prevention
and intervention, culture shock/adjustment, linguistic diversity, immigration, eco-
logical/systemic perspectives of schools, broader perspectives of identity, cultural
diversity of students, group counseling for diverse youth and development of counselor self-awareness; (9) writing in a style that is less abstract and more applied; and
(10) inclusion of up-to-date statistical data where available.

FOREWORD

In the aftermath of the September 11, 2001 terrorist attacks on the World Trade Center in New York City and the Pentagon in Washington, D.C., our nation has been stunned and shocked by the magnitude of the horrific events. We have naturally reacted angrily against our tormentors and are motivated to bring the culprits to justice. The threat to our nation's way of life also has led to an increase in patriotism. Our patriotic fervor has resulted in many symbolic acts that express our love of country: multiple displays of the U.S. flag, increased vigor in saying the pledge-of-allegiance, new meaning attached to the singing of the national anthem, and the recording and playing of patriotic songs by popular artists. While the spirit of patriotism can pull us together as a nation, give us feelings of comfort and pride, and reaffirm cherished democratic ideals, it also can be misinterpreted in an ethnocentric and restrictive manner. In some educational circles, for example, there has been a suggestion that "multiculturalism" is unpatriotic and that the study of other cultural groups in America is unAmerican. Those of us who have been in the forefront of civil rights, who dissent or protest against unfair practices in our society, especially those dealing with racial/cultural differences, now encounter increased accusations of being disloyal.

Nothing could be further from the truth. I submit that "multiculturalism," instead of proving to be a hindrance or burden to mutual understanding, is, rather, an answer to society's polarizing perceptions of religious, racial, ethnic, and sociodemographic differences. While the terrorists should be condemned and brought to justice, we must not allow our urge for revenge prevent us from national and deliberative actions that remain true to our democratic values and ideals. To diminish the values of inclusion, respect, fairness, and protection of the innocent for the sake of expediency is a dangerous path for us to take. Only through multicultural education, for example, can we make it clear that there is a major difference between Muslims and the terrorists, and that Islam does not condone the taking of innocent lives. Our Muslim brothers and sisters cannot become scapegoats for our nation's miseducation, just as events in World War II did to our many law-abiding Japanese American citizens.

There has never been a more urgent period in our history for a text like *Multicultural Counseling in Schools: A Practical Handbook* edited by Paul B. Pedersen and John C. Carey. First, the text reaffirms the social reality that we are indeed a multicultural, multiracial, and multilingual society. All the contributing authors seem to echo a common theme: Existence in a pluralistic society requires mutual understanding, respect for differences, sharing common goals, and allowing for equal access and opportunity for all groups in society. Second, the authors all stress that much of the racial and cultural problems of our society do not reside with multiculturalism, but in racism, classism, and the uneven power relations in our society and schools. As such, counseling in the schools is seen in relationship to families, communities, and the wider society. Third, but of preeminent importance, is that the hope for our future lies in our children, and the nature of our eduational system. It is probably fair to say that our school systems have done a poor job in educating our students to understand issues of diversity, cultural differences, bias, and prejudice because the curriculum and services are monocultural and ethnocentric in nature. Pedersen and Carey obviously believe that any educational system that does not help students develop the awareness, knowledge, and skills to function in a pluralistic society is derelict in its educational responsibilities. Multicultural education and multicultural counseling in the schools is not only good for our nation but also absolutely essential if we are to survive and prosper.

Multicultural Counseling in Schools: A Practical Handbook is among the best in the field—not only because of the points raised in the last paragraph, but also because of its inherent strengths:

- The editors have brought together some of the most renowned authors in the field whose knowledge and expertise are obvious in the chapters they have written. All are multicultural experts whose perspective of school counseling extends beyond the counselor's office or even the classroom. Because of this orientation, the chapters are not simply a collection of isolated contributions, but flow from one to the other, are conceptually integrated, and read with a consistent point of view. The four parts of this second edition start from a conceptual/developmental framework to greater specificity of issues.

- The text is written in a highly readable manner. While theory and research are presented, it actively translates multicultural and counseling issues into concrete practical applications. Case studies are used generously to give human richness to the concepts, chapters list specific objectives for readers, and "thinking questions" aid readers to organize the chapters and reflect upon what they have learned. Readers will walk away from this text with specific counseling suggestions and guidelines to work with a culturally diverse student population.

- There are an increasing number of texts devoted to the topic of multicultural counseling and therapy. There are, however, a paucity of relevant publications on multicultural school counseling. In the past, educators have had to rely on general multicultural texts, in which the subject matter has been more appropriate to clinical settings. Schools were shortchanged as a distinct and different setting with their own unique issues and problems. MCS2 recognizes the distinctiveness of counseling in a school setting and the unique counseling issues and interventions that arise from working in an educational environment. Strangely enough, many of the chapters advocate psychoeducational approaches that are increasingly found to be effective in other nonschool environments as well. It appears, therefore, that our counseling practices can be enriched by an understanding of multicultural school counseling. This text definitely fills a void in the professional literature.

- This is a state-of-the-art text. While integrating a body of literature that has withstood the test of time, it also presents the most recent up-to-date data, statistics, findings, and conceptual models in multicultural school counseling. The depth and breadth of the individual chapters are refreshingly rich. Readers will find the text a valuable resource in building their general fund of knowledge about multicultural school counseling and will walk away with many helpful ideas to develop or improve their school counseling skills.

Derald Wing Sue, Ph.D.
Professor of Psychology and Education
Teachers College, Columbia University

PART ONE

Developmental and Conceptual Issues

1. *School Counselor Involvement in Culture-Centered Education Reform* (Colbert and Magouirk Colbert)
2. *Cultural Identity Groups and Cultural Maps: Meaning Making in Groups* (Washington et al.)
3. *Racial Identity in the Social Environment* (Helms)

The first three chapters describe the developmental and conceptual context of multicultural counseling in schools. Our assumption is that a multicultural perspective is not exotic but is rather generic to all K–12 school systems. When culture is defined broadly to include ethnographic, demographic, status, and affiliation variables, each school classroom is multicultural in composition. To ignore the diversity of cultures in a school is to interpret behaviors outside the cultural context where those behaviors were learned and are being displayed. Accurate assessment, meaningful understanding, and appropriate intervention requires the school counselor to make culture central rather than marginal.

Each of the three chapters in Part One provides a different developmental and conceptual perspective. The first important theme is that of "developmental change." In Chapter 1 Colbert and Magouirk Colbert provide a role-specific framework for making cultural issues central to the process of educational reform through nontraditional approaches to school counseling. The school counselor role is to lead toward positive change through the school community at the local and district levels. The authors present this perspective through a participant-observer field study involving cooperation between the counselors, teachers, administrators, and others in the school community. The focus is developmental change in the "student accountability movement" and in the "development of standards for professional preparation."

The second important theme is "identity" presented in Chapter 2. Washington et al., describe how Cultural Identity Groups (CIGs) can help students find out who they are more accurately. The making of cultural maps is described as one technique whereby the students draw meaningful symbols and tell stories to explain their identity in their own multicultural context. Guidelines are suggested with which counselors can match their interventions with the appropriate stage of cultural identity development for each student, and those guidelines are illustrated by case examples. The implications for self-esteem and consequences for positive growth are predicted. Chapter 3 by Helms develops the notion of racial identity development in schools by providing a framework with which to design and evaluate interventions already in place that shape the educational climate both inside and outside the classroom.

1

School Counselor Involvement in Culture-Centered Education Reform

ROBERT D. COLBERT
University of Connecticut

MARGE MAGOUIRK COLBERT
University of Massachusetts, Amherst

OBJECTIVES

1. To provide a framework for exploring school counselor role(s) in culture-centered education reform
2. To increase understanding of a nontraditional foundation for the redesign of school counseling programs in the context of education reform
3. To provide school counselors with direction for leadership roles that promote and create culture-centered school and district-level change
4. To offer direction for future research, school counselor education, and school counselor practice

Introduction

A partnership with one school district has provided us with the opportunity to participate in education reform and develop a school counselor education and practice model grounded in reality. In this chapter we present a detailed discussion of an ongoing, participant observation field study which involves a collaboration between counselor educators, school administrators, school counselors, and teachers aimed at developing and implementing a school change initiative. The study has implications for further investigation and development of the model that provides a framework for school counselor educators and school counselors who play a collaborative, leadership role in culture-centered education reform.

Two major developments in education have converged to create a new cultural context for school counselors in today's public schools. The first, the student accountability movement, is evidenced in enormous pressure from the public and policymakers for educators to improve student academic achievement levels. This shift attempts to target all students, inclusively, to ensure the extension of educational advantages which have traditionally been available primarily to middle- and upper-class white students. Education reform initiatives such as the development of higher standards for all students, increased focus on assessment of learning, and the identification of strategies to address persistent academic disparities between different cultural and economic groups of students continue to emerge across the nation.

The second, and closely related development, has been an intensified focus on educator preparation and practitioner quality that has similarly resulted in the development of standards for professional preparation programs for educators and increased attention on assessment for accountability. In this new context, school counseling students will be expected to provide evidence of having developed proficiency in the standards set by the profession while practicing school counselors will strive to effectively demonstrate that they can indeed carry out their roles in an effective manner. Everyone involved with school counseling and change must work to ensure that education reform is truly culture-centered and that changes are made with an all-inclusive multicultural focus.

The American School Counselor Association (ASCA) has responded to these developments by articulating National Standards for School Counseling Programs (Campbell & Dahir, 1997). The ASCA "encourages school counselors to become catalysts for school change, and to assume or accept a leadership role in education reform" (p. 3). In order to do so, the ASCA recommends that school counselors: (1) coordinate comprehensive developmental guidance programs for all students; (2) advocate for all students navigating through the school system in preparation for post–high school options; (3) call attention to those factors in the school system that enhance or hinder student academic success for every student; (4) utilize achievement data to identify patterns and behaviors that facilitate academic success for all students; and (5) act as leaders to identify the issues that need to change in the school and help develop change strategies for the benefit of each and every student.

Although these recommendations are a beginning point, school counselors are left with questions of how to carry out these changes. What does it mean to coordinate school counseling programs in contrast to being the sole deliverer of programs? What schooling factors are related to and facilitate student success? How does a school counselor draw attention to such factors? What does the role of change leadership entail?

Similarly, counselor educators are faced with the task of identifying what school counseling students need to know in order to carry out these roles. What changes will occur in school counselor education programs? What will school counselor education in the 21st century consist of? To answer these questions, counselor educators must create and implement new, all-inclusive multicultural counselor education and practice frameworks that direct school counselors to the factors and processes associated with culture-centered education reform. In order to do so, they must consider what school counselors will do to function effectively in this new context.

New Realities for School Counselors

The growing pressure on school counselors requires a rethinking of current job descriptions, the school counselor's role, and, in turn, school counselor education. There are three major transitions inherent in the new school counselor roles. First, they require a shift from focus on service delivery to individual students, their families, or a small subgroup of students, to a focus on whole-school concerns. Traditional school counselor education models have largely encouraged the development of skills and knowledge related to individual student and small-group intervention. Many experts agree however, that when the counseling focus is on the individual student, the tendency is to identify the problem as being solely in the student (Ivey, 1986; Ivey, Ivey, & Simek-Morgan, 1993; Pederson & Ivey, 1994; Sue & Sue, 1990) rather than in the schooling process. School counselors who act as advocates, organizational change facilitators, and consultants focus on deep-level issues such as school organization, group dynamics, communication, and other factors within a school system that affect student learning (Comer, Haynes, Hamilton-Lee, Boger, & Pollack, 1986; House & Martin, 1998). There are indications that such alternatives, broadly defined in more inclusive roles, may prove to be more effective (Atkinson, Thompson, & Grant, 1993; Sue, 1995; Sue & Sue, 1990).

A second major transition requires that school counselors shift from a primarily responsive service orientation to school counseling partnerships that are proactive and developmental. Although the literature has for years recommended that school counseling programs focus on prevention (Baker, 1996; Borders & Drury, 1992; Gerler, 1992; Paisley & Borders, 1995), current research continues to document that school counselors spend the majority of their time conducting responsive services (Whiston & Sexton, 1998). Increasingly, research documents the influential role of sociocultural factors in creating many student problems (Carey, Boscardin, & Fontes, 1994; Nieto, 1993; Pianta & Walsh, 1996; Weiner, 1993; Wheelock, 1993; Whelage, 1990). School counselors frequently find themselves in a position of working with students whose "problems" reflect school practices and policies that work to undermine student motivation (House & Martin, 1998) and engagement, alienate parents, and create barriers for community involvement (Rivera, 1988). Although working with troubled students is necessary, "our task will be an endless and losing venture unless the true sources of the problem (stereotypes, prejudice, discrimination, and oppression) are changed. Would it not make more sense to take a proactive and preventative approach by attacking the cultural and institutional basis of the problem?" (Sue, 1995, p. 476).

The research, paired with the reality of increasing diversity in schools, leaves little room for argument that school counselors refocus their energy to building proactive partnerships. Given that school counselors have been educated for more than two decades to develop and implement comprehensive developmental programs and focus primarily on responsive services, a shifting of attention within the context of today's schools will not be a simple matter.

A third transition which is required, is that school counselors move from working primarily as individuals, to focus on joint work in building professional communities. Individual work reflects norms that are often based on individualism (Sue & Sue, 1990), isolationism, and privatism (Lortie, 1975) which are no longer sufficient in today's schools. School counselors will work with others to facilitate the building of a school context that values collegiality, openness, and trust over counselor marginality and territoriality (Sue, 1995). Teamwork among school staff, community members, parents, and others is a constant factor that emerges in research findings of successful education reform changes, especially in schools that have high minority and low-income populations (Weber, 1971). School counseling experts highlight this transition in their recommendations that "the school counselor and school counseling program use a collaborative model as their foundation. Counselors do not work alone; all educators play a role in creating an environment which [sic] promotes the achievement of identified student goals and outcomes. The counselor facilitates communication and establishes linkages for the benefit of students. . . ." (Campbell & Dahir, 1997, p. 9).

The field is missing a mechanism and process that enables school counselors to make these transitions. The purpose of this chapter is to describe the qualitative inquiry study of a foundational counselor education and practice model that provides a theoretical grounding for the development of new school counselor roles. In the following subsections, the model is described, followed by a discussion of the collaborative implementation of the model in a school district that was implementing changes related to education reform. The chapter ends with implications for school counselor practice and education and recommendations for future research.

The Foundational Model

The schooling process provides a significant cultural context for understanding, describing, and explaining the complexities of school counselor roles in relationship to education reform, student development, and learning. Most traditional school counselor educators and researchers have emphasized academic learning and student development from the perspective of the child, the family, or the school. The discourse has largely been silent in terms of interactions, communication, and relationships among all participants in the schooling process. This is interesting in light of educational literature and research that continues to inform us that the educational reforms that produce the most significant change in student outcomes are those that are comprehensive and targeted at multiple factors (Holtzman, 1992; Pianta & Walsh, 1996; Schorr, Both, & Copple, 1991). While a multiple-factor model may be cumbersome to investigate, the complexity can facilitate the development of alternative conceptual models from which reform actions based in contemporary reality emerge (Pianta & Walsh, 1996). In reflecting upon the complex changes that must be made in school counseling, the notion of change process and levels of change is important. The next section describes the change-related underpinnings of the foundational model.

The Change Process

Pope's (1992) Multicultural Change Intervention Matrix (MCIM) provides a basis for conceptualizing change within individuals or groups of students, staff, parents, or others in a school community. The MCIM, adapted by the authors, rests on principles of organized systemic change and multicultural development in organizations, and consists of two dimensions, each with three targets for change (see Fig. 1.1).

Dimension One defines three potential change targets: individual, group, and school system. Dimension Two distinguishes between first-order change and second-order change. First-order change is defined as "change without change—or any change in a system that does not produce a change in the structure of the system" (Lyddon, 1990, p. 122). Change that occurs in the internal state of an individual, group, or institution, including change in a group's membership, without altering its basic structure, and that still maintains the coherence of the system is considered first-order change (Lyddon, 1990). This type of change assumes that innovations must fit within the individual, group, or school's current beliefs and operating principles and is the most common type of change that occurs in schools. Many experts have hypothesized that numerous research-based, powerful educational innovations have failed due to the fact that they were implemented as first-order changes.

Second-order change is "change of change—a type of change whose occurrence alters the fundamental structure of the system" (Lyddon, 1990, p. 122). When individuals, groups, and/or schools make changes that actually transform the structure and basic ways of operating, they have implemented second-order change. First-order changes may continue to occur, but they occur within a new structure.

As shown in Figure 1.1, the adapted MCIM identifies six ways to view and structure change efforts in a multicultural school context (Pope, 1992). Cell A change

Types of Change

Change Targets	1st-order Change	2nd-order Change
Individual	A. Knowledge or skill level with no attempt to change fundamental beliefs or perceptions.	B. Work with an individual with a focus on worldview or paradigm shifts.
Group	C. Change without change in norms goals of group.	D. Might involve complete reconceptualization and transformation of existing school counseling program.
School System	E. Involves programmatic interventions aimed at the school district or school building level but does not alter the underlying assumptions and propositions.	F. Requires addressing underlying structural issues such as values, goals, beliefs, and propositions which guide day-by-day operations in the district.

FIGURE 1.1   The Multicultural Change Intervention Matrix.

Source: Adapted from Pope, 1992.

efforts (first-order change, individual) typically "involve education at the awareness, knowledge or skill level" (Pope, 1992, p. 75) with no attempts to change fundamental beliefs or perceptions. Cell B change efforts (second-order change, individual) are characterized by work with an individual with a focus on worldview or paradigm shifts. These shifts go beyond the information sharing of Cell A and may be process oriented, challenging underlying assumptions. Cell C change efforts (first-order change, group) focus on group-level changes in composition, but not in group structure, norms, or goals. Cell D change efforts (second-order change, group) involve complete restructuring and transformation of the group (i.e., school counseling program), including new visions, norms, members, and goals. Cell E change efforts (first-order change, school district) involve programmatic interventions aimed at the school district or school building level that do not alter the underlying assumptions and propositions. Cell F change efforts (second-order change, school district) require addressing underlying structural issues such as values, goals, beliefs, and propositions which guide day-to-day operations in the district. These are specifically analyzed and connected to school change initiatives.

Although the cells of the adapted MCIM are presented independently, their relationship is characterized by fluidity and interconnectedness. One type of change is not necessarily better than another, they all must be incorporated into change efforts depending on the context and particular needs. The adapted MCIM helps clarify the complexities and provide direction in the school change process and school counselor role transitions. Additional direction comes from The Schooling Process Model presented in the following section which is predicated on a basic understanding of the change levels.

The Schooling Process Model

The Schooling Process Model is built on the assumption that education is a political subsystem with a constant interplay among external and internal factors that influence the classroom, student retention, and achievement (see Fig. 1.2).

External and Internal Schooling Process Factors.   As shown in Figure 1.2, external factors, which include legislative mandates, parent group demands, and the like, exert pressure on schools to teach competencies that will lead to graduation and future societal contribution. In most school districts, school boards/committees incorporate these external pressures into their administrative directives. The superintendent is then charged with the responsibility of ensuring that school board/committee wishes are communicated to building-level administrators who translate these into rules, roles, and operating procedures.

At the single-school level, the resources provided to meet the goals, a building administrator's interpretation of the district's desires, his/her creativity in integrating them into the school, and a host of unknowns influence teacher functioning and student outcome (Coleman & Collinge, 1991; Fuller, Wood, Rapport, & Dornbusch, 1982). The external factors are intertwined with internal schooling process

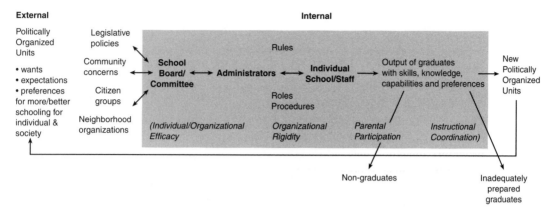

External

Politically
Organized
Units

• wants
• expectations
• preferences
for more/better
schooling for
individual &
society

Legislative
policies

Community
concerns

Citizen
groups

Neighborhood
organizations

Internal

Rules

**School
Board/
Committee** ←→ **Administrators** ←→ **Individual
School/Staff** → Output of graduates
with skills, knowledge,
capabilities and preferences

Roles
Procedures

*(Individual/Organizational
Efficacy*

*Organizational
Rigidity*

*Parental
Participation*

*Instructional
Coordination)*

New
Politically
Organized
Units

Non-graduates

Inadequately
prepared
graduates

FIGURE 1.2   Schooling as a political subsystem.

Adapted from "In the Web: Internal and external influences affecting school improvement," by P. Coleman and J. Collinge, 1991, *School Effectiveness and Improvement, 2 (4)*, p. 262–285.

factors that exist within individual school settings. Once the external factors are incorporated into the school system, they interact with and influence the internal factors and vice versa. This merging of the two types of factors results in the practices, procedures, and rules within the school district and buildings that ultimately affect the students.

Previous researchers have identified four factors that are related to student learning (Pollard, 1989), are significant in the schooling process, and are consistent with school counselor transitions. The identification and monitoring of the influences that these four factors have at all levels of change in a district is critical to the success of change efforts. The four factors, organizational and individual performance efficacy, organizational rigidity, parental participation, and instructional coordination require brief definitions.

Organizational Efficacy.   This term refers to the degree to which an organizational member feels efficacious in gaining valued outcomes by influencing another person at the same or different level of the organization. Organizational efficacy is intertwined with individual performance efficacy and attempts to change one can influence changes in the other (Fuller et al., 1982).

Individual Performance Efficacy.   This concept is reflected in one's sense of confidence toward achieving successful outcomes in day-to-day roles, as outlined in one's job description. The nature of the relationship between organizational and individual efficacy must be understood in order to clarify the many threats and facilitative forces that influence school change implementation efforts.

Researchers have identified two categories of mediating variables associated with organizational and individual performance efficacy within the context of complex change efforts such as education reform (Petty, Beadles, Lowery, Chapman, & Connell, 1995). Category one, structural differentiation and convergence, is concerned with how interdependent work roles exist between people at different organizational levels. The variables of role clarity, mandated tasks, shared vision, caring relationships, resource exchange, and relevancy make up this category. Category two, social evaluations and sanctions, includes soundly based evaluation, incentives, and influence in evaluation criteria, and is concerned with how much involvement staff have in determining evaluation criteria, fairness, and procedures (Fuller et al., 1982).

Parental Participation. This third factor refers to the participation of families/ guardians in developing and maintaining academic and related knowledge and competencies in concert with other members of the school community. Effective school, family, and community partnerships are focused on changing school culture so that more people, through their interactions with one another, can have a positive influence on student learning. School, family, and community interactions are manifested in six major ways: (1) parenting skills, understanding of child/adolescent development, home conditions for learning, and the school's understanding of its families; (2) communications from home to school, and from school to home about programs and student progress; (3) the organization, schedules, and use of volunteers at and for the school, and the opportunities and schedules for audiences at school for student events; (4) family involvement in learning activities at home, including homework, class work, curriculum-related interactions, and decisions; (5) family involvement in school decisions, committees, school-based management, advocacy, and other practices of participation; and (6) community collaborations and resources for students, the school, and families (Colbert, 1996; Epstein, 1992).

Organizational Rigidity.   The degree to which schools require rigid adherence to rules and regulations affects school change. Administrators convert external demands to standard rules and operating procedures (see Fig. 1.2), and subsequently communicate them to teachers. The manner of communication influences how they are perceived and implemented by teachers. Rule rigidity or flexibility is related to level and type of parental involvement which influences academic achievement (Hoover-Dempsey, Bassler, & Bissie, 1987). Parents volunteer more in rule-flexible schools than in rule-rigid schools and teachers report greater degrees of minority parental support in schools that are less organizationally rigid (Colbert, 1993). This is important knowledge in that research demonstrates that as the socioeconomic level in schools decreases (Hoover-Dempsey et al., 1987) and ethnic and racial diversity increases (Colbert, 1993), the organizational rigidity level increases.

Instructional Coordination.   This factor refers to the planned activities implemented by school personnel to ensure that the instructional practices within and across grade and school levels are consistent. Curriculum that is clearly coordinated across grade levels enhances student learning and is associated with teacher perceptions that parents carry out suggested home school programs and that nonminority parents support their teaching efforts (Colbert, 1993). The remaining sections of this chapter focus on a research investigation of a two-year collaboration with one school district which afforded the opportunity to study the schooling process and factors at both the administrative and at the individual school level during the planning and implementation of education reform.

The Research

Research Questions

The research was focused on examination of the following specific questions: (a) What happens when the Schooling Process Model and identified factors are used to facilitate understanding of, and communication about, a district's education reform efforts at the administrative and individual school levels? and (b) What are the implications of the findings for school counselor education and practice?

The Partnership District

The School Counselor Program at the University of Massachusetts at Amherst has as its partner district, the Amherst-Pelham Regional Public Schools. There are five elementary schools in this community of 36,000, spanning a wide range of socio-economic (SES) levels. Median income is $26,000, while per capita income is approximately $11,100. Approximately 17 percent of households have an income below $10,000, with 30 percent of households having incomes in the range of $10,000 to $25,000. In addition, 26 percent of households have incomes between $25,000 and $50,000, while approximately 27 percent of household incomes are above $50,000. The district comprises, primarily, students identified as white (75 percent), with significant percentages of students who are identified as Asian (8 percent), Black (8 percent), and Hispanic (8 percent). Similar to other districts in the country, Amherst has experienced a significant growth in the number of low-income and minority students over the past two decades.

The implementation of the Massachusetts Education Reform Act in 1993 required that all schools in Massachusetts analyze their schooling processes and implement changes to address their weaknesses. About the same time, the Amherst Regional Schools and the NAACP entered into a consent decree to work together to respond to an NAACP lawsuit over the issue of academic tracking in the secondary schools.

In light of these external changes, the Amherst school committee identified two beginning target change areas. The first focus was on equitable practice in terms of academic achievement for all students. To date, good faith efforts have been made and the district is working to eliminate the disproportionality of African American and Hispanic students' enrollment in less rigorous courses and their underrepresentation in honors-level courses. The second focal area revolved around a request for more effective communication regarding student learning. The school committee directed administrators to focus on development of methods to increase effective communication throughout the district, especially with parents who had expressed the need to better understand curriculum, instruction, and other schooling processes.

The Overall Approach

A flexible, participant observer field study and interviews were utilized to investigate the research questions. This qualitative inquiry research design, which assumes that the context and setting have value, allowed us to gain a deep understanding of the experiences of school administrators, counselors, and teachers engaged in education reform in the presence of crucial contextual variables. This method holds unique strengths for the type of descriptive analysis we had as our goal and allowed us to maximize the possibility of thoughtful responses to our questions (Zelditch, 1962). Such qualitative inquiry methods have been praised for contributions to research that is designed for examining complexities and processes in depth, exploring innovative models, exploring disconnection between policy and local practice, examining informal, unstructured links and processes in organizations, and identifying relevant variables (Marshall, 1985, 1987). These methods retain the flexibility necessary to allow the research focus to evolve during the process (Marshall & Rossman, 1995).

Administrative Level Data Collection and Analysis

A leadership academy was held with the school district superintendent, curriculum director, elementary principals, and two university faculty members, the first author a counselor educator and Dr. Jerri Willett, a teacher educator. The focus of the academy was to develop a plan and strategic focus for education reform in the district. The university faculty members worked in a consultation role with the goal of assisting the administrators to develop an action plan for addressing the target areas of equity and communication.

We participated in ongoing dialogue with the administrators, speaking to the process as it was happening, helping all to reflect on what they were doing, and making decisions periodically about whether the direction and process was consistent with their goals for school change. A primary component of our role was to determine and point out how individual ideologies, social relations, and identities were being constructed in open dialogue, what was influencing them, and how they, in turn, were shaping potential new educational practices (J. Willett, personal communication, March, 1998). In addition, we provided written reports with our analysis of the work we were involved in, which served as evaluative tools that were utilized for direction and decision making by the administrators. The reports were based on an understanding of the schooling process conceptual framework and factors. One of our goals was to create and implement a model that would be applicable in the realities of a school counselor's day-to-day context; hence, we continuously consulted with and sought feedback from practicing school counselors and school counseling graduate students in our meaning-making dialogues.

Data Collection and Analysis at the School Building Level

After two summer sessions, the Leadership Academy devised a conceptual framework for maintaining strategic focus and change efforts were moved into each elementary school. University faculty agreed to continue participation at the building level. Once school change efforts became located in the schools, school counselors and other school staff were involved. The group decided that school counseling graduate students should also be included in the process. We saw this as a rich, contextual educational opportunity for our students in collaboration with practicing school counselors, and we were interested in seeking answers to our second research question, What are the implications for school counselor education and practice? Our efforts were intended to help school personnel in the ongoing real-life process of school reform while simultaneously working to develop and refine models for educating school counselors to function as professionals involved in the study and practice of education reform.

Open-ended qualitative interviews (Seidman, 1998) with teachers and other staff members by the first author and two graduate students were structured around the school change framework that the administrators had articulated. After one year of the implementation of the school district's framework at the school-building level, staff members were interviewed at their school during their planning periods and after school. The interviews lasted between thirty minutes and one hour. Interview notes were analyzed according to the constant comparative method for analyzing inductively gathered data (Conrad, 1978; Glaser & Strauss, 1967; Hoshmand, 1989). Staff members were asked to provide their level of awareness of the school change framework and asked to share their thoughts about the change process.

The Findings

Question A

> What happens when the Schooling Process Model and identified factors are used to facilitate understanding of, and communication about, a district's education reform efforts at the administrative and building levels?

In this section we trace the events that took place during the academy which illustrate specifically what happened when the schooling process and factors were used as a conceptual base. The outcome of the leadership academy was to develop a response to the school committee's charges related to equity and communication. The administrative team was working toward the articulation of a framework for promoting equity and communication about student learning. The administrators wanted to ensure that their plan would not compromise any participants' individual role and responsibility at their individual job/position level. Using the schooling process model, the first author made the interpretation—and administrators agreed—that a clash existed between internal and external factors, to the point that educators across all levels of the district were feeling significantly ineffective in their ability to communicate their contribution to student learning. For instance, principals were in agreement that they found it difficult to engage in meaningful exchange with staff regarding the educational process, which had resulted in their inability to elevate exemplary models of teaching and pinpoint areas for staff improvement. This sentiment is illustrated by one administrator who stated, "I know that some of my staff are already doing the kind of work with students the district is complaining about, yet it's just real difficult to bring these to the surface." At each level of the schooling process, people had become isolated in their own role and function. The superintendent, principals, parents, teachers, and the school committee (to a significant degree) all felt as though they were "playing on different teams."

When attempts to improve the situation took place, resistance was the common response. The wonderful ideas and the many demonstrations of competence were not enhancing education across the district as they should. It was clear that communication barriers needed to be addressed. The team had to ask, What has contributed to the barriers and isolation, and how will it affect the process of school change? Drawing from the model, the first author's interpretation was that administrators felt such communication barriers would indeed affect reform efforts by reducing organizational and individual performance efficacy (Fuller et al., 1982). One principal noted that "we need to find a common language that everyone (parents, teachers, administrators, school committee members, etc.) can use as a reference when we get into dialogue about what we're doing to ensure that each and every student succeeds. This would certainly help facilitate communication about student learning and improve morale so that staff would be more willing to collaborate around successful learning for all students." The group agreed to work toward the goal of opening communication channels throughout the district.

The university faculty consultants helped the administrators clarify all the potential communication channels and possible barriers in the district as depicted in Figure 1.3. The administrators realized that successful education reform relies on open vertical, horizontal, and diagonal communication throughout the district. They felt that if open communication existed, all school members would feel that their perspectives were, at a minimum, heard and at best understood by others, particularly those at different levels of authority. Subsequently, individual performance efficacy would be enhanced by the school change framework. These understandings facilitated the dialogue and provided direction for the administrators to work with others at the building level in attempting to develop more effective communication.

The administrators slowly began to break down the barriers among themselves (vertical communication, Fig. 1.3) and continually worked to maintain openness. For example, early on, much time was spent grappling with competing beliefs regarding educational ideologies, pedagogy, and school culture through an initial competition for the right of the "best" to dictate the group's directions. Through dialogue, the group identified commonalities among their differing philosophies and agreed to "live" with the differences. Throughout the next two years, each time the group worked to establish consensus in a number of areas, new discussions were necessary as new challenges emerged.

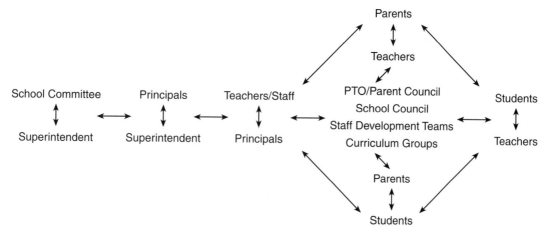

FIGURE 1.3   School system communicating channels.

During the middle stage of the work, members began to listen to one another, and were able to hear each other's concerns. The administrators were attending to both external and internal influences simultaneously and with equal energy. An illustration of this forward movement took place when the superintendent acknowledged his concerns about not having the necessary language to translate the groups' consensus for the project in such a way that he could effectively communicate it to the school committee (horizontal–vertical). For the first time during the process, members worked at helping someone at a different level in the administrative hierarchy address a concern without claiming a similar need themselves. This highlighted the importance of conceptualizing aspects of the school change well enough to apply them within the context of day-to-day functioning. The model helped administrators gain an enhanced ability to cooperate with one another in developing a school change strategy.

Administrators' common conceptual understanding of the schooling process and factors and their enhanced sense of cooperation led to a focus on the broader school system. From that point on, they began to focus their efforts on how to conceptualize the developing aspects of their work at the individual classroom and school committee levels, as well as at all points in between. The administrators wondered how their efforts might work toward removing communication barriers at all levels of the system. The team then developed an action plan for realizing their goal to remove the communication barriers across the district while framing the reform initiative within a structure that also addressed the school committee's initial concerns. The administrators realized that their first-order change effort of attempting to remove communication barriers would be more effective if they attended to the underlying structure (a second-order change). The primary concern they addressed through the removal of communication barriers was how to help all involved understand the "whats" and "hows" of effective student learning. Through their discussions, the administrators articulated steps to advance their goal.

The schooling process model and factors provided a common conceptual framework and language for the administrators. They stated that the model exactly reflected their day-to-day roles and the work that was occurring in the leadership academy. Once they perceived that their ideas of school culture and school change were validated and valued by others, and that their contributions would be taken seriously and utilized for the good of the whole, they began to cooperate effectively. All wanted to obtain a certain level of influence within the group, or achieve a sense of organizational efficacy (Fuller et al., 1982). The ability to openly communicate and empathize with other members was a very important part of the process and without it the group would have had difficulty moving forward to develop an action plan.

The model provided a means for attending to the individual performance efficacy within the context of organizational efficacy (Fuller et al., 1982) and a lens for viewing the change process. In addition, it gave faculty consultants a means by which to frame reports pertaining to what had occurred during the open dialogue process. The later stage of the collaboration with the administrators revolved around the development of a framework that allowed the administrators to function in their respective roles while leading others toward promoting equity in learning for all students and more open communication about student learning throughout the school community. Administrators knew that the key to addressing the district's concerns was for them to stay well focused on their collective philosophies, vision, mission, and means for achieving successful learning for all students.

The district's education reform vision and plan was developed from a collective set of ideas and principles that reflected the practices and beliefs of different staff. The primary goal of the plan was successful learning for all students and included: (1) ensuring high expectations for all students (with appropriate scaffolding); (2) constant questioning regarding what students are learning and how that is known; (3) helping students share responsibility for learning; and (4) creating shared dialogue and reflection among staff and other school community members. The administrators proposed that the school change vision and plan serve as a guideline for examining proposed curriculum or instructional initiatives, meetings, curriculum days, and study groups, as well as for developing individual staff member instructional objectives. Administrators began implementing the plan with their building level staff. Interviews were conducted with teachers and other staff after one year of planning and implementation.

School Staff Interview Results.   Three themes emerged from the interviews:

1. Staff members expressed a need to have their ideas, practices, and voices acknowledged.
2. The different strategies for implementing the framework needed to be integrated.
3. Staff wanted to have input into the tasks for implementing the framework.

Staff Members Expressed a Need to Have Their Ideas, Practices, and Voices Acknowledged. This theme reflects shared vision and resources, two of the eight mediating variables related to organization and individual performance efficacy. Previous research has demonstrated that as all members of the change process perceive that their vision is aligned with their superiors' vision, a greater sense of cooperation occurs (Fuller et al., 1982). One staff member's statement exemplifies this need: "This is a top-down initiative and what we need is more bottom-up activities [*sic*] where our own ideas and methods can be part of the plan and there is peer pressure helping the entire staff to be supportive of school change."

The Different Strategies for Implementing the Framework Need to be Integrated. The second theme also revolved around shared vision and resources. Teachers/staff spoke about their concern that it is important to them to have the "big picture" regarding how all the activities associated with the framework are connected. This includes those that occur within their building and at the central administration level. One teacher stated that, "I did not see the framework as part of a bigger plan, I thought it was a fly-by-night program. It is hard to see the larger school happening from a teacher's vantage point, all parts need information, and if more parts of the school system had awareness of the whole we'd get a better sense of where we are headed."

Another teacher likened the need for staff to know the whole of the change framework to the auto manufacture industry in stating, "It's like General Motors versus Toyota wherein General Motors tells its workers that your role involves only this area here. On the other hand, Toyota seeks input from its front line workers on the entire car, not just the area that they are responsible for." These themes are also consistent with previous research (Fuller et al., 1982) which documents that staff want opportunities to be resources in the school change process, not only in relation to their designated roles, but at all levels of the school system.

Staff Wanted to Have Input into the Tasks for Implementing the Framework. This last theme refers to the influencing area of specific or mandated tasks for implementing the school change framework. One teacher, reflecting on current practices regarding a framework component, stated, "The system-level math testing a few times a year is a weak link in this component area. We don't have assessment that is more authentic or embedded in what we are doing. The current assessment is not useful in that it does not reflect math that the students are doing at low levels; there seems to be a void. We [staff] need training around observing and interpreting what we are seeing. This would help give authenticity to our assessment of what students are learning." Staff members had plenty to say about the details of specific tasks pertaining to each of the framework components, and requested that time be allotted for them to work on restructuring the tasks to fit their realities. Staff members' sense of influencing others at different levels could be positively affected through opportunities for input into the entire process (Fuller et al., 1982). The outcome of enhanced efficacy may facilitate the district change process.

Interview Results Sharing

The anonymous interview results were shared with administrators and were used as feedback for determining the next steps in the school change process. The interviews indicated that the processes at the building level were highly similar to those at the administrative level. We communicated to administrators that staff members would need extensive time to process and openly communicate their thoughts, beliefs, and feelings concerning the school change framework. This recommendation emerged from our observations that the administrators' success in developing the school change plan hinged on time spent actively engaged with each other in open communication. Each building principal was given the freedom to choose how he or she would incorporate staff feedback into specific school change activities. As the process unfolded, it was clear that the schooling process model helped the administrators identify facilitative and inhibitive conditions related to their efforts. The better able they were to identify the factors and ensure facilitative conditions, the better their chance of success.

The Schooling Process Model facilitated a recursive process of communication and monitoring of change efforts which included an ongoing dialogue between the building level teams and the administrative team. The identification of influencing factors and mediating variables at the district and building levels led to the delineation of change efforts to address them. Once implementation of the change goals had begun, information was shared back and forth and used to monitor their effectiveness. This led to the identification of additional variables that needed to be addressed, additional change efforts, additional information sharing and dialogue, and so on. The implementation of this model in the complex context of education reform has illuminated many implications and possibilities for school counseling practice and education.

Discussion

Our application of the Schooling Process Model required that we consistently incorporate knowledge and skills in group dynamics, communication, cooperation, collaboration, group problem solving, advocacy, facilitation, and monitoring of the change process. Continued synergistic research efforts including real-world application of the model by school counselors will further inform our processes and are a necessary next step. To date, the school district administrators continue to report success in their beginning efforts to implement the model in their particular school buildings. Our interviews with teachers and continued discussions with school counselors lead us to believe that the model holds much promise as a tool to provide direction for school counselor role in culture-centered education reform.

A major implication emerging from this work is that of the importance and necessity of making the transition to collaboration as a foundation for the implementation of both first- and second-order changes in the school and the school counseling program. Our experiences in using the Schooling Process Model led to the delineation of a framework for school counselor collaboration which is visually depicted in Figure 1.4. The framework has two levels at which school counselors might operate.

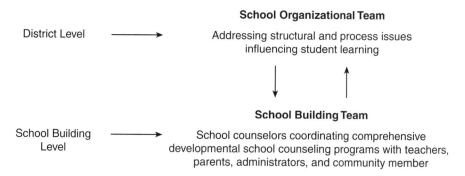

FIGURE 1.4   District and school building level roles for school counselors in culture-centered educaton reform.

The first level, School Organizational Team (SOT), requires that school counselors envision themselves in action as members of a team that constantly works to address district-level structural and process issues which affect student learning and development. The second level, School Building Team (SBT), requires that school counselors work as collaborators in a school-building team that includes teachers, parents, administrators, students, and other community members who work together to develop and implement the comprehensive developmental school counseling program.

By applying the Schooling Process Model, school counselors work with their respective SBTs to identify the factors and mediators that are affecting school change, student learning, and development. The school counselors from each building then collectively pool their information at the SOT level, leading to identification of priority-influencing factors for each building and for the larger district. Such clarification provides direction for the education reform teams and facilitates decisions related to first- and second-order change efforts.

At the SBT level, school counselors coordinate, consult, and work with others to continuously monitor the factors to ensure that they are being addressed in the implementation of the change process and to evaluate their impact on student learning and development in relation to the established outcomes of the counseling program. This should be a recursive process as school counselors from each SBT continuously bring information back to the SOT, adding to the ongoing evaluation of the district-level change process. The SOT continually monitors student impact as student needs change over time as the district changes. The SBT continually works to monitor, reassess, and maintain or change aspects of the counseling program when necessary.

Applying these ideas to the real-life case of this school district, school counselors might work, through collaboration and consultation, toward addressing the factors and monitoring the effects of changes in order to facilitate organizational and individual efficacy. A building's school counselor can inform building staff of the existing communication barriers, communicate the impact on students, and collaborate to develop a means to address them. If the building is characterized by isolation in contrast to teamwork, as some were in this study, the school counselor can facilitate cooperation and teamwork, helping all work together toward the common goal of student success and well being. If teachers and others feel that their voices are not heard at the district level and desire input into the change process as the teachers noted, the school counselor can advocate and coordinate to ensure that their input into the school's vision, education reform framework, and operating procedures is considered seriously. The school counselor could monitor the process through facilitating ongoing data collection such as interviews, surveys, group dialogue, and observation, and provide periodic written reports to building staff as well as the SOT. These strategies provide a foundation for counselors to take a leadership role focused on the support and facilitation of successful learning for all students within the changing cultural context of education reform. Using such strategies, the school counselor can maintain a focus on ensuring that their districts' education reform efforts are being designed to meet the needs of all students.

Conclusions and Implications

The Schooling Process Model holds much potential for providing direction to school counselors as they engage in culture-centered education reform. Although much research remains to be conducted, it appears that the model might aid school counselors to function in proactive, developmental partnerships which are focused on whole-school concerns and the promotion of positive student outcomes for all students (Campbell & Dahir, 1997).

Professional Development

Culture-Centered Education Reform Opportunities.   Practicing school counselors who decide to take a leadership role in their schools' education reform efforts can begin by participating in the opportunities available for staff involvement. Simultaneously, school counselors should engage in staff development in order to gain knowledge that will enhance their participation efforts. Many districts have a central-level committee (i.e., school committee or restructuring committee) charged with the development and monitoring of reform endeavors. Individual school buildings often have one or more committees or groups responsible for planning, implementing, and evaluating building-level input at the district level. These groups may fall under the title of school councils, site-based committees, diversity committees, school improvement plan committees, etc.

Workshops.   National-, regional-, and state-level school counseling conferences are beginning to provide opportunities for professional development consistent with the school counselor's role in culture-centered education reform. School counselors should work to remain aware of current initiatives around the nation. For example, Reynolds and Hines (2000) work with building-level steering committees that initiate whole-school reform.

University/College Course Offerings.   The model in this chapter draws primarily from multicultural organizational development and counseling—theory, consultation, and multicultural group and individual skills and practice. All practicing school counselors are familiar with counseling theories for intervening with individuals and groups. In the context of culture-centered education reform, school counselors will need to learn to apply these skills in different ways and may need further work in the area of multicultural counseling. Helpful courses would be those that focus on multicultural organizational development with an emphasis on multicultural school development and change.

University/College Partnerships.   Partnerships with local colleges and universities are viable mechanisms for practicing school counselors to learn more about culture-centered education reform while at the same time participating in the education of school counseling students. Many counselor education programs are considering, or are in the midst of, restructuring (Hayes, Dagley, & Horne, 1996) and could benefit greatly from the opportunities such partnerships afford. Many counselor educators prefer professional service opportunities in their local communities and would welcome practicing school counselors who are willing to collaborate.

School Counselor Education

Education reform requires that counselor educators work with practicing school counselors to ensure that school counseling students graduate with the necessary skills, knowledge, and ability to implement new roles. While future research will be focused on specificity of skills, knowledge, and abilities, our experiences alert us to new directions for counselor education that are rich with possibilities.

In order to participate in education reform, school counseling students will need to:

- understand the schooling process from a systems perspective;   → school Process Model
- understand the potential internal and external factors that can influence student learning and development, and how the school environment influences learning;
- have knowledge and ability to analyze the potential interactional dynamics among the factors and potential mediators;
- engage in group problem solving in order to identify opportunities and barriers to change, and to develop innovative strategies and ideas;
- understand the change process, the issues involved in complex change, and how to facilitate effective change;
- engage in group action planning, implementation, and evaluation;
- apply relationship building, group dynamics and knowledge about communication to adults working in a school context;
- apply collaborative consultation skills;
- apply abstract concepts and theory to their work in a real-world context and effectively communicate processes and ideas to others;

- facilitate teamwork among school staff, parents, and others who may have differing and/or competing ideologies and agendas; and,
- be knowledgeable of resources and how to coordinate and develop collaboration among a wide variety of potential resources.

The fact that education reform is occurring across the nation provides a rich context full of real-life issues and opportunities for school counseling students to learn new roles and participate in working partnerships. Involving school counseling students in a school district's education-reform efforts gave us insight into the further development of relevant field experiences for application of new knowledge. At the same time, the school district benefited from the students' work by having additional professional expertise as the students learned to collaborate with the school professionals. Such reciprocal relationships hold much potential for counselor education.

Implications for Research

Future research will address the implementation of the model by school counselors at the building level. Potential research questions focus on the following: (1) model implementation—What happens when school counselors implement the model at the building level? Does the model facilitate change at the building level in the same way as it did at the administrative level? Can specific parallels and differences be identified? What changes are necessary for the model to be an effective tool for school counselors? What happens when the model is implemented in a different school district with different characteristics? (2) factors and mediators—Are there patterns across districts in the factors identified as priorities? Are there other factors and mediators of import in different districts? What specific changes do school districts devise to address the factors? How do they influence student outcome? Can assessment instruments be developed to increase efficiency of factor identification and monitoring? (3) the change process—How do the factors influence the change process? What methods do school counselors utilize to facilitate change? First-order change? Second-order change? (4) counselor role—What happens when school counselors attempt to change their roles in a school district? Are there specific strategies school counselors can use to help develop receptivity to the changes in their relationships? What kinds of relationships do school counselors develop with school administrators, and other members of the school community through utilization of the model? How do new school counselor roles affect student learning and development? How do teams co-construct new organizational procedures and processes? (5) school counselors as researchers—Would instruments facilitate school counselors' ability to do research on their practice which can inform the field? What implications do changes in school counseling practice have for school counselor education?

School counselors have unique expertise and skills that are essential for successful change in diverse school settings. Our work informs us that we cannot wait for the transitions of the 21st century to occur. The time is now. Let us begin.

DISCUSSION QUESTIONS

1. Discuss the importance of culture-centered education reform.

2. Identify opportunities and challenges (in training and/or practice) that emerge from ASCA's recommendations that school counselors "become catalysts for school change, and assume or accept a leadership role in education reform (Campbell & Dahir, 1997)."

3. Why is it important to consider levels and types of change when planning and implementing culture-centered education reform?

4. Consider a school or district with which you are familiar. What roles do the school counselors play in the school or district? Brainstorm other possible roles they might play.

5. Reflect on your answers to question #4. If the school counselors decided to change their roles, what are some suggestions you could give them?

6. What challenges will you have in implementing school counselor roles as suggested in this chapter?

7. What benefits do you see in implementing school counselor roles as suggested in this chapter?

8. Share this chapter with a practicing school counselor and hold a discussion regarding his/her perceptions of the ideas. Share your notes with other school counseling students. What do you think about what you hear?

9. Design and conduct an action research project on a particular point or concept raised in the chapter that interests you.

10. Attend a local districts' school board meeting or access media reports of a local meeting. Document changes in school policy, procedures, etc. that are being discussed. Apply the adapted MCIM to identify the levels and types of change being considered. Identify other types and levels of change that might be applied in this district.

11. Consider the staff members at the building level who were discussed in this chapter. Discuss how you would address their concerns with the district's culture-centered education reform initiative. Draw upon one or more of the three transitions needed for school counselor role changes as you answer this question.

12. How would you use the Schooling Process and adapted MCIM models to enhance your ability to do what you discuss in question #10?

13. What would you do as a school counselor to involve students and parents in your work?

14. What would you do to involve others in the community in your work?

15. "When will theory meet practice? I've got 450 kids, one-fourth of whom are pregnant, one-fourth of whom are on drugs, and another one-fourth of whom never even show up for school and you ask me to work in a proactive leadership role where I develop and maintain collaborative efforts to facilitate culture-centered education reform? Give me a break!"
    State whether you agree or disagree with this school counselor and explain your response.

16. Using the concepts in the chapter, write a dialogue for a presentation that you could give to convince a school board or committee that they should support your requests for changes in the school counselor's role in the district.

17. Brainstorm changes in school counselor education that are needed in order for school counselors to carry out the leadership roles recommended by ASCA.

REFERENCES

American School Counselor Association. (1995, January/February). Changing directions: School counselors collaborating for student success. *The ASCA Counselor, 32,* 1–10.

Atkinson, D. R., Thompson, C. E., & Grant, S. K. (1993). A three-dimensional model for counseling racial/ethnic minorities. *The Counseling Psychologist, 21,* 257–277.

Baker, S. (1996). School counseling for the twenty-first century (2nd ed.). Columbus, OH: Merrill.

Borders, L. D. & Drury, S. M. (1992). Comprehensive school counseling programs: A review for policy makers and practitioners. *Journal of Counseling and Development, 70,* 487–498.

Campbell, C. A. & Dahir, C. A. (1997). *The national standards for school counseling programs.* Alexandria, VA: American School Counseling Association.

Carey, J. C., Boscardin, M. L., & Fontes, L. (1994). Improving the multicultural effectiveness of your school. In P. Pedersen & J. C. Carey (Eds.), *Multicultural counseling in schools: A practical handbook.* Needham Heights, MA: Allyn & Bacon.

Colbert, R. D. (1996). The counselor's role in advancing school and family partnerships. *The School Counselor, 44,* 100–104.

Colbert, R. D. (1993). Relationships between teacher perceptions and minority parental involvement. *Journal of Communications and Minority Issues, 1*(1), 15–20.

Coleman, P. & Collinge, J. (1991). In the web: Internal and external influences affecting school improvement. *School Effectiveness and School Improvement, 2*(4), 262–285.

Comer, J. P., Haynes, N. M., Hamilton-Lee, M., Boger, J., & Pollock, D. (1986). *Academic and affective gains from the school development program: A model for school improvement.* Paper presented at the annual meeting of the American Psychological Association, Washington, DC.

Conrad, C. F. (1978). A grounded theory of academic change. *Sociology of Education, 51,* 101–112.

Epstein, J. L. (1992). School partnerships: Leadership roles for school psychologists. In S. L. Christenson & J. C. Conoly (Eds.), *Home-school collaboration* (pp. 499–515). Colesville, MD: National Association of School Psychologists.

Fuller, B., Wood, K., Rappaport, T., & Dornbusch, S. M. (1982). The organizational context of individual efficacy. *Review of Educational Literature, 52,* 7–30.

Gerler, E. R., Jr. (1992). What we know about school counseling: A reaction to Borders and Drury. *Journal of Counseling & Development, 70,* 499–501.

Glaser, B. G. & Strauss, A. L. (1967). *The discovery of grounded theory: Strategies for qualitative research.* Chicago, IL: Aldine/Atherton.

Hayes, R. L., Dagley, J. C., & Horne, A. M. (1996). Restructuring school counselor education: Work in progress. *Journal of Counseling & Development, 74,* 378–384.

Holtzman, W. H. (1992). *School of the future.* Washington, DC: American Psychological Association.

Hoover-Dempsey, K. V., Bassler, O. C., & Bissie, J. S. (1987). Parent involvement: Contributions of teacher efficacy, school socio-economic status, and other school characteristics. *American Educational Research Journal, 24,* 417–435.

Hoshmand, L. L. S. T. (1989). Alternate research paradigms: A review and teaching proposal. *The Counseling Psychologist, 17,* 3–79.

House, R. M. & Martin, P. J. (1998). Advocating for better futures for all students: A new vision for school counselors. *Education, 119,* 284–291.

Ivey, A. E. (1986). *Developmental therapy.* San Francisco: Jossey-Bass.

Ivey, A. E., Ivey, M. B., & Simek-Morgan, L. (1993). *Counseling and psychotherapy: A multicultural perspective.* Boston: Allyn & Bacon.

Lortie, D. (1975). *Schoolteacher.* Chicago: University of Chicago Press.

Lyddon, W. J. (1990). First- and second-order change: Implications for rationalist and constructivist cognitive therapies. *Journal of Counseling and Development, 69,* 122–127.

Marshall, C. (1985). Appropriate criteria of trustworthiness and goodness for qualitative research on education organizations. *Quality and Quantity, 19,* 353–373.

Marshall, C. (1987, March 24). *Report to the Vanderbilt policy education committee.* Vanderbilt University, Nashville.

Marshall, C. & Rossman, G. B. (1995). *Designing qualitative research.* (2nd ed.), Thousand Oaks, CA: Sage.

Nieto, S. (1993). Creating possibilities: Educating Latino students in Massachusetts. In R. Rivera & S. Nieto (Eds.), *The education of Latino students in Massachusetts: Issues, research and policy implications.* Boston, MA: The University of Massachusetts Press.

Paisley, P. O. & Borders, L. D. (1995). School counseling: An evolving specialty. *Journal of Counseling & Development, 74*, 150–153.

Pederson, P. & Ivey, A. E. (1994). *Cultured-centered counseling and interviewing skills.* New York: Greenwood.

Petty, M. M., Beadles, N. A., Lowery, C. M., Chapman, D. F., & Connell, D. W. (1995). Relationships between organizational culture and organizational performance. *Psychological Reports, 76,* 483–492.

Pianta, R. C. & Walsh, D. J. (1996). *High-risk children in schools.* New York: Routledge.

Pollard, D. S. (1989). Against the odds: A profile of academic achievers from the urban underclass. *Journal of Negro Education, 58,* 297–308.

Pope, R. L. (1992). An analysis of multiracial change efforts in student affairs. (Doctoral dissertation, University of Massachusetts at Amherst, 1992). *Dissertation Abstracts International, 53,* 3457A.

Reynolds, S. & Hines, P. L. (2000). *The Indiana Student Achievement Institute: Guidance-centered whole school reform.* Paper presented at the National Symposium on the Role of School Counseling in Meeting the Needs of Students in the Twenty-First Century, National Association for College Admission Counseling, Washington, DC.

Rivera, R. (1988, June). *Latino parent involvement in the Boston public schools: Preliminary notes from the field.* Boston, MA: University of Massachusetts, William Monroe Trotter Institute.

Schorr, L. B., Both, D., & Copple, C. (1991). *Effective services for young children.* Washington, DC: National Academy Press.

Seidman, I. (1998). *Interviewing as qualitative research: A guide for researchers in education and social sciences* (2nd ed.). New York: Teachers College Press.

Sue, D. W. (1995). Multicultural organizational development: Implications for the counseling profession. In J. G. Ponterotto, J. M. Casas, L. A. Suzuki, & C. M. Alexander (Eds.), *Handbook of multicultural counseling.* Thousand Oaks, CA: Sage.

Sue, D. W. & Sue, D. (1990). *Counseling the culturally different: Theory and practice.* New York: John Wiley.

Weber, G. (1971). *Inner-city children can be taught to read: Four successful schools.* CBE Occasional papers, No. 18. Washington, DC: Council for Basic Education.

Weiner, L. (1993). *Preparing teachers for urban schools: Lessons from thirty years of school reform.* New York: Teachers College Press.

Wheelock, A. (1993). The status of Latino students in Massachusetts public schools. In R. Rivera & S. Nieto (Eds.), *The education of Latino students in Massachusetts: Issues, research, and policy implications.* Boston: The University of Massachusetts Press.

Whelage, G. C. (1990). The problems of identifying at-risk students. *River East Division Journal, 2*(1), 1–10.

Whiston, J. & Sexton, P. (1998). Outcome Research of Comprehensive Developmental Guidance Program. *Journal of Counseling and Development, 80,* 487–498.

Zelditch, M. (1962). Some methodological problems of field studies. *American Journal of Sociology, 67,* 566–576.

AUTHORS' NOTE

Our deepest and most sincere gratitude to the teachers, administrators, and school counselors in the Amherst-Pelham Regional School District for letting us join with them in revisioning their schools. In particular we want to thank Dr. Gus Sayer, Dr. Russell Vernon-Jones, Dr. Paul Wiley, Dr. Lenore Carlisle, and Derek Shea. We would also like to thank Dr. Jerri Willett, professor in the Department of Teacher Education and Curriculum Studies at the University of Massachusetts in Amherst for her wisdom, guidance, and mentoring during this project. Finally, we want to thank graduate students Veronica Williams, Vera L. Stenhouse, Gabrielle Glorioso, Paula Verson, and Judith Wides who expended considerable time and effort in assisting with this project.

Robert D. Colbert is an assistant professor at the University of Connecticut, Neag School of Education, Department of Educational Psychology, and Counseling Psychology Program. Colbert's primary scholarly interests are research-based school counselor practice in culture-centered education reform and the application of an ecological perspective to the consultation process. Colbert is an active member of state and national counseling associations. He recently served on the Governing Board of the Massachusetts School Counselor Association, the Professionalization Committee of the American Counseling Association, and the Editorial Board of *Professional School Counseling*.

Marge Magouirk Colbert teaches in the Department of Teacher Education and Curriculum Studies at the University of Massachusetts at Amherst. Her work focuses on education reform models and the redesign of teacher and counselor education programs. Current research involves case studies of fourteen school districts that are restructuring around Career Pathways models and the development of alternative supervision models for teacher education.

2 Cultural Identity Groups and Cultural Maps: Meaning Making in Groups

ERNEST D. WASHINGTON, TRICIA CROSBY,

MAYRA HERNANDEZ, RUSS VERNON-JONES,

RENEE MEDLEY, BRENDA NISHAMURA, and

DIANA TORRES

University of Massachusetts, Amherst

OBJECTIVES

1. To provide a framework for the implementation of cultural identity groups
2. To use cultural identity groups as a mechanism for helping children cope with prejudice in schools
3. To provide an instrument to assess meaning making in cultural identity groups
4. To introduce the emotional climate scale as a way of assessing the emotional climate of schools

"They won't like us no matter what we do!" said a young Asian girl about race relations in her school. Is she wrong? Let us take seriously the possibility that she is telling the truth. How can we help this young girl meet the challenges of exclusion in her school and community?

A gifted young African American boy sits terrified in his fifth-grade social study class because he believes the teacher is going to call on him to discuss slavery. He knows lots of things but he does not know anything about slavery.

A young fourth grade African American boy is not doing well at his new school. He has been referred to the speech therapist because his speech is almost incoherent. What kinds of stress is this youngster experiencing as he makes an adjustment to his new school and community?

A racial epithet is shouted at a young Puerto Rican child on the school bus. He complains to his teacher, and nothing is done about the incident because the other child denies the incident. A young African American boy is punched by a white boy in his class. This goes on for a period of time. The teacher does not interpret the experience as having racial overtones; instead, she sees it as a matter of choosing friends.

Cultural identity groups (CIGs) are designed to intervene in the recurring rituals of prejudice that cause pain to children of color. The strengthening of individual and group identity is therapeutic and helps the children cope with the anxieties and pains caused by prejudice. Through the synergy of shared story telling in small groups, children of color learn their individual and collective strengths. Pride is the thread that connects individual self-esteem and group identity because pride emerges from self-esteem. Identification with a group draws upon self-esteem and pride in the group.

The purpose of this chapter is to outline the procedures for implementing cultural identity groups in schools. Cultural identity groups are a developmental model of group counseling for children of color which utilizes narratives of identity to counter prejudice and racism in our schools and communities. These groups are a safe group environment in which children can tell their stories of family, identity, culture, race, class, and even discuss things such as music, sports, and movies. The group sessions are designed so that children utilize the experience of their peers and capitalize upon their acceptance and support.

The steps in creating these groups will be described so that a counselor can use this technique. The procedures begin with understanding the developmental stage of identity, self, and emotions of the child, and the appropriate intervention strategy. Next comes administrative and parental approval to participate in the groups. The roles and responsibilities of the group facilitator will be explained. A description of the story telling approach is used in the cultural identity groups following. The facilitation of the sessions will be explained through the use of story telling and a technique we call "cultural maps." Cultural maps are drawn by children on sketch pad paper. At the beginning of the session each child chooses a symbol, draws the symbol, and explains the symbol to the other members of the group. The maps are a sociometric representation of the meaning that the members of the group make of the stories that they tell and the connections that they make between the stories in the group. They scribble notes on the paper in front of them as they draw lines connecting the stories. The evaluation of the CIG process is accomplished through two instruments: the Emotional Climate Scale, which uses a seven-point Likert scale, and a cognitive assessment of individual and group identity using a traditional Likert scale.

Choosing the Appropriate Intervention/Group Strategy

The most important step is the first, where we identify the student's stage of identity development, take account of his cognitive and emotional skills and of the development of the self, and then choose the appropriate intervention strategy. At each cognitive stage of development children encounter different forms of prejudice and racism that affect the development of the self. The self is an awareness of the systems of goals that we set for ourselves (Table 2.1). The concept of identity includes the perception of the self and the cognitive and affective identification which set the standards toward which each individual aspires. Children learn pride as they develop self-esteem. Group identity is related to closeness and acceptance by groups in the community.

TABLE 2.1 Matrix of Intervention Factors and Strategies

Identity	Prejudice	Cog/Self	Emotions	Intervene
Family sets standards	Anxious when separated from sig. others	Self-aware, attached to family	Right from wrong, happy, sad, anger, interest	Soothed by family to whom she is attached
Standards by family, friends, preschool, forbid violence	Hitting, name-calling exclude	Concrete friendships, comparing the self, aware of skin color, no concept of race, magical thinking	Fear, sad, anxiety, shame, guilt, can't separate self from emotions	Groups not appropriate, behavior, intervene, play therapy, concrete examples, pride in self
Standards by family, friends and early elem. school (ages 5–9), late elem. (ages 10–12), peers conform	Name-calling, hitting, exclusions subjective curriculum, aware of race	Ages 5–9 able to separate emotions from thought, ages 10–12 share, connect subjective experience	Insecurity, indiv. pride in achievement, inferiority, anxiety, guilt	Ages 5–9 emphasize concrete, visual and sensations, ages 10–12 emphasize story telling/reduce anxiety (cultural I.D. groups)
Preoccupation with standards of peers and self	Physical violence, subjective curriculum, racial separation dating	Multiple identities and cognitive dissonance	Confidence, pride, depression, guilt	Group counseling, individual therapy, cultural identity groups

Prejudiced acts produce anxieties in children of color. Other emotions such as fear, embarrassment, anger, and sadness occur but the key emotion is anxiety. Anxiety is an existential emotion; that is, its presence is a threat to our existence in the world (Lazarus & Lazarus, 1994). Anxiety threatens our sense of self and our connections to our group identities. Anxiety is not a reaction to a specific act but an uneasiness, a worry and apprehension. When we are anxious, we cannot do the things that make us feel good about ourselves. Pride, not the pride of sin and hubris, but the pride of affirmation of something well done, something that increases our sense of self-esteem is the antidote to anxiety and is therefore the other key emotion that we use in our discussions. As children meet the challenges of each stage of identity development, their experiences will be shaped by their balancing of pride and anxiety-producing events. Pride and anxieties are the key indicators in our decisions about the interventions that can best help children of color cope with prejudice.

The first stage of identity development is the period in which the family sets the standards for the development of the child. Children in this stage process information though the senses and organize this information into motor experiences. They develop increasingly complex motor patterns that are used to accommodate them to the social world. Children become attached to the significant others who soothe them when they are anxious and make them happy when at play. During the first year children experience joy, interest, anxiety, anger, and fear which help them evaluate the world. During the second year children experience sadness and, under extreme circumstances, depression. During this period children show an awareness of self that is unmistakable and that is bounded by the moral standards of the family. According to Kagan (1986) moral standards begin to emerge toward the end of the second year when the ability to gauge right and wrong appear. These standards are based on emotional responses to a discrepant event, on the capacity for empathy, and on an awareness of standards and the recognition the child has the ability to meet that standard.

At the second stage of identity development children ages three to five are egocentric and believe that others see the world the way that they do. There is magic in their thinking, and implausible events and causal relations are acceptable to them. They identify with significant others in their worlds and form increasingly complex emotional relationships. They show pride in what they accomplish as individuals but they do not recognize the concept of race or ethnicity. They do notice the concrete facts of skin color, however. During the third and fourth years guilt, anxiety, and shame emerge, often because there is a need to protect younger children from the violent behavior of older siblings (Kagan, 1986). For example, at this age children are quite capable of violence, and it is important for them to accept the standard that violence should be interrupted. They recognize that they have a choice, and they can choose which actions to take. In order for the child to be accepted by the social groups, they have to inhibit behaviors that are disapproved of by adults.

By the fourth year children have an unconscious appreciation of some of their psychological qualities, and an identification with others that includes the acknowledgment that some of the distinctive qualities they perceive in significant others also belong to themselves. The other person can be a parent, sibling, relative, friend, or even a television character. A girl realizes that she and her mother have the same family name and the same hair and nose. The child goes beyond these facts to assume that the self must share other psychological qualities with the parent. This going beyond the facts to make an inference about unobserved qualities is a universal tendency (Kagan, 1986). Children during this period compare themselves with others. They are aware of racial differences, that their skin is darker, and that they are different in appearance. They also learn that these differences may make them unwelcome.

The preschool years are the times when children of color, like all children, go to preschool, and they first experience the violence of racial discrimination. This is also the time for the emergence of one aspect of a sense of self which consists of conscious awareness of intentions, feelings, standards, and the ability to attain a goal. Children of this age live in a rich fantasy world as they are experiencing the pain of name calling and hitting. There is wishful thinking as children want to be accepted by their peers, and they are willing to deny and put out of their minds yesterday's negative racial experiences. We must hesitate in attributing an adult mind to a child. Some four-year-old youngsters are not exactly sure that girls will grow up to be women, and boys will grow up to men. Some think these things may change. Many five-year-old children have imaginary friends to whom they listen.

The responsibility of the counselor at this age is to help children grow in self-esteem, and pride, which every child should experience as part of every school day. Children believe in their teachers and want to please them. At the same time if the child is experiencing anxieties then it is the responsibility of the teacher and counselor to identify the cause of the anxiety and reduce and prevent the consequent crying, clinging, hitting, withdrawals, and yelling that are often seen in preschools. Therapeutic interventions should be concrete and behaviorally oriented. Models, dolls, and concrete representations are excellent teaching strategies which can help children absorb the rules and behaviors for becoming students in school.

The third stage of identity development spans ages five to twelve, and there is a great shift in those with whom the child identifies. Children continue to identify with friends and teachers but during the late elementary school years there is a shift towards the standards of the peer group. The rich fantasy worlds of the preschool era have been left behind. This age range reaches from the kindergartner who does not have the full cognitive skills to become a literate reader, to the sixth grader who is beginning to develop intellectual interests in disciplinary ways of knowing about the world. Some sixth-grade girls are physically young women and are experiencing menarche. The period of concrete operations is divided into two age ranges: the latency period, five through seven, and middle childhood, ages eight through twelve.

The period from five to nine is the time period in which children value conformity and enjoy repetitive tasks (Gilantzer-Levy & Cohler, 1993). The preferences for normality, conformity, and repetition by primary-age youngsters are ways that youngsters protect themselves from anxiety. For the first time they see themselves as members of a valued group. No bad qualities belong to their group, those bad qualities belong to other groups. During this period children continually compare themselves to their friends, and this is a break with the dominance of the family in framing standards. Children crave the approval of their teachers. The emotions that emerge during the fifth and sixth year are insecurity, inferiority, humility, pride, and confidence. These emotions have as their purpose the evaluation of the self in comparison with others. This is a time when children are comparing themselves with others. They have standards for abilities, attractiveness, honesty, bravery, dominance, and popularity, and they rank themselves in relation to their peers. The cognitive advance at this age is the ability to make this evaluation.

Remember that schools are not very pleasant for many students. In addition to the fears of academic failure, children face the forms of violence that we associate with bullying, sexual harassment, classism, homophobia, and racism in schools. Locked into egocentrism children think only of themselves. When they experience racism, it comes as a surprise, and, of course, it does not occur to them that others have had similar experiences. Children live with the anxieties that they are the only ones experiencing discrimination and racism.

The teacher and counselor need to be especially vigilant that children of color grow in self-esteem, pride, and identity as students during the early elementary years. At this age they are under the spell of conformity, and most of all they want to be like their peers. Labeling, name-calling, stereotyping, and exclusionary acts are anxiety-producing acts that can demoralize a beginning student. Again it is crucial that children experience success as they begin to learn the role of student so that they can develop pride in their work. Interventions are directed toward both the elimination of the offensive acts and concrete discussions with the offending party about what is acceptable. Kindergarten and first-grade teachers are powerful role models to their students, and teachers who model accepting behavior send a most important message to children.

The years between nine and twelve are times of work in schools. Children begin to experience the grueling repetitive nature of schoolwork. Metacognitive skills emerge at about eight years of age, and children are able to monitor their own thinking, memory, knowledge, emotions, actions, and goals. Children put these new skills to work in the service of conformity and the avoidance of anxiety. Youngsters who do not fit in are treated cruelly. Children at this age protect their sense of self by hostile treatment of others. The attribution of undesirable characteristics to others is a common response to those who are different. Racial and color lines are increasingly drawn in schools both formally and informally.

Children of color in the upper elementary grades become vigilant in their concerns about discrimination as they experience symbolic violence. Ironically, the ability to experience symbolic violence is one of the heirs to the increasing cognitive complexities of the thinking of adolescents. Symbolic violence is the imposition of a set of symbols in such a way that they are perceived to be legitimate, and yet these same symbols cause pain and discomfort (Jenkins, 1993). An all-white staff and an all-white curriculum in multiracial schools is a form of symbolic violence that children of color faces. No single age group is as aware of or sensitive to the impact of the symbols of their peers, teachers, and parents as are adolescents who strive to be like their high-status peers.

Teachers and counselors recognize that peer-group influences and standards intensify during the preteen years. This is a time when children of color, particularly males, become disengaged from their identities as students. Their anxieties and defensiveness with regard to their achievements have all but immobilized them. They are undergoing anger and sadness as they continually underachieve. The conundrum for the counselor and teacher is how to find something for the youngster to be proud of when he sees the racial and the achievement divides as unpassable.

The adolescent applies a new set of standards to her actions in addition to the standards set by parents, teachers, and peers. She is examining her own beliefs to detect consistencies and inconsistencies in her thoughts, beliefs, and actions. A new phase of the development of the self emerges as she becomes fixed on comparing herself to others. Now the adolescent ascribes to herself a position on a psychological or physical dimension that reflects her perception of the degrees to which she possesses a particular quality relative to others. It is during this pre-adolescent period that there is a preoccupation with monitoring and regulating her subjective world and comparing it with that of others.

The teen years mark a decisive turning point in the racial relationships of young people. Dating and interest in the opposite sex becomes a priority. The color line along which dating takes place is rigid though an increasing number of young people challenge that division. The cognitive ability of adolescents to strive toward consistency reinforces the influence of informal peer groups that separate groups and sustain dating patterns. These peer groups are easily recognized in almost all schools (Castleberry & Arnold, 1988; Classen & Brown, 1987). Castleberry and Arnold identified the informal groups as: O.P. Gang (Black guys), Junior Rockers (Black girls), Punk Rockers, Nerds, Preps, Jocks, Goody-goodies, Christians, Depressed People, Bullies, Pot Heads, and Good Friends in a middle school. In junior high school Classen and Brown found the Brains, Druggies, Jocks, Loners, Normals, Outcasts, Populars, Toughs, special interest groups (Farmers, Band Buddies), hybrids (Preppie-Brains), and the unassignable.

Teachers and counselors have as their greatest challenges to help those children of color who reach the teen years and for whom school has always been a place where they had little to be proud of and where they had experienced anxieties, fears, and sadness. The bad news is that it is not going to be easy to help these youngsters; the good news is that it can be done. Group counseling interventions are a most powerful and useful first step in helping these youngsters. They will need to find some part of schooling about which they can be proud, and they must also begin to become desensitized to some of the pain and failure experiences that they have had in school. Cultural identity groups are an appropriate strategy to help these youngsters share their secrets, conflicts, and successes. Youngsters at this age continue to value peer approval, and efforts to improve attendance and achievement should have a group component. Students need to hear the stories of struggle and achievement from their friends.

Group identity is a continuing process of negotiating the different developmental challenges and standards of the groups in their communities. Amidst the complexities of development there is continuity. As children move from one stage of identification to the next they take their memories with them. The pains and anxieties from previous stages are past but not forgotten, and the same can be said for the successes and the accomplishment of previous stages. It is important for the counselor and teacher to remember that previous experiences influence current behavior.

Methodology

Getting Started

The implementation of the cultural identity groups requires the cooperation of public school administration, teachers, parents, and children. The first step—getting administrative approval—is a challenge because there is an unofficial silence around the issues of ethnicity, race, and racism. These issues can be discussed, of course, but only within the prescribed control of the school. To implement cultural identity groups requires strength and a bit of courage by an administrator. (A parent once complained to a superintendent that children were being segregated by the principal.) Counselors should be aware that administrators are very concerned about publicity that reflects badly on them.

The next step in the process is a meeting with the teachers. To enlist their support and cooperation, a memo is sent to the teachers inviting them to the next inservice training meeting. Teachers usually have seen programs come and go, and they have an initial skepticism to new programs coming into the schools, so it is important to make it clear at the outset that this is a program that is designed to help children who need social and academic support.

Asking for and getting parental permission and support is delicate and vital. A letter to parents and a subsequent parent meeting are required prior to beginning the cultural identity process. Parents need help and support in exploring with their children the issues of ethnicity, race, and racism. Most parents quickly become firm supporters and there are a few parents who remain skeptical about the "recreation of segregation in schools." Parent meetings are well attended and a vigorous, powerful, and thoughtful discussion often occurs as parents reveal their concerns and share their painful experiences with racism in our society. At one discussion a parent told of the experiences of her young Asian American boy, "who was told he could not become president because he was Asian." At another parent meeting a parent introduced the metaphor of the cultural identity group as creating an orchestra. He explained, "Before you rehearse the entire orchestra, you have to rehearse the different sections separately and after they have learned their parts, then it is time to bring them together in harmony."

The facilitators for the groups can be experienced teachers, counselors, or college students. Of course, it is helpful if the facilitator has had experience with groups. Nevertheless, the structure of the cultural identity group process makes it possible for new counselors to quickly grasp the routines for conducting the groups. It is important for the facilitator to be familiar with the literature on racial identity theory, adolescent development, and racism and how ethnicity and culture impact human development. There should also be discussions of future alternative topics, group processes, ethical guidelines for working with groups, and the role of the group in the school.

Facilitating a Group

Getting started is a bit daunting but surprisingly easy. It is important to begin the CIGs with warm-up exercises because the children often do not know each other, and certainly, they have not participated in this kind of group together. Examples of warm-up or ice-breaker exercises are standard activities in group work and are widely available.

The children need to get to know each other, and it is important to improve and increase group cohesion as quickly as possible. A number of strategies have proved useful. It is appropriate to begin with choosing a name for the group. (One interesting group name chosen recently was Chocolate Swirl. The group consisted of four African American girls and one European American girl.) Rituals such as a handshake are also a good way to begin a session. And, it is important for the children to be involved in creating a set of rules for participation in the group. Group products should be produced and shared with the school.

As the Chocolate Swirl group demonstrates, not all members of a group have to be from the same ethnic group. Though a counselor from the same ethnic group as the students can be helpful, it is not a requirement. The research literature indicates that, all things being equal, ethnic minority participants prefer an ethnically similar counselor though many weigh attitudes, values, education, and experience as more important (Atkinson & Lowe, 1994). Children of color are often taught by white teachers and it is our experience that white facilitators can effectively work with any group of children.

Selecting the scope and sequence of topics for the session depends upon the group's members, their relationships, and the politics of the school. The sequence of topics should be tailored to the cultural backgrounds of the group. Likewise, culturally specific topics should be included in the curriculum to affirm the members of the group. When members do not know each other, it is critical to allow them time to build trust and cohesion. The politics of the school and school district is always a consideration. In some schools discussions of racism must be handled carefully because they can be difficult for children. It can be an even more difficult task for school administrators and parents. It is certainly a topic that should be set aside until trust and cohesion have been built within the groups.

Suggested Session Topics
1. Getting to know each other/Setting goals
2. Who am I?
3. Family and identity
4. Heroes and sheroes
5. Music
6. Fairness in our school
7. Discrimination in our town

Day one of the cultural identity group sessions is busy. There is the process of collecting the members of the group in one room and making them mindful of the time and day when the group meets. Two or three sessions are required before the children can be relied upon to bring each other to the sessions. Group members have to be introduced to each other because some of them are very shy and not used to talking. The evaluations have to be done prior to the beginning of the sessions.

The first order of business is to talk to the children about what a story is. Giving the students an example of a story and its structure helps them to understand how to tell a story. Discussions of setting, characters, plot, facts, and conclusions follow. During the first few sessions children learn to participate and they sometimes follow a scheme in their story telling. The facilitator reminds the children of the importance of context in appreciating the action in a story.

During each session each child is encouraged to provide music. Youngsters usually express a preference for rock and rap, though some students prefer classical music. There might be spirited discussions about the different kinds of rap.

A Story-Telling Perspective

Story telling is the perspective of choice for cultural identity groups, and it is used in such diverse areas as psychotherapy with adolescents (Biever, McKenzie, Wales-North, & Gonzalez, 1995), counseling with elementary school children (Cabello & Terrell, 1994; Webb-Mitchell, 1995), pastoral counseling (Ruard, 1993), and counseling theory (Spence, 1993). Learning to tell a different story is the therapeutic goal that these studies have in common. In short, the purpose of therapy is not to change some inner state of the individual but to help the individual learn to tell different and more productive stories about themselves.

This approach to story telling is modeled upon autobiographical memory research or the memories of the stories about ourselves and others (Conway & Pleydell-Pearce, 2000). The rationale for using this approach is that memory research tells us about the essential dimensions of a story. Their theory of story telling includes a global self, the emotions that monitor and guide the development of the self, and the content of the stories, which are clusters of memories. The global self organizes the overall goals toward which the individual works, and can be subdivided into different sets of selves: an actual self (an accurate representation of one's goals or self), an ideal set of goals/self and an ought self (goals set by parents, peers, teachers, ethnic communities, and others). There is accumulating evidence that goals and memories are organized into groups around such issues as work, school, synagogue, recreation, etc. The memory system thus has access to groups of memories rather than individual goal/memory states.

An emotional system monitors and guides the global self system, which produces the emotional reactions we have to story telling. Positive emotions indicate that the discrepancies between the actual and ideal selves are being reduced while negative emotions indicate that there is an increasing discrepancy between the actual and ideal selves. The emotions that come from the discrepancies between actual and ideal selves tell us about individual self-concept. The discrepancies between our actual self and our ought self results in the multiple selves that include our work, school, synagogue, and recreation selves. These multiple selves are the result of our multiple involvements and identification with the different complex institutions of our modern society.

Story telling comes alive when we adopt a dynamic dual self-system that includes emotions and cognitions. The complex interplay of knowledge and the emotions that are so typical of story telling is made readily visible in story telling. This approach is also aligned with our everyday experiences in which we experience emotions as we go about attempting to meet our daily challenges. It is commonplace to describe the plot of a story with its settings, characters, plots, and intrigues. The inclusion of the emotions in story telling invites us to examine the human experiences in all of their complexities.

Story Telling and Cultural Maps

Story telling is not one but a series of three different narratives that together create a therapeutic result. The three narratives include a narrative of self-disclosure, a narrative of connecting and scaffolding, and a narrative of change in which students create new narratives. The first stage of the process is self-disclosure. A recent review of this literature finds that self-disclosure promotes physiological health and well being, and is related to positive self-reports of health, records of use of health services, immune system efficiency, mortality, cardiovascular illness, and symptoms of emotional stress. Cook (2000) finds that self-disclosure is a necessity for existence because it is through this process that we enact and simultaneously recreate "self." Others play a crucial role in the enactment of the self in its different settings.

The second stage of the narrative process is the making of connections between the stories told by the different members of the group. This stage builds on the first stage and confirms and supports the different members of the group as they go about the process of recreating themselves. As they go about making connections and meanings, it is interesting to notice that each individual is free to choose the meanings that they will make of the stories that have been told. One student may choose to connect because of an identification with a certain character, experience, or outcome. Because there is a shared background of experience, the connections made by the students have a cultural coherence. The example used here is from a blended group of African American and European American children who are discussing Learning about Different Cultures (Box 2.1). The facilitator begins the construction of the Cultural Map by drawing her symbol (Fig. 2.1).

The third stage of the narrative process is the creation of a new narrative based upon new learning. This summing up refers to the understanding achieved by the students in the groups. Understanding is the scaffolding of knowledge and subjective experiences into a new narrative. This new form of knowing rises above bare knowledge to include subjective experiences with a continuing process of an

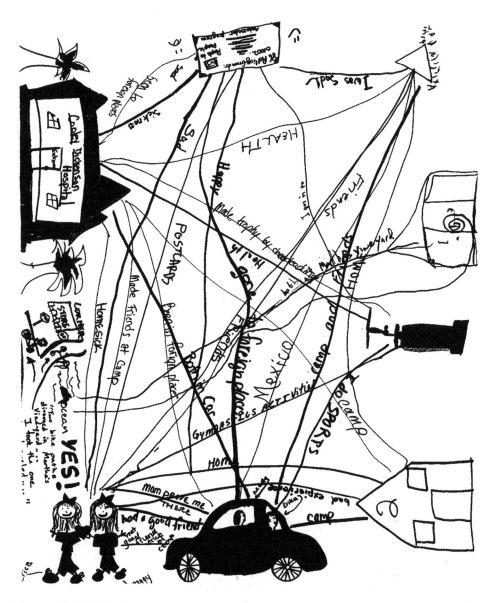

Figure 2.1 A cultural map.

appraisal. Penrose (1994) claims that understanding has its locus in the complex interplay of cerebral activity. Understanding presupposes a working self that has access to subjective experiences. According to Penrose, at about twelve years of age the corpus collosium matures and connects the two hemispheres of the brain making possible the linking of thought and subjective experiences.

BOX **2.1**

A Cultural Map: An Example

The facilitator begins with, "Today we are going to share stories about learning from other cultures. We all find ourselves in situations where we have to adjust to new situations and cultural experiences. It is normal to feel anxiety about being in a new learning situation but it can be exciting and fun.

"My symbol is a green mountain with green grass because I was in the city of eternal spring. (In Figure 2.1 her mountain looks more like a triangle!)

"I had an opportunity to study in Mexico a few years ago. I was studying Spanish. And I wanted to improve my speaking ability. I went to stay in the home of a Mexican family for six weeks. I was excited yet fearful at the same time. I was afraid because I was going to live in a strange house. I traveled to Mexico and after the first week I was fine. I learned that when you live in a culture and you respect the experience there's a lot of fun to be had. I met some wonderful people with whom I became friends. I am a better person for the experience."

As each student participates in the session, they tell their stories and draw their individual symbols. After the first round, the facilitator begins by saying, "I see a connection between my story and John's story because we have both had health problems." The teacher writes down the reason for the connection. "I see a connection between my story and Rachael's story because we have both spent time in a foreign country." Again, the teacher writes down the reason for the connection. This procedure continues until all have finished. The next round of story telling asks the students to identify the common themes and learnings that they have learned that day. Some examples of the curriculum or themes from the group include the feelings one has in a new place, health, friends, and family.

The facilitator ends the session by explaining, "We can look at the Cultural Map and remind ourselves of how similar we are. We have the building blocks for learning to understand each other. Let us continue to listen with open minds and have fun."

Evaluation Instruments

Story telling has emotional and cognitive components, and the evaluation is designed to assess these two different areas. The Self-Esteem Scale focuses on cognitive appraisals of individual and group self-esteem as well as on identity as a student, while the Emotional Climate Scale (ECS) yields a profile of the emotional responses of student participation in the CIG, of individual identity, group identity, and identity as a student. You will notice that the instruments assess virtually the same variables, one from a cognitive perspective and the other from an emotional perspective.

The ECS yields a profile of the ratings of emotions by children to the different aspects of their educational environment. The emotions included in the scale are: anger, sadness, anxiety, fearful, happiness, hopeful, pride, and excitement, each of which is rated on a seven-point scale. We learn about emotions by being engaged in the world in which hurtful experiences challenge those about whom we care. Negative emotions are the reactions to the hurts experienced by those we care about while positive emotions result when plans are successful. There is then a complementary relation between positive and negative emotions (Solomon, 1995). It is the case that the more we care for another person, the more likely we are to react with strong, negative emotions when that person is harmed or threatened.

Emotional Climate Scale

Instructions.   In a few minutes I am going to ask you to answer the questions to the Emotional Climate Scale. First we have to fill out the first page which asks for some background information from you. This is the Emotional Climate Scale. You will evaluate your participation in the groups, your classes in school, and other experiences using eight different emotions. You will rate your emotional reactions on a seven-point scale (one = low and seven = high). On each of the following pages there are a title and list of eight emotions each with seven dots. Read the title and circle or put an X over the dot to represent your choice along the scale, from high to low.

Following is an example of the responses of an African American student.

When I Am Learning About Racism I Feel

	Low						High
1. Excited	.	.	.	.	.	.	X
2. Sad	X	.	.	.	.	.	.
3. Pride	X	.	.	.	.	.	.
4. Anxious	X	.	.	.	.	.	.
5. Fearful	.	.	.	.	X	.	.
6. Hopeful	.	.	X	.	.	.	.
7. Angry	.	.	.	.	.	.	.
8. Happy	.	.	.	X	.	.	.

Here is an example of an African American student's responses to the Emotional Climate Scale. As you can see, this youngster has an array of emotional reactions to discussions of racism. Some of them are rather disheartening.

The Emotional Climate Scale consists of eight items on which responders rate their feelings: When I Am In The African American Group, When I Am Learning About Racism, When I Am On The Playground, Eating In The Cafeteria, When I Am On The Bus, When It Is Reading and Writing Time, In Math, and As A Student. Of course, the different items can be changed to fit the needs of the students and the counselor.

The Self-Esteem Scale

The Cognitive Self-Esteem Scale measures the cognitive assessment of group and individual self-esteem, and it goes on to assess the student's participation in the cultural identity group and perceptions of ethnic group membership.

Instructions. I would appreciate it very much if you would complete the Self-Esteem Questionnaire. It is an instrument that measures your reactions to the cultural identity group, group identity, personal self-esteem, and school. Answer these items on a seven-point scale (one = low and seven = high). Here is a copy of the Self-Esteem Scale. Do you have any questions?

The test items are listed below:

Group Identity
1. I feel proud of being African American.
2. I feel safer with African Americans.

Personal Self-Esteem
3. I am happy to be me.
4. I am proud of myself as a person.
5. I feel good about myself.

Cultural Identity Group
6. I feel good about belonging to the cultural identity group.
7. I feel like I belong to the African American group.
8. I enjoy learning about the African American experience.
9. I enjoy working with members of the African American group.

School
10. I am proud of my school work.
11. I am proud of the things that I can do.
12. In our school everyone is treated equally.
13. In sports all children are treated equally.

The purpose of this approach to evaluation is to bring a balance of emotion and cognition to the study of culture and story telling. Heretofore, the study of identity and story telling has emphasized the cognitive. The use of the Emotional Climate Scale makes plain that it is possible to study children's emotional responses to their school experiences. The Emotional Climate Scale makes it possible to study the patterns of emotional responses to the different settings within a school. We take for granted that emotions are a critical dimension to identity and story telling, and this makes it possible to identify the different patterns of responses that different groups of children have toward ethnicity, themselves, and their schools.

Implications

We began this paper with a series of vignettes in which children of color were confronted with racism, discrimination, and prejudicial behavior. A young Asian American girl asked, "What can we do about it?" The answer is that we cannot change the society in which we live. What we can do is help our children live more productive lives at school in a country that has racism as one of its founding principles.

Through the cultural identity groups we can help students tell their stories of racism, discrimination, home, family, friends, and school. Telling their stories will help them take ownership of their experiences and make concrete their sense of identity and self-esteem. They will become clearer about the pride that they have in themselves, their families, and their cultural backgrounds. Talking about painful experiences will make them less anxious and more willing to discuss difficult issues.

The cultural identity group process can be used with a wide range of student groups. It can be used with girls to discuss issues of gender, with children who have learning disabilities, children with behavioral problems, and so on. Most importantly there are different components of the cultural identity group process that can be helpful. The lessons to be learned are:

1. Emotional development and cognitive development are equally important in the educational process. Each can be evaluated and used effectively in the group process.

2. The Cultural Map provides a useful record of meaning-making in a group. It is helpful to have a visual representation of the goings-on in a group. This record can be used by the participants and the group leader to review the accomplishments of the group.

3. The Emotional Climate Scale can be used effectively to assess how children feel about the groups they attend, their classes, and their experiences in school and community.

4. One of the major problems in groups is that a few group members often do most of the talking. Changing the procedure so that all members of the group are expected to talk can alter the dynamic of the group, and can empower those who are least likely to be heard.

Good luck with your cultural identity groups.

DISCUSSION QUESTIONS

1. Why is it necessary to have cultural identity groups?

2. Are there developmental differences in the ways in which children cope with prejudice?

3. Why does cognitive development influence how children respond to prejudice?

4. Why is it important to have an objective instrument to record meaning making?

5. Why is it important that every child have an opportunity to participate in the process of meaning making?

6. What are the consequences of silence in the presence of prejudice?

7. What can we learn from the emotional climate scale?

8. What areas of a school should be included in the emotional climate scale?

9. Are cultural identity groups only necessary in schools with culturally diverse populations?

REFERENCES

Atkinson, D. R. & Lowe, S. M. (1990) The role of ethnicity, cultural knowledge, and conventional techniques in counseling and psychotherapy. In J. G. Ponterotto, J. M. Casas, L. A. Suzuki & C. A. Alexander (Eds.), *Handbook of Multicultural Counseling* (pp. 387–414). Thousand Oaks, CA: Sage.

Biever, J. L., McKenzie, K., Wales-North, M., & Gonzalez, R-C. (1995). *Adolescence, 30*, 491–499.

Cabello, B. & Terrell, R. (1994). Classroom interaction, *29*(1), 17–23.

Castlebury, S. & Arnold, J. (1988). Early adolescent perceptions of informal groups in a middle school. *Journal of Early Adolescence, 8*(1), 97–107.

Classen, D. R. & Brown, B. B. (1987). Understanding peer pressure in the middle school. *Middle School Journal, 19*(1), 21–23.

Conway, M. A. & Pleydell-Pearce, C. W. (2000). The construction of autobiographical memories in the self-memory system. *Psychological Review, 107*(2), 261–288.

Galatzer-Levy & Cohler, B. J. (1993). The Essential Other: A developmental psychology of the self. New York: Basic Books.

Jenkins, R. (1992). Pierre Bourdieu, New York: Routledge.

Kagan, J. (1984). The Nature of the Child. New York: Basic Books.

Lazarus, R. S. & Lazarus, B. N. (1994). Passion and reason: Making sense of our emotions. New York: Oxford University Press.

Penrose, R. (1994). Shadows of the mind: A search for the missing science of consciousness. New York: Oxford University Press.

Ruard-Ganzevoort, R. (1993). Investing life stories: Personal narratives in pastoral psychology. *Journal of Psychology and Theology, 21*, 277–287.

Spence, D. (1993). Narrative truth and historical truth. New York: Norton.

Webb-Mitchell, B. (1995). The importance of stories in the act of caring. *Pastoral Psychology, 43*(3), 215–225.

AUTHORS' NOTE

A note of appreciation is due to Mary Branford Ivey, Allen Ivey, and Phyllis Brown who were involved in implementing the first Cultural Identity Groups.

Ernest D. Washington is currently a professor of education at the University of Massachusetts, Amherst. He received his Ph.D. from the University of Illinois in Educational Psychology. His major interests are in culture, methodology, and the philosophical foundations of education. His current research is focused upon the use of aesthetics as the foundations of methodology.

3

Racial Identity in the Social Environment

JANET E. HELMS
Boston College

OBJECTIVES

1. To present Helms's (1990–1995) racial identity theories as conceptual frameworks for analyzing the racial dynamics that impinge upon the educational climate, including but not limited to the classroom.
2. To present Helms's People of Color and White theories to describe the characteristics of students, educators, and parents at an individual level.
3. To present interaction theory as the framework for designing interventions and evaluating interventions already in place.

In the school system, the unresolved race-relations issues that prevail in the society more broadly are acted out at various levels of interaction. Because there are few commonly accepted theoretical models for resolving these issues in society, there are also few models for structuring the educational environment so that it becomes a climate facilitative of personal and interpersonal growth rather than of damaged personal self-esteem and destructive interpersonal relationships.

In this chapter, Helms's (1990, 1995) racial identity theories are presented as conceptual frameworks for analyzing the racial dynamics that impinge upon the educational climate, including but not limited to, the classroom. Her People of Color and White theories will be used to describe the characteristics of students, educators, and parents at an individual level, and her interaction theory will be used as the framework for designing interventions and evaluating interventions already in place.

Racial Identity Development Theory

Racial identity theory concerns a person's racial self-conception as well as her or his beliefs, attitudes, and values vis-à-vis the self relative to racial groups other than her or his own. Helms (1990) proposes that a person's racial identity is composed of three interacting components, personal, affiliative, and reference group. The personal component is the self-conception or "who am I?" aspect of racial identity. The affiliative component of racial identity concerns the extent to which the person believes that what happens to other members of his or her racial group also happens to him or her, whereas the reference group component refers to the person's level of conformance to the norms of his or her ascribed racial group(s).

During the formative years of childhood and adolescence, each of these three aspects can be shaped and influenced by a variety of environmental factors including: (1) societal messages about the individual's worth as well as that of her or his group; (2) parental socialization concerning race relations; (3) peer influences; and (4) educators' communications about race and racial differences.

Racial identity theory uses a social rather than a biological definition of "race." Accordingly, in this country, by custom and/or fiat, some combinations of certain observable characteristics including, but not limited to, skin color or quantity of melanin, facial features, and/or language are assumed to distinguish various *racial* groups. By the age of three or four years, children generally know to which group they belong (P. Katz, 1976), and consequently, one must assume that by the time they enter elementary school, the implications of belonging to one group rather than another have already become salient for them.

It is not clear to what extent pre–secondary-school children have developed a racial identity of their own. At this stage of life, it is most likely that they reflect the racial identity climate evident in their home environment(s). In other words, adult role models (e.g., parents) initially influence how the child feels about him- or herself (personal identity), whose values are assumed to be worth imitating (reference group orientation), as well as influence the child's role within her or his racial community (affiliative identity). Teachers and peers may eventually influence the child's racial identity development in alternative directions, but it is the familial environment that provides the foundation for the child's subsequent development.

Therefore, it is important for teachers to be familiar with the models of adult racial identity development so that they will recognize imitative childhood racial identity development whether the behavior being imitated derives from the home or the school environment. Helms's models of adult racial identity development differ depending upon whether one is describing the development of melaninated persons or White persons. The former group has the task of developing a healthy positive racial identity in environments in which they are often the survivors of racial oppression, whereas the latter's developmental tasks occur in environments in which they are usually the beneficiaries of racial oppression. Nevertheless, even in these markedly different environments, analogous racial identity characteristics can develop and these may be expressed in various kinds of social interactions.

Racial Identity and People of Color

Racial identity theorists have begun to discuss the racial identity development of members of various groups of color including Asian Americans (Alvarez & Helms, 2001; Lee, 1988), Latinos/Latinas (Delgado-Romero, 2001), and Native Americans (Lowrey, 1983). However, most of the contemporary theories and empirical research continue to focus on Black Americans (Helms, 1990; McAdoo, 2002; Nghe & Mahalik, 2001). Nevertheless, in proposing the People of Color model of racial identity, Helms (1995) noted that virtually all of the models of racial or ethnic identity propose at least some similar as well as some unique developmental processes. Consequently, the People of Color model is intended to describe the racial identity developmental process as it pertains to the shared themes of development rather than to replace the models that describe unique racial socialization experiences of members of the groups of color.

Racial identity is assumed to develop via a maturational process in which the person potentially can come to use increasingly more complex cognitive-affective ego statuses to perceive not only herself or himself as a racial being, but also the racial dynamics of members of her or his affiliative and reference groups. Schemas are the overt manifestations of racial identity statuses. The five statuses are the not conscious or automatic states of the person's ego that define the nature or theme of the person's race-related cognitions, feelings, and behaviors (i.e., schemas). Because the statuses and, consequently, the schemas develop in response to racial socialization in which White people and/or the White group has the most power, the central racial identity developmental task for a Person of Color is to resolve intrapsychic conflict involving Whites as the contrast group. (It is conceivable that racial identity may also involve resolution of internal conflict with respect to disempowered groups other than one's own, but this issue has not yet been addressed in the racial identity literature). In the People of Color model, the five racial identity statuses (and related schemas) are Conformity, Dissonance, Immersion/Emersion, Internalization, and Integrative Awareness.

Conformity

The Conformity status is characterized by the general theme of superiority of Whites and White culture and the denigration of "color" and of the culture of Peoples of Color. A Conformity personal identity is expressed by the child who (or whose parents) attempts to emphasize "White" physical characteristics and de-emphasize or eliminate the characteristics that mean color in this society. Thus, some examples of parental behaviors that might contribute to the child's imitative Conformity identity include shaving the child's head (e.g., getting rid of the "bad hair"), forcing the child to wear long sleeves so that her or his skin will not be darkened by the sun, using skin lighteners. Teachers reinforce Conformity personal identities when they favor light-skinned children and stereotype and/or ignore their darker skinned counterparts.

A Conformity reference group orientation is reflected in the child and parent's beliefs that educational achievement is a foreign value among their racial group. Thus, as the argument goes, in order to be comfortable with achieving academically, the child must reject own-group values and adopt those of Whites. Educators can reinforce a Conformity RGO by not providing contradictory information. That is, to the extent that textbooks and lesson plans do not include information about the scholastic achievements of People of Color, to the extent that scholastic achievers of color are not acknowledged and rewarded by the educational environment, then the child's Conformity RGO remains unchallenged.

A lack of a variety of other People of Color in the school environment (that is, peers, teachers, administrators) reinforces children's Conformity affiliative identity. That is, they do not learn much about the diversity of people in their own racial group. Moreover, they may not learn the social skills for interacting with their own group, but will learn the skills of White culture. Consequently, what appears to be rejection by one's group coupled with ostensible acceptance by Whites may contribute to a child's belief that Whites *are* better.

Dissonance

The Dissonance status involves confusion about how one regards one's racial group. On the one hand, there is considerable societal exposure to the theme that "White is best," but because of some personally meaningful events, individuals may begin to realize that they are not really members of the White group. Yet a lack of exposure to the benefits of belonging to one's own group can leave individuals with no racial group with which to identify. Often Dissonance is expressed as euphoria as individuals first realize that their own culture represents an alternative to White culture. Dissonance may also be expressed as anxiety and/or depression as individuals become aware of their marginality with respect to the available racial/ethnic groups.

During childhood and adolescence, Dissonance may be expressed through unpredictability as children act out their questions about belongingness. On some days children expressing Dissonance will conform to the racial norms of the classroom; on other days, they may try to get attention in ways that focus on their "differentness." Treating such children's behavior as merely a disciplinary problem without acknowledging their core identity issues decreases the likelihood that these children will learn that they can value themselves because they belong to a particular racial group. Moreover, failure to address their needs in identity-enhancing ways strengthens the children's beliefs that the school system does not value members of their group, and decreases the chances of unconflicted identification with Persons of Color. Consequently, Dissonant children may internalize racial stereotypes with respect to their own racial group and will not be able to recognize and evaluate the norms of their racial group. Under these circumstances, their associations with members of their own will be based on automatic negative rather than positive predispositions.

Thus, the sensitive teacher will provide opportunities for positive acknowledgement of the child's racial group membership without making the child an oddity. In other words, it can generally be assumed that all children in a classroom are learning something about racial identity whether explicitly or implicitly. The Dissonant child may be merely expressing the class's confusion around racial issues.

Immersion/Emersion

The basic theme of the Immersion/Emersion status and schema are idealization of the group of color and denigration of Whites. This status has essentially two aspects, Immersion and Emersion. The first involves a withdrawal from everything assumed to reflect White culture in response to anger generated by one's increasing awareness of the consequences of racial oppression. The second involves intensive attempts to learn about one's own racial group.

With respect to personal identity, children using this schema emphasize their racial group membership particularly in appearance and behavior. Often Immersion children's interpretation of what characterizes their racial group is naive because it is likely to be an enactment of society's view of the group. The child's reference group may also become group members who "live up" to the group's stereotype, and the political oppression experienced by other members of the racial group is reacted to "as if" it were personally experienced. Thus, at times, the child's affective reaction to seemingly trivial events may appear grossly exaggerated. The Emersion aspect of this status allows a great opportunity for helping children develop a positive view of their racial group as well as of self with respect to the group. When the children's racial reactions are motivated by Emersion, then they are receptive to the influence of positive role models from their own racial group. They are generally interested in and stimulated by classroom activities that increase their knowledge about the positive attributes of their racial group. Such information provides them with the cognitive tools to resist societal racial stereotypes and to build a positive mental representation of their own group.

Thus, the teacher's task when confronted with students using this schema is to help them channel their anger and energy into positive group-affirming activities and assignments. Teachers who become frightened by this newly developing racialism often respond by discouraging the child's burgeoning racial development, which, of course, increases the child's perception that institutions and authority figures are racist.

Internalization

Children who can use the Internalization schema interact with others with a positive sense of themselves as racial beings. The values that are most important are those of their own racial group and the children recognize their debt to members of their racial group who preceded them. Generally, Internalizing children are the ones who are capable of functioning across racial groups and are often put in the role of mediator when racial conflicts arise among peers.

Teachers often feel uncomfortable with racial issues themselves and so rely on the child with a positive sense of racial identity to teach the other students about the student's group. Other times this student is used as the role model for other racial group members or is viewed as the "exception" by members of the other group(s). This can be overwhelming to the Internalizing child in this stage because it emphasizes her or his "differentness." It may also assume knowledge that the child does not yet have, which may leave the child feeling inept. The same sorts of racially appropriate enrichment experiences available to the Immersion/Emersion child should be available to the Internalization child as well. Additionally, teachers or other appropriate adult role models should assume the responsibility of teaching about race relations as they do other subjects of importance. Such teachings can be readily worked into classes concerning history, art, science, languages, and math.

Integrative Awareness

The general themes of the Integrative Awareness status (and schema) are the integration and resolution of issues pertaining to one's various demographic identities (e.g., racial, gender, sexual orientation) and the recognition of shared conditions of oppression or advantage with a variety of groups that society accords differential statuses. Although it is unusual to find children or adolescents who have developed so inclusive a humanistic orientation toward others, it does happen occasionally.

Adults and other children are often threatened by children who can accept and value aspects of themselves and other people that are distasteful to them. Sometimes such children are teased and ostracized because they in effect are challenging racial group and peer group norms. Teachers need to learn to value a wide range of diversity themselves so that they will be prepared to foster a classroom climate where valuing of diversity is the norm rather than the exception.

White Racial Identity Theory

White racial identity theory is a relatively recent approach for explaining the pathways to a healthy identity for White people (cf., Helms, 1990, 1995; Silvestri & Richardson, 2001). However, students from this group are more likely to need such a model given that when schools are integrated, children of color generally move into "White environments" rather than the converse. Also, because White identity and "racism" are often treated as synonyms, White people's exposure to racial issues generally has others (non-Whites) as the focus, and does not help them understand how unresolved racial developmental issues affect their personal adjustment and well-being.

In my model (Helms, 1995), White identity is assumed to progress via a six-status model: Contact, Disintegration, Reintegration, Pseudo-Independence, Immersion-Emersion, and Autonomy. As was the case with the previous model, each status involves conceptions of the self as a racial being as well as conceptions of self relative to other racial groups. However, because Whites (regardless of socioeconomic status) have greater privilege and sociopolitical power, they can more readily avoid working through issues of racial identity development than can other groups (cf. Phinney, 1989). The combination of opportune avoidance and adult role models, who frequently have no conception of the meaning of a positive White identity themselves, means that White children often seemingly enter the school environment unaware that race still exists as a volatile issue in the society, or that they can "choose" what kind of White person they will be. In general, the teacher has the task of expanding their awareness of identity options and raising growth-promoting questions.

Contact

The general theme of the Contact status is lack of consciousness of one's own race and either naive curiosity or timidity with respect to other groups. Children using or imitating the Contact schema generally either have been directly taught to pretend that racial differences do not matter or they have acquired these beliefs indirectly due to lack of meaningful contact with members of other groups or by being raised in a familial environment in which such issues just are not discussed.

Thus, Contact children may be aware of their appropriate racial self-label (White), but may have very little reality-based sense of what it actually means to be White. Interestingly, the reference group orientation of these children is usually White, but not deliberately so. Many children in this group may adopt another group affiliative identity as they attempt to role-play being non-White. This other-group enactment is generally naive and focuses on superficial characteristics of the other group (e.g., hair styles, clothing).

The classroom interventions for children in this stage should involve providing accurate and honest information about various racial/ethnic groups as well as "safe" exposure to various groups via guests, outings, and media. Moreover, because Whites and White culture are dominant in this society, it is often easy for students (and teachers) to be unaware of the dimensions of White culture and to focus exclusively on the cultural dimensions of other racial groups. A lack of any focus on White culture leaves the White child feeling that other groups are more exciting than one's own and probably retards one's willingness to explore the issues of White racial identity development.

Disintegration

The primary theme of this status is guilt and confusion. This status represents the White person's ongoing acknowledgment that being White has social implications that often force the White person to face moral dilemmas that arise from being considered to be better than other groups. As far as personal identity is concerned, children may express guilt and anxiety when racial issues are discussed. They may also attempt to avoid any such interactions. The Disintegrating child's affiliative identity becomes more deliberately White, though it is not usually an unconflicted identification. That is, the child may embrace immoral racial values and beliefs because these are the norms of that part of the child's White group to which he or she is exposed. The reference group aspect of identity may also become exclusively White as the child tries to escape from the painful feelings associated with this status.

For children using the Disintegration schema, teachers should design interventions that help the children distinguish personal responsibility from group responsibility. Thus, via role-plays, readings, and discussions, children might be helped to analyze how different behaviors impact self, members of other groups, as well as other Whites in their environment. Ideally, these strategies should help children understand their own feelings as well as empathize with others.

Reintegration

As a means of resolving the intrapersonal conflict aroused by the confusion of Dissonance, the Reintegrating person adopts an orientation in which everything White is considered to be superior to everything that is not. When using this schema, the tendency is to negatively stereotype other groups and to exaggerate the differences between one's own group and others.

As far as personal identity is concerned, Reintegrating children appear to be rather rigid in their beliefs. They generally have learned rules for explaining to themselves why they are better than members of other groups and why Whites and White culture should dominate the school environment. The reference group for children motivated by this status is Whites, and often Whites who hold racially oppressive values and beliefs, in particular. Whites are also the group that defines one's affiliative identity with respect to this status and schema. In general, the group identifications associated with this schema are based on shared views of White superiority (which need not be explicitly expressed) and denigration and hostility directed toward other groups. When children use this schema, they may engage in behaviors such as name-calling designed to make the other racial group members feel uncomfortable; they may also engage in behaviors, such as wearing the Confederate flag, in an attempt to express a White identity—albeit a dysfunctional one.

Reeducation should be educators' primary focus when students use this schema. Reeducation should be aimed at eliciting the stereotypes of all the racial groups within the environment (including Whites) and providing contrary information. Via analyses of the histories of their own groups, students could be helped to discover the source of prevailing stereotypes and the social consequences of maintaining them. In their books, Helms (1992), Helms and Cook (1999), and J. Katz (1978) provide a number of experiential exercises that can be adapted for children in need of interventions to assist them in working through this phase of the racial identity developmental process.

Pseudo-Independence

This status represents an immature positive nonracist identity. Here, the basic themes are intellectualization and paternalism. That is, the person attempts to control tumultuous feelings aroused by thinking about other groups' racial problems and trying to help them acculturate to White culture. That is, the person not only still believes that White culture is best, but also tends to believe that the Person of Color's racial issues can be resolved by learning White culture and/or gaining access to it through associations with Whites. For these reasons, I sometimes call Pseudo-Independence the status of "White liberalism."

Children who use this schema generally have a positive view of themselves as White persons, and though this view is still tinged with superiority, it is not consciously so. The reference group for these children is generally "good Whites," that is, other Whites who believe that assimilation into White culture is a desirable goal for People of Color. The child's affiliative identity is often multiracial, reflecting comfort with certain members of other groups (i.e., those receptive to learning White culture). Moreover, the child motivated by this status may be involved in volunteer work that helps individuals perceived to be underprivileged.

Because thinking about racial issues is a crucial dimension of Pseudo-Independence, teachers and educators can help strengthen use of this schema by encouraging and devising activities that stimulate the child's curiosity and critical thinking about racial issues. Stimulating activities include diaries, field trips to cultural events or places, volunteer work, book reports about People of Color, and panel presentations involving people of various races. Each of these activities should be structured to encourage the child to develop critical thinking skills with respect to members of racial groups including her or his own group. Exposing them to a variety of situations that contradict prevailing White stereotypes about People of Color should facilitate this process.

Immersion/Emersion

The search for personally meaningful definition of Whiteness and re-education of other White people about race and their contribution to racism characterize this status and schema. In children and adolescents, this status is often expressed as an unsophisticated form of social activism.

Thus, children are consciously aware of being White and so their personal identity is White when they have either developed the Immersion/Emersion status themselves or can imitate the relevant schema as exhibited by significant adults in their lives. However, they often lack a clear affiliative or reference group identity. On the one hand, they know that they should identify with other Whites, but often the adult Whites in their environment have not resolved their own racial identity issues, and consequently cannot help the child. Thus, the child frequently lacks adequate White role models. As far as affiliative identity is concerned, the child is probably confused here as well. Children using this schema attempt to grapple with the moral dilemmas that are not talked about by adults in their environments. As a consequence of these efforts, they are filled with "why" questions. White adults sometimes have their patience tried by having to respond to complex issues which they may not have resolved themselves. Consequently, these children may turn to peers of color to help them resolve their discomfort with the "immorality" of Whiteness (as they see it).

Educators can facilitate children's quest for answers by encouraging them to analyze race-related current events with an eye toward clarifying the moral dilemmas, helping them think of creative ways to educate themselves and other Whites about racism and racial issues, and encouraging the child to recognize the positive aspects of Whiteness through events such as White ethnic awareness days or events.

It is important to realize that children who are developing this status may become quite angry with White adults who are perceived as having deceived them about racial issues. Therefore, the educator's task is to become an ally in helping the child examine who the child is.

Autonomy

This is the most cognitively and affectively complex status of White identity development and might best be thought of as an ongoing process of refinement of one's racial identity. The primary themes of this status are internalizing, nurturing, and applying a more complex personal definition of Whiteness to interpret life events.

When using this schema, individuals' personal identities are nonracist; they are able to conceive of being White without also being racist. Their affiliative identity is also White in that they recognize that their core values and beliefs are absorbed from White culture. Nevertheless, by being able to use critical thinking skills to actively question the tenets of White culture, the Autonomous individual is developing the capacity to choose those aspects of White culture that feel right. When using the Autonomous schema, the person's reference group orientation is multiracial as well as multicultural. Not only does his or her friendship network include people representing a wide range of so-called races, but he or she is also sensitive to the commonalities inherent in various forms of oppression (e.g., sexism, poverty, ageism). This sensitivity permits the person to avoid blaming the victims of oppression for their adverse circumstances and gives the person evolving an Autonomous racial identity a focus for changing systems to eliminate oppression from society.

Autonomous children are generally quite cognitively flexible and open to new information and new ways of thinking about racial and cultural variables. In some sense, the educator's job is easiest when children can use this schema because they can often think of their own self-enrichment experiences. Therefore, the educator can often act as a consultant who helps children channel their energies into practicable goals and activities.

So far, my discussion has focused on using racial identity theory to "diagnose" the child's status and develop interventions that are congruent. In addition, to these ideas, the reader might also wish to consult Feldstein's (2001) identity interventions for educators as well as Banks' (1981) ideas for curriculum reform using identity models.

Racial Identity Interaction Theory

Perhaps it has not been evident that *everyone* with whom the child comes in contact in the school environment (including teachers, peers, support staff) is also using some racial identity schema. Racial identity interaction theory hypothesizes that the child's level of identity in combination with others' (e.g., teachers) identities can result in qualitatively different educational experiences for the child.

Three types of potential interactions seem relevant here: parallel, regressive, and progressive. Interactions are conceptualized from the perspective of the person with less social power (in this case, the student). "Social power" is defined according to social roles, numerical presence, and/or sociopolitical histories of the racial groups within the environment. Thus, in general, teachers, principals, and similar figures have more social power than students, and Whites generally have more than People of Color. However, members of the numerical majority (Whites) within a particular environment may have less social power than does the numerical minority.

A parallel relationship is defined as one in which the educator and the student in the interaction use the same (if they are of the same race) or analogous (if they are of different races) racial identity schemas. Thus, participants share the same types of racial attitudes, and it is unlikely that the educator can help the student develop beyond where the student already is. Of course, the more advanced each participant's level of development is, the more influential will a parallel relationship be. In other words, a relationship that is parallel with respect to Autonomy or Internalization ought to be more beneficial to both participants than one that is parallel with respect to Contact or Conformity, for example.

A Regressive relationship is one in which the educator is less developmentally advanced with respect to racial identity development than the student. Because such an educator is less comfortable facing racial issues than is the student, the educator attempts to change the student's thinking and behavior in directions that feel wrong to the student. As a consequence, Regressive relationships are often characterized by varying degrees of disharmony, conflict, tension, and rebellion. With less direct control over the quality of the interaction, a student may engage in acting out and/or passive aggressive behaviors to express discomfort with the quality of the relationship. For their part, educators may engage in punitive (both overt and covert) activities whose purpose, perhaps unconscious, is to coerce the student to think as the educator does. If the educator does not realize that the student is merely expressing resistance to coercion, then the educator also will feel emotional distress and attempt to find ways to escape from or terminate the relationship.

The most beneficial type of interaction is a Progressive one—the educator's identity status is more advanced than the student's. If the educator can recognize the developmental issues of the student, then the educator can offer experiences and creative role-modeling that will help the student consider alternate ways of being. Progressive dyads can be mutually beneficial to those involved. Because the educator is functioning in the expected role of teacher and has the greater social power, the student is likely to be responsive to alternative educational experiences advocated by the educator.

In any particular educational setting, the educator may become involved in different kinds of interactions with different students. When the setting involves more than one student, students may form coalitions (i.e., smaller subgroups) based on similarity of expression of racial identity statuses. In these instances, the interaction is classified according to the coalition and educator's manner of interacting with one another concerning racial issues. Thus, Parallel interactions would occur when the coalition expressed a level of racial identity development similar to the educator's level; a Progressive interaction would occur when the educator's racial identity development is more advanced that the coalition's expressed level; and a Regressive interaction would occur when the coalition's expressed developmental level is more advanced than the educator's.

An example might illustrate how this interaction theory can be used to analyze the factors affecting the racial climate in one's school. The situation is real, though I have disguised it somewhat so as not to identify the school that was involved. School X is predominantly White (about 80 percent) and is located in a White upper-middle-class neighborhood. Ten percent of the students are Black, 7 percent are Asian, and 3 percent are Latina/Latino. The students of color come from families whose socioeconomic status ranges from lower to upper middle class. The administration at school X likes to view itself as a success story where integration is concerned. Students of all of the racial groups perform better than the national average on achievement tests and there is little obvious conflict between the various racial/ethnic groups.

One day, several of the White boys in the school show up wearing Confederate flag lapel pins. When the Black students observe this, many of them become angry and start arguments in hallways and classrooms with the offending White students.

When Principal X (a White man) discovers the cause of the sudden conflict, he calls the boys to his office, confiscates the pins, and forbids them to wear anything of the sort in the future. When the students explain that the flags are a symbol of membership in a social club and ask why they cannot wear them, Principal X says, "because they upset the Black students."

Teacher X (a White woman) has several of the boys involved in class. When she discovers that the White boys were prohibited from wearing the pins, she believes that they were unfairly treated and so the next day, she wears a Confederate flag pin to school. Although Principal X orders her to remove her pin as well, it is too late: several factions of students, parents, and teachers have formed. On one side are those who feel the White students' freedom of speech has been violated; on the other are those who feel that the Black students' right to a nonracist educational environment has been violated.

Although there are a number of interactions we could examine, we will focus on Teacher X's interactions with students in her class. First, we can "guesstimate" Teacher X's level of identity based on her manner of reacting to the situation—either Contact or Reintegration. Based on the available information, Contact seems the most likely because the teacher acts as though there are no racial issues involved in this situation and that the Black students are not even present in the environment. A person who was expressing a Reintegration identity would probably recognize that race was a critical issue in this situation, but find a way to blame the Black students (as Principal X does).

The White students also could be expressing either Contact or Reintegration identities. The students seem to be trying to find a way to bond together as White students without perhaps recognizing that they are doing so. They also do not seem to be aware of the racial implications of the situation, though perhaps they are. Conscious awareness of any racial implications of their behavior would suggest that Reintegration describes them better than Contact. However, the educator would have to do some creative interviewing to discover which is more accurate. In any case, for our purposes, we will assume that the pin-wearers were using the Contact schema. Thus, the pin-wearers were in a coalition themselves and with other students in the class who viewed the situation as merely a freedom of speech issue.

Teacher X and the Contact coalition are in a Parallel interaction. Thus, though they all feel righteous in their political stance and feel supported and understood by one another, it is unlikely that their racial attitudes will change as a result of one another's influence. They are "unaware" of race, so they are incapable of helping each other analyze their contribution to the racial tensions in this situation.

Teacher X and the Black student protestors are in a Regressive interaction. Though the Black students are aware of racial issues, they have less social power in this situation than Teacher X in a variety of ways. Of course, the student role gives them less power. They also are numerically underrepresented in the student body and do not have access to educators who can help them articulate their feelings in ways that help others respect their point of view.

In Regressive interactions, one expects covert and overt fights about racial issues, as was the case at School X. One also expects that little student growth will result from this situation because the teacher has lost her credibility with the Black students. And, the teacher probably becomes frightened by a perspective she does not understand. In Regressive interactions the teacher and coalition(s) become entrenched in their respective positions and find ways to "fight" each other until their relationship ends or is ended.

Although I only focused on one level of a complex school environment, teacher–student interactions, perhaps it is clear that one could use the model to examine issues at other levels (e.g., teacher–principal; principal–pin-wearers) as well. Additionally, the model can be used to examine the quality of students' educational experiences with those aspects of the situation that symbolize the teacher (e.g., books).

In the situation described, the commonality across the kinds of interactions is a lack of attention to race and its implications for how students treat one another. In retrospect, an educator who was at a higher level of identity development than either of the foregoing educators demonstrated might have used this "opportunity" to expose students to learning experiences that would facilitate healthy identity development. An even better solution would be to integrate such experiences into one's ongoing curriculum so that the student body does not confront these important issues only when there is a crisis.

Of course, educators who intend to introduce regular racial identity developmental experiences into the school environment must be amenable to self-examination with respect to these issues as well. One cannot be a part of Progressive relationships if one's self has not "progressed." The works of Helms (1990, 1992, 1995), Helms and Cook (1999), and Takaki (1993) might be useful in facilitating this process.

DISCUSSION QUESTIONS

1. What do you think television programming for children teaches children and adolescents about racial identity?

2. Design a school curriculum that you think would facilitate healthy racial identity development.

3. How would you intervene to help a child whose racial identity development is more advanced than her or his teacher's racial identity development?

4. Some people believe that racial tensions in U.S. society would not exist if everyone would just stop talking about racial differences. What do you think?

5. How can parents facilitate thier chilren's healthy racial identity development?

6. What, if anything, is wrong with teaching all children (regardless of race or ethnicity) to adapt to White culture?

7. Identify some racial "moral dilemmas" with which children in today's society might have to cope.

8. Use racial identity interaction theory to analyze a school or other educational environment in which you function.

9. How could Principal X have better handled the situation described in the chapter?

10. What strategies would you use to evaluate your own racial identity development?

REFERENCES

Alvarez, A. N. & Helms, J. E. (2001). Racial identity and reflected appraisals as influences on Asian Americans' racial adjustment. *Cultural Diversity & Ethnic Minority Psychology. Special Issue: Asian American acculturation and ethnic/racial identity. Research innovations in the new millennium, 7,* 217–231.

Banks, J. A. (1981). The stages of ethnicity: Implications for curriculum reform. In J. A. Banks (Ed.), *Multi-ethnic Education Theory and Practice* (pp. 129–139). Boston: Allyn & Bacon.

Delgado-Romero, E. A. (2001). Counseling a Hispanic/Latino client—Mr. X. *Journal of Mental Health Counseling. Special Issue: Counseling racially diverse clients, 23,* 207–221.

Feldstein, M. (in press). Teaching about racism and oppression in predominantly White elementary schools. In J. E. Helms (Ed.), *Proceedings of the First Annual Diversity Challenge: How to survive teaching courses on race and culture.* Boston College: Institute for the Study and Promotion of Race and Culture.

Hardiman, R. (1982). *White identity development theory.* Unpublished doctoral dissertation, University of Massachusetts, Amherst, MA.

Helms, J. E. (1990). *Black and White and White racial identity: Theory, research, and practice.* CT: Greenwood Press.

Helms, J. E. (1992). *A race is a nice thing to have: A guide to being a White person or understanding the White persons in your life.* Topeka, KS: Content Communications.

Helms, J. E. (1995). An update of Helms's White and People of Color racial identity models. In J. G.

Ponterotto, J. M. Casas, L. A. Suzuki, & C. M. Alexander (Eds.), *Handbook of Multicultural Counseling* (pp. 181–191). Thousand Oaks, CA: Sage.

Helms, J. E. & Cook, D. A. (1999). *Using race and culture in counseling and psychotherapy: Theory and process.* Boston: Allyn & Bacon.

Katz, P. A. (1976). The acquisition of racial attitudes in children. In P. A. Katz (Ed.), *Toward the elimination of racism* (pp. 125–150). New York: Pergamon Press.

Katz, J. (1978). *White awareness: Handbook for antiracism training.* Norman: University of Oklahoma Press.

Lowrey, L. (1983). Bridging a culture in counseling. *Journal of Applied Rehabilitation Counseling, 14,* 69–73.

McAdoo, H. P. (Ed.). (2001). *Black children, social, educational and parental environments* (2nd ed.). Thousand Oaks, CA: Sage.

Nghe, L. T. & Mahalik, J. R. (2001). Examining racial identity statuses as predictors of psychological defenses in African American college students. *Journal of Counseling Psychology, 48,* 10–16.

Phinney, J. S. (1989). Stages of ethnic identity development in minority group adolescents. *Journal of Early Adolescence, 9*(1–2), 34–49.

Silvestri, T. J. & Richardson, T. Q. (2001). White racial identity statuses and NEO personality constructs: An exploratory analysis. *Journal of Counseling & Development, 79,* 68–76.

Takaki, R. (1993). *A different mirror: A history of multicultural America.* Boston: Little, Brown.

A U T H O R   N O T E

Janet E. Helms is a professor of Counseling Psychology and director of the Institute for the Study and Promotion of Race and Culture at Boston College. Dr. Helms is a Fellow in Division 17 (Counseling Psychology) and Division 45 (Ethnic Diversity) of the American Psychological Association (APA) and is co-chair of the Joint Committee on Testing Practices as APA's representative. She is a member of the Association of Black Psychologists.

Dr. Helms serves on the editorial board of the *Journal of Psychological Assessment* and she is a member of the Council of Research Elders for the *Journal of Cultural Diversity and Ethnic Minority Psychology*. She has written over 50 empirical and theoretical articles and four books on the topics of racial identity and cultural influences on assessment and counseling practice. Her books include *A Race Is a Nice Thing To Have*, and (with Donelda Cook) *Using Race and Culture in Counseling and Psychotherapy: Theory and Process* (Boston, MA: Allyn & Bacon).

Dr. Helms has been acknowledged for her work with awards that include an engraved brick in Iowa State University's Plaza of Heroines and the Distinguished Career Contributions to Research award from the Society for the Psychological Study of Ethnic Minority Issues, awarded at the APA convention. In 1991 she was the first annual recipient of the Janet E. Helms Award for Mentoring and Scholarship in Professional Psychology. This award was inaugurated in her honor by Columbia University Teachers College.

PART TWO

Multicultural Family Issues

The five chapters in Part Two define the heart of this book by emphasizing the profoundly important connection between the school student and the family/community context in which that student lives. Far too few school counselors are trained for family interventions and in many schools contact with the student's family is discouraged. When the family is bicultural, this tension frequently results in a tug-of-war between the family and the school simultaneously pulling the student in two different directions. These chapters demonstrate the importance of cooperating with the student's family and being sensitive to the multicultural family issues.

Each chapter in Part Two is focused on a different multicultural family issue relevant to school counseling. One important theme is "worldviews" which is highlighted in Chapter 4 by Roysicar-Sodowsky and Frey. This chapter focuses on the specific context of immigrant populations but the issue is also relevant for other populations as applied to the student's subjective assumptions and culturally learned perceptions. The tradition of immigration and increased rates of recent immigration make this chapter particularly relevant. Recent immigrants from non-Western cultures have had more difficulty assimilating than European immigrants of previous generations. Case examples are discussed and a variety of models are presented for understanding worldview values and dimensions as applied to school counseling. Chapter 5 by Bemak and Chung continue the same theme by helping school counselors provide effective counseling to immigrant students. Meeting the needs of immigrant students requires counselors to take on a new and different role from their work with nonimmigrants. This chapter points out that while the school changes the immigrant, the immigrant student also changes the school in return, and especially school counseling. A Multi-level Model of Psychotherapy (MLM) is described along with fifteen other recommendations for counseling immigrant students. Chapter 6 by Casas, Furlong, and Ruiz de Esparza focus on the worldviews of Hispanic students and families as they influence school counseling. Given the rapid increase in the number of Hispanic students in U.S. schools this specific population requires special attention. Hispanic parents will have considerable influence on the educational success or failure of their children. In schools that marginalize the role of families this becomes a serious problem. The chapter reviews specific programs and suggests ways that school counselors can include Hispanic parents in the educational process.

A second important theme in Part II is that of the "family–school partnership." It is not necessary for the family and the school to compete with one another for the student. A partnership of shared rights and responsibilities is much preferred. Chapter 7 by McKenna, Roberts, and Woodfin describes such a partnership model as a means of supporting school counselors in their work. The collaboration between the school and the family recognizes that each has different values and needs and makes different assumptions, so developing a partnership is not easy. However, the authors point out the disastrous consequences of not having a partnership as well. A key factor is developing a framework for the partnership ahead of time. Specific examples illustrate the problems and opportunities of partnership. Chapter 8 by Juntunen, Atkinson, and Tierney continues the partnership theme by looking at school–home–community liaisons. This liaison is particularly important in schools with more ethnic diversity and, as more and more U.S. schools become explicitly diversified, the need for a strong partnership increases. Schools typically lack the resources for such a liaison, which also might not be welcomed by some cultural groups. However, the many sources of acculturative stress require that a partnership be developed, however difficult that might be. Specific guidelines for developing and implementing a liaison are discussed.

CHAPTER

4

Children of Immigrants: Their Worldviews Value Conflicts

GARGI ROYSIRCAR-SODOWSKY
Antioch New England Graduate School

LISA L. FREY
University of Oklahoma

OBJECTIVES

1. To provide a rationale for understanding and serving Asian and Latino/Hispanic children of immigrants within the school system
2. To identify the differences in psychological characteristics, adaptation to U.S. society, values orientation, and ethnic identity issues of immigrant children from different generation groups
3. To discuss the influence of U.S. culture on immigrant youths' family interactions
4. To identify possible coping strategies and other resources of immigrant children as they experience difficulties of immigration and subsequent individual acculturation adaptations
5. To understand the construct of worldviews and the ways in which worldviews may be translated into specific cultural values, behaviors, and practices
6. To identify and explain specific worldview dimensions from various theoretical frameworks
7. To discuss the importance of worldview assessment of a school student, as well as of the self-awareness of a counselor of his or her own worldviews value orientations, as part of the counseling process in the school and community

Since the 1960s the United States has experienced an influx of immigrants from Asia, Latin America, and the Caribbean (Rumbaut, 1997). The children of foreign-born, first-generation immigrants have, in turn, begun to change North American society with their visible numbers. Zhou (1997) noted that since the 1980s immigrant children have become the fastest growing and the most ethnically diverse segment of America's child population. The rapid growth of immigrant children and adolescents is also being felt in the school systems across North America, especially in the major urban areas. However, limited information is currently known about both first-generation immigrant children and of U.S.-born second-generation children of immigrants

(Portes, 1997a). Currently, research on new immigrants and refugees has largely been on adults (e.g., see Kuo & Roysircar-Sodowsky, 1999; Roysircar-Sodowsky & Maestas, 2000; Sodowsky & Carey, 1988; Sodowsky & Lai, 1997; Sodowsky, Lai, & Plake, 1991). Rumbaut (1994) noted:

> Less is known about the subjective aspects of the children's experience, as processed within their phenomenal field. What we refer to here as the 'crucible within.' This includes their modes of ethnic or national self-identification, perceptions of discrimination, aspirations for their adult futures, cultural preferences, forms of intergenerational cohesion or conflict within their families, self-esteem and psychological well-being, and how these may be related to more objective indices of their experience, such as their school and work performance and language shifts from the mother tongue to English. (p. 752)

Ten years earlier, Aronowitz (1984) had also observed the lack of conceptual efforts in examining and understanding the effects of migration on children. A similar concern has now been raised about the increasing presence of international adolescent students in U.S. and Canadian high schools and middle schools (Pedersen, 1991; Wilson, 1983). Literature on international students has been on adults, specifically college and graduate student populations (e.g., Berry, 1985; Kwan, Sodowsky, & Ihle, 1994; Sodowsky, 1991; Sodowsky, Maguire, Johnson, Ngumba, & Kohles 1994; Sodowsky & Plake, 1992; Suthakaran & Roysircar-Sodowsky, in press). Pedersen (1991) observed:

> The emphasis has been entirely on counseling international students in U.S. colleges and universities. There . . . [has been] very little reference to counseling international high school or elementary school students. This very limited but growing literature is an area demanding much new research. (p. 51)

Children of Immigrants: Some Defining Demographics

Portes (1997b) pointed to a number of reasons for the scholarly neglect of post–World War II immigrants: (1) the relative youth of this group owing to their post–1965 immigration to the United States; (2) the obscurity of census and official data concerning them; and (3) the general invisibility of immigrants of color until the recent dramatic increase in birth rates in immigrant groups.

Two significant points concerning immigrants in the United States and Canada must be noted. First, Asian and Latin American immigrants constitute the majority of immigrants to the United States since 1970 (Rumbaut, 1997). Asians and Pacific Islanders showed a 35-percent population increase from 1990 to 1996 (U.S. Bureau of the Census, 1998). In Canada, the Asian presence was even stronger than in the United States, with slightly over 7 percent of the total Canadian population being represented by Asians (Statistics Canada, 1996). The Statistics Canada (1996) indicated that Asian-born immigrants accounted for 57 percent of the recent immigrants in Canada between 1991–1996. Hong Kong, the People's Republic of China, India, the Philippines, and Sri Lanka led the list for most recent immigrants.

Second, Asian immigrants are characterized by their relative youth. Oropesa and Landale's (1997) analyzes of the 1990 U.S. Census indicated that 90 percent of Asian American children and 60 percent of the Latino children belonged to the first or second generation (that is, they were new immigrants), as compared to 6 percent of the non-Latino African American children and 5 percent of non-Latino European children (Oropesa & Landale, 1997). Among Asian American children, 47 percent of Japanese Americans, 91 percent of Chinese Americans, and 99 percent of Vietnamese and of Asian Indians belonged to the first and second generations. Japanese Americans have historically come to the United States before most Asian groups, and, therefore, they have fewer first- and second-generation youth than do the other groups. Age cohorts determined by time-related trends in immigration can be further illustrated: 30 percent of Chinese American children were first generation, 61 percent were second generation, and 9 percent were third generation (Oropesa & Landale). In Canada, one third (33 percent) of the immigrant population consisted of children and adolescents under age 24 (Statistics Canada, 1996). For South Asians, Chinese, Koreans, Japanese, Southeast Asians, and Filipinos, 22 percent were reported to be between the ages of 0–14, and another 16 percent to be between the ages of 15–24 (Statistics Canada, 1996). Furthermore, the configuration of the foreign-born versus native-born immigrants in Canada indicated that 65 percent of the Japanese were reported to have been born in Canada, while that was true only for 29 percent of the South Asians who are relative new comers.

There is another even more neglected subgroup of Asian adolescents. Young sojourners from Asian countries (e.g., China, Hong Kong, Taiwan, and South Korea) live and study in the United States and Canada without being accompanied by their parents (Hong, 1998; Kim, 1998; Lin, 1998). In 1990, an estimated 30–40,000 Taiwanese unaccompanied minors between 8 and 18 years were reported to be living in the United States (Forden, 1990). In 1993, approximately 10,000 of these adolescents were in Southern California alone (Lin, 1998). In Canada, approximately 12,000 foreign students from Asian countries were studying in Canadian elementary and secondary schools from 1995 to 1996 (Canadian for International Bureau Education, 1997), most of whom were in Canada without their parents.

Information on East Asian unaccompanied adolescents is obscured by insufficient official records, paucity of research, and negative portrayal of Asians by the mass media (Kim, 1998). Limited available research on Chinese unaccompanied sojourners points to their acculturation-related difficulties, such as cultural adjustment difficulties (Kuo & Roysircar-Sodowsky, 1999; Lin, 1992), education-related concerns (Lee, 1994), and psychological and emotional problems (Cheng, 1994; Chung, 1994).

Mental Health of Adolescent Immigrants: Differences between Cohorts

Important differences exist between immigrant children of different cohort groups. Those who immigrate as children (called the 1.5 generation) and the U.S.-born second-generation children of immigrants differ significantly in their psychological characteristics, adaptation to school and society at large, and values orientation toward their cultural origins. Among the first-generation children, there are also differences between those who immigrated early and those who immigrated as adolescents. These differences are noted by the studies discussed here.

Significant differences were detected in self-reported identity between foreign- and native-born Chinese Canadian adolescents (Lay & Verkuyten, 1999). The participants' self-identification (including ethnic identification), collective self-esteem, and personal self-esteem were measured. Foreign-born Chinese Canadian adolescents were more likely to call themselves Chinese as opposed to Chinese Canadian or Canadian Chinese than were the Canadian-born adolescents. They were also more inclined to make references to their ethnicity regarding who they were (i.e., their responses to a "Who Am I" questionnaire). For the foreign-born, personal self-esteem was related to more positive evaluations of their ethnic group and a greater sense of being good members of their ethnic group. For native-born Chinese Canadians, no significant relationship was found between personal and collective self-esteem. Lay and Verkuyten suggested that foreign-born adolescents may have been more allocentric than their Canadian-born counterparts. That is, the foreign-born individuals were more focused on in-group characteristics, such as ethnicity, religion, and gender, when defining and describing themselves, as compared to more idiocentric Canadian-born Chinese individuals.

Rosenthal and Feldman (1990) investigated whether Western culture influenced Chinese immigrant youth's perception of their family patterns. High school students in tenth and eleventh grades from three countries were surveyed: the United States (i.e., first-generation Chinese, second-generation Chinese American, and Euro-American adolescents); Australia (i.e., first-generation Chinese, second-generation Chinese Australians, and Anglo-Australians); and Hong Kong (i.e., Chinese adolescents born in Hong Kong, Canton, or China). An increased accommodation to the autonomy-promoting norms of Western society (the United States and Australia) occurred in the family dynamics of all Chinese immigrants in the United States and Australia. However, despite increasing endorsement of the autonomy value over time, both first- and second-generation Chinese immigrants reported more structured, controlling family environments than did the White nonimmigrant groups. More specifically, the first-generation Chinese Australian adolescents perceived their family environment to be "structured." Their second-generation Chinese Australian counterparts perceived their family environment to be "controlling" and "conflictual," thus suggesting negative reactions to Asian parental authority. The second-generation Chinese Americans perceived their parents to be regulatory, to be monitoring their activities, and to be taking responsibility in decision making, more so than did the first-generation Chinese Americans.

While a loosening of family boundaries was observed in both immigrant samples in the United States and Australia, conformity to family values was still maintained. The authors concluded, "even in long-standing immigrant families, certain traditional aspects of Chinese family life are maintained, despite evidence of acculturation to individualistic norms over time" (p. 512).

Chiu, Feldman, and Rosenthal (1992) investigated the influence of immigration on parental behavior and child distress and the relationship between these two variables for Asian adolescent immigrants. Their findings were similar to those of the previously cited study (Rosenthal & Feldman, 1990). Immigrant and nonimmigrant adolescents from the United States, Australia, and Hong Kong differed in their perceptions of parental control and involvement, but they did not differ in their view of parental warmth (Chiu et al., 1992). The second-generation Chinese reported less "harmony," more "rule setting," and more "attempted monitoring" with regard to parental behaviors than did the first-generation immigrants. On the other hand, the first generation immigrants reported more emphasis on "order keeping" by their parents compared to the second generation. Again, the implication was that the second generation might have family conflicts with their foreign-born first-generation immigrant parents. With regard to perceived distress, first-generation Chinese American and Chinese Australian adolescents were found to have more symptoms of emotional distress (e.g., anxiety, depression, low self-esteem), while second-generation participants had more psychosomatic complaints (e.g., headache, fatigue, loss of appetite). Thus both generation cohorts experienced difficulties, albeit manifesting different symptoms.

Feldman and Rosenthal (1990) conducted another cross-national (the United States, Australia, and Hong Kong) study of five groups of adolescents, consisting of tenth and eleventh graders. There were two Chinese immigrant groups and three nonimmigrant groups. The study assessed participants' expected ages for behavioral autonomy in a variety of everyday life management domains. First- and second-generation Chinese immigrant adolescents were shown to be different from American and Australian adolescent samples and the nonimmigrant Chinese adolescent sample in Hong Kong. For the Chinese immigrant adolescents, the core aspects of Chinese culture, such as children's level of autonomy, might have been less susceptible to change than external adaptations, such as in the domains of language, food preference, and clothing styles. Rosenthal and Feldman concluded that Chinese adolescent immigrants appeared to be selective and modest in making accommodations to the values of individualism of the West, while maintaining a continuity of their traditional culture.

In a third study, Rosenthal and Feldman (1992) studied the ethnic identity of first- and second-generation Chinese Australian and Chinese American adolescents. Ethnic identity was assessed with a multifocus approach in terms of ethnic identification, an individual's engagement in culturally expected behaviors and knowledge of his or her ethnic culture, the importance of maintaining these behaviors, and the value ascribed to one's ethnic origin. In both the U.S. and Australian samples, first-generation Chinese immigrant adolescents indicated greater familiarity with Chinese behaviors and cultural knowledge than did their second-generation counterparts. However, the two groups considered maintaining cultural practices to be equally important, and regarded ethnic-group membership in equally favorable terms. Rosenthal and Feldman concluded that the external aspects of ethnic identity may be more prone to attrition over time, but internalized ethnic identity is more resistant to change. This finding was supported by a study of South Asian Hindu and Muslim adult immigrants in the United States (Suthakaran & Roysircar-Sodowsky, in press).

In a study (Lay & Nguyen, 1998) with sixty first-generation Vietnamese students, "in-group" hassles were defined as stressful events and conflicts that stem from immigrants' interaction with their ethnic peers (for example, perceived lack of fluency in their language of origin, or difficulties in understanding and conducting oneself confidently in the context of one's cultural origin). In-group hassles originated from the differences in values and desires between the second-generation Vietnamese immigrant children and their first-generation network, such as one's family, friends, fellow workers, neighbors, voluntary associations, and community services.

Padilla, Alvarez, and Lindholm (1986) studied the impact of generation status on stress. They used a 66-item, self-report stress scale, the Social, Attitudinal, Environmental Stress Scale (SAFE). The immigrant participants were categorized into four groups: early immigrants (immigration prior to the age of 14); late immigrants (immigration after the age of 14); second generation; and third/later generation. The late immigrant students experienced the greatest stress. They showed lower self-esteem and were more externally controlled than the other groups. On the other hand, the early immigrants scored lower on stress and higher on self-esteem and internal control than did the late immigrants. There was another striking finding. There were similar profiles between the late immigrants and the second generation, and similar profiles between the early immigrants and the third/later generation. The implication was that children who immigrate early are predisposed to healthy biculturalism, benefiting equally from both worlds they live in—their ethnic families and the dominant society—while skipping the problems of late immigrants' acculturation to the new society and preventing the ethnic identity confusions and cultural marginalization of the U.S.-born second generation.

In view of the aforementioned findings, it is evident that immigrant adolescents have to deal with several psychological issues: acculturation change attitudes and behaviors, ethnic identity, perceptions of family and parent–child relationships, interpersonal tensions between cohort groups, self-esteem, anxiety, depression, and stress. All these dimensions importantly include the cultural values of immigrant ethnic communities. However, the salience of each dimension varies across different generations of minority children and adolescents.

Adolescent Immigrants' Ways of Coping

Owing to their developmental characteristics, social resources seem critically important to coping for all adolescents universally, specifically in their being able to rely on adults to a great extent for survival and in investing in close friends (Compas, 1987; Patterson & McCubbin, 1987). However, immigrant children, who feel different from their parents, other cohorts groups within their ethnic society, and peers from the dominant group who reject them, could be leading lonely lives without much social support. Yet social support is a critical cultural variable in collectivistic societies. There is evidence on the importance of community and social support in affecting the stress experiences of minority individuals, as will be discussed.

An investigation on first-generation Korean immigrants who immigrated to Canada after the age of 16 studied the relationships among stressors, psychological resources, and social resources (Noh & Avison, 1996). The investigators construed social resources in terms of support coming from the immigrants' own ethnic communities as well as from the host community. Social support from outside the Korean community had no effect on the immigrants' psychological health. However, social support from one's own ethnic group had greater impact on the well-being of the immigrants. In addition, psychological resources that included self-esteem and mastery constituted a significant factor in affecting psychological distress.

Based on their review of the literature on Hispanic stress and coping, Cervantes and Castro (1985) pointed out that the presence or absence of supportive extended family kinships, religious/spiritual affiliations, supportive versus nonsupportive work relationships, and the nature of available social services and/or health services agencies serve as external mediators of stress. These resources serve as a kind of buffer in mitigating stressful life events for minority individuals (Smith, 1985) and may help to reduce psychiatric symptoms (Dressler & Bernal, 1982; Dyal & Dyal, 1981).

It is conceivable that accessing collective resources may be fundamental to the coping responses of ethnic minorities. The notion that coping and social resources are separate constructs, according to the general coping literature (e.g., Parker & Endler, 1996; Pearlin & Schooler, 1978), may not be relevant for ethnic minority individuals whose lineal–hierarchical and collectivistic values orientations may predispose them to using coping resources outside themselves.

Olah (1995) examined the coping strategies utilized by 720 adolescents, between the ages of 17 and 18, from five countries (Hungary, Italy, Sweden, India, and Yemen). European participants from Hungary, Italy, and Sweden showed a preference for assimilative, operative, confrontational behaviors when facing stressful circumstances. Assimilative coping represents a coping strategy that attempts to shape environmental forces to be in line with what one wishes. On the other hand, the non-European participants from India and Yemen reported a greater preference for accommodative, emotion-focused coping responses. In accommodative coping, an individual directs the changes upon oneself, such as one's emotions (e.g., denial, avoidance), in order to meet the demands of external situations. Olah attributed these nationality differences in coping to different cultural influences.

Hispanic and Anglo adolescents seem to cope differently (Copeland & Hess, 1995). Participants were 189 Anglo students and 55 Hispanic students from an urban area. Hispanic adolescents reported greater use of social activities and seeking spiritual support than their Anglo counterparts. Humor was more prevalent among the Anglo students than the Hispanic students.

Cervantes and Castro (1985) noted that Mexican Americans with different acculturation levels (e.g., low, bicultural, high) experience clusters of potential stressors that are unique to their acculturation. Acculturation variables such as language, level of adaptation to White American ways, and degree of adherence to traditional and non-traditional values function as "internal mediators" that affect stress responses. Similarly, Laosa (1990) observed that characteristics of the community of origin, characteristics of the new community of settlement, characteristics and lifestyle of the Hispanic child and family prior to and after migration, life changes associated with the immigration process, accumulated stressors during relocation, school characteristics in both the community of origin and the community of settlement, and the child and family's cognitive appraisal of immigrant stressors all serve as complex interacting variables that shape immigrant children's choice of coping strategies and long-term adaptation in the new environment.

Mena, Padilla, and Maldonado (1997) studied coping mechanisms among four generation groups of immigrant college students. The late immigrants utilized a more active and individualistic coping strategy than did their early-immigrant and second- and third-generation counterparts. The early-immigrant, second-, and third-generation respondents used more social networks as coping mechanisms than did the first-generation group. Mena et al. attributed the individualistic coping of the first-generation immigrant group to their lacking a social network or to their unfamiliarity with their new cultural environment.

Zheng and Berry (1991) found similar coping in a Chinese sojourner group. They compared local Chinese students in China, Chinese sojourners in Canada, Chinese Canadian students, and non-Chinese Canadian students in Canada. The Chinese sojourner group was found to utilize more active ways of coping than both the Chinese Canadian and the non-Chinese Canadian students. Coping strategies such as tension reduction, information seeking, less self-blame, and less wishful thinking were identified more by the Chinese sojourner students than the other two groups. Differences in stress-coping responses between the two groups of Chinese participants in Canada were clearly evident. The authors of this chapter suggest that sojourners and first-generation immigrants, having few social contacts, might need to be self-reliant, instrumental, and agentic for survival reasons, behaviors quite contrary to the values of communal living, relationship affiliations, and passive resignation espoused by their original collectivistic cultures. Such behavioral transgressions under duress can cause much stress and mental health problems to the newcomers.

Differences in the cultural values of individual youth and their values-oriented understanding of situations, along with the differential impact of their adaptations to a new culture, result in a complex array of experiences and responses within adolescent students. Two case studies are used to illustrate the stresses of immigrant youth and their ways of coping.

School Counseling Cases
Case Study 1

A math teacher notices that Linh, a 14-year-old boy from Viet Nam, who immigrated   to the United States with his family two years ago, has done poorly on several tests and has fallen asleep several times in class. This is unusual for Linh, who had previously seemed very interested in the class and had received good grades on his math tests, especially in comparison to his work in English and social studies. The teacher approaches Linh to discuss this new pattern. Linh tells her that he has had trouble concentrating on studying in all his classes for the past few months, apologizes for his test grades, and says he will try harder. The teacher continues to press Linh about what might be causing his concentration difficulties, but Linh is reluctant to talk about it. The teacher, however, remains concerned and sends Linh to the school counselor, Mr. Malborough.

When Linh apologetically tells Mr. Malborough that he has had trouble concentrating, Mr. Malborough suspects that there may be more to the situation, especially because Linh has also been falling asleep in class. However, Mr. Malborough is also aware that Linh may view the school counseling situation as strange because Linh may associate school only with learning from teachers. In addition, Linh's reluctance to respond to his teacher's persistent questioning indicates to Mr. Malborough that privacy and emotional restraint may be important values to Linh. Mr. Malborough decides the most respectful approach would be to respond to Linh's expressed problems with concentration and help him explore solutions to this problem.

Mr. Malborough makes arrangements with an ESL volunteer tutor to work with Linh in study hall. Mr. Malborough hopes that making such an intervention will help to build the trust and rapport needed for Linh to communicate any other concerns which are underlying his school problems. In addition, he believes that an active, structured approach will help Linh to better understand what counseling can offer.

Mr. Malborough meets with Linh several times, giving Linh a chance to get to know him better. One day Linh tells Mr. Malborough that his mother is quite ill and was diagnosed with cancer four months ago. Linh reports that he helps to take care of her and wishes he could stay with her all day, but his parents want him to focus on his studies. Linh's father works at two jobs, and because Linh is the oldest child and a male, he thinks he has special leadership responsibilities of overseeing his younger siblings' conduct in his father's absence. Linh knows that his success in school is important to his mother and father, but he says he worries about his mother too much to concentrate. He watches T.V. at night because he cannot sleep.

Mr. Malborough considers a number of factors in trying to determine the ways in which he can be most helpful to Linh. One of Mr. Malborough's immediate considerations is assessing ways in which he may be able to provide Linh with academic support during his school day. In addition to arranging for a tutor, Mr. Malborough, while maintaining the confidentiality of Linh's specific family concerns, discusses with ESL teachers and other subject teachers whether they would be able to spend a little extra time with Linh in order to decrease the amount of schoolwork Linh takes home. Most teachers are generously responsive to the idea. Mr. Malborough limits the number of courses to the minimum necessary and reorganizes Linh's schedule. Creative solutions specific to Linh's difficulties might be necessary. For example, if Linh is falling asleep in class because of family commitments and worries which are limiting his sleep, arrangements might be made for Linh to nap in the counselor's office during the lunch hour and at other possible times.

Another factor that Mr. Malborough considers is the possibility that Linh may have experienced other significant losses in his life. Mr. Malborough is aware of the history of conflict and violence in Linh's native land. He knows that Linh may have experienced previous personal losses and separations from family members or may have heard stories about such events from older members of the family, and these may be now contributing to his distress about his mother. In addition, Mr. Malborough knows that the process of immigration itself is difficult and stressful, and the probability exists—that the family left loved ones behind—grandparents, uncles, aunts, and cousins—who lived close by before Linh and his family relocated to the U.S. These possible losses may also be contributing to Linh's distress. Additionally, Linh may be more affected by the threat these losses present to the integrity of the family as a whole than by their effect on him as an individual member of the family.

One option that Mr. Malborough might consider is to explore with Linh the helpfulness of informing key people in the school support system about his situation and, if so, how to best inform them. Linh may want their understanding and support but not want to explain the situation repeatedly or answer lots of questions. In the individualistic U.S. society, where there is an emphasis on "talking out" emotions, asking questions about someone's personal crises is a way of showing concern. In less individualistic cultures, however, people may depend on friends and relatives to act as intermediaries to communicate personal information among their reference group. Being required to continually answer questions and provide information about the personal crisis may be experienced as stressful, draining, and invasive.

A related issue that Mr. Malborough might consider is associated with Linh's values regarding the directness of verbal communication. Perhaps Linh would feel less threatened and more at ease expressing his thoughts and feelings symbolically, which could include describing how he spends his weekend at home with his family; accompanying Mr. Malborough to the school library and finding pictorial books and fiction on Viet Nam, which Linh and Mr. Malborough could refer to briefly in later sessions; drawing pictures of festive occasions that are held in the Buddhist temple which Linh and his family attend; exchanging information with Linh about Vietnamese festivals and celebrations and about holidays that are observed in the United States; asking Linh to bring in family pictures; asking Linh to list any friends that he might have, both Vietnamese and White American, and describing what he likes most about them, etc. Such symbolic communication may also provide Linh, an ESL student, with a tool to express the depth and intensity of experiences and feelings, which he is unable to convey verbally through the use of English.

Talking to Linh about how he and his family would deal with the situation of his mother's health if they were still in Viet Nam might provide Mr. Malborough with some information about how to best support Linh at this time. In addition, Mr. Malborough might be able to engage Linh in problem solving regarding ways to adapt culture-specific coping mechanisms that he might have used in Viet Nam to his current environment. This might involve spiritual practices and seeking social support. Developing an increased understanding of Linh's beliefs about illness and even death would also give Mr. Malborough direction regarding how to provide culturally appropriate help for Linh. For example, if Linh's worldview includes a belief that life is primarily determined by external forces, Linh may believe that the outcome of his mother's illness depends on fate and must be endured stoically. This information would help Mr. Malborough to better understand and empathize with Linh's grief responses and, as a result, assist him in determining what interventions would be the most effective in helping Linh to cope and derive meaning from his experience.

Case Study 2

Maya is a 12-year-old Asian Indian girl who was born in the United States. Her parents are first-generation immigrants from India. Maya is experiencing considerable pressure from her parents. They have high expectations for her academic performance, and even after she finishes her homework, they require her to study for extended periods of time with additional help from private tutors. Maya also takes piano lessons and learns classical Indian dancing. Maya's parents want her to comply with their rules for filial respect, a vegetarian diet, a traditional female gender role, familiarity with her first language and Hinduism, and frequent participation in Indian parties that her parents attend and in activities in the Hindu Temple. Even though Maya's mother shows a lot of attention and care to Maya, Maya finds her mother cold. Maya thinks her father has no time for her and comments that he works all the time. Maya has referred herself for counseling.

In this instance, if the counselor pressures Maya for disclosures about family disagreements over different values and expectations across two generations, the counselor may show disrespect for the cultural value of family loyalty that is highly valued by Asian Indians. The counselor's pressure may also set in an antitherapeutic process, causing Maya to comply with the counselor's authority and speak reluctantly, a hierarchical process in which she is already enculturated by her immigrant parents. This counselor–client interaction of demand-and-comply is likely to evoke in Maya the same concerns she has at home about authority figures.

Instead, the counselor can provide an affirmative interpersonal experience in counseling which is different from Maya's experiences with older family members. Being of the second generation, Maya is acculturated to verbal communications and affective expressions and may even like such behavioral interactions to some extent. At the same time, the counselor keeps in mind the core taboo about family betrayal. The counselor could thus say, "You don't need to talk to me about the difficulties you're having at home. I am wondering what might happen at home if you were to talk to me about this problem. Can we talk about what your mother might say or what your father might do because you have come to see me? Is there a family member you might feel better talking to?"

Or if Maya is trying hard to please the counselor, the counselor can say, "I feel as though I'm like the older people in your family, making you feel that you must agree with me. What can I say or do that will make you speak your mind?" By helping Maya to identify and resolve her concerns about talking freely, without feeling disrespectful, Maya may begin to talk. Still, owing to her family loyalty, Maya may speak selectively, which boundary the counselor respects. Through her interactions with the counselor, Maya is empowered to speak for herself rather than to merely comply. Such a process, based on an understanding of the client's cultural values, allows for an authentic person-to-person interaction, which encourages meaningful change in the client.

However it is important to note that because a particular counselor's response evolves out of an understanding of cultural values, the same response that helps one child may hinder another child. For instance, a counselor who self-discloses difficulty in solving a problem may be seen as lacking expertness and showing unprofessional behavior by Asian clients, but may be welcomed by clients from another culture group because the counselor is seen as human and less judgmental.

These case studies illustrate the importance of understanding and therapeutically translating the value-based meanings that immigrant children give to situations. In the case of Linh, a first-generation (sometimes also known as 1.5) immigrant who came to the United States in middle school, counseling consisted of educational services and structured, problem-solving methods of help. He was provided friendly, confidential support and mentoring rather than involved in self-disclosing, talk therapy. His deep sense of obligation to his parents, his separation loss from his extended family in Viet Nam, other potential threats of loss, and his stressful immigration process were affirmed and included in the understanding of his school difficulties. In the case of Maya, a U.S.-born second-generation immigrant, counseling consisted of interpersonal dynamic therapy, a mainstream orientation, which was modified to make the counselor culturally empathic to issues of Asian Indian family hierarchy and his or her own authority status as a school official. Maya's self-empowerment occurred through the opportunity offered by the counselor for free and safe self-expressions and communications, with the core Asian Indian value of family loyalty being protected, at the same time, even though Maya was frustrated with her less acculturated and traditional first-generation parents.

Immigration and subsequent individual acculturation to the host society impact a child's worldviews in a variety of ways. For example, the youth may reject culturally prescribed values and behaviors as a response to the expectations of the host culture to conform. On the other hand, reliance on culturally sanctioned strategies and the resultant rejection of the host society's norms and values could also occur. Additionally, it is possible that the child's required school involvement could potentially expose her to frequent and intense contact with those outside her cultural reference groups, much more than her parents are exposed to. The parents, however, exercise more control over interpersonal contacts outside school. Significantly discrepant communications occur in the family as family members' worldviews change, evolve, and mutate differently, causing much stress to the structure and fabric of the immigrant family.

Information about children of immigrants has been provided to underscore the importance of counselors understanding the construct of worldviews. If an individual's worldviews are not taken into account in the counseling that is provided within the school, the picture of the child's complete experience will be obscured. In the following section, we address value assumptions in worldviews so that counselors can understand why immigrants think, value, and behave differently.

Cultural Values Assumptions in Worldviews

Values have importance to societies in a broader sense, especially in the context of the current U.S. society where new immigrants from collectivistic cultures are bringing with them strong value codes. By climbing down from its power status as the dictator of norms, the United States could become a world community based on an understanding of common values among its dominant and minority cultures and in cooperative action for fulfilling those values.

Worldviews, a values-based construct (Ibrahim, Roysircar-Sodowsky, & Ohnishi, 2001), has gained attention in recent years. Worldviews has been defined in various ways, but this paper is influenced by Baldwin and Hopkins' (1990) description: "A people's worldview includes, at its core, their [sic] system of basic assumptions and guiding beliefs about life-existence" (p. 41). D. W. Sue (1981) stated, ". . . in a broader sense, we can define a worldview as how a person perceives his or her relationship to the world (nature, institutions, other people, etc.)" (p. 73). Sodowsky and Johnson (1994) see worldviews as principles of living and explanations that develop within the context of how a person is affected by other people and the groups with whom he or she identifies. They say, "This worldview is related to the person's individual perceptions and to social, moral, religious, educational, economic, or political inputs shared with the members of one's reference groups, such as one's culture group racial/ethnic group, family, state, or country" (p. 59).

McKeon (1950) observed that in order for people to cultivate cultural values, they must first experience satisfaction of a minimum of material needs. But the means by which needs are satisfied is determined by what is considered a value in the culture. Similarly F. Kluckhohn and Strodtbeck (1967) postulated that common existential dilemmas, such as what should one's relationships be like, have different solutions, which are determined by the worldviews values orientation of a particular group of people.

Lee (1959) proposed that culture mediates values for the individual. She observed that cultures are structured in a way that they maintain and enhance social values and furnish for the individual experiences that are rich in a particular societal value. Lee studied the culture of the Arapesh of New Guinea, describing them as being infused with certain social values, as demonstrated by their attitudes and behavior patterns. Everything the Arapesh did had a social purpose behind it. For example, food was always shared with others, items found and picked up in the forest were donated to others for building their homes, and the kill from the hunt was never kept by the hunter, but given away to relatives or friends (Lee).

In a collectivistic culture, as opposed to an individualistic culture, there is a societal value in communal sharing. Lee (1959) also researched the Oglala Indians of this country, who imparted value to the individual experience through a societal lens. In the Oglala culture, relatedness was considered the ultimate value. Development of the self was emphasized, but the goal of that development was to benefit relatedness and the social unit. Oglala children were encouraged and taught to pay attention to self-development and growth, not in a self-centered way, but as a means of enhancing the society and the culture. In another collectivistic culture, India, self-actualization is sought for the benefit of one's society.

Baldwin and Hopkins (1990) provide data on values from a cultural perspective. Baldwin and Hopkins (1990) confirmed their hypothesis that African Americans and European Americans have distinct cultural worldview differences in harmony with nature (African Americans) versus control over nature (European Americans); spiritualism (African Americans) versus materialism (European Americans); collectivism (African Americans) versus individualism (European Americans); strong religious orientation (African Americans) versus weak religious orientation (European Americans); and interdependence (African Americans) versus separateness (European Americans).

Sodowsky et al. (1994) conducted a cross-cultural study in which they investigated the worldviews of White Americans, mainland Chinese, Taiwanese, and Africans. They used F. Kluckhohn and Strodtbeck's (1961) model of five existential questions: (1) What is the character of innate human character? (2) What are human beings' relationships with other human beings? (3) What is the relationship of human beings to nature and the supernatural? (4) What is the temporal focus of human life? and (5) What is the modality of human activity? Sodowsky et al. (1994) showed that differences between the international students and the White American students were greater than the differences among the international groups, although the latter also differed from each other. White American students were primarily interested in individual goals, and preferred the "being" modality to the "doing" modality which brings external rewards. The mainland Chinese and Taiwanese students saw human relationships as lineal–hierarchical and collateral–mutual. They believed that human nature is evil; that natural phenomena need to be controlled; that life needs to be lived with a future focus; and those activities which result in accomplishment are preferred. In all these ways, the international students from developing nations differed from White Americans. The African students were similar to the mainland Chinese and the Taiwanese students in all these values, except in their time preference which focused on the past.

D. W. Sue (1981) proposed a model of worldviews which is based on the concepts of locus of control and locus of responsibility. According to Sue, people learn one of two worldviews regarding the exertion of control: that locus of control rests either with the individual or with external forces. Regarding the two worldviews about responsibility or accountability, people learn either that responsibility or blame should be placed on the individual or on the system. In a model showing the intersection of these two worldviews on two orthogonal axes, four variants are indicated: IC-IR— internal locus of control, internal locus of responsibility; IC-ER—internal locus of control, external locus of responsibility; EC-ER—external locus of control, external locus of responsibility; or EC-IR—external locus of control, internal locus of responsibility. While those subscribing to an internal locus of control perceive themselves as in control of their life, those with an external locus of control perceive that the control of their life is outside of them. People with an internal locus of responsibility perceive personal responsibility, and those with an external locus perceive responsibility to lie in other people or in the environment. D. W. Sue pointed out that the worldviews of many White Americans are based on perceptions of internal locus of control and internal responsibility, while internal locus of control and external locus of responsibility are the worldviews of well-functioning Asian American individuals. These Asian Americans may view themselves in a very positive way, but also view realistically the institutional racism surrounding them.

There is some empirical support for D. W. Sue's conceptualization. Students in a study (Betancourt, Hardin, & Manzi, 1992) were asked to react to vignettes describing either an academic and social success situation, or an academic and social failure situation. Students' perceived controllability of attributions that they made for the actor in the vignettes was assessed. Students who had been classified as control-oriented attributed successful outcomes in social settings to more controllable causes than did students who had been classified as subjugation-oriented. The control value orientation had a similar effect for attributions concerning failure in achievement situations. The control-oriented groups also reported more positive feelings than did the subjugation-oriented group toward the actor who experienced social success and more negative feelings toward the actor in the case of academic failure.

Values as Moral and Ethical Behavior

In a study designed to examine the relationship of worldviews to a sense purpose in life, Molcar and Stuempfig (1987) assessed worldviews of students from the perspective of belief in God and also assessed students' purpose in life. They affirmed their hypothesis that people who subscribed to worldviews consisting of a personal belief in God expressed more purpose in life than did those whose worldviews did not include a transcendent being. This study on the relationship between religious worldviews and purposeful living is important for therapy because having a life purpose in life-threatening and uncontrollable situations has been related to hopefulness and positive personal adjustment (Frankl, 1969).

The religious worldviews perspective is concerned with moral and ethical behaviors. Many of the concepts that psychology is trying to understand about people, such as how they perceive human nature, time, activity, and relationships (Kluckhohn & Strodtbeck, 1961) were traditionally part of religious belief systems. Over time, religious views on human values became part of the study of cultural worldviews as Western thought became more secularized (Sodowsky & Johnson, 1994).

Religion has traditionally been one of the major shapers of morals and values. In fact, significant portions of any of the world's major religions are moral–ethical teachings. The world's most straightforward account of the relationship of Eastern enlightenment (characterized as peace of mind and wisdom) with ethics and morals, is found in the first sermon of the Buddha. Buddha's insights were that all existence is marked by suffering, that suffering has a cause, that suffering can be brought to an end, and that there is specific pathway of temperance that leads to enlightenment, ending suffering. Many Southeast Asian and South Asian immigrants in the United States follow these teachings. The Bible is a powerful influence on the values of people following the Christian tradition, and it is difficult to exaggerate its role in many people's motivation and behavior. Many Christians regard the Bible as divinely inspired, the very word of God. Books of the Old Testament exemplify values and moral instruction, and the New Testament's Sermon on the Mount is a list of ethical teachings. The venue of religious teachings has changed dramatically over the years, however. The ethical, moral, and values teaching once done through the church is now given to the home and public schools because fewer people today attend church and Sunday school. Religious teaching is also made popularly available through conservative political groups, the media, and Christian psychological counseling. Thus the religious worldviews perspective is commonly practiced in most societies and needs recognition in psychological help.

Specific Worldviews Dimensions

Several theorists have sought to define specific worldviews dimensions that are reflective of the social and cultural difference in social behavior and relationships. Three sets of these dimensions are explored here: mechanism and organicism, individualism and collectivism, and normativism and humanism. As shown in Table 4.1, the similarities and differences among these sets of constructs in values and expectations can easily be delineated.

Pepper (1942) presented a taxonomy of four philosophical worldviews, or fundamental ways of knowing the world. He associated each of these worldviews with a specific causal assumption about events in the world: (1) formism, which is based on realism; (2) mechanism, is based on materialism; (3) contextualism, based on pragmatism; and (4) organicism, based on idealism. Later, factor analysis of worldview inventories (e.g., Botella & Gallifa, 1995; Johnson, Germer, Efran, & Overton, 1988) have suggested that these four categories are reducible to two, with mechanism subsuming

TABLE 4.1   **Similarities and Differences Among Worldviews Dimensions**

Mechanistic	Organismic	Individualistic	Collectivistic	Normativistic	Humanistic
Stability; simplicity	Complexity	Complexity	Stability	Stability; simplicity	Complexity
Objectivism; realism	Constructivistic	Abstract	Objectivism; realism	Objectivism; realism	Constructivistic
Particularistic; reductionistic	Rationalistic	Rationalistic; universalistic	Particularistic	Factual; reductionistic	Rationalistic
Conforming; orderly	Self-differentiating; creative; changing	Hedonistic; creative	Polite; obedient; conforming	Polite; obedient; conforming	Nonconforming; creative
Dependent	Autonomous	Independent	Dependent on group	Dependent	Individualistic
Interpersonally passive	Emotionally expressive	Affectionate	Self-controlled	Self-controlled	Emotionally expressive

Note: The six rows provide descriptors for how each worldviews dimension understands human existence. Row 1, philosophical query into the nature of life and being. Row 2, investigation into the nature and origin of knowledge. Row 3, explanations offered for a cause. Row 4, whether a person should conform to rules or find fulfillment by breaking away from rules. Row 5, whether a person is considered to be dependent on a group or independent of groups. Row 6, a person's outward manifestation of an emotional state. Similarities and differences in descriptors among three sets of worldviews constructs are delineated: (a) mechanism and organicism (Pepper, 1942); (b) individualism and collectivism (Triandis, 1993); and (c) normativism and humanism (de St. Aubin, 1996). It appears that Mechanistic, Collectivistic, and Normativistic classifications share some descriptors, and that Organismic, Individualistic, and Humanistic do as well.

formism (i.e., mechanism/formism) and organicism subsuming contextualism (i.e., organicism/contextualism). These two categories will be identified simply as mechanism and organicism.

Mechanism

The mechanistic worldview is based on the metaphor of the machine (Pepper, 1942) and "assumes that the universe, like a machine, can be analyzed into parts that can be understood in isolation from the whole" (Johnson et al., 1998, p. 824). These discrete parts are understood as static, and the relationships between them are the units to which all objects, events, and experiences can be reduced (Johnson et al.). According to the mechanistic viewpoint, only particulars exist and reality is external to the knower (Pepper).

Johnson et al. (1998) found that individuals preferring the mechanistic worldview tend to be reactive, interpersonally passive, orderly, stable, conventional, conforming, dependent, and objective and realistic in their cognitive style. In a study exploring congruence between worldview and counseling approach preference in 90 college undergraduate students, Lyddon and Adamson (1992) found a preference for behavioral counseling among persons with a mechanistic worldview. Modern examples of this philosophical worldview are manifested in the approach of behaviorists and in stimulus-response associationistic models of memory.

Organicism

The root metaphor of the organismic worldview is the complex, integrated organic process (Pepper, 1942) and assumes that the universe is composed of complex, interrelated processes that are constantly active and changing (Johnson et al., 1988). According to the organismic worldview, the part is embedded in, and has no existence independent of, the whole. Pepper describes the principle of organicity in two ways: (1) ". . . an organic whole is such a system that every element within it implies every other"; and (2) ". . . is such a system that an alteration or removal of any element would alter every other element or even destroy the whole system" (p. 300).

Johnson et al. (1988) found that individuals preferring the organismic worldview tend to be fluid, changing, creative, nonconforming, individualistic, active, purposive, autonomous, and integrated into their interpersonal environment. Lyddon and Adamson (1992) found a preference for constructivistic counseling approaches among persons with an organismic worldview. Current examples of this worldview can be found in the work of developmental and humanistic psychologists, general systems theorists, and information processing models of memory.

Individualism and Collectivism

The individualism-collectivism dimension of cultural variation describes the relationship between the individual and the cultural group in which he or she lives. According to Triandis (1993), individualism and collectivism are cultural modes of living and provide an organizing theme for a particular culture. In individualism, the organizing theme is the "centrality of the autonomous individual" (Triandis, p. 156); in the case of collectivism, the organizing theme is "the centrality of the collective" (Triandis, p. 156). As such, the worldview of the individual will reflect the culture's individualistic or collectivistic orientation.

Triandis (1990) summarized the primary contrasts between individualism and collectivism: (1) in individualism, there is an emphasis on the private self rather than on the person's family and reference group (i.e., ingroup); (2) in collectivism there is an emphasis on long-term time perspectives, while the time frame in individualism tends to be short term; (3) collectivism emphasizes the importance of hierarchy and harmony within the group; and (4) collectivistic individuals tend to be emotionally attached to only a few ingroups and are intimately involved with them, while the individualistic tend to have many ingroups with whom they interact superficially.

Triandis (1993) emphasized that there is not a single attribute by which an individual or society can be classified as individualistic or collectivistic. Rather, a number of attributes must be considered in order to operationalize the constructs, including child-rearing practices, the defining self, social perceptions, intergroup relations, political systems, and so on. Collectivistic attributes include a focus on the group as the basic unit of social perception, attribution of failure to lack of effort, an emphasis on ingroup harmony, an emphasis on ascribed roles, and shame (rather than guilt) as an organizer of social life. In contrast, individualistic attributes include a focus on the individual as the basic unit of social perception, attribution of failure to factors external to the individual, the acceptance of debate and confrontation, an emphasis on achieved roles, and guilt (rather than shame) as an organizer of social life (Triandis).

Normativism and Humanism

Personal ideology is defined by de St. Aubin (1996) as a philosophy or beliefs about how life should be lived and how human living is influenced. This ideology is evidenced in areas such as child-rearing philosophy, political orientation, religiosity, value systems, and assumptions regarding human nature. De St. Aubin stated, "Personal ideology is the *weltanschhaung*, or worldview, that encompasses these and other value-laden components of personality" (p. 152).

The personal ideology of an individual, group, or culture can be understood through the dimensions of humanistic and normativistic ideologies (Tomkins, 1965). The humanistic orientation views humankind as "an end in itself, an active, creative, thinking, desiring, and loving force" (de St. Aubin, 1996, p. 153); the normativistic orientation "maintains that reality exists prior to and independent of humankind and that human beings must struggle towards this (unattainable) potential through conformity to norms and set rules" (de St. Aubin, p. 153). Tomkins operationalizes these constructs through delineating specific values, affects, and behaviors such as: (1) a belief in equal opportunity for all and the importance of creativity, daring, and open-mindedness (humanistic); (2) a belief in the importance of respect, admiration, tidiness, courtesy, restraint, and self-discipline (normativistic); (3) a view that one should be loved and respected only if worthy (normativistic); and (4) a view of human nature as trustworthy and independent (humanistic).

Worldviews and Counseling

With worldviews having become an interest of various disciplines and thought systems, it is not surprising that counseling psychology has begun to examine the client and the counselor's respective worldviews. The interaction of the client–counselor worldviews has been hypothesized to affect the counseling process (Ibrahim, 1991; Ihle, Sodowsky, & Kwan, 1996). Highlen and Hill (1984) conducted a review of research dealing with factors that influence client change and concluded "the assumptive worlds of both the counselor and client, and the unique relationship that ensues, will affect the array of the therapeutic change factors" (p. 364). Ibrahim (1991) pointed out that by approaching psychotherapy through the assessment of worldviews, the therapist can eliminate trying to guess the client's beliefs. Assessment of worldviews in psychotherapy facilitates the counseling process by making explicit the client's beliefs, and aids the process of determining goals for the counseling process which are appropriate for the client (Ibrahim, 1991; Ihle, Sodowsky, & Kwan, 1996). Sue, Arredondo, and McDavis (1993) stated that multiculturally competent counselors must also make explicit their own worldviews, so that they can become aware of their own value bias and, consequently, prevent themselves from overlooking their clients' preferred values.

Sodowsky, Kuo-Jackson, and Loya (1997) added that only when counselors develop their own cultural self-awareness can they learn to affirm their clients' cultural differences and, thus, gradually gain access to their clients' assumptive worldviews, meanings, and epistemologies. Sodowsky et al. (1999), using the multicultural counseling competencies model, proposed that the intersection of the counselor's and client's worldviews and how the counselor negotiates through this interface are major determining factors of the multicultural counseling relationship and treatment process. While keeping a check on their own worldviews, counselors maintain the integrity of their clients' worldviews in order to facilitate the counseling relationship and treatment (Sodowsky et al., 1999). Because peoples' worldviews influence almost all responses, it is likely that the assessment of worldviews of both the client and the counselor will provide essential information for the counseling process.

DISCUSSION QUESTIONS

1. You are a counselor in a middle school that is part of the public school district in a large metropolitan area. Your school is ethnically and racially diverse and, over the past ten years, has seen a significant increase in the number of immigrant children, particularly children of Asian and Latino/Hispanic American descent. You are in the process of planning psychoeducational support groups for these students with the goal of facilitating the adaptation of the youth within the school. In organizing a presentation for the school administration regarding such groups, you must be prepared to respond to the following questions:

   a) What are your objectives for the group?
   b) How will you select participants for the group? Will participation be voluntary (explain why) or based on specific criteria developed by teachers and school counselors (explain why)? If based on specific criteria, what will they be? Will you make the group open to European immigrant students (e.g., from Bosnia, Russia) and/or to White nonimmigrant students (explain why)?
   c) What content would you cover in the group?
   d) How would you structure the group (e.g., size, age range, length, and duration, in-school or after-school meetings, etc.)?
   e) What would be key multicultural attitudes, interventions, and personal characteristics of the group leaders?
   f) How would you involve the students' families in the planning process and in other activities related to the groups?

2. What key dimensions would you consider in assessing a student's worldviews? Identify specific questions that would provide appropriate information in assessing worldview dimensions of a student. Identify ways in which these worldview dimensions might also be demonstrated by teachers and the administration within the school setting. If you wanted to gather information regarding worldview values through observation of a student in the school environment, in what specific settings would you observe this student? What information could you gather through observation that would help you to better understand the student's worldviews and help him or her?

3. You are a counselor in the only high school of a small, rural public school district. A student who is the second-generation child of immigrant parents from India moves into your school district after her father is recruited by the community as a family physician. You are interested in assisting this student in her transition into the school, which currently has no teachers or students of color. How

would you approach this student and/or her family regarding providing her with assistance? What aspects of school life would you focus your interventions on? Identify specific ways you might consider intervening with teachers and administrative personnel.

4. Review the worldview dimensions of mechanism and organicism, individualism and collectivism, and normativism and humanism. Discuss your own worldview values and assumptions within the framework of these three models. How are these value orientations expressed in your approach to school counseling?

5. What are some of the defining demographics of children of Asian immigrants?

6. What are some of the differences among cohort groups of immigrant children and adolescents with reference to the relationships of generational statuses with different psychological responses and difficulties? Seven studies were reviewed to illustrate these differences.

7. How do immigrant children and adolescents cope with their difficulties? Six studies were reviewed to broadly illustrate their coping strategies and other resources.

8. Give your reactions to the two case studies.

REFERENCES

Aronowitz, M. (1984). The social and emotional adjustment of immigrant children: A review of the literature. *International Migration Review, 26,* 237–257.

Baldwin, J. & Hopkins, R. (1990). African-American and European-American cultural differences as assessed by the worldviews paradigm: An empirical analysis. *The Western Journal of Black Studies, 14*(1), 38–52.

Berry, J. W. (1985). Psychological adaptation of foreign students. In R. Samuda & A. Wolfgang (Eds.), *International counseling and assessment* (pp. 235–248). Toronto: C. J. Hogrefe.

Betancourt, H., Hardin, C., & Manzi, J. (1992). Beliefs, value orientation, and culture in attribution process and helping behavior. *Journal of Cross-Cultural Psychology, 2,* 179–195.

Botella, L. & Gallifa, J. (1995). A constructivist approach to the development of personal epistemic assumptions and worldviews. *Journal of Constructivist Psychology, 8,* 1–18.

Bureau Canadian de l'education Internationale (1997). *Profil des étudiants étrangers au Canada 1996–1997.* Ottawa: Bureau Canadian de l'education Internationale.

Cervantes, R. C. & Castro, F. G. (1985). Stress, coping, and Mexican American mental health: A systematic review. *Hispanic Journal of Behavioral Sciences, 7,* 1–73.

Chataway, C. J. & Berry, J. W. (1989). Acculturation experiences, appraisal, coping, and adaptation: A comparison of Hong Kong Chinese, French, and English students in Canada. *Canadian Journal of Behavioral Science, 21,* 295–309.

Cheng, C. H. (1994). *Assessment of depression and risk factors among adolescent Chinese immigrants: A comparative study of accompanied and unaccompanied minors.* Unpublished doctoral dissertation, California School of Professional Psychology-Los Angeles.

Chiu, M. L., Feldman, S. S., & Rosenthal, D. A. (1992). The influence of immigration on parental behavior and adolescent distress in Chinese families residing in two western nations. *Journal of Research on Adolescence, 2,* 205–239.

Chung, C. L. E. (1994). *An investigation of the psychological well-being of unaccompanied Taiwanese Minors/parachute kids.* Unpublished doctoral dissertation, University of Southern California, Los Angeles.

Compas, B. E. (1987). Coping with stress during childhood and adolescence. *Psychological Bulletin, 101,* 393–403.

Compas, B. E. (1998). An agenda for coping research and theory: Basic and applied developmental issues. *International Journal of Behavioral Development, 22,* 203–219.

Copeland, E. P. & Hess, R. S. (1995). Differences in young adolescents' coping strategies based on gender and ethnicity. *Journal of Early Adolescence, 15,* 203–219.

de St. Aubin, E. (1996). Personal ideology polarity: Its emotional foundation and its manifestation in individual value systems, religiosity, political orientation, and assumptions concerning human nature. *Journal of Personality and Social Psychology, 71*, 152–165.

Dressler, W. W. & Bernal, H. (1982). Acculturation and stress in a low-income Puerto Rican community. *Journal of Human Stress*, 32–38.

Dyal, J. A. & Dyal, R. Y. (1981). Acculturation, stress, and coping. *International Journal of Intercultural Relations, 5*, 301–328.

Feldman, S. S. & Rosenthal, D. A. (1990). The acculturation of autonomy expectations in Chinese high schoolers residing in two western nations. *International Journal of Psychology, 52*, 259–281.

Forden, R. W. (1990). Taiwan's "Little overseas students." *NAFSA Newsletter, 41*, 7–10.

Frankl, V. (1969). *The will to meaning: Foundations and applications of logotherapy.* New York: World Publishing.

Highlen, P. S. & Hill, C. E. (1984). Factors affecting client change in individual counseling: Current status and theoretical speculations. In S. D. Brown & R. W. Lent (Eds.), *Handbook of counseling psychology* (pp. 334–396). New York: Guilford.

Hong, K. H. (1998). Overseas study by unaccompanied Korean minors: Current issues and future strategies. In J. C. H. Lin (Ed.). *In pursuit of education: Young Asian students in the United States* (pp. 27–43). CA: Pacific Asia Press.

Ibrahim, F. (1991). Contribution of cultural worldviews to generic counseling and development. *Journal of Counseling & Development, 70*, 13–19.

Ibrahim, F. A., Roysircar-Sodowsky, G., & Ohnishi, H. (2001). World view: Recent developments and needed directions. In J. G. Ponterotto, M. C. Casas, L. A. Suzuki, & C. M. Alexander (Eds.), *The handbook of multicultural counseling* (2nd ed.) (pp 425–456). Thousand Oaks, CA: Sage.

Ihle, G. M., Sodowsky, G. R., & Kwan, K. (1996). Worldviews of women: Comparisons between White-American clients, White-American counselors, and Chinese international students. *Journal of Counseling and Development, 74*, 306–312.

Johnson, J. A., Germer, C. K., Efran, J. S., & Overton, W. F. (1988). Personality as the basis for theoretical predilections. *Journal of Social Psychology, 55*, 824–835.

Kim, S. C. (1998). Young Korean students in the United States. In J. C. H. Lin (Ed.), *In pursuit of education: Young Asian students in the United States* (pp. 44–54). CA: Pacific Asia Press.

Kluckhohn, F. & Strodtbeck, F. (1961). *Variations in value orientations.* Evanston, IL: Row, Peterson.

Kuo, B. C-H. & Roysircar-Sodowsky, G. (1999, August). *Effects of acculturation variables on adjustment of Taiwanese unaccompanied minors: A path analysis study of sojourners.* Paper presented at the 107th Annual Conference of the American Psychological Association, Boston, MA.

Kuo, P. Y. & Roysircar-Sodowsky, G. (1999). Cultural ethnic identity versus political ethnic identity: Theory and research on Asian Americans. In D. S. Sandhu (Ed.), *Asian and Pacific Islander Americans: Issues and concerns for counseling and psychology* (pp. 71–90). New York: Nova Sciences.

Kwan, K., Sodowsky, G. R., & Ihle, G. M. (1994). Worldviews of Chinese international students: An extension and new findings. *Journal of College Student Development, 35*, 190–197.

Laosa, L. M. (1990). Psychological stress, coping, and development of Hispanic immigrant children. In F. C. Serafica, A. I. Schwebel, R. K. Russel, P. D. Issac, & L. B. Myers (Eds.), *Mental health of ethnic minorities* (pp. 38–65). New York: Praeger Publishers.

Lay, C. & Nguyen, T. (1998). The role of acculturation-related and acculturation non-specific daily hassles: Vietnamese-Canadian students and psychological distress. *Canadian Journal of Behavioral Science, 30*, 172–181.

Lay, C. & Verkuyten, M. (1999). Ethnic identity and its relations to personal self-esteem: A comparison of Canadian-born Chinese adolescents. *The Journal of Social Psychology, 139*, 288–299.

Lee, D. (1959). Culture and the experience of value. In A. Maslow (Ed.), *New knowledge in human values.* New York: Harper & Bros.

Lee, P. L. M. (1994). *Hong Kong visa students in secondary schools in metropolitan Toronto.* Toronto: Joint Center for Asian Pacific Studies.

Lin, J. C. H. (1998). Young Taiwanese students in the United States. In J. C. H. Lin (Ed.), *In pursuit of education: Young Asian students in the United States* (pp. 4–17). CA: Pacific Asia Press.

Lyddon, W. J. & Adamson, L. A. (1992). Worldview and counseling preference: An analogue study. *Journal of Counseling & Development, 71*, 41–47.

McKeon, R. (1950). Conflicts of values in a community of cultures. *The Journal of Philosophy, 47*, 197–210.

Mena, R., Padilla, A. M., & Maldonado, M. (1987). Acculturative stress and specific coping strategies among immigrant and later generation college students. *Hispanic Journal of Behavioral Sciences, 9*, 207–225.

Molcar, C. & Stuempfig, D. (1987). Effects of world view on purpose in life. *The Journal of Psychology, 122*, 365–370.

Noh, S. & Avison, W. R. (1996). Asian immigrants and the stress process: A study of Koreans in Canada. *Journal of Health and Social Behavior, 37*, 192–206.

Ol'ah, A. (1995). Coping strategies among adolescents:

A cross-cultural study. *Journal of Adolescence, 18,* 491–512.

Oropesa, R. S. & Landale, N. S. (1997). Immigrant legacies: Ethnicity, generation, and children's familial and economic lives. *Social Science Quarterly, 78,* 399–416.

Padilla, A. M., Alvarez, M., & Lindholm, K. J. (1986). Generational status and personality factors as predictors of stress in students. *Hispanic Journal of Behavioral Sciences, 8,* 275–288.

Parker, J. D. A. & Endler, N. S. (1996). Coping and defense: A historical overview. In M. Zeichner & N. Endler (Eds.), *Handbook of coping: Theory, research, and application* (pp. 3–23). New York: John Wiley & Sons.

Patterson, J. M. & McCubbin, H. I. (1987). Adolescent coping style and behaviors: Conceptualization and measurement. *Journal of Adolescence, 10,* 163–186.

Pearlin, L. I. & Schooler, C. (1978). The structure of coping. *Journal of Health and Social Behavior, 19,* 2–21.

Pedersen, P. (1991). Counseling international students. *The Counseling Psychologist, 19,* 2–21.

Pepper, S. C. (1942). *World hypothesis: A study in evidence.* University of California Press: Berkeley.

Portes, A. (1997a). Preface. In A. Booth, A. C. Crouter, & N. Landale (Eds.), *Immigration and the family: Research and policy on U.S. immigrants* (pp. ix–x). Mahwah, New Jersey: Lawrence Erlbaum.

Portes, A. (1997b). Introduction: Immigration and its aftermath. In A. Booth, A. C. Crouter, & N. Landale (Eds.), *Immigration and the family: Research and policy on U.S. immigrants* (pp. 1–7). Mahwah, New Jersey: Lawrence Erlbaum.

Rosenthal, D. A. & Feldman, S. S. (1990). The acculturation of Chinese immigrants: Perceived effects on family functioning of length of residence in two cultural contexts. *Journal of Genetic Psychology, 151,* 131–151.

Rosenthal, D. A. & Feldman, S. S. (1992). The nature and stability of ethnic identity in Chinese youth: Effects of length of residence in two cultural contexts. *Journal of Cross-Cultural Psychology, 23,* 214–227.

Roysircar-Sodowsky, G., Liu, J., Webster, D., Yang, Y., Germer J., Lynne, E. M., Kerr, G. C., Blodgett-McDeavitt, J., & Palensky, J. E. J. (1999). *Empirical validity of multicultural competencies: Counselor, client, and supervisor self-reports.* Paper presented at the 107th Annual Convention of the American Psychological Association, Boston, MA.

Roysircar-Sodowsky, G. & Maestas, M. V. (2000). Acculturation, ethnic identity, and acculturative stress: Evidence and measurement. In R. Dana (Ed.), *Handbook of cross-cultural and multicultural personality assessment* (pp. 131–172). Mahwah, New Jersey: Lawrence Erlbaum.

Rumbaut, R. G. (1994). The crucible within: Ethnic identity, self-esteem, segmented assimilation among children of immigrants. *International Migration Review, 28,* 749–794.

Rumbaut, R. G. (1997). Ties that bind: Immigration and immigrant families in the United States. In A. Booth, A. C. Crouter, & N. Landale (Eds.), *Immigration and the family: Research and policy on U.S. immigrants* (pp. 3–46). New Jersey: Lawrence Erlbaum.

Sodowsky, G. R. (1991). Effects of culturally consistent counseling tasks on American and international student observers' perception of counselor credibility: A preliminary investigation. *Journal of Counseling and Development, 69,* 253–256.

Sodowsky, G. R. & Carey, J. C. (1988). Relationship between acculturation-related demographics and cultural attitudes of an Asian-Indian immigrant group. *Journal of Multicultural Counseling and Development, 16,* 117–136.

Sodowsky, G. R. & Johnson, P. (1994). Worldviews: Culturally learned assumptions and values. In P. Pedersen & J.C. Carey (Eds.), *Multicultural counseling in the schools: A practical handbook* (pp. 59–79). Boston: Allyn & Bacon.

Sodowsky, G. R., Kuo-Jackson, Y. P., & Loya, G. J. (1996). Outcome of training in the philosophy of assessment: Multicultural counseling competencies. In D. Pope-Davis & H. Coleman (Eds.), *Multicultural counseling competencies: Assessment, education and training, and supervision* (pp. 3–42). Thousand Oaks, CA: Sage.

Sodowsky, G. R., Kwan, K. K., & Pannu, R. (1995). Ethnic minority of Asians in the United States: Conceptualization and illustrations. In J. Ponterotto, M. Casas, L. Suzuki, & C. Alexander (Eds.), *Handbook of multicultural counseling* (pp. 123–154). Newbury Park, CA: Sage.

Sodowsky, G. R. & Lai, E. W. M. (1997). Asian immigrant variables and structural models of cross-cultural distress. In A. Booth, A. C. Crouter, & N. Landale (Eds.), *International migration and family change: The experience of U.S. immigrants* (pp. 221–234). Mahwah, New Jersey: Lawrence Erlbaum.

Sodowsky, G. R., Lai, E. W., & Plake, B. S. (1991). Moderating effects of sociocultural variables on acculturation variables of Hispanic and Asian Americans. *Journal of Counseling and Development, 70,* 194–204.

Sodowsky, G. R., Maguire, K., Johnson, P., Ngumba, W., & Kohl, R. (1994). Worldviews of White

American, mainland Chinese, Taiwanese, and African students: An investigation into between-group differences. *Journal of Cross-Cultural Psychology, 25*, 309–324.

Sodowsky, G. R. & Plake, B. S. (1992). A study of acculturation differences among international people and suggestions for sensitivity to within-group differences. *Journal of Counseling and Development, 71*, 53–59.

Statistics Canada (1996). *Census: Immigration and citizenship.* The Daily, Statistics Canada. Available: http://www.statcan.ca/Daily/English/971104/d971104.httm#ART2.

Sue, D. W. (1981). *Counseling the culturally different: Theory and practice.* New York: John Wiley & Sons.

Sue, D. W., Arredondo, P., & McDavis, R. J. (1992). Multicultural competencies and standers: A call to the profession. *Journal of Counseling Development, 70*, 477–486.

Suthakaran, V. & Roysircar-Sodowsky, G. (in press). Religious orientation and cultural identity retention: Differences between Asian Muslims and Hindus. *Cultural Diversity and Ethnic Minority Psychology.*

Tomkins, S. S. (1965). Affect and the psychology of knowledge. In S. S. Tomkins & C. E. Izard (Eds.), *Affect, cognition, and personality: Empirical studies* (pp. 72–97). New York: Springer.

Triandis, H. C. (1993). Collectivism and individualism as cultural syndromes. *Cross-Cultural Research: The Journal of Comparative Social Science, 27*, 155–180.

U.S. Bureau of the Census (1998). *Census Bureau Facts for Features.* The U.S. Census Bureau's Public Information Center. Available: http://www.census.gov/Press-Release/ff998-05.html.

Zheng, X. & Berry, J. W. (1991). Psychological adaptation of Chinese sojourners in Canada. *International Journal of Psychology, 26*, 451–471.

Zhou, M. (1997). Growing up American: The challenge confronting immigrant children and children of immigrants. *Annual Reviews of Sociology, 23*, 63–95.

AUTHORS' NOTES

Gargi Roysicar-Sodowsky is a professor in the Department of Clinical Psychology and Director of the Multicultural Center for Research and Practice (ANE MC Center, www.multiculturalcenter.org) at Antioch New England Graduate School. She does research on the interface of acculturation and ethnic identity with the mental health of immigrants and ethnic minorities; worldview differences between and within cultural groups; multicultural competencies and training in professional psychology; and multicultural assessment and instrumentation. She is a fellow of the American Psychological Association (APA), President of the Association of Multicultural Counseling and Development, and former chair of the Section on Ethnic and Racial Diversity of APA's Division 17 (Counseling Psychology). She is a senior associate editor of the Journal of Multicultural Counseling and Development, a consulting editor of Cultural Diversity and Ethnic Minority Psychology, and the editor of APA's Division 17 Newsletter. At the ANE MC Center, she integrates clinical services with research, consultation, and education.

Lisa L. Frey is an assistant professor in the counseling psychology program of the Department of Educational Psychology at the University of Oklahoma. Her research interests are in the perceptions of trauma in children and adolescents as related to ethnocultural and sociocultural influences; characteristics of female sexual offenders; and relational health in women. She has a private consulting and clinical practice and consults in both educational and clinical settings. Her clinical interests are in traumatized youth, sexual offender treatment and assessment, and multicultural and diversity practices. She obtained her Ph.D. from the University of Nebraska-Lincoln and did her pre-doctoral internship at the University of Texas at Austin.

5 Multicultural Counseling with Immigrant Students in Schools

FRED BEMAK

RITA CHI-YING CHUNG

Graduate School of Education
George Mason University

OBJECTIVES

1. To assist the school counselor in understanding and providing effective multicultural counseling for immigrant students
2. To provide an understanding for a new role and practice for school counselors working with immigrant students within the context of public educational policies and practices
3. To provide a context for school counseling within the framework of changing demographics, premigration, and acculturation
4. To understand the impact of schools on immigrant youth and the resultant importance of school counseling, inluding inequities, racism, discrimination, and mainstream policies and procedures
5. To redefine the school counselor's role to more effectively advocate and work with immigrant students

Migration trends have shown that, since the late twentieth century, the pattern of migration has been from developing to more developed countries (Bemak, 2000), and it is estimated that this trend will continue (Coleman, 1995). Migration is a global issue caused by international problems such as political instability, economic and social pressures, natural disasters, and local, state, and civil wars that occur frequently throughout the world, especially in developing countries (Bemak & Chung, 2000). The increasing number of immigrants arriving in the United States has been well documented over the past decades, dramatically changing the demographics of the U.S. population (e.g., Aponte & Crouch, 2000; O'Hara & Felt, 1991). Current estimates project that approximately 10 percent of the U.S. population are from a migrant background (U.S. Bureau of Census, 1997). Although the focus of this chapter is on multicultural counseling with immigrant youth in U.S. schools, it is important to note that this is a global issue relevant to all resettlement countries. Furthermore, this chapter is focused on permanent and not temporary immigrants, such as international students. The latter group has its own unique set of issues and challenges (Leong, in press).

Given the rapid increase of immigrants in U.S. schools, it is critical that school counselors work effectively with this population. In order to achieve this school counselors need to: (1) have awareness, understanding, and appreciation for the historical, sociopolitical, cultural, and educational issues encountered by this group; and (2) redefine their roles and responsibilities in schools. Thus, this chapter will provide information and recommendations for school counselors. To fully understand this population the chapter will begin with an overview of the immigration patterns to the United States, examining demographics and the characteristics of this group, followed by a discussion on cultural adaptation issues encountered by young immigrants and their families. To provide a context for understanding counseling with immigrant student groups, a discussion of multicultural educational practices and challenges will be presented, as well as subsequent multicultural counseling strategies and the school counselor's role in addressing challenges facing immigrant youth. The chapter will conclude with recommendations for school counselors.

Migration: Status, Patterns, and Characteristics

It has been estimated that there are seventy to one hundred million migrants in the world today (United Nations, 1995) which could be viewed as an unrecognized "shadow continent" that is defined by its mobility (P. B. Pedersen, personal communication, July 15, 2000). Although all migrants (e.g., immigrants, refugees, sojourners) have some commonality in their experiences it is important to highlight the two major distinctions in migration status to fully understand the experiences of each group. Murphy (1977) delineated two primary categories in migration status: "forced" (involuntary) and "free" (voluntary). Refugees are migrants who were forced to involuntarily leave their home country most often due to political, religious, or ethnic persecution and/or war. Their involuntary departure was without preparation, plan, or choice. In comparison, immigrants who voluntarily left their home countries typically left due to economic hardship, lack of resources, or in search of a better life for their family (Bemak & Chung, 2000). There are differences in postmigration adjustment between voluntary and involuntary immigrants including school experiences where, for example, it has been documented that involuntary minorities' academic performance is poorer than that of voluntary minorities (Gibson, 1997; Ogbu & Simons, 1998).

Given the large numbers of immigrants entering the United States, it has been noted that the first and second generations of this population remarkably account for most of the ethnic population growth in the United States during the last several decades (Aponte & Wohl, 2000; De Vita, 1996; O'Hara, 1992; Passel & Edmonston, 1992) with estimates that almost 3,000 immigrants arrive daily (Aponte & Wohl, 2000). Although the United States continues to accept approximately one million new legal and illegal (unauthorized) immigrants annually (Aponte & Wohl, 2000), there are restrictions in policies related to immigrants that limit their rights. Immigration data indicate that of 3,705,400 immigrants to the United States (U.S. Department of Commerce, 1997) most were from North America (51.2%), Asia (30.0%), Europe (11.8%), South America (5.1%), and Africa (2.5%). There were significant numbers from Mexico (1,286,500), the Caribbean (337,000), and Central America (226,800) while the majority of the Asian immigrants were from Vietnam (192,700), Philippines (188,100), China (137,500), and India (121,000).

Immigrants cluster in different relocation areas in the United States (more than four of five students with Limited English Proficiency (LEP) live in California, Florida, Illinois, New York, and Texas) (Gonzalez & Darling-Hammond, 1997) where concerns about bilingual education have been highly controversial given the rapid ethnic changes. An example of substantial changes in students can be found in Florida's Dade County where 25 percent of the students are foreign born with a monthly average of 1,322 new students (Schnaiberg, 1996). This data is important information for schools because it is estimated that similar immigration patterns will probably continue (Aponte & Wohl, 2000).

It is important to acknowledge that although immigrant youth in the United States share some degree of similar resettlement and adjustment experiences in schools, there are substantial intragroup and intergroup differences. Variations are based on geographic location, race and ethnicity, language, religion, voluntary or involuntary migration, discrimination, socioeconomic status, social networks, and community support systems.

Demographic Profile of Immigrant Children Aged 5–18

United States schools have faced the challenge of educating immigrant students for more than a century. Almost 20 percent of the immigrants arriving in the United States in 1998 were under 15 years of age, with an additional 32 percent being between the ages of 15 and 29 (U.S. Department of Justice, 1999). In 1990 it was estimated that 16–18 percent of 50 million students in elementary and secondary schools were first- or second-generation immigrants (Rong & Preissle, 1998). For school counselors to understand the immigrant student it is important to gain a broader perspective about home life. Seventy-eight percent of 5- to 18-year-old foreign-born children lived with parents or adopted parents, 4 percent lived with siblings, and 7 percent lived with other relatives. Of those living with parents, 71 percent lived with two parents, 14 percent lived in female-headed households, and 7 percent lived in male-headed households. Mexican and Asian children are currently the main immigrant groups entering school systems (Rong & Preissle, 1998).

The impact of families on education requires schools and school counselors to re-examine policies and practices on how to best serve this culturally diverse population. It is also important to note that 50 percent of foreign-born children in the United States have been resettled less than 5 years and 33 percent less than 3 years so that language and cultural adaptation for these children must be learned quickly because approximately half of these children are of high school age, between 14 and 18 (Rong & Preissle, 1998). Thus, adaptation requires not only learning English and overall adjustment to U.S. culture, but also adapting to the school culture which may include peer pressure and possibly antischool culture found in many U.S. inner city schools (e.g., Fordham, 1996). Given the need for acculturation and language skills, educators and school counselors must develop effective and culturally sensitive strategies to support immigrant children while understanding the unique challenges they face.

Cultural Adaptation

Cultural Mastery

For an immigrant student, entering a new culture requires the mastery of a new set of skills and competencies, and in order for the school to become truly bicultural and/or multicultural that must be understood by the school counselor. Bemak (1989) developed a three-phase bicultural model of acculturation whereby immigrants initially rely on previously established skills to adjust to the new culture, but eventually must learn and test new skills. The new skills are then integrated with old paradigms as a student becomes bicultural and integrates the past, present, and future. This model is important when considering new-student adjustment to schools and education as defined by the dominant culture in the resettlement country. Mastery of these skills is crucial to functioning and succeeding in the school environment, but it must not be at the expense of their primary culture skills, knowledge, and identity. This is especially important because there is usually school pressure on the immigrant student to conform to the dominant culture, which also impacts acculturation in other life domains.

Immigrant students' responses to these pressures and their ability to maintain bicultural identities have a lifelong impact on each individual's cultural and personal development. If acculturation and bicultural identity are not supported and developed, there is a danger that immigrant students may reject the school culture in an attempt to maintain their native culture, thereby defying school rules and staff authority (Fordham & Ogbu, 1987; Gibson, 1997; James, 1997). One example of this was with immigrant African Caribbean students where a devaluation of their ethnic and racial identity in schools resulted in a disregard for school norms and authority and a rejection of standards for academic success (James, 1997).

Changing Family Dynamics

Typically children of immigrant families acculturate faster than their parents which may precipitate changes in the family dynamics. This situation must be understood by school counselors in order for them to work effectively with immigrant students. School life exposes the students to the norms and values of the host country on a daily basis, requiring them to speak English, interact with U.S.-born staff and students, and become further immersed in the resettlement country's culture. Due to this intensified exposure and the demand that they adjust to school and subsequently the larger society, immigrant students often learn English and the new culture more rapidly than do the adults in their families. This places them in the unique role of being depended upon as the language and cultural translator for adults, as they assume responsibility for translating, filling out forms, making telephone calls, knowing about resources, and so on. This changing role of the child within the family may create tension, especially in traditional cultures where men are the head of the household. Being dependent on their children may lead to increased frustration and a sense of powerlessness, resulting in domestic violence that may not have occurred in the home country (Chung & Okazaki, 1991). Thus, paradoxically, as children acculturate and adopt the values of the new culture their roles may shift, causing tension in the family and problems in school.

There is also the inevitable conflict between traditional and new culture values that could be addressed by the school counselor. Children may challenge their parents on issues such as the importance of school, dating, gender roles, religious practices, and general social activities. They may also feel embarrassed to be with their parents and/or family in social settings especially if the family members are not fluent in English. To further complicate matters, immigrant families may be faced with new laws regarding discipline and punishment (Bemak & Chung, 2000) and not know about childrearing without using methods of discipline that were sanctioned in their home country. For example, hitting a child or locking them in a room may have been an acceptable practice in one's home country, but both are characterized as child abuse in the resettlement country. These parent–child relationship issues are crucial to the child's adjustment, behavior, attitude, and motivation within the school environment and contribute to an increased risk of failure in school by immigrant students.

Language

More than 6.3 million students are foreign born or are children of recent immigrants, with over one third reporting difficulties in speaking English (Martin & Midgley, 1994) since many came from countries where English was not the official language (Rong & Preissle, 1998). Regardless of English proficiency, about 80 percent of migrant groups in the United States do not speak English at home including 90 percent of Spanish speaking Cubans, El Salvadorians, and Mexicans and 90 percent of Chinese, Filipinos, Koreans, and Vietnamese (U.S. Bureau of Census, 1993). The first and second largest groups of foreign-born students in the United States speak Spanish and Chinese respectively.

Although there has been a history of controversy and philosophical differences about teaching English to foreign-born students in U.S. schools, the past 100 years of immigration have led to the development of various teaching strategies (Montero-Sieburth & LaCelle-Petersen, 1991). Even so, a major challenge for educators working with immigrant youth is not only to balance teaching English language skills and the maintenance of student's native language, but also to balance the impact of how language training is constructed in schools and the ensuing psychological ramifications, an area where school counselor's can play a crucial role. In fact, learning English as a second language has been called a form of social control (Gonzalez & Darling-Hammond, 1997) whereby a forced and intensive language training approach could precipitate feelings of powerlessness and restimulation of premigration trauma, accompanied by frustration, anger, withdrawal or confusion, and consequently poor school experiences.

Although the acquisition of a new language is one of the most important factors in acculturation, it is highly complicated and is symbolic of negative consequences of adjustment, such as the direct or indirect rejection of native languages or cultures. An example of this is the first author's observation of a school counselor who was insistent that her Vietnamese students not speak Vietnamese during group activities. The overt and authoritative rejection of the students' language and culture had multiple negative effects on the students that went far beyond an arbitrary rule made by the counselor.

Language is a metaphor for cultural pluralism and promotes respect and receptivity to differences. Even so, many immigrant students find themselves in classrooms with poor and untrained language instructors. In fact the National Center for Educational Statistics (1997) reported that a sparse 2.5 percent of U.S. ESL teachers in public schools have an academic degree in bilingual education or ESL courses. Further examination found that less than one of three teachers (30 percent) who taught immigrant students have any formal training in that area (Gonzalez & Darling-Hammond, 1997). The lack of formalized teacher training in addressing students with poor English in content or language classes can have dire consequences; immigrant students might be confused by their lessons and the social order and norms of the school, and unsure of their role and relationship with counselors and teachers. Even so, schools require that immigrant students express thoughts and develop personalities within the context of two cultures, while simultaneously mastering academic content in a new language (Lucas, 1999). Awareness of these issues by school counselors can be instrumental in developing institutional and individual appreciation for other languages and cultures and in facilitating the development of a teaching methodology that is more culturally and psychologically sensitive.

School counselors also can present research to school administrators to assist immigrant students. For example data that show how students who study English as a second language often have lower grades and teacher expectations for academic performance (Gonzalez & Darling-Hammond, 1997) would be important information for school counselors to present and discuss. In addition, poor language skills and poor instruction together cause student boredom and inattention. Thus the mastery of English in schools is a far more complex process than simply one of becoming language proficient, and it correlates to the quality of one's educational experience and career path. These issues are critical in redefining school counselor's roles and will be discussed in *Recommendations*.

The Impact of Schools on Immigrant Youth

Historically, the role of U.S. public schools (primarily urban schools) as a cultural bridge for immigrant youth has had mixed success. Leading educators contend that education is central to acculturation, for school policies and practices are similar to those of the larger society (Gonzalez & Darling-Hammond, 1997). The dramatically increasing numbers and nature of today's immigrants require new and different methods with which schools and communities respond to immigrant students' needs.

Although many immigrant youth are able to transcend cultural, social, economic, and linguistic barriers and have successful school experiences, there are large numbers of immigrant students who perform poorly, drop out, or are chronically truant—all issues of concern for school counselors. For example, 20 percent of students studying high school English in the United States and 12 percent at the junior high level have missed two or more years of school since the age of six. This results in 27 percent of high school and 19 percent of middle school students being assigned at least two grade levels below their age norms (Gonzalez & Darling-Hammond, 1997). Equally alarming, 95 percent of foreign-born children between the ages of 12 and 18 have completed only 5 years of elementary school, causing a disparity in graduation rates. Only 32 percent of 18-year-old immigrant students graduate, a figure significantly lower than the percentage of U.S.-born children (Rong & Preissle, 1998). This is consistent with findings that immigrant children are more likely to drop out of school than are U.S.-born children (Rong & Preissle, 1998). This may be attributed to personal, cultural, and societal factors such as the fact that in home countries, low-income students do not have the same access to quality formal education that wealthier students do. This results in a nominal premigration educational experience and feelings of estrangement from public education in resettlement countries.

It is important to note that there are intergroup and geographical differences between immigrant students. For example, within the Asian immigrant group, it has been well established that Chinese and Vietnamese students succeed academically but Cambodians, Filipinos, Laotians, and Hmong students are less successful. It is also striking that different school districts have disparate results; in San Diego, Southeast Asian students had higher grades than did a parallel group in Boston, where dropout rates among Cambodian and Laotian students is high, more than doubling since the 1980s (Hsia & Peng, 1998; Root, 1997).

In addition, there are other barriers to immigrant students' academic success that are inherent to the school culture. Problems in impoverished schools include teacher prejudice, poor academic tracking that simply clusters immigrant students in classes, poor instructional placements for immigrant youth, low academic performance, a disparity between home and school life, poor facilities, deficits in instructional materials, racism and discrimination, unmotivated teachers, and standardized curriculum that has little relevance to immigrants (Gibson, 1997). In addition, there are overcrowded classrooms, accentuated social tensions, untrained teachers and inferior instruction, and curriculum debates that have spilled over into the classroom (McDonnell & Hill, 1993), as well as cultural biases in testing and assessment (Dana, 2000), all of which have impacted placement, performance, and career options for immigrant students. There is potential for school counselors to have a major impact in addressing these issues in a redefined role as discussed in *Recommendations*.

Minority Immigrant Students and Educational Inequities

Over one half of immigrant children in the United States are from minority backgrounds (Portes & Rumbaut, 1996). This is important when considering that the treatment of ethnic minorities in society reflects their treatment in the public education system (Ogbu & Simons, 1998), particularly seen in the unequal distribution of power and resources in the school system (Gibson, 1997). Thus, immigrants not only face adjustment and discrimination issues (American School Board, 1998), but also must contend with the comparative lack of resources in poorer school districts (Comer, 1980; Goodlad, 1984; Kozol, 1991). The alarming nature of these inequalities and the discrimination resulted in a national call to U.S. public schools by the Stanford Working Group to provide equitable public education opportunities for immigrants (Gonzalez & Darling-Hammond, 1997). Inequities in education are attributed to unqualified personnel who more frequently find jobs in poorer urban school districts, to the lack of equipment and resources, ranging from books to computers, to the lack of knowledge about curricular alternatives for immigrant students with minimal prior education and poor literacy skills, and to a paucity of research on how to counsel or teach immigrant students who are struggling with acculturation, language, and premigration issues (Gonzalez & Darling-Hammond, 1997).

Monoculturalism Versus Multiculturalism

A long-standing controversy about how to educate and incorporate immigrant students into the school culture is the basis of monoculturalism versus multiculturalism. Monoculturalism emphasizes assimilation, aiming to eliminate ethnic and cultural boundaries and differences so that everyone is viewed as similar. This unidirectional model requires conformity by everyone, regardless of their ethnic, racial, or cultural backgrounds, to a mainstream White European American model. A diametrically different approach is based on pluralism, maintaining that multicultural perspectives are essential in incorporating ethnic and cultural differences (Cornbleth & Waugh, 1995; Phelan & Davidson, 1993) that celebrate and respect cultural and linguistic differences. Examples of countries whose national public education systems value multiculturalism are the Netherlands, where equality and cultural importance for all cultures is valued, and Israel, where schools are openly concerned with social adjustment and cultural identity (Gibson, 1997).

Despite research findings that minority students are more successful in schools when they feel rooted in their cultural identities, the debate of multiculturalism versus monoculturalism continues, thus engendering significantly different outcomes for immigrant youth (Gibson, 1997). Our belief is that school counselors could significantly contribute to this debate, developing programs, researching, documenting, and disseminating the efficacy of multicultural counseling perspectives.

School Success: A Mainstream Culture Paradigm

In the United States school success has been socially constructed and defined by mainstream culture. It focuses on U.S.-born students without taking into account the broad spectrum of students who migrate from diverse cultures around the world, most often without language skills, and needing to intensively deal with postmigration adjustment while coming to terms with premigration experiences. Therefore, in reviewing the experience of immigrant children in public education, it is critical for school counselors to become leaders in redefining educational success for immigrant students, rejecting linear Eurocentric middle-class values that reflect Western models and standards. Not only are these models inappropriate for many immigrant students, but they raise serious questions for many immigrant children about the purpose and motivation to pursue the rigor and demands of education for long-term gain.

Interestingly, some cultures reject the notion of "getting ahead" as the basis for success. This is evident in societies that sanction traditional gender roles expecting marriage at an early age or cultures like Japan where studying to accomplish more than classmates may be viewed as egotistical and personally embarrassing. Thus, immigrant students find themselves in an educational paradigm that values individual competitive success based on grades, test scores, self-performance, tracking, class rank, and winning rather than one that examines qualitative measures of success such as enjoyment, excitement, interest (Hertzberg, 1998), acculturation, healthy social networks, and cultural mastery.

Perceived Benefits of Education for Immigrant Students

Many migrant students and/or their families do not perceive the long-term benefits of education (Gibson, 1997). For many, the daily struggle to survive and deal with more immediate social and economic stress is far more important than are the benefits of a seemingly abstract and far-reaching goal of graduation (Bruner, 1996; Dryfoos, 1994). Furthermore, there are questions about whether hard work in school results in better jobs and wages (Ogbu & Simons, 1998), in sharp contrast to the belief held by many immigrant students' parents and extended families that hard work, sacrifice, and self-discipline leads to significant and more immediate rewards. This is evident when first-generation Asians fail in school because they adopt negative behaviors based on negative experiences in school (Lee, 1994), or when Mexican immigrants reject school because they perceive no benefit in it (Hayes,

1992), or with Chinese Americans who resist school norms and academics, identifying with African American and Latino "homeboys" (Goto, 1997). School counselors are in an ideal position, given their background and skills, to address these poignant questions.

Basic Survival Skills in Schools

For those immigrant students who do choose to succeed in school, learning basic school survival skills is essential to acquire English skills, pass proficiency tests and general examinations, and select an appropriate career track. Despite this, public education most often bypasses the survival skills and disregards the multiple contributing factors that impact on a student's ability to concentrate, study, get along with peers, pass standardized tests, sit quietly in a classroom, or participate in classroom discussions. Critical school survival skills for immigrant students would include: (1) an overall adjustment to the school culture given their lack of experience with premigration educational institutions; (2) balancing assertiveness that is demanded in U.S. public schools with one's own culture; (3) resolving discomfort with co-ed activities; (4) providing study skills rather than focusing only on language-learning difficulties; (5) developing adequate career paths for ESL students that are not solely based on their performance in classes and tests; (6) understanding their own cultural values as cultural norms; (7) coming to terms with students' home-based responsibilities such as caring for younger children or working in a family business; (8) pragmatically balancing home responsibilities that are highly demanding and often take priority over schoolwork; (9) coming to terms with premigration trauma and difficulties in postmigration adjustment; and (10) dealing with difficulties and family transitions. All of these areas are within the scope of training and skills of school counselors and could be addressed by them in training classes and seminars. The lack of a concerted effort to address these important issues facing migrant students is deplorable—one could easily be spearheaded by school counselors who are in a unique position of having the skills to provide leadership and be social change agents within educational systems.

Core Issues in School Adjustment

Ecosystems: A Contextual Base

When immigrant children enter a new country the world is strange and different. People's names, street names, and store and office locations must be learned, the community looks unmanageable, school classrooms are confusing, stores all look alike, formal and informal rules about appropriate behavior in the community and school must be learned, there are odd tastes and smells to the foods, and people dress differently. All this is encountered while they study a new language, learn how to act within a school and how to learn, and then actually learn the academic content.

There is great variation in immigrant students' responses to their education, which relates to a number of factors such as country of origin, race, ethnicity, culture, gender, religion, educational background prior to migration, age at time of migration, family support, family educational level, and family perception of the importance and benefit of education. Important in adjusting to school is the transition from, and interrelationship with, families and communities—an area where school counselors could play an instrumental role. As mentioned, the treatment or mistreatment of ethnic minorities within public education systems is shaped by policies (Ogbu & Simons; 1998) and therefore determines how ethnic minorities adapt. Policies, practices, and pedagogy impact how migrant children shape and form their experience within schools.

The ecological context of families and communities as it relates to immigrant students' educational experiences is critical information for school counselors who are in an ideal position to be liaisons. The impact of community and family life on school life may be more accentuated for immigrant children, who rely on their cultural traditions as a foundation and anchor of security (Bemak, 1989) as they are exposed and gradually learn about the school environment. Families and communities provide immigrant students a safe cultural haven from which to explore school, as they attempt mastery over their new culture, which would warrant close ties to the school via the school counselor.

School counselors may easily access community support systems and centers because migrant groups typically live in clusters to provide a base of social and cultural support. The structure of the community buffers and supports younger members as they transition to the larger society, and thus would be a beneficial link for the school counselor to use. Over time there is a developmental shift in the relationship between youth and their families and communities as they achieve increased understanding and mastery over their expanding world and school. The role of the communities and families may shift from being "*all* important" to "important" for students, accentuating the role of the school counselor in this developmental transition.

Interpersonal Relationships: Counselors, Teachers, and Students

The relationship immigrant students have with school counselors and teachers is an important bridge to their school experience. This is even more significant for immigrant students because a majority come from collectivist societies where interpersonal relationships within different social contexts provide a foundation for the culture. The concatenation to the classroom, which is facilitated by the teacher, is central to learning content areas and establishing norms and practices. This is established through edict, negotiation, and definition (Hertzberg, 1998). In contrast, school counselors can promote linkage with the wider school culture (including teachers). If the patterns of behavior and expectations in school are inconsistent between the classroom and home/community this may create problems, especially when academic success is determined on the basis of a socially constructed definition of learning (Hertzberg, 1998). Thus, the teacher expectations that contribute to student performance and assist in redefining and interpreting learning and school success may be examined and discussed with school counselors.

School counselors may also facilitate successful participation in school by assisting immigrant students and teachers understand the impact of premigration, and in many instances trauma, on their lives (Kaprielian-Churchill, 1996). For example, the authors encountered an Ethiopian student in a U.S. middle school who was terrified to go on a nature walk with her class. Talking with the student, it became clear that in her experience, people were killed in the "bush," hence her strong reaction to a supposedly leisurely walk. Understanding this issue was crucial for the school counselor to be able to work with the student and teachers. In this capacity the school counselor is the doorway into the world of school and in a larger sense, the world of the resettlement country, contributing to students' successful psychosocial adjustment.

Despite the importance of positive relationships between school personnel and immigrant students, personnel often feel that having an impact on students is beyond their reach. For example, it has been reported that school personnel attribute the high truancy and dropout rates of immigrant students (Goldberg, 1999) to individual, community, and family factors that remain outside the school's control (Ziesemer, 1984), leading to a sense of hopelessness among the staff, who in turn, transmit this message to students. The school counselor is in a vital position to take a leadership role in addressing these kinds of issues, facilitating coordination between students, families, and communities, and attending to staff frustration.

Student Peer Relationships

Because school is the institutional bridge to a new culture for immigrant students, healthy and positive relationships with peers are essential to their positive adjustment to school and the larger community. Cultivating an accepting school climate with peers that celebrates diversity generates a sense of belonging and welcoming, rather than a heightened sense of difference and alienation. Efforts to promote healthy peer relationships could be led by school counselors who, with skills in group dynamics and interpersonal relations, could introduce peer cross-cultural sharing and learning that helps immigrant students adjust, rather than focus only on academics. The school counselor could introduce cooperative learning activities that integrate both shared group tasks and group learning, which support academics as well as social and cultural adjustment. School counselors could simultaneously educate other students and promote positive interethnic group relations in the school environment.

Redefining the Role of School Counselors

To meet the unique needs of immigrant students it is imperative that school counselors clearly redefine their roles to effectively work with this rapidly expanding multicultural population. This requires a paradigm shift that includes not only the knowledge of multicultural counseling, but also new responsibilities such as assuming leadership positions, working in a multidisciplinary and multiagency framework within the larger community, data collection (Bemak, 2000; Hobbs & Collison, 1995; Keys & Bemak, 1997), and assuming the role as a social change agent by challenging existing systems (Bemak, 1998). It is only with this redefined role that school counselors can be effective and assist immigrant students toward healthy and positive adjustment to public education and a successful school experience. These responsibilities are briefly described here because they are cornerstones for the re-definition of the school counselor.

Multicultural Counseling

Immigrant students come from a wide variety of countries with diverse ethnic and racial groups. Working with this population requires an exemplary foundation in cross-cultural awareness and counseling as well as a proactive initiative to learn more about the history, sociopolitical, and cultural issues, and challenges of immigrant groups. Thus, it is imperative for school counselors to deeply understand concepts and applications of multicultural counseling, especially in the context of immigrant groups.

Leadership

School counselors must become leaders to address the institutional barriers encoun-tered by immigrant youth. Group leadership skills are conducive to fostering institu-tional leadership skills that value social justice and social responsibility leading to equity and equal opportunity for all students.

Multiagency and Multidisciplinary Collaboration

Immigrant students' needs are complex and different than those of U.S.-born students. To address these complex needs, it is essential that school counselors work collaboratively, across disciplines and service systems (Bemak, in press; Keys & Bemak, 1997). This requires work with social services, mental health, housing, public health, and juvenile services, religious institutions, and business organizations and will be discussed further in *Recommendations*.

Data Collection and Dissemination

To ensure that effective practices are documented with immigrant students, it is essential that programs are evaluated. The documentation and dissemination of mea-surable outcomes of prevention and intervention programs provides guidelines to a better understanding of what does and does not work.

Social Change and Advocacy

The increasing numbers of immigrant students and the failure of schools to ade-quately educate and acculturate them requires an examination and challenging of existing educational policies and practices. School counselors are in a position to have broad perspectives that are inclusive of all aspects of schools, families, and communities in determining how to best meet the needs of this population. To support and assist immigrant students, there must be accompanying institutional change derived from a foundation of multicultural counseling. School counselors are well positioned to advocate for equal education, personal and family adjustment, and resolution of premigration problems by assuming the role of social change agent.

Recommendations for School Counselors

To be competent with culturally diverse immigrant student populations, school counselors must take an active leadership role; they must become change agents, advocates, and leaders in public education. To accomplish this goal we would propose the following fifteen recommendations for the multicultural school counselor:

1. *Accurate assessments and ongoing review for student placement in classes.* It is well established that ethnic minority students are placed in remedial courses at far greater rates than are White students (The Education Trust, 1998). The same is true for immigrant students, who are placed in less rigorous academic or vocational classes (Lucas, 1999) based on poor testing or language skills. School counselors can challenge these placements by taking into account cultural differences and learning styles, language barriers, and migration adjustment issues in determining classroom assignments, career paths, and job placements for migrant students (Lucas, 1999), and recommending the use of nontraditional measures that may be more accurate in assessing the abilities of this group. It is also critical that they continue to assess the academic tracking of migrant students and reevaluate their classroom placements since initial placements usually become permanent.

2. *Reevaluate terms of success in schools.* As described, success that emphasizes only academic achievement, test scores, and passing proficiency tests does not account for the complex and multifaceted needs of immigrant students. We would recommend that school counselors assume a leadership role in helping school cultures understand the nature and dynamics of migration and the impact of pre- and postmigration issues on the education of immigrant students. For example, it may be helpful to introduce in-service training to educators on cultural survival and the impact of premigration trauma on learning.

3. *Teach basic survival skills in schools.* As previously stated, there is a need to establish a foundation of basic survival skills for migrant students by teaching them about things that are fundamental to school systems. We would suggest that school counselors become forerunners in making these skills a critical component of school curriculum for immigrant students. Counselors could provide leadership and coordination with activities that have already been introduced in some programs, such as introducing Intake Centers or Parent Information Centers where oral and written information is disseminated in multiple languages (Lucas, 1999). They could also design programs to orient immigrant students to school rules and expectations related to time, using bathrooms, using school lockers, changing classes, procedures for being absent and getting excuse notes, the purpose and meaning of report cards, and fire drills. School counselors could also introduce citizenship classes as well as address basic food, housing, and clothing needs and coordinate community outreach for families needing assistance.

4. *Promote cooperative small group learning.* Most immigrant students come from collectivist societies where social relationships and cooperation are highly valued. Cooperative learning in small groups would greatly benefit immigrant students (Gibson, 1997) and maintain cultural synchronicity. Given school counselors' background and training in group work, their skills could be used as consultants for teachers in developing culturally relevant cooperative learning groups. The groups could emphasize learning activities with heterogeneous student groups focused on cooperative activities where educational activities could be learned simultaneously with language. The emphasis on collaboration rather than on coercion would be culturally appropriate, based on interpersonal relations rather than competition (Gibson, 1997).

5. *Coordinate study skills training.* Coming with varied backgrounds from other cultures, migrant students may need academic support to maintain or reach their grade level. School counselors can assist in assessing their needs and coordinating these efforts. This could take the form of tutorial programs, summer programs, weekend and afterschool programs, or special academies with a focus on the specialized adjustment *and* academic needs of students.

6. *Build on students' strengths rather than focus on English as the primary factor in academic success.* Many immigrant students are resilient and have learned how to survive in highly complex and confusing worlds, both during pre- and postmigration. School counselors could capitalize on these strengths to enhance students' adjustment to schools, educational performance, and learning, rather than ignore this repertoire of coping strategies and strengths that has developed. For example, if students come from a small village in Somalia where technology is nonexistent, they may be artful in storytelling. The school counselor could assist teachers in infusing storytelling into lessons, whereby the strengths of those students become part of the instructional pedagogy. Furthermore, school counselors can support and advocate the rights of students to use their native languages freely in schools and communities (Gonzalez & Darling-Hammond, 1997), supporting their strengths as bilingual speakers. It is important to not erase the past of immigrant students, but rather to incorporate information and experiences from their home life and country to instill a sense of belonging and infuse the school climate with an inclusive multicultural perspective.

7. *Promote students and families to the school as resources for information about their home cultures.* The school experts on other cultures are the immigrant students themselves, as well as their families. School counselors can play a crucial role in promoting a rich cultural diversity and respect for the diverse backgrounds of students by inviting them and their families to become cultural informants and resources about their home countries. Counselors could facilitate students and family to make presentations, decorate classrooms and hallways, develop exhibits of traditional dress, bring in traditional foods, share special holiday practices, etc.

8. *Cultivate a climate of respect for cultural diversity.* It has been discussed previously how public education in the United States is based on European American mainstream values and outcomes. Yet for a healthy adjustment of the expanding population of immigrant students, there is a need for a multicultural identity. Given the important role that schools play as the first institution of contact for immigrant youth, respect for the diverse cultures that students bring would be important in their education and long-term adjustment. It is recommended that school counselors play a vital role in promoting a culture of dignity, appreciation, and respect for cultural diversity, building on the background of immigrant students to support their cultural identity while supporting academic success (Davidson, 1996; Hertzberg, 1998). This may be achieved through consultation with teachers about classroom activities, coordinating diversity appreciation days within schools, and working with student councils, parents, and the community to generate schoolwide and community-linked activities that honor and pay tribute to cultural traditions and practices.

9. *Teach, consult, and educate staff.* To create a school culture that appreciates and respects cultural diversity and the differences that immigrant students bring, school personnel, from custodians to principals, must contribute and share similar values. Given the importance and acknowledgment of multiculturalism in the counseling field, the school counselor has the knowledge and skills to organize and lead diversity workshops and seminars for *all* school personnel. A core value system in the school at multiple levels has the potential to promote a culture that truly respects, welcomes, and embraces diversity.

10. *Collaboration with communities.* Collaboration with communities is important for immigrant student school adjustment and success. As students master the world of public education, their healthy adaptation is contingent upon a broadening understanding beyond the school to the larger community. The school counselor can play an important role in linking communities and schools, facilitating work opportunities, finding and maintaining sensitive internship placements, and linking with human service agencies that can offer other necessary services. By doing so, the school counselor is also educating the wider community about its members, creating an appreciation and understanding of cultural diversity, and therefore promoting positive interethnic group relations.

11. *Collaboration with families.* It is well documented that collaboration with families assists students in their school performance improving academic achievement, attendance, and reducing dropout rates (Comer, 1980; Fine, 1995; Teachman, Day, & Carver, 1995). Research also suggests that parents make valuable contributions to their children's social and emotional development (Comer, 1980). This is important for parents or family members from different ethnic groups (Herring, 1997; Myrick, 1997), especially because schools are constructed within the framework of mainstream culture. If families require counseling, it is likely that they will be more comfortable visiting the school counselor and discussing the concerns within a school context, rather than be dishonored and embarrassed by the stigma of the mental health system (James, 1997).

12. *Provide counseling to resolve premigration trauma and loss and postmigration difficulties that are barriers to education.* The school counselor is in a singular position to identify and counsel children with mental health problems. Their attention to barriers to school success such as premigration trauma, family loss, culture shock, and ethnic identity confusion is a major step toward acculturation for immigrant students. For example, the first author was requested to consult in a school where a middle-school Bosnian student became afraid and refused to come out from under his desk. The school psychiatrist recommended that the child be medicated. The first author met with the child and determined that the class discussions and assignments related to family triggered painful memories of his mother's death and the acute fears he has about loss of other significant family members. Rather than medication, sessions with the school counselor and later with a clinician in a nearby mental health center helped the child understand and come to better terms with unresolved issues and fears.

A Multilevel Model of Psychotherapy (MLM) for refugees and immigrants has been developed as a culturally sensitive psychotherapy model for this population. The model addresses issues such as cultural empowerment, cross-cultural psychoeducation, racism and discrimination, incorporating traditional healers, and culturally applicable individual, group, and family therapy. For more information regarding the MLM model refer to Bemak, Chung, and Pedersen (in press).

13. *Promote a climate of safety for exploration and adjustment.* School counselors can assist immigrant students in establishing the personal, social, and environmental security that is necessary to gain a sense of mastery of living in their world. Gaining the knowledge and skills to feel safe in the context of schools will assist the immigrant student with adjustment, as well as in academic and career success, and may require nurturing and caring (Hertzberg, 1998). For example, the first author consulted in a school where a school counselor decorated her room with pictures, words (in the native language), items, and images of the cultures represented by immigrant students. When students entered her room they described feeling safe and welcomed, and readily shared their struggles and problems. Another important issue in cultivating safety is to deal with discrimination toward immigrant students.

14. *Social change agents and advocates.* To truly address the larger scope of issues facing immigrant students there must be change made on personal, familial, community, and institutional levels. School counselors are the best equipped to understand change in school systems. It is therefore recommended that school counselors challenge existing paradigms, not only on counseling levels that involve individuals, families, and groups, but also within educational institutions that continue to perpetuate discriminatory and unequal practices.

15. *Data collection and evaluation.* Many school counselors do good work with immigrant students. Unfortunately, this work often goes unnoticed except by the school principal or colleagues. In order to document the efficacy of best practices and good work, it is strongly suggested that school counselors who develop and implement programs with immigrant students and families evaluate and disseminate outcomes to colleagues and school systems. For example, a school counselor who designs a program based on cooperative learning concepts could measure academic performance, attendance rates, acquisition of English, and adjustment outcomes as a result of the activities. This information would be invaluable to educators and school systems for better understanding what works.

Summary

In conclusion, it is critical that school counselors redefine their role so as to be effective with the dramatically increasing immigrant school population. It is essential that school counselors know about pre- and postmigration challenges encountered by immigrant students and the interrelationships between immigration and school policy and multicultural counseling. To be effective multicultural counselors they must assume leadership roles, work collaboratively, evaluate their work, and become social change agents to assist immigrant students with successful educational experiences.

DISCUSSION QUESTIONS

1. What are the causes of migration?

2. What are the differences between voluntary and involuntary migration? How do these differences impact the school counselor's work with immigrant and refugee students?

3. Discuss cultural mastery for immigrant students. What is the role of the school counselor in facilitating cultural mastery?

4. What are some of the changing family dynamics for immigrant students?

5. Discuss the importance of language in cultural adaptation and psychosocial adjustment for immigrant students and implications for school counselors.

6. Given the poor academic performance of many immigrant students what is the role of the school counselor in improving academic success and school performance for this group?

7. What role does the school counselor play in ensuring that immigrant students have a positive and successful school experience?

8. What are some of the educational inequities that immigrant students face? How can the school counselor effectively address these issues?

9. As a school counselor how would you define success in schools for immigrant students? How does this differ from success in mainstream populations?

10. What are the basic survival skills for immigrant students that school counselors must address?

11. Discuss the school counselor's role in working with immigrant families to enhance academic success for their children.

12. Discuss the importance of redefining the school counselor's role in working with immigrant students and their families.

13. Why is it important for the school counselor to assume the role of a social change agent and advocate for immigrant students?

14. There are fifteen recommendations listed in this chapter with which the multicultural school counselor can effectively work with immigrant students. Discuss the changing role of the school counselor as it relates to each of these recommendations.

15. What are the components of the Multilevel Model of Psychotherapy (MLM) for this population?

REFERENCES

American School Board. (1998, May). *American School Board Journal*, 20–21.

Aponte, J. F. & Crouch, R. T. (2000). The changing ethnic profile of the United States in the twenty-first century. In J. F. Aponte & J. Wohl (Eds.), *Psychological interventions and cultural diversity* (pp. 1–17). Boston: Allyn & Bacon.

Aponte, J. F. & Wohl, J. (2000). *Psychological interventions and cultural diversity*. Boston, MA: Allyn & Bacon.

Bemak, F. (2000). Migrants. *Encyclopedia of psychology* (pp. 244–247). American Psychological Association and Oxford University Press.

Bemak, F. (2000). Transforming the role of the school counselor to provide leadership in educational reform through collaboration. *Professional School Counseling, 3*(5), 323–331.

Bemak, F. (1998). Interdisciplinary collaboration for social change: Redefining the counseling profession. In C. C. Lee & G. R. Walz (Eds.), *Social action: A mandate for counselors* (pp. 279–292). Alexandria, VA and Greensboro, NC: American Counseling Association and ERIC Counseling and Student Services Clearinghouse.

Bemak, F. (1989). Cross-cultural family therapy with Southeast Asian refugees. *Journal of Strategic and Systemic Therapies, 8*, 22–27.

Bemak, F. & Chung, R. C.-Y. (2000). Psychological intervention with immigrants and refugees. In J. F. Aponte & J. Wohl (Eds.), *Psychological intervention and cultural diversity* (pp. 200–213). Boston: Allyn & Bacon.

Bemak, F., Chung, R. C.-Y., & Pedersen, P. (in press). *Counseling refugees: A psychosocial cultural approach to innovative multicultural interventions.* Westport, CT: Greenwood Press.

Bruner, J. (1996). *The culture of education.* Cambridge, MA: Harvard University Press.

Chung, R. C.-Y. & Okazaki, S. (1991). Counseling Americans of Southeast Asian descent: The impact of the refugee experience. In C. C. Lee & B. L. Richardson (Eds.), *Multicultural issues in counseling: New approaches to diversity* (pp. 107–126). Alexandria, VA: American Association for Counseling and Development.

Coleman, D. A. (1995). International migration: Demographics and socioeconomic consequences in the United Kingdom and Europe. *International Migration Review, 29*(1), 155–180.

Comer, J. P. (1980). *School power: Implications of an intervention project.* New York: The Free Press.

Cornbleth, C. & Waugh, D. (1995). *The great speckled bird: Multicultural politics and education policy making.* New York: St. Martin's.

Dana, R. H. (2000). Psychological assessment in the diagnosis and treatment of ethnic group members. In J. A. Aponte & J. Wohl (Eds.), *Psychological intervention and cultural diversity* (pp. 59–74). Boston: Allyn & Bacon.

Davidson, A. L. (1996). *Making and molding identity in schools: Student narratives on race, gender, and academic engagement.* Albany, NY: SUNY Press.

De Vita, C. J. (1996). The United States at mid-decade. *Population Bulletin, 50*(4), 1–48.

Dryfoos, J. G. (1994). *Full-service schools.* San Francisco, CA: Jossey-Bass, Inc.

Fine, M. J. (1995). Family–school intervention. In R. H. Mikesell, D.-D. Lustermann, & S. H. McDaniel (Eds.), *Integrating family therapy: Handbook of family psychotherapy and systems theory* (pp. 481–495). Washington, DC: American Psychological Association.

Fordham, S. (1996). *Blacked out: Dilemmas of race, identity, and success at Capital High*. Chicago: University of Chicago Press.

Fordham, S. & Ogbu, J. U. (1987). Black students school success: Coping with the "Burden of Acting White." *Urban Review, 18*(3), 176–206.

Gibson, M. A. (1997). Complicating the immigrant/involuntary minority typology. *Anthropology & Education Quarterly Review, 28*(3), 431–454.

Goldberg, M. E. (1999). Truancy and dropout among Cambodian students: Results from a comprehensive high school. *Social Work in Education, 21*(1), 49–63.

Gonzalez, J. M. & Darling-Hammond, L. (1997). *New concepts for new challenges: Professional development for teachers of immigrant youth*. Washington, DC: Center for Applied Linguistics.

Goodlad, J. I. (1984). *A place called school*. New York: McGraw-Hill Book Company.

Goto, S. T. (1997). Nerds, normal people, and homeboys: An accommodation and resistance among Chinese American students. *Anthropology & Education, 28*, 70–84.

Hayes, K. G. (1992). Attitudes toward education: Voluntary and involuntary immigrants from the same families. *Anthropology & Education, 23*, 250–267.

Herring, R. D. (1997). *Counseling diverse ethnic youth: Synergetic strategies and interventions for school counselors*. Fort Worth, TX: Harcourt Brace College Publishers.

Hertzberg, M. (1998). Having arrived: Dimensions of educational success in a transitional newcomer school. *Anthropology & Educational Quarterly, 29*(4), 391–418.

Hobbs, B. B. & Collison, B. B. (1995). School–community collaboration: Implications for the school counselor. *The School Counselor, 43*, 58–65.

Hsia, J. & Peng, S. S. (1998). Academic achievement and performance. In L. C. Lee & N. W. S. Zane (Eds.), *Handbook of Asian American Psychology* (pp. 325–358). Thousand Oaks, CA: Sage Publications.

James, D. C. S. (1997, November). Psychological risks of immigrant students. *Journal of School Health*, 50–53.

Kaprielian-Churchill, I. (1996). Refugees and education in Canadian schools. *International Review of Education, 42*(4), 349–365.

Keys, S. G. & Bemak, F. (1997). School–family–community linked services: A school counseling role for changing times. *The School Counselor, 44*, 255–263.

Kozol, J. (1991). *Savage inequalities*. New York: Crown Publishers, Inc.

Lee, S. J. (1994). Behind the model-minority stereotype: Voices of high- and low-achieving Asian American students. *Anthropology and Education Quarterly, 25*, 413–429.

Leong, F. (in press). Counseling international students. In P. B. Pedersen, J. G. Draguns, W. J. Lonner, & J. E. Trimble (Eds.), *Counseling across cultures* (5th ed.). Thousand Oaks, CA: Sage Publications.

Lucas, T. (1999, January/February). Promoting secondary school transitions for immigrant adolescents. *The High School Magazine*, 40–41.

Martin, P. & Midgley, E. (1994). Immigration to the United States: Journey to an uncertain destination. *Population Bulletin, 49*(2), 2–46.

McDonnell, L. M. & Hill, P. T. (1993). *Newcomers in American schools—Meeting the educational needs of immigrant youth*. Santa Monica, CA: RAND.

Montero-Sieburth, M. & LaCelle-Peterson, M. (1991). Immigration and schooling: An ethnohistorical account of policy and family perspectives in an urban community. *Anthropology and Education Quarterly, 22*, 300–325.

Murphy, H. B. (1977). Migration, culture and mental health. *Psychological Medicine, 7*, 677–684.

Myrick, R. D. (1997). *Developmental guidance and counseling*. Minneapolis, MN: Educational Media Corporation.

National Center for Educational Statistics. (1997). *A profile of policies and practices for limited English proficient students: Screening methods, program support, and teacher training* [SASS 1993–1994]. NCES 97-472. Washington, DC: U.S. Government Printing Office.

Ogbu, J. U. & Simons, H. D. (1998). Voluntary and involuntary minorities: A cultural-ecological theory of school performance with some implications for education. *Anthropology & Education Quarterly, 29*(2), 155–188.

O'Hara, W. P. (1992). America's minorities—The demographics of diversity. *Population Bulletin, 47*(4), 1–47.

O'Hara, W. P. & Felt, J. C. (1991). *Asian Americans: American's fastest growth minority group*. Washington, DC: Population Reference Bureau.

Passel, J. S. & Edmonston, B. (1992). *Immigration and race: Trends in immigration to the United States*. Washington, DC: Urban Institute.

Phelan, P. & Davidson, A. L. (Eds.). (1993). *Renegotiating cultural diversity in American schools*. New York: Teachers College Press.

Portes, A. & Rumbaut, R. G. (1996). *Immigrant America: A portrait* (2nd ed.). Berkeley: University of California Press.

Rong, X. L. & Preissle, J. (1998). *Educating immigrant students: What we need to know to meet the challenges*. Thousand Oaks, CA: Corwin Press.

Root, M. P. P. (Ed.) (1997). *Filipino Americans: Transformation and identity*. Thousand Oaks, CA: Sage Publications.

Schnaiberg, L. (1996, September). Immigration plays key supporting role in record-enrollment drama. *Education Week, 16*, 24–25.

Teachman, J. D., Day, R. D., & Carver, K. P. (1995). The impact of family environment on educational attainment: Do families make a difference? In B. A. Ryan, G. R. Adams, T. P. Gullotta, R. P. Weissberg, & R. L. Hampton (Eds.), *The family–school connection* (pp. 155–203). Thousand Oaks, CA: Sage.

The Education Trust. (1998). *Education watch 1998: State and national data book, Vol. II*. Washington, D.C.: Author.

United Nations. (1995). *Notes for speakers: Social development*. New York: Department of Public Information, United Nations.

U.S. Bureau of Census. (1997). *Current population reports: Special studies*, P23–193. Washington, DC: U.S. Government Printing Office.

U.S. Bureau of Census. (1993). *1990 census of population and housing—Public use microdata samples 5%*. Washington, DC: Author.

U.S. Department of Commerce. (1997). *Statistical abstract of the United States: 1997*. Washington, DC: U.S. Government Printing Office.

U.S. Department of Justice, (1999). *Legal immigration, Fiscal Year 1998*. Washington, DC: Author.

Ziesemer, C. (1984). Student and staff perceptions of truancy and court referrals. *Social Work in Education, 6*, 167–178.

AUTHORS' NOTES

Fred Bemak is a professor and the program coordinator of the Counseling and Development Program in the Graduate School of Education at George Mason University. He has provided consultation, training, and done research throughout the United States and in 30 countries and has published widely in the areas of cross-cultural counseling, youth identified as being at risk, and the mental health and psychosocial adjustment of refugees and immigrants. Dr. Bemak has been a Fulbright scholar, a Kellogg Foundation International fellow, and World Rehabilitation Fund International Exchange of Experts fellow.

Rita Chi-Ying Chung is an associate professor in the Counseling and Development Program in the Graduate School of Education at George Mason University. She has researched and published extensively in the areas of mental health and psychosocial adjustment of refugees and immigrants, interethnic group relations and racial stereotypes, coping strategies in dealing with racism and its impact of psychological well-being, and cross-cultural and multicultural issues in mental health, achievement motivation, and aspirations. Dr. Chung has lived and worked in China, Brazil, and New Zealand.

6

Increasing Hispanic Parent Participation in Schools: The Role of the Counselor

J. MANUEL CASAS

MICHAEL J. FURLONG

CHRISTOPHER RUIZ DE ESPARZA
University of California, Santa Barbara

OBJECTIVES

1. To explore the role that Hispanic parents' participation plays in the school success of their children
2. To review the educational challenges facing Hispanic students; discuss parent participation and its positive effects on student learning; review programs and suggestions to assist school counselors in increasing Hispanic parent participation

In many urban areas and the Southwest, Hispanic children now are the majority group in public elementary and secondary schools (California Basic Educational Data System, 2000). These children come from a variety of backgrounds and represent challenges to educators because schools must respond to new social, cultural, and linguistic diversity. Research continues to show that one important key to enhancing the educational progress of all students is to create a school environment that enables parents to participate in the schooling process. As key student support personnel, school counselors have the group process and interpersonal communication skills required to facilitate activities to bring this about—they are natural leaders in the school setting who can advocate for an increase in parent participation and facilitate the increased empowerment of Hispanic parents.

This chapter explores the role that Hispanic parent participation plays or can play in the school success of their children. We begin by examining the challenges facing educators working with Hispanic students and their parents. The discussion then moves to a review of the research about parental participation and its positive effects on student learning. The next section focuses on what is known about Hispanic parent participation in schools. After showing that Hispanic parents do place a high value on education, several model programs designed to increase Hispanic parent school participation are reviewed to provide inspiration for what might be possible in schools serving Hispanic children and their families. Finally, to bring all of the information together and to provide some direction for follow-up activities, a comprehensive planning process to increase Hispanic parent participation that can be spearheaded by school counselors is presented.

Hispanic Educational Challenges

For years it has been widely recognized that the Hispanic population is destined to become the largest racial/ethnic minority in the United States because it is the fastest growing and increasingly important segment of the U.S. population. Hispanics totaled 31.3 million in 1999, an increase of 40 percent since 1990. The total U.S. population grew much more slowly, increasing by less than 10 percent during the same period (U.S. Census Bureau, 2000). Currently, Hispanics represent approximately 11.5 percent of the total population; however, because of their high representation among urban, low socioeconomic, and undocumented groups, the undercount of Hispanics by the census may be quite high (Ramirez, 1999).

Projections by the U.S. Census indicate that in 20 years about 1 in 6 U.S. residents will be of Hispanic origin, and by the middle of this century—when today's young children are middle aged—this ratio will increase to about 1 in 4 (2000). The future productivity of the U.S. labor force hinges to a considerable degree on our nation's ability to provide high-quality education for Hispanic young people who will play a vital role in the labor market.

The dramatic pattern of growth is expected to continue because of three major factors. First, it is expected that, given the dire socioeconomic conditions prevalent in Mexico, Central America, and South America, the high level of immigration from these countries will continue. Second is the relative youth of the Hispanic population. In 1999, the median age of the Hispanic population was 26.5 years, about 9 years lower than the median age of the national population, which was 35.5 (U.S. Census Bureau, 2000). Third is the high fertility rate among several Hispanic subgroups, most notably Mexican Americans and Puerto Ricans. The total fertility rates for most Hispanic groups are well above the replacement level of 2.1, the rate required for a generation to replace itself, after allowing for deaths. In 1995, the total fertility rate ranged from 3.3 for Mexicans to 1.7 for Cubans. Cubans were the only major Hispanic group with a fertility rate below the replacement level (Ventura, Martin, Curtin, & Matthews, 1997).

It is not surprising that, given this growth, Hispanics are having and will continue to have a tremendous impact on social, economic, political, and educational institutions. Nowhere is the impact of Hispanic growth more apparent than in elementary schools. Hispanic children represent a significant proportion of the school-age population in a number of urban school districts, and in some they are already the majority. Between 1972 and 1996, Hispanic enrollment in public schools rose from 6 to 15 percent. In 1996, approximately one out of every four students who lived in a central city and who attended public schools was Hispanic, up from approximately 1 out of 10 students in 1972 (National Center for Education Statistics, 2000). In the state of California, Hispanic students represented 42 percent of the total statewide enrollment for the year 1999–2000 (the largest single ethnic group in the state). And in Los Angeles County alone, there are 966,699 Hispanic students, or 58.6 percent of the countywide enrollment (California Basic Educational Data System, 2000).

Although Hispanic children are highly represented in elementary schools, they are severely underrepresented at the secondary and higher educational levels. According to Casas and Furlong (1986), one of the reasons for this under representation is that Hispanics are plagued with alarming dropout rates. The Hispanic dropout rate has averaged 30 percent over the past 25 years, and is 2.5 times the rate for Blacks and 3.5 times the rate for non-Hispanic Whites (Kaufman, Kwon, Klein, & Chapman, 2000). Between 1972 and 1996, the dropout rate for non-Hispanic Whites and Blacks decreased, while the dropout rate for Hispanics was not significantly different. Although the dropout rate for Blacks decreased at a faster rate than that for non-Hispanic Whites, Blacks and Hispanics were still more likely to drop out of school than their non-Hispanic White peers (U.S. Department of Education, 2000). According to the Hispanic Dropout Project (HDP) (Lockwood & Secada, 1999), varied reasons have been put forth to explain the high Hispanic dropout rate. The two that have received a significant amount of attention are immigration status and low socioeconomic status. The HDP report contains the following facts that serve to show that such explanations are more complex than they appear to be on the surface.

1. Dropout rates for Hispanics are higher than for non-Hispanics of similar immigration and generational status. Among foreign-born immigrants, 43 percent of Hispanics between the ages of 16 and 24 (young adults) have dropped out of school versus 8 percent of non-Hispanics. Among first-generation U.S.-born young adults, 17 percent of Hispanics versus 6 percent of non-Hispanics have dropped out. Second- or later-generation U.S.-born young adults show even higher dropout rates—24 percent of the Hispanics in this group have dropped out of school versus 11 percent of non-Hispanics (National Center for Education Statistics, 1998).

2. While many Hispanic students live in conditions of severe poverty, Hispanic dropout rates are at least double those of other Americans at the same income level. That is, wealthy Hispanics are *twice* as likely as wealthy whites or wealthy African Americans to not obtain a high school diploma (National Center for Education Statistics, 1998). Although the dropout rate is measured in various ways, no matter how it is measured, Hispanics are more likely to drop out of school than are non-Hispanics who are similarly situated (National Center for Education Statistics, 1998).

Given the dropout trends of Hispanics it is not surprising that they are severely underrepresented at the secondary and higher educational levels (Casas & Furlong, 1986; National Center for Education Statistics, 1996; National Center for Education Statistics, 2000). Other school-related reasons contribute to this under representation. In California, the percentage of Hispanic students completing the required courses for University of California and/or California State University entrance is the lowest of any ethnic group's at 22.1 percent, compared to the state average of 35.6 percent (California Basic Educational Data System, 1999). Even when Hispanics do complete the required courses, they are very often not "competitively" eligible for admission because of lack of access to advanced placement classes (i.e., courses in key content areas that prepare students to take Advanced Placement exams, and potentially give students college credit for course work in the content area), honor courses, and actual college courses offered at local community colleges. With respect to Advanced Placement courses, limited accessibility is due to the fact that these courses are often offered in private schools and suburban high schools with mostly non-Hispanic White or Asian American students than in urban high schools whose student bodies are mostly Hispanic and/or Black. Non-Hispanic White and Asian American students are also more likely to take SAT preparation courses whose fees can run as high as $800. Needless to say, without access to these courses, Hispanics are more likely to score poorly on this test, which is used by 90 percent of four-year colleges and universities to help pick their freshman class (Weiss, 2000, August 30).

The severity of the ongoing problem is well exemplified by the following statistics. The proportion of Hispanics who graduate from 4-year colleges is less than half that of non-Hispanic Whites. At a conference sponsored by the University of California System in 1988 that dealt with increasing racial/ethnic minority student representation in the system, it was noted that the University's graduating class of the year 2000 was in the fourth grade at that time and Hispanics represented more than 32 percent of all students in California. It was then hypothesized that if current trends remained unchanged, the following educational patterns could be expected for the fourth-grade Hispanic students (most current data available follows in parentheses; California Basic Educational Data System, 1996; Pachon, Mejia, & Bergman, 1997 December).

Number who will enter the ninth grade	144,000
(Actual number of Hispanic 9th graders in 1995–96)	(168,000)
Number who will graduate from high school	70,000
(Actual number who graduated from high school)	(78,000)
Number who will be qualified to enter the University of California	13,500
(Actual number who qualified to enter the UC system)	(17,529)
Number who will actually enroll in the University of California	1,700
(Actual number who enrolled in the UC system)	(3,209)

Number who will graduate or still be enrolled in the year 2000   1,100
(Predicted graduation based on 1997 data)   (1,925)

Number who will earn a doctorate from the University of California   19

The Impact of Hispanic Educational Challenges

The educational challenges that continue to confront Hispanics have a detrimental impact on their socioeconomic advancement. It has been widely acknowledged for some time that education is an important means to economic progress (Carter & Segura, 1979; Ford Foundation, 1984; Lockwood & Secada, 1999). The economic rewards for education are on the rise. The importance of educational outcomes for Hispanics is underscored by the increasing value of education in the labor market. Two decades ago, a male Hispanic college graduate earned 67 percent more than a Hispanic male with no high school education, an earnings premium that has increased to 146 percent today (The Council of Economic Advisers, 2000).

In 1998, 85 percent of people in the United States between the ages of 18 and 24 had a high school diploma or a General Equivalency Diploma (GED). For young Hispanics, just 63 percent had a diploma or GED—compared with 88 percent of non-Hispanic Whites and African Americans—suggesting that 37 percent of Hispanic young people are sent into the workforce of the information age without a high school education (U.S. Department of Education, 2000). Given the dropout and educationally related statistics as well as these workforce statistics, it is not surprising that Hispanics continue to be at the lowest levels of professional status, income, and net worth.

More specifically, relative to their representation in the workforce of the information age, Hispanics are greatly underrepresented in today's high-paying information-technology (IT) sector. While Hispanics are 11 percent of employed workers, only 4 percent are workers in IT occupations. This Hispanic "digital divide" exists because the relatively low educational level of many Hispanics hinders entry into the IT labor market. This underrepresentation contributes to an economy-wide Hispanic pay gap because these IT jobs pay considerably more than other jobs (The Council of Economic Advisers, 2000).

Given the rapid growth of the U.S. Hispanic population, the gap in educational achievement and the disparity relative to representation in the workforce between Hispanics and their non-Hispanic peers is a matter of critical importance for Hispanic young people and society in general. Given this state of affairs, there is a potential for the deterioration of the labor force, resulting in a decline of U.S. economic competitiveness, a loss in sales and profits, as well as a decline in the nation's tax base (McEvoy, 1988).

Public and private efforts to provide resources for the development of innovative programs that increase the likelihood of academic success for Hispanic students have been motivated by an increased awareness of the seriousness of these problems and the significant social and economic role that the Hispanic population is destined to play in this country. For instance, in 1995, the Department of Housing and Urban Development (HUD) launched a community-based effort to encourage the development of resource and computer learning centers in HUD-assisted and/or -insured housing. Today more than 600 centers are in operation around the country and program centers include computer training, Internet access, job readiness support, micro enterprise development, GED certification, health care and social services, adult education classes and youth services (Neighborhood Networks, 1998).

In June 2000, the U.S. Department of Education announced the award of $25.8 million to fund 76 new grants to Hispanic Serving Institutions (i.e., colleges or universities where Hispanics represent at least 25 percent of the student population and at least half of those students are low income) to improve their facilities, academic programs, and student services. U.S. Secretary of Education Richard W. Riley stated:

> The goal is to increase the college graduation rates of Hispanics. These grants will enable colleges that serve large numbers of Hispanic and disadvantaged students to offer an enriched academic experience that will go a long way toward making that goal a reality. (U.S. Department of Education, 2000 June 15, online)

Vice President Gore added:

> This program is part of a larger, overall effort to increase the achievement of Hispanic students at all levels of education, from preschool through college. Education can open a new world of opportunity for Hispanics and other minorities, and this administration is committed through this program and others like it to help those dreams become a reality. We must reduce the Hispanic dropout rate in America. And I will not rest until we do. (U.S. Department of Education, 2000, June 15, online)

At the same time, President Clinton highlighted a partnership between the Department of Housing and Urban Development (HUD), Department of Health and Human Services (HHS), and the White House Initiative on Educational Excellence for Hispanic Americans to provide English- and Spanish-language materials and educational forums to parents of young children through HUD's Neighborhood Networks and other community-based programs. Parents receive information on early brain development research, parenting tips, how to access childcare subsidies and tax credits, how to choose a childcare center, what Head Start has to offer, and other family supports. Since the summer of 2000, this effort is being piloted in six Hispanic-serving community locations across the country (U.S. Department of Housing and Urban Development, 2000).

As an example from the private sector, the Kellogg Foundation recently launched an initiative that focuses on and provides resources to the emerging group of Hispanic-Serving Institutions (HSIs) and other institutions serving Hispanics. The initiative directs attention to these institutions as the catalysts for stimulating grassroots community efforts to strengthen the educational pipeline for Hispanic children. More specifically, the Foundation is interested in catalyzing and supporting actions that increase academic success, access to higher education, and graduation from high school and college (Kellogg Foundation, 2000).

What Is the Impact of Parent Participation in Schools?

Henderson, Marburger and Ooms (1986) suggested two major barriers to successful parental involvement: logistical and attitudinal. Logistical barriers include time, money, and childcare concerns. Attitudinal barriers include uncertainty about roles, anxiety about how others perceive them, disagreements regarding educational policies, dissatisfaction with their own home involvement, and communication problems. The actual impact of these barriers can vary depending on the type of involvement that the parents might think of undertaking or might be asked or expected to undertake.

Ascher (1987) defined parental participation as a range of activities promoting the value of education in the home to the actual role of team decision maker in policy, curriculum, and instructional issues. According to Ascher, parents can participate at various levels, including taking advocacy roles like sitting on councils and committees, participating in the decisions, and operation of schools. Parents can serve as classroom aides, can accompany a class on a field trip, or assist teachers in a variety of other ways. Parent participation may also include parents initiating learning activities at home to improve their children's performance in school, for example, reading to them, helping them with homework, playing educational games, or discussing current events.

Involving parents in their children's education and in educational decision making is a relatively new activity in U.S. public schools. During early efforts to involve parents in education, schools saw parents as agents of service for the school rather than as equal partners in the educational endeavor (Bermudez, 1994). Schools determined the areas for assistance and how parents would assist.

Today, much more value is placed on parents' participation in their children's education and research supports involvement as a means to improved academic outcomes. One of the most promising ways to increase achievement is to involve their families (Henderson & Berla, 1994). At the elementary school level, a range of studies demonstrates an association between parent involvement and improved child outcomes. In particular, more parent involvement has been found to be associated with fewer behavioral problems (Comer, 1984), lower dropout rates (National Center for Education Statistics, 1992), higher student achievement (Klimes-Dougan, Lopez, Nelson, & Adelman, 1992; Kohl, 1994; Muller, 1993; Reynolds, 1992; Stevenson & Baker, 1987), and increases in children's perceived level of competence (Wagner & Phillips, 1992).

The combination of these pre-existing beliefs in the value of parent participation and research demonstrating an association between such participation and a variety of positive child outcomes has led policy makers and educators to assume that parent involvement programs will have the same salutary effects on student outcomes. This is based on the observation of the higher achievement levels of students whose parents, independent of any program, involve themselves in their children's education. As a result, increasing parent–school participation has become part of the Federal government's Goals 2000, and parent involvement programs devoted to improving children's outcomes may be found in schools of every type throughout the country. (For an overview of Goals 2000, visit the U.S. Department of Education's website: http://www.ed.gov/pubs/hispanicindicators/.)

What Do We Know about Hispanic Parent Participation in the Schooling of Their Children?

The importance of increasing the level of educational attainment for Hispanic Americans through parental involvement attracted national attention when, in September 1994, President Clinton established the White House Initiative on Educational Excellence for Hispanic Americans. As part of the White House Initiative activities, a national conference series started in San Antonio in October of 1998. This series included "Excelencia en Educación: The Role of Parents in the Education of Their Children" and focused on improving the education of Hispanic youth by better engaging Hispanic parents (White House Initiative on Educational Excellence for Hispanic Americans, n.d.).

Such involvement was strongly underscored by the following two overarching findings and recommendations contained in the Hispanic Dropout Project monograph (Lockwood & Secada, 1999).

1. Schools and school staff must connect themselves—both institutionally and personally—to Hispanic students and their families. They should provide Hispanic students with a high-quality education based on rigorous standards, and provide backup options to push both students and staff past obstacles that come up on the way to achieving those rigorous standards.

2. Students and their families deserve respect. In many cases, this means that school staff and other educational stakeholders must change long-held conceptions of Hispanic students and their families. These stakeholders need to see Hispanic students as central to the future well being of the United States rather than as foreign and unwelcome. They also need to recognize that Hispanic families have social capital on which to build. Hispanic students deserve genuine opportunities to learn and to succeed in later life—rather than being dismissed as deficient because of their language and culture.

In spite of the importance given Hispanic parent involvement in the schooling of their children, there continues to be little substantive information regarding the dynamics associated with such participation. More specifically, there is very limited research examining the factors that increase or enhance their participation (Casas & Furlong, 1994). Without objective information about Hispanic parent participation, conditions are ripe for the proliferation of stereotypic and subjective attitudes and opinions about their willingness to participate.

To many, Hispanic parents' lack of involvement in their children's education is frequently seen as reflecting a lack of interest or an indifference to their children's education. Other stereotypic reasons used to explain the low level of Hispanic parental involvement include, but are not limited to: "moving too frequently, not speaking or wanting to learn how to speak (read, or write) English, and being too undereducated to properly educate their children. Parents and families also are often portrayed as victims unable to do anything about the racism they experience and unable to understand American cultural norms. Parents are said to be ignorant, poor, products of bad schools, in conflict with their children, and in general, culturally deprived" (Lockwood & Secada, 1999, p. 7).

Based on the extensive work conducted by the Hispanic Dropout Project (HDP) (Lockwood & Secada, 1999), such stereotypes have been challenged with evidence that shows that small segments of Hispanic parents do value learning and do all that they can to support their children in school. In the research conducted by the HDP it was found that Hispanic parents are involved in a variety of ways in the schooling of their children—for example, tutoring, volunteering as instructional assistants, fundraising, and helping to implement educational programs.

Before the HDP, Montecel et al. (1993) presented evidence that Mexican American parents do care about their children's education. The reasons identified for limited involvement included beliefs that the roles of home and school are sharply delineated. Mexican American parents see their role as being responsible for providing basic needs as well as instilling respect and proper behavior. They see the school's role as instilling knowledge (Nicolau & Ramos, 1990). They believe that one should not interfere with the job of the other. Nicolau and Ramos compare Mexican Americans' respect for teachers with the awe that most Americans have (or used to have) for doctors or priests. Hispanic parents may view educators with high regard and defer to their experience/professional development in questions regarding their own children's best interests.

Casas, Furlong, Carranza, Solberg, and Jamaica (1986) conducted a comprehensive study to better understand the educational values of Hispanic parents. Their findings challenge the stereotypical beliefs that Hispanic parents do not value education or that they prefer to have their children enter the workforce before high school graduation. To the contrary, Hispanic parents expressed a high value in education, wanted increased levels of participation in their child's schooling process, and expressed a willingness to become involved. However, the parents in their sample did not participate in school activities at a high rate. The low levels of participation appear to be related to a misunderstanding of the school operational structure as well as a lack of knowledge regarding the availability of resources that they can access in order to increase the educational successes of their children (Casas & Furlong, 1994).

More recently, Navarette (1996) reports that while parents understand the importance of homework, they may not realize the academic importance of everyday activities like children talking to adult members of the family, reading and writing for fun, playing board games, or participating in sports. Azmitia et al. (1994) found that although parents held high aspirations for their children, parents had varying amounts of information about how to help them attain these aspirations. While some parents were aware that school grades were important, none of the parents who hoped their children would become doctors, lawyers, and teachers were aware that these professions require a graduate education.

A rather troubling reason put forth by Hispanic parents regarding their limited involvement in the schooling of their children is their perceptions of teachers and experiences with resistance and hostility on the part of schools relative to such involvement. To this point, the HDP monograph provides two very poignant vignettes.

> At almost every city visited by Project managers, Hispanic parents said that their children's schools did not take them or their concerns very seriously. One mother recounted being told of her child's suspension hearing just 30 minutes before it was held. Risking her job, she rushed to the school, only to wait all morning in the school office and to be told abruptly that the meeting had been postponed. One father did, in fact, lose his job because of the time he spent trying to keep his daughter from, in his words, being pushed out. Another mother reported—in flawless English—how her child's principal would not speak directly to her, supposedly because her accent made it too difficult for school personnel to understand. (p. 7)

Finally, from an applied and comprehensive perspective, studies show that Hispanic parents are more active when they feel "empowered" by the school. More specifically, when Hispanic parents are empowered with the knowledge of how to work cooperatively with school personnel to resolve issues pertaining to their children, they become more active in school (Delgado-Gaitan, 1994). In a similar vein, the HDP (Lockwood & Secada, 1999) found that when Hispanic parents are able to see their children benefiting because of their involvement and the meaningful roles and responsibilities they are given, they are more than willing to do their part. To this point, Rumberger and Larson (1995) conducted a longitudinal study of a successful dropout prevention program and found that Hispanic parents cooperated much more readily with the program's recommendations than did the schools and the teachers.

What Is Currently Being Done to Involve Hispanic Parents in the Schooling Process?

A variety of innovative programs has made an effort to enhance the quality of Hispanic parent participation. This section describes a few programs that are representative of different approaches to addressing this need.

Using Fotonovelas to Improve Hispanic Parent Participation

Modeling has been found to be an effective way to encourage behavior change among Hispanic adults. Sabido (cited in Bandura, 1986), for example, used modeling in Mexico to motivate adults to become involved in a national literacy drive. A popular soap opera was used as the medium. In one episode, the actors were shown becoming involved in literacy-promoting activities. During the year before the airing of the episode, 99,000 individuals were involved in the campaign. During the year immediately after the episode, this number rose to 840,000 and remained at 400,000 two years later. This suggests that models combined with a story format may be an effective way to teach and encourage parents to become more involved in children's education.

Although filmed role models may be powerful, the resources needed to create such material are too prohibitive for schools. However, in Hispanic cultures there is a related communication medium, fotonovelas, which offer a more cost-effective alternative. Fotonovelas are pictured novelettes that can be used to show Hispanic parent models engaging in the behaviors and skills needed to deal effectively with school-related issues (Fig. 6.1). These fotonovelas can be an effective means of disseminating information within the Hispanic community by instructing parents about new ways of thinking, feeling, and acting about school-related issues. They can also motivate parents into action by demonstrating the positive and negative consequences of engaging in a given behavior.

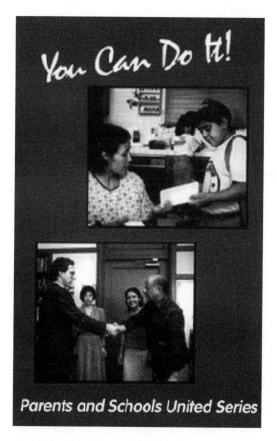

FIGURE 6.1   Fotonovela designed to encourage purposeful parent participation in their child's education.

The fotonovela format has been used as a culturally appropriate medium to transmit a variety of information related to AIDS (Delouya, 1989; Matiella, 1989; Muñoz & Green, 1989; Novela Health Foundation, 1988a, 1988b), drug abuse and prevention (Mattos, 1984), sex education (Chiapella & Matiella, 1989a, 1989b; Gonzalez, 1984), and genetic counseling (Novela Health Foundation, 1990). Drawing on the use of the fotonovela in the health education field, Casas, Furlong, Martinez, McClintock, and Benoit (1991) developed a fotonovela designed to present information to Hispanic parents to help them learn to participate more assertively in their child's education. The use of a familiar and culturally appropriate communication medium also enhances the impact of the behaviors modeled by the actors in the fotonovela (Casas & Furlong, 1994).

Parent Institute for Quality Education

California's Parent Institute for Quality Education (PIQE), a nonprofit organization, is implementing programs to help Hispanic parents develop the skills necessary to play an active part in their child's learning. In 1987, PIQE was formed in San Diego County to assist low-income parents and limited-English-speaking families to assume the role of teachers of their children, connecting parents with their community schools, increasing home–school communication, and establishing an effective home/school-support team. PIQE works directly with participating families through intermediary organizations, usually public schools at the K–9 grade levels. PIQE stresses an active relationship with schools and community organizations to create a full partnership between parents and schools on behalf of their children. The work of PIQE is inclusive and consciously seeks to integrate the schools, administrators, instructors, and family members into a communication and coordination network responsive to issues of change and empowerment.

The program is an eight-week course for parents and is conducted at individual school sites. Currently, there are over 140,000 graduates of the program in California, with 10 offices serving 16 counties. The course covers such topics as positive communication, self-esteem, obstacles that get in the way of school success (including learning disabilities), how the school system works, high school curriculum, and college and career planning. A recent grant provided by the California Endowment, the state's largest health foundation, will allow PIQE to incorporate a health module into its eight-week program. The health module will focus on educating parents on ways they can access low- and no-cost health care services, address common health problems and proper nutrition, as well as teach parents the importance of preventative care.

MALDEF Parent Leadership Program

The Mexican-American Legal Defense and Educational Fund (MALDEF) is a national nonprofit organization that protects and promotes the civil rights of Hispanics in the United States. Launched in Los Angeles in 1989, MALDEF's Parent Leadership Program is designed to improve the academic achievement of Hispanic students through greater parental involvement in schools. The Parent Leadership Program heightens awareness of how to effect positive change in their children's schools while addressing local, state, and national issues of critical importance to Hispanic children. Schools are selected according to the following criteria: high percentage of low-income students, low-test scores, and a need for increased parent involvement. Participants must be willing to serve on local educational committees, parent councils, and boards and become part of a network of MALDEF program graduates. In 1998, MALDEF's second site in San Antonio, Texas, completed its five-year program cycle, graduating 432 parent leaders. The Los Angeles Parent Leadership Program, now in its eleventh year, has so far graduated over 900 participants. In addition, in 1999, MALDEF launched two new locales of the program in Houston, Texas, and Albuquerque, New Mexico.

The Parent Leadership Program consists of two phases. Phase I is a beginning course that meets for two hours each week for ten weeks. Parents, usually 20 to 30 in a class, learn about the importance of their participation in their children's education, parental rights in schools, the administrative structure of schools, how to effectively problem solve in school bureaucracies, how schools are financed, holding elected school officials accountable, and guiding a child toward college. Many of these classes feature guest speakers, such as the school principal. In the six weeks of Phase II, parents develop advanced leadership skills, including learning to access community resources for school and neighborhood projects, organize a meeting, make public presentations, use the media, and increase parent involvement at their school.

ASPIRA Parents for Educational Excellence (APEX) Program

The ASPIRA Association, Inc. is the only national nonprofit organization devoted solely to the education and leadership development of Puerto Rican and other Hispanic youth. ASPIRA takes its name from the Spanish verb *aspirar*, meaning "to aspire." In 1994, through an initial three-year grant from the DeWitt Wallace–Reader's Digest Fund, the ASPIRA Parents for Educational Excellence Program (APEX) reached out to Hispanic parents who desire to become involved in their children's education, but may not have a clear approach or a starting point from which to begin such a venture. The program began at ASPIRA offices in Chicago and Philadelphia. With a second-level grant, APEX eventually expanded to Miami, New York, Puerto Rico, New Jersey, and Connecticut.

The APEX program consists of two basic components—the APEX workshop series and one-on-one technical assistance. The 10-session workshop series addresses such topics as self-esteem in parents and children, school structure, helping children improve their study habits, communication skills for the home, parents' rights in the schools, group dynamics, and leadership skills. Easy-to-read manuals exist in both Spanish and English. With the increased awareness of educational issues and support, parents have a base from which to begin advocating their children and community's education. Because one of the main goals of the APEX program is to enhance parent leadership in the Hispanic community, the program design allows parents who have graduated from the APEX program to be trained further to conduct the APEX workshop series themselves. In this way, APEX reaches its goal of training parents to pass on their knowledge to other parents.

Parent Empowerment Program-Students Included/Padres en Poder-Sí (PEP-Sí)

PEP-Sí was a demonstration program with a strong research component developed collaboratively by the University of California, Santa Barbara (UCSB), and the Santa Barbara School Districts to facilitate the transition of Hispanic at-risk students from elementary to junior high school (Casas, Furlong, & Solberg, 1988). This is a particularly crucial time to intervene in the lives of adolescents who have greater-than-average odds of dropping out of school before receiving a diploma.

PEP-Sí addressed the needs of at-risk students by working directly with the students and by systematically reaching out to encourage the participation of parents in the educational process. The program was based on the belief that meaningful change in the educational careers of at-risk students is more likely to occur when a comprehensive intervention and prevention model is used.

The comprehensive components for the PEP-Sí program included four areas of program and service delivery that were coordinated through the site school counselor.

Student Development Component.   This component involved providing direct support services to 15 students. The services provided included: (1) orientation to junior high school prior to the start of the 1987–88 school year; (2) weekly individual and group sessions to encourage the development of academic self-confidence, positive classroom behavior, study habits, and self-esteem; and (3) regular consultation with school staff to integrate PEP-Sí activities with regular school activities.

Parent Outreach Component.   Parents of 11 students participated in this part of the PEP-Sí program. In this component, four home visits were made during the school year. Information concerning grades, graduation requirements, strategies for helping with homework, and sources of information at school were discussed. Parents were also given a special orientation at the back-to-school night in October and were invited to participate in a parent-training program held at the targeted junior high school.

Tutorial Component.   The students in the program received one-to-one tutoring from a UCSB student during the spring semester. Eight UCSB students volunteered to do the tutoring. The majority of these students was of Hispanic background and was able to provide positive role models for the students. This was particularly noticeable when the program took the PEP-Sí students to UCSB for a field trip.

Community Component.   Working from a community-oriented perspective, support for the PEP-Sí students and their parents was sought from local businesses and agencies. Generous and varied support was received from these businesses: Von Markets, Safeway Stores, Longs Drugs, McDonald's, Burger King, Center for

Community Education and Citizen Participation, La Casa de la Raza, Radio KHTY, and the *Santa Barbara News Press.*

The outcome of this program was very positive. Of the students who participated, 85 percent earned credit in all of their academic courses; 85 percent also indicated that graduating from high school was "very important" to them. All the parents involved in the program expressed a desire to have the program continue as well as a willingness to help their children succeed in school. According to Casas et al. (1988), the parents were most willing to participate if they saw a direct relationship to helping their child. Finally, given the success of this demonstration program, it should be noted that many of its components were subsequently incorporated in the ongoing services provided at the targeted junior high school to at-risk students.

What Can School Counselors Do to Facilitate Hispanic Parent Participation in Schools?

"The challenge of the '90s is to make sure that all parents are respected, all cultures are valued, all parents and citizens set the agenda for the education of our youth" (Bamber, 1990, p. 1). This sentiment could not be stated more clearly and remains true today. This is the challenge for all educators, and school counselors can take the lead in promoting this agenda. Before we discuss what can be done to facilitate the involvement of Hispanic parents and citizens in the schooling process, a philosophical foundation about parental involvement in communities with diversity needs to be established. We have reviewed research showing that Hispanic parents value education and want their children to succeed. Other research has clearly shown that everyone benefits from high rates of parental involvement in school. Yet, we strongly believe that even if the research was not as favorable, the goal of parental involvement is still desirable. In a democratic society, public schools belong to the parents and citizens of the community. From this perspective, we, as educators, are actually public servants who are being entrusted to use our expertise to help create the best school system possible—every child has a right to attend an effective school. However, we cannot lose sight of the fact that the schools are not ours—they belong to the community. We use our knowledge and skills as a resource to help the community build effective schools. Herein lies the critical need for parental involvement: parents must be involved because the schools belong to them.

We also need to be aware of pressures to view parental involvement from a manipulative perspective. In some instances, programs to increase parental participation in school activities are developed because they will make the educational task easier from the educator's perspective. Ideally, programs to increase parental participation have the ultimate objective of setting positive conditions that facilitate parental involvement and eliminate barriers to their continuing involvement. Only if this vision supports a parent participation program will it realize long-term gains in parental ownership of the schooling process.

As demonstrated by the research at the National Committee for Citizens in Education, there does not appear to be a "magic bullet" to increase the participation of Hispanic parents in the schooling process. The key clearly seems to be to do what-ever is necessary to get the parents involved. Although specific programs certainly provide inspiration and possible direction, it is increasingly clear that if Hispanic par-ents are to become more fully involved in the schooling process, schools will need to systematically re-evaluate their commitment to parent participation. We feel strongly that school counselors can take a strong advocacy position for parents by taking steps to ensure that the school community engages in an ongoing parent participation plan-ning process to improve school climate (Kaplan & Geoffroy, 1990). Such a planning process can have eight stages or steps, a discussion of which follows.

Creating a Vision of Hispanic Parental Participation

We feel strongly that school counselors can take a strong advocacy position for parents by taking steps to ensure that the school engages in a parent participation, planning, and implementation process that is comprehensive, ongoing, dynamic, self-correcting, and culturally sensitive and responsive. Such a process could consist of specific steps such as the eight that follow.

Step 1: Identify and Recruit All Key School and Community Personnel.   What we particularly want to point out to school counselors is that programs to increase parent participation much too often begin by conducting a needs assessment or by immediately jumping into the identification of priorities and development of an ac-tion plan. We believe that jumping into such action can be counterproductive to the success of any parental participation programs that aspire to be comprehensive and ongoing in nature and in particular, those earmarked for Hispanic communities.

Prior to taking any programmatic action, it is vitally important that all key school and community personnel be identified. Identifying the school personnel may be an easy task; however, the fact is that in many Hispanic neighborhoods there has traditionally been very little ongoing contact between the school and the community, making the identification of the key personnel in the Hispanic community much more of a challenge. Consequently, the individual given the task of identifying the key com-munity personnel must have and/or quickly acquire a good working knowledge of those individuals in the community who are indispensable to the success of imple-menting a parent participation program.

Even in those communities in which there is some ongoing contact with a group of Hispanic parents, it is vitally important when seeking to expand parental participa-tion to examine the representativeness of this group of parents vis-à-vis the total com-munity. If the group is solely representative of one segment of the community (e.g., more educated, more affluent), which is likely to be the case, then efforts must be ex-pended to reach as many of the other segments as possible. Success in reaching these segments will necessitate not only knowledge of the community and its key players but also knowledge of those recruitment and marketing methods that are most culturally appropriate and effective in reaching the less visible, less vocal, and more traditional segments of the targeted Hispanic community.

For instance, mailing out invitations to parents to attend a meeting or providing information relative to the important role that they can play in the schooling of their children may be effective in more middle-class, higher SES communities; however, the same may not be the case for more traditional, low-income communities. For these communities a personal contact via telephone and/or home may be more appropriate. Delivering the invitation through persons who are highly respected in the community (e.g., principals, ministers, priests, or medical doctors) or providing the information in conjunction with an important cultural or social community event may be more effective. Suffice it to say, the broader the base of parent participation and the stronger the spirit of community involvement, the greater likelihood of success in attaining parent participation goals.

Step 2: Assess and Develop the Climate for Parent Participation. Once all target key school and community personnel have been identified, then steps should be immediately taken to develop a climate that is conducive to the type of parent participation that all key players (i.e., parents, teachers, and administrators) would like to achieve. Developing such a climate will require that such personnel take the necessary steps to establish open communication and a trust level that is conducive to both team and consensus building. To this end, school counselors can utilize their group and communication skills to help the school and parent community through critical stages that focus on mutual understanding and team/consensus building (steps 2 and 3 in the planning process that we are describing) and that are so often overlooked.

More specifically, they can facilitate the discussion between school personnel and parents regarding why parent participation is important, what their fears are in engaging in the planning process, and what their hopes are with respect to parent participation. Given their skills in the area of assessing personal and group needs, they can play a vital part in assessing the existing climate for parent participation. Parent involvement has been perceived as falling on a continuum from passive (e.g., parent home newsletter) to active roles (parent as partner in decision making). In order to attain successful outcomes for desired parental involvement programs, it is essential that the key players, especially teachers and administrators, identify where they fall on the type of involvement they desire to promote. To this end, there is a need to ask and get answers to very basic questions such as Is the desire for an increase in or change in the nature of parental participation naturally occurring or is it being spearheaded by a few? Is the staff open to increasing and expanding the options for parents to participate in their children's schooling? And if so, what exactly are these options?

If the options include participation in the governance and decision-making process, questions such as those proposed by Kershner and Connolly (1991) need to be asked: What power should parents have relative to school policies and practices? How should these powers be exercised? What should be the parents' role in the education of their own children? How much choice should parents have about what kinds of schools their children will attend?

The importance of getting direct answers to these questions cannot be overemphasized. The answers should help provide an accurate measure of the existing climate and receptivity with respect to parent involvement. To assume that such involvement, especially as it relates to governance and decision making, is desired by all key players is to set one's self up for failure. For example, various kinds of parent involvement were evaluated by elementary teachers in a six-state regional survey (Williams & Stallworth, 1983). The outcome of this survey showed that, in general, teachers were not enthusiastic about parent participation in curriculum development, instruction, or school governance. However, they did support other forms of parent involvement, such as assisting with homework or tutoring children—ones that make their job as an instructor more effective.

A comparison survey of elementary school principals in the same six states obtained similar results (Williams & Stallworth, 1983). Supporting these findings, in an NEA poll (1981) over 90 percent of teachers in all parts of the country and at all grade levels stated that more home–school interaction would be desirable (i.e., parents working at home to help their children become better learners). Even in states that have mandated citizen participation (e.g., California, Florida, and South Carolina), there is evidence showing that the attitude of principals to the shared governance role has tended to be at best indifferent and at worst negative (Foster, 1984).

Needless to say, assessing and/or developing the desired climate for parent participation needs to occur within a positive climate that is open and safe and that encourages critical review. Establishing and nurturing such a climate in many Hispanic communities can be quite a challenge. This should not come as a surprise. A high level of distrust may exist in such communities as a result of the past failures of the educational system relative to meeting the educational needs of Hispanic students. Diminished trust may also arise out of past negative interactions with school personnel who may have been less than hospitable to "the new Hispanic" kids on the block, and/or negative experiences with any agencies or services tied to the "establishment." Should this be the case, before taking any action, the counselor should be prepared to address this distrust that is reflected in such questions that parents might ask, such as Why are they really doing this? What do they really want? What's it going to cost us? Will I have to take time off work to help the schools teach my kids? How is my attendance at meetings going to help my son to learn? I've gone to parent meetings before where we told them what our kids need and nothing happened—will this be any different?

Step 3: Dispel Existing Beliefs that Work Against Parent Involvement.   Once the climate has been assessed and the parameters for the type of parental involvement desired articulated, then it is necessary to identify barriers to parent participation. School counselors will want to pay close attention to attitudinal barriers that might exist among teachers, administrators, and even the parents that impede attaining desired objectives. With teachers and administrators it may be necessary to challenge any preconceived notions regarding what Hispanic parents are interested in and capable of doing. As previously stated, there is a prevailing belief that Hispanic parents "just don't care." Research provides empirical evidence to the contrary.

Relative to what parents are capable of doing—and in particular those with lower levels of education—the prevailing belief is that their level of skills limit their involvement in their children's education to passive and peripheral roles. For instance, with respect to ability, a significant number of teachers report that the general ideal of parent involvement is a good one; however, many have serious doubts about the success of practical efforts to involve parents in learning activities (Becker & Epstein, 1982). Teachers report concern regarding whether or not parents have sufficient skills to teach their children to read or to solve problems and whether parents want to know more about the school curriculum than they are usually told (Becker & Epstein, 1982). According to Becker and Epstein, the belief that poorly educated parents cannot help seems more a consequence of not having used the diversity of options that are available to involve parents. This should not be surprising given the fact that few teacher-training programs focus on how to involve parents in the education of their children.

Given such findings, it would appear that counselors are in key positions to organize and provide culturally sensitive training programs that would help school personnel get beyond the commonly held stereotypes of parents—"pushy" upper middle-class parents, "helpful" middle-class parents, and "incapable" lower-class parents. Such programs could give specific attention to the prevailing stereotypes that work against and even impede attaining substantive Hispanic parent involvement.

Focusing on the Hispanic parents themselves, given their level of education and frequently less-than-positive past experiences with the educational system, their self-perceptions may be that they lack the necessary knowledge and skills to become active partners in their children's schooling. Given available information, such an all-encompassing perception is simply not true. Although some Hispanic parents may not be ready to assume certain skill-based forms of involvement (e.g., helping their child master algebraic concepts), all Hispanic parents are capable of getting involved in one form or another in their children's education. The task of the counselor could be to help the school community identify the level at which parents feel most comfortable and to provide them with various participation options. Invite parents to take the initial steps to get involved at this level. Take steps to ensure that such involvement is rewarding to both the parents and the children and develop a plan of action to help the parents develop those skills and knowledge that might help them to assume more active involvement roles in the future. Overall, the school counselor should provide the kinds of experiences that empower the parents to assume such roles—experiences that engender a "can-do" attitude.

Step 4: Address Parental Participation within Existing School Improvement Efforts. A primary issue here is not to reinvent the wheel. Undoubtedly, there are a number of parents already involved in various capacities in the school. Counselors should try to build on these resources while reaching out to parents who are underrepresented. As noted with respect to nonparticipating Hispanic parents, it is recommended that they be invited to join all kinds of ongoing efforts, but in particular those in which they feel more comfortable.

It is important to solicit broad parental participation and to integrate such participation with other school planning efforts. If this is not done, then the staff and other parents may perceive efforts to create a plan to increase parent participation as "Just another thing to do." At this stage of the planning process, it is critical that efforts be made to encourage collaborative planning. This will function as a model of how parents can become more involved in school-level decision making.

Step 5: Collect and Analyze Data (a.k.a., Information). This is often where traditional change efforts in schools take off. With the added information gathered by the team-building process, however, the collection of data for a needs assessment can be more focused on the particular needs of the school. The overall goals should be to assess existing levels and types of parent involvement among the diverse segments of the school population. Because it is likely that some positive things are happening on campus with respect to parent participation, a needs assessment should also identify areas of pride and strength in addition to specifying areas for improvement or change. Henderson, Marburger, and Ooms (1986); McGrail, Wilson, Buttram, and Rossman (1987); and Furlong, Morrison, Bates, and Chung (1998) provide assessment tools for this stage of the planning process.

Step 6: Develop a Plan—Set Priorities. Once the school community has a clear understanding about the areas that need change or improvement, it is important to list the high-priority concerns and needs, explore possible barriers to parental participation, and identify the resources needed and those available to respond to these needs. Only after these issues are discussed should a specific action plan be developed, which includes strategies for implementation, evaluation criteria, and reasonable time lines.

Step 7: Select and Implement Activities to Increase Parent Participation. Here, we finally go to the part of the planning process that involves the specific program that will be used to increase parent participation. Once again, we believe the literature is quite clear in showing that it is not prudent to observe a successful program in one school/community context and then develop plans to "replicate" that program in another school/community context. Model programs certainly do provide inspiration, motivation to take action, and food for creative thought. What they do not offer is a "manualized" way to increase parent participation at your school. For the sake of effectiveness, each community must develop its own unique plan of action. The specific strategies and actions for facilitating parental participation should include proposed time lines and completion dates; clearly assigned responsibilities among staff, parents, and community; and a process to monitor progress.

Step 8: Evaluate the Plan to Increase Parent Participation. Systematic efforts to increase and maintain high levels of parent participation never really end. The model described herein is really an ongoing process that continually seeks to make the school more responsive to the needs of the community. At this stage of the planning cycle, it is critical to determine if parental participation has actually increased in quantity and quality. Staff and parents can be surveyed about their attitudes and perceptions of the school in general and parent participation in particular. Parents and staff should discuss the successes and difficulties of the program and explore ways that it can be strengthened or revised. And, as you might have surmised, with this information, return to step 4.

Those joining in the planning process should be encouraged to think broadly about how best to involve parents in a way that respects the hopes and wishes of the school community. There are different types of ways that parents can participate in schools, including the following: audience, child advocate, school helper, learner, partner in school governance, expert consultants, and co-teachers.

Conclusion

The impact of the educational problems that plague Hispanics can have on the social and economic well-being of this nation is forcing educators and policy makers to urgently seek solutions to these problems. In this chapter, we briefly identified some of these efforts, and have given specific and detailed attention to those efforts that are presently receiving a great deal of attention and that emphasize the importance of local input and control of educational decision making. Many recognize that the success of these efforts will ultimately depend on the participation of parents in all aspects of their children's education. As emphasized in this chapter, it is our belief that school counselors have the kinds of skills that place them in a unique position to work closely with teachers, administrators, and communities to facilitate and maximize parental participation in all aspects of their children's education.

Working from this perspective, a major thrust of this chapter was to arm counselors with basic knowledge regarding the impact that parents can have on their children's learning and on the schooling process in general. To correct some stereotypic misconceptions regarding the willingness and/or capability of Hispanic parents to be involved in the education of their children, we provided recent research findings showing that Hispanic parents value education, want increased levels of participation in their children's schooling process, and express a willingness to become involved at school.

From a more pragmatic perspective, we have provided examples of programs that are successfully working with Hispanic parents. Along this line, we presented guidelines that provide directions on how school counselors can help initiate a systematic planning procedure to truly integrate Hispanic parents into the total schooling process. Finally, reflecting the research on parent participation, we strongly admonished throughout the chapter that there is no *specific* correct program to reach this end. Rather, we strongly advocate the development of programs that are comprehensive, ongoing, dynamic, self-correcting, and culturally sensitive and responsive to the needs of Hispanic parents.

Endnote

Before addressing the focus of the chapter, the following prefatory comments are necessary. While the generic term *Hispanic* is used throughout the chapter, this is done solely for the sake of brevity, and should in no way be interpreted as implying that the Hispanic population is a homogeneous entity. On the contrary, the Hispanic population is a very heterogeneous entity, comprised of differing racial, ethnic, and national groups.

In addition to the diversity that is reflective of these racial, ethnic, and national groups, the Hispanic population also varies across numerous mutually nonexclusive and frequently interacting variables, including the following: demographic (e.g., mean and median age, family size and composition, geographic distribution); sociohistorical (e.g., length of time in the United States, impetus for immigration to the United States, experiences with racism); sociopolitical (e.g., immigrant/citizen status, level of political participation); socioeconomic (e.g., educational attainment, labor force participation, individuals and family income); and sociopsychological (e.g., acculturation level, actual and perceived power, and self-entitlement; intragroup similarity and cohesion).

Finally, it should be noted that although most of the recommendations contained in this chapter may have applicability for a significant number of Hispanics, they are particularly applicable for those Hispanic subgroups that have lower levels of educational attainment and higher levels of educational dropouts (e.g., Mexican Americans and Puerto Ricans), are found at the lower level of the socioeconomic stratum, and are less acculturated into the mainstream U.S. culture. Furthermore, recent research findings underscore the fact that at-risk Mexican American and Puerto Rican students and their parents share many similar characteristics (see Casas et al., 1986; Rosado, 1991).

DISCUSSION QUESTIONS

1. What are ways to facilitate parent involvement in your school? For example: are programs and materials bilingual? Is babysitting provided, are there fees, and are times and locations of meetings convenient for parents? Is transportation available? Are interpreters available?

2. What are some effective ways to solicit parent involvement? Consider impersonal efforts—letters, flyers, announcements, etc.—versus face-to-face conversations with parents in their primary language in their homes. How can you add that necessary *personal touch*?

3. What climate and environment can you create for first-time parent volunteers? Is it possible to hold the first meeting at a site familiar to the parents? What impacts can a social atmosphere have over a more formal event?

4. How can teachers and counselors communicate with parents in nonjudgmental ways? How can parents be supported for their strengths, not judged for perceived failings?

5. How can the school counselor incorporate the involvement of teachers, staff, and administration alike? Are policies flexible and accommodating? Is the school administration and staff totally committed to accomplish a successful program?

6. Is staff development at your school focused on Hispanic culture? Do teachers understand how key features of Hispanic culture impact their students' behavior and learning styles?

7. What methods of community outreach are available in your area, for example: family literacy programs, vocational training, ESL programs, improved medical and dental services, and other community-based social services. How can the school serve as a resource and referral agency to support the overall strength of the families involved?

8. How can teachers and counselors take into account Hispanic values and expectations? How can teachers and counselors demonstrate an understanding of both the importance of *respecto* and the individual's dignity?

REFERENCES

Ascher, C. (1987). *Improving the school–home connection for poor and minority urban students.* New York: ERIC Clearinghouse on Urban Education Institute for Urban and Minority Education, Teachers College, Columbia University.

Azmitia, M., Cooper, C. R., Garcia, E., Ittel, A., Johanson, B., Lopez, E., Martinez-Chavez, R., & Rivera, L. (1994). *Links between home and school among low-income Mexican-American and European-American families.* Santa Cruz, CA: The National Center for Research on Cultural Diversity and Second Language Learning.

Bandura, A. (1986). *Social foundations of thought and action: A social cognitive theory.* Englewood Cliffs, NJ: Prentice-Hall.

Becker, H. J. & Epstein, J. L. (1982). Parent involvement: A survey of teacher practices. *Elementary School Journal, 83,* 85–102.

Bermudez, A. (1994). *Doing our homework: How schools can engage Hispanic communities.* Reston, VA: ERIC Clearinghouse on Rural and Small Schools.

California Basic Educational Data System. (1999). *Numbers of 12th grade graduates in California public schools completing all courses required for U.C. and/or C.S.U. entrance by gender and by ethnic group for the year 1998–1999,* [Online]. California Department of Education. Available: http://data1.cde.ca.gov/dataquest/.

California Basic Educational Data System. (2000). *Statewide enrollment in California public schools by ethnic group for the year 1999–00,* [Online]. California Department of Education. Available: http://data1.cde.ca.gov/dataquest/.

Carter, T. & Segura, R. (1979). *Mexican-Americans in school: A decade of change.* New York: College Entrance Examination Board.

Casas, J. M. & Furlong, M. J. (1986). In search of an understanding and responsible resolution to the Mexican-American educational dropout problem. *California Public School Forum, 1,* 45–63.

Casas, J. M. & Furlong, M. J. (1994). School counselors as advocates for increased Hispanic parent participation in schools. In P. Pederson & J. C. Carey (Eds.), *Multicultural counseling in schools: A practical handbook* (pp. 121–155). Boston, MA: Allyn & Bacon.

Casas, J. M., Furlong, M. J., Carranza, O., Solberg, S., & Jamaica, P. (1986). *Santa Barbara student success study: Profiling successful and at risk junior high school students.* Final report submitted to the Santa Barbara School District Board of Education, Department of Education, University of California, Santa Barbara.

Casas, J. M., Furlong, M. J., Martinez, M. I., McClintock, E., & Benoit, C. (1991). *You can do it! (¡Sí se puede!).* Santa Barbara, CA: University of California, Department of Education.

Casas, J. M., Furlong, M. J., & Solberg, V. (1988). Parent Empowerment Program (PEP-Sí). Unpublished manuscript, University of California, Santa Barbara.

Chiapella, J. & Matiella, A. C. (1989a). *La quinceañera.*

Santa Cruz, CA: Networks Publications, ETR Associates.

Chiapella, J. & Matiella, A. C. (1989b). *Papi, ¿què es el sexo?* Santa Cruz, CA: Networks Publications, ETR Associates.

Comer, J. (1984). Home–school relationships as they affect the academic success of children. *Urban Society, 16*, 323–337.

Delgado-Gaitan, C. (1994). *Empowerment in Carpinteria: A five-year study of family, school, and community relationships* (CDS Report No. 49). Baltimore, MD: Johns Hopkins University Center for Research on Effective Schooling for Disadvantaged Students.

Delouya, N. (1989). *Tres hombres.* Seattle, WA: Novela Health Foundation.

Ford Foundation. (1984). *Hispanics: Challenges and opportunities.* New York: Author.

Furlong, M., Morrison R., Bates M., & Chung, A. (1998) School violence victimization among secondary students in California: Grade, gender, and racial-ethnic group incidence patterns. *California School Psychologist, 3*, 71–87.

Gonzalez, M. (1984). *The danger of love (El peligro del amor).* Santa Barbara, CA: Santa Barbara County Health Services, Health Promotion and Education Division.

Henderson, A. T. & Berla, N. (1994). *A new generation of evidence: The family is critical to student achievement.* Washington, DC: National Committee for Citizens in Education.

Henderson, A. T., Marburger, C. L., & Ooms, T. (1986). Beyond the bake sale: An educator's guide to working with parents. Columbia, MD: National Committee for Citizens in Education.

Kaplan, L. S. & Geoffroy, K. E. (1990). Enhancing the school climate: New opportunities for the counselor. *School Counselor, 38*, 7–12.

Kaufman, P., Kwon, J. Y., Klein, S., & Chapman, C. D. (2000). *Dropout rates in the United States: 1998* (Statistical Analysis Report No. 2000022). Washington, DC: National Center for Education Statistics.

Kellogg Foundation. (2000). *A W.K. Kellogg Foundation Initiative for Hispanic Higher Education,* [Online]. Author. Available: http://www.wkkf.org.

Kershner, K. & Connolly, J. A. (1991). *At-risk students and school restructuring.* Philadelphia, PA: Research for Better Schools.

Klimes-Dougan, B., Lopez, J., Nelson, P., & Adelman, H. (1992). Two studies of low-income parents' involvement in schooling. *The Urban Review, 24*, 185–202.

Kohl, G. (1994). *Correlates of parent involvement in urban elementary school children.* Paper presented at the Annual Meeting of the American Psychology Association, Los Angeles, CA.

Lockwood, A. T. & Secada, W. G. (1999). *Transforming education for Hispanic youth: Exemplary practices, programs, and schools* (NCBE Resource Series No. 12). Washington, DC: National Clearinghouse for Bilingual Education, George Washington University.

Matiella, A. C. (1989). *Amigos y amantes.* Santa Cruz, CA: Network Publications, ETR Associates.

Mattos, A. (1984). *El toque del diablo.* Santa Barbara, CA: Santa Barbara County Health Care Services, Alcohol and Drug Prevention Program.

McEvoy, A. (1988). Student development and exclusion. *School Intervention Report, 1*, entire issue.

McGrail, J., Wilson, B. L., Buttram, J. L., & Rossman, G. B. (1987). *Looking at schools: Instruments and processes for school analysis.* Philadelphia, PA: Research for Better Schools.

Montecel, M. R., Gallagher, A., Montemayor, A. M., Villarreal, A., Adame-Reyna, N., & Supik, J. (1993). *Hispanic families as valued partners: An educator's guide.* San Antonio, TX: Intercultural Development Research Association.

Muller, C. (1993). Parent involvement and academic achievement: An analysis of family resources available to the child. In B. Schneider & J. Coleman (Eds.), *Parents, their children, and schools* (pp. 77–113). San Francisco, CA: Westview Press.

Muñoz, S. & Green, B. (1989). *Chicos modernos. Vol. III.* West Hollywood, CA: Core Program.

National Center for Education Statistics. (1996). *Digest of education statistics.* Washington, DC: U.S. Government Printing Office.

National Center for Education Statistics. (1992). *A profile of American eighth-grade mathematics & science instruction* (NCES No. 92-486). Washington, DC: U.S. Government Printing Office.

National Center for Education Statistics. (1998). *Dropout rates in the United States: 1996* (NCES No. 98-250). Washington, DC: U.S. Government Printing Office.

National Center for Education Statistics. (2000). *The condition of education, 1999* (NCES No. 2000-005). Washington, DC: U.S. Government Printing Office.

Navarette, Y. G. (1996). Family involvement in a bilingual school. *The Journal of Educational Issues of Language Minority Students, 6*, 77–84.

Neighborhood Networks. (1998). *About neighborhood networks,* [Online]. U.S. Department of Housing and Urban Development. Available: http://www.hud.gov/nnw/nnwfs002.html.

Nicolau, S. & Ramos, C. L. (1990). *Together is better: Building strong relationships between schools and Hispanic parents.* New York: Hispanic Policy Development Project.

Novela Health Foundation. (1988a). *El despertar de Ramón.* Seattle, WA: Author.

Novela Health Foundation. (1988b). *Face to face with AIDS.* Seattle, WA: Author.

Novela Health Foundation. (1990). *La gran decisión de Armida y Manuel.* Seattle, WA: Author.

Pachon, H. P., Mejia, A. F., & Bergman, E. (1997, December). *California Latinos and Collegiate Education: The Continuing Crisis.* Paper presented at the Harvard University Civil Rights Project conference on "The Crisis in Latino Civil Rights," Los Angeles, CA, and Washington, DC.

Ramirez, R. (1999). *The Hispanic population in the United States* (Current Population Reports No. P20-527). Washington, DC: U.S. Census Bureau, Population Division, Ethnic and Hispanic Statistics Branch.

Reynolds, A. J. (1992). Comparing measures of parental involvement and their effects on academic achievement. *Early Childhood Research Quarterly, 7,* 441–462.

Rosado, J. (1991). Being good at being bad: The Puerto Rican student overachieving at underachieving. *Urban Education, 25,* 428–434.

Rumberger, R. W. & Larson, K. A. (1998). Toward explaining differences in educational achievement among Mexican American language-minority students. *Sociology of Education, 71,* 68–92.

Stevenson, D. L. & Baker, D. P. (1987). The family–school relation and the child's school performance. *Child Development, 58*(5), 1348–1357.

The Council of Economic Advisers. (2000). *Educational attainment and success in the new economy: An analysis of challenges for improving Hispanic students' achievement.* Washington, DC: United States Government Printing Office.

U.S. Census Bureau. (2000). *Resident population estimates of the United States by sex, race, and Hispanic origin,* [Online]. Population Estimates Program, Population Division, U.S. Census Bureau. Available: http://www.census.gov/population/estimates/nation/intfile3-1.txt.

U.S. Department of Education. (2000). *Key indicators of Hispanic student achievement: National goals and benchmarks for the next decade,* [Online]. Author. Available: http://www.ed.gov/pubs/hispanicindicators/index.html.

U.S. Department of Education. (2000, June 15). *Riley announces grants to Hispanic colleges to expand access and educational opportunities,* [Online]. Author. Available: http://www.ed.gov/PressReleases/06-2000/0615.html.

U.S. Department of Housing and Urban Development. (2000). *HUD announces two new partnerships to provide digital opportunity, technology-based education programs* (HUD No. 00-136). Washington, DC: Author.

Ventura, S. J., Martin, J. A., Curtin, S. C., & Matthews, T. J. (1997). *Report of final natality statistics, 1995* (Monthly vital statistics report; Vol. 45, No. 11). Hyattsville, MD: National Center for Health Statistics.

Wagner, B. M. & Phillips, D. A. (1992). Beyond beliefs: Parent and child behaviors and children's perceived academic competence. *Child Development, 63,* 1380–1391.

Weiss, K. R. (2000, August 30). SAT gap for Latinos and Blacks grows. *Los Angeles Times,* p. A-1.

White House Initiative on Educational Excellence for Hispanic Americans. (n.d.). *The Creation of Excelencia en Educación,* [Online]. U.S. Department of Education. Available: http://www.ed.gov/offices/OIIA/Hispanic/eec/creation.html [2000, September].

Williams, S. & Stallworth, J. (1983). *Parent involvement in education project: Executive summary of the final report.* Austin, TX: Southwest Educational Development Laboratory.

AUTHORS' NOTES

J. Manuel Casas received his doctorate from Stanford University with a specialization in counseling psychology. Currently, he is a professor in the Counseling, Clinical, and School Psychology Program at the University of California, Santa Barbara. He has published widely and serves on numerous editorial boards. He is the coauthor of the *Handbook of Racial/Ethnic Minority Counseling Research* (Charles C Thomas, 1991) and is one of the editors of the *Handbook of Multicultural Counseling* (Sage, 1995). His most recent research and publication endeavors have focused on Hispanic families and children who are at risk for experiencing educational and psychosocial problems, including drug and alcohol abuse. His research in this area gives special attention to the resiliency factors that can help Hispanic families avoid or overcome such problems. His expertise and that of his colleagues in this area have brought numerous research grants to the campus. He also serves as a consultant to various private and governmental agencies and organizations.

Michael J. Furlong received his doctorate from the University of California, Santa Barbara in 1980. After working as a school psychologist in Hawaii and California, he returned to the University of California, Santa Barbara in 1990 to help coordinate the school psychology credential program. Currently, he is affiliated with the Counseling, Clinical, and School Psychology degree program. He has focused on research that addresses pressing needs of children and adolescents, particularly as they inhibit the schooling process. These projects are carried out in collaboration with local community agencies, schools, county mental health, county juvenile probation, child protective services, among others. To provide research and service opportunities for his students, he has been quite active with state and national school psychology organizations, having recently served as the president of the California Association of School Psychologists. He is an advisory panel member of the California Healthy KIDS Survey Project, and the USOE Safe and Drug-Free Local Education Agency Implementation Survey. He is the recipient of the 2001 Saundra Goff Memorial Award.

Christopher A. Ruiz de Esparza is a doctoral student in the Counseling, Clinical, and School Psychology Program at the University of California, Santa Barbara. He is coauthor of the chapters "Machismo Revisited in a Time of Crisis: Implications for Understanding and Counseling Hispanic Men" (*The New Handbook of Psychotherapy and Counseling with Men*, 2001) and "Counseling and Latina/o: A Guiding Framework for a Diverse Population" (*Counseling Across Cultures*, 5th ed., in press). Given his experience as the first from his family to graduate from college, Christopher has focused his research efforts on assisting other disadvantaged students and youngsters achieve their goals through education.

7 Working Cross-Culturally in Family–School Partnerships

NORMA McKENNA
Mountain View Elementary School, East Longmeadow, MA

JANINE ROBERTS
University of Massachusetts, Amherst

LIBBY WOODFIN
Brattleboro Area Middle School, Brattleboro, Vermont

OBJECTIVES

1. To describe how initiatives for inclusive, cross-cultural family–school partnerships at the elementary or high school level can be used to develop new links between families and schools that can sustain and support the daily multicultural work of school counselors

2. To present a framework that highlights the bi-directional nature of family–school collaboration—where both families and schools are seen as contributing essential resources, rather than the school "knowing best" and "directing" families on what to do

3. To articulate dilemmas in doing this work considering the often differing values and beliefs, cultural and class backgrounds, needs, time tables, and agendas of people in schools, families, and university training programs

4. To recommend specific, doable actions to address such dilemmas that readers can incorporate into their work

Kick That Ball Together: Applebrook Elementary

The evolution of a family–school partnership program at Applebrook Elementary School over a three-year period has demonstrated that fostering a multicultural environment in a school system is complex and multilayered. The Family–School Resource Project (F.S.R.P.), composed of a group of parents, school staff, and university interns, was established at this K–6 school of approximately three hundred students to strengthen the relationships between *all* families and the school. The F.S.R.P.'s objectives have been to help give a voice to parents who lack empowerment in the school culture and to create networks of understanding and communication between families who come from different cultural and socioeconomic backgrounds. We have found that there are no prescribed solutions for creating an inclusive community that is free from cultural biases and assumptions. Instead, positive change toward a functioning multicultural system requires small initiatives on many levels to build understanding, trust, and commitment between all who are members of the community. Constantly looking for modest openings, pairing up with allies, and keeping a focus on the time-limited, doable projects that would have ripple effects helped to ensure the success of the F.S.R.P.

Some programs set up by the F.S.R.P. have directly served the needs of students from so called "minority" backgrounds and have helped "majority" families connect with them differently. One such activity that met with great success was coordinating the inclusion of a group of second-grade Latino students into a recreational soccer league. The classroom teacher was keenly aware that six of her Spanish-speaking students frequently played soccer at recess but rarely joined in with their English-speaking classmates who also enjoyed this sport at recess. When she discovered that all of the Anglo children played soccer together on a recreational league outside of school, she approached the F.S.R.P. for assistance in finding a way to enroll the Latino children on the same league. The constraints that limited participation for these children included language barriers, financial needs, and transportation issues.

In response, the Family–School Resource Project was able to coordinate a group of bilingual parents who could help Spanish-speaking parents fill out applications, raise funds to cover the costs of application fees, and organize the placement of Latino students on teams that some of their classmates were members of. The outcome was community building at its best on the soccer fields. Transportation to practices and games was set up by parents through an elaborate carpooling system and became a way for families to interact regularly. Both cultural groups discovered new and comfortable ways of communicating and new friendships between students and between parents blossomed. It was the sentiment of many Anglo and Latino parents that the opportunity for their children to join together outside of school for a common interest gave them insight into ways to overcome cultural barriers.

Trying to Find a Place for Parents: Kinhaven High School

Through the process of opening a parent center at Kinhaven, a large regional high school, families, school staff, and the school counselor intern-coordinator struggled to define a structure that would make a meaningful place for parents in the culture of the school and for school staff in the culture of the community. The structure needed to respect the tremendous demands, time constraints, and importance of the work parents, teachers, and administrators do in today's society. What exactly would the parent center do to facilitate new links between families and school at the high school level? What did it mean that it was functioning primarily with parent volunteers whereas the school staff were paid and part of a clear hierarchy of evaluation and promotion? Who should supervise the student intern? How would facilitators and decision makers be identified and selected from the community and from the school, and how would decisions be made?

These kinds of questions surfaced with each initiative made by the parent center or with a request from the school to the center. For example, parents carefully surveyed the parents, stepparents, and guardians of the entire student body and culled from them a list of over 80 parents willing to do things in and for the high school. These names were given to school staff but over the year only a few parents were called upon to help in activities such as after-school homework support and tutoring. It did not help staff–parent relationships when the parent center was given the teacher's lounge for its space in the school. The teachers felt pushed out.

When other parents came together in committees according to stated interests to work on issues such as disseminating information about resources at the high school to families, and advocacy for students and families, some committees worked well and others got bogged down because of lack of time that people could commit, or because of people's personal agendas. The school counselor intern-coordinator struggled to find a way to support these committees, but ultimately he had no power to enforce things getting done in a timely manner.

The parent volunteers and student coordinator were trying to define roles, create new bi-directional links between families and schools, and find a home within the culture of the school at the same time that they needed the scaffolding of roles, structure, and space to help them do the work. Each move they made determined aspects of hierarchy, membership, and who was in and out of the group.

Frameworks for Family–School Partnerships

The ongoing multicultural work of school counselors can have greater impact if it is done in an environment that is inclusive of all the different families found in any given school community. A key way to effect school culture is with family–school partnerships that are bi-directional and communicate to families that their unique backgrounds are a resource for the school staff, other families, and students. If the two main systems in students' lives—the school and the family—respect and honor the different world views they each encompass, the daily work of school counselors with groups, individuals, families, school staff, and classrooms will be enhanced. By putting effort into developing family–school partnerships, school counselors will also be able to influence and reach out to more than the twenty or thirty families that a counselor might be able to work with directly in any given year.

The two opening vignettes describe issues in trying to create inclusive, cross-cultural family–school partnerships at the elementary and high school levels. We will come back to Applewood Elementary and Kinhaven High School to look more closely at similarities and differences in creating partnerships at each of these levels. But first, what frameworks are essential to developing vibrant, cross-cultural family–school connections?

There are many variables at work when forging new links or maintaining existing links between school systems and family systems, including many implications for how school counselors can meet with success when working at the junction of these two systems. Knowledge of a system's framework, an understanding of the benefits of solid family–school partnerships including bi-directional links, a working definition of cross-cultural counseling and communication, and a commitment to viewing school counselors as agents of social change are important places to start.

A Systems Framework for Schools and Families

A child's dual membership in school and within a family means that he or she must mediate the similarities and differences in routines, rules, schedule, and expectations between his or her culture at home and the culture of the school. For example, a fifth-grade girl, Roxanna, who spent the first part of her life in South America, was having difficulty finishing her work on time. She also experienced the relationship with her teacher, Mr. Allen, as somewhat distant. Roxanna's mother and father coached her on some ways to structure her time differently but she continued to have the same problem. So, her parents asked to speak to the teacher.

As they talked with Mr. Allen it became clear to Roxanna's mother that he was working with a very different notion of time than Roxanna. She tried to explain. "You know, Mr. Allen, the first six years of her life Roxanna lived in a culture where time was more relaxed and fluid for people. Getting things done on time seems very important to you. This can be important for Roxanna too, but it really helps if she feels connected to the people she's doing tasks for. That's more motivating for her than deadlines and due dates. I think there are some cultural differences here." Mr. Allen replied dismissively, "Children don't have culture—they're just kids. Only adults have culture."

Roxanna's mother was trying to mediate between these two important systems in her daughter's life. If her mother had not done this, Roxanna would have been left to make the necessary adaptations without the help of adults. This can greatly impair a child's chances for success in school. When there is not a good working alliance between families and schools, the student is often the one who bears the brunt of tensions, misunderstandings, and conflicts. In Roxanna's case, because the teacher was not able to change his perceptions, the child and family were left with the burden of accommodating to his world view.

The Importance of the Family–School Connection

The National Standards for Education Reform, as well as a host of state reform initiatives, mandate that schools institute programs to increase parental involvement. Goal 8 of the National Education Goals states, "By the year 2000, every school will promote partnerships that will increase parental involvement and participation in promoting the social, emotional, and academic growth of children" (U.S. Department of Education, 1994). This decree makes it obligatory for school systems to reach out to families, especially to those parents who have historically been less involved, in a broad effort to provide conditions that are the most conducive to learning for all students.

Henderson and Berla (1994) provide a comprehensive review of the research focusing on the benefits for children of parental involvement. In their review of sixty-six studies, they conclude that the most accurate predictor of student achievement is the extent to which a family is involved in its child's education from the preschool years through high school. They also find that efforts to improve student outcomes are much more effective when the family is actively involved in the child's school. In an earlier review of the research (Henderson, 1987), community interest in high quality education is stressed as a critical factor in supporting the relationships between home and school. The research also documented that school-based programs that help parents without access to economic resources to work with their children are highly effective for improving language skills, test performance, school behavior, and increasing a student's general interest in school.

Children whose parents are not involved in their education are often at risk of not achieving success in school. This includes a higher likelihood of failing courses, repeating grades, not enjoying school, and lessened participation in extracurricular activities (Moles, 1996). Populations that most often fall into this category include racial and ethnic "minorities," those with limited English proficiency, and those with a lower socioeconomic status (Moles, 1996). It has been shown that most parents, regardless of their background, need information and invitations from schools on ways to be productively involved in their children's learning (Moles, 1996; Epstein & Dauber, 1991; Epstein, 1986).

The research of Epstein and her colleagues (Becker & Epstein, 1982; Epstein, 1986; Epstein & Dauber, 1991) on school practices of parent involvement programs indicate that the way in which teachers and counselors reach out to parents, especially to those with less access to economic resources is a major determinant for a program's success. When teachers make parent involvement a part of their regular teaching practice, parents increase their interactions with their children at home, feel more positive about their abilities to help their elementary school children, and give higher ratings to the classroom teacher. In addition, student's positive attitudes about school increase, and their achievement improves (Becker & Epstein, 1982; Epstein, 1986).

Further studies show that counselor and teacher attitudes and practices are crucial for informing and involving parents, guardians, and grandparents who have had less access to education, economic resources, or who are single heads of households. For success with involving these families, teachers and administrators must relinquish stereotypes and develop a high frequency of reaching-out strategies (Epstein & Dauber, 1991). They suggest that school policies and programs reflect the literature base documenting that children's outcomes are improved if families partake actively in their education. The U.S. Department of Education's (1997) data on school climate supports this claim. In its massive study on father involvement, it was found that both mothers and fathers are more likely to be involved in their children's school if the schools welcome parental involvement and make it easy for parents to be active participants. Involvement is also higher if classroom and school discipline are maintained and if students and teachers respect each other.

When making family–school connections, it is essential, especially when working cross-culturally, that these connections be bi-directional in nature. Too often the work done at the interface of family–school relationships includes an undertone that the school "knows best" and that people from that system will train parents in the "right ways" to supervise homework, talk to their teen, or discipline their child.

Parents and communities are not always seen as composed of numerous resources that can in turn inform schools about cultural values, beliefs, parenting and educational practices, and the unique lived experience of each student. A bi-directional relationship between families and schools may help schools avoid "events" at the school that are not attended by families of color. For example, a school may assume that Latino parents could benefit from a workshop on ways to encourage their children to read at home only to find out that such a workshop is simply uninteresting or not useful to those families. Instead, by talking to these same parents, the school counselor or a teacher might discover that what would really make these parents feel more connected to the school would be invitations to come into the classroom and read stories in Spanish, share oral history, or teach Spanish songs.

Taking time to discover the real needs of families can help bridge the gap between the school and family systems. Further, a bi-directional relationship between a family and a school will assume that neither is the expert but will instead allow each system to learn from the other in hopes of a more cohesive working relationship.

Families and Schools Working Cross-Culturally

An important aspect of bi-directional relationships between families and schools is an understanding of and sensitivity to how this work demands flexibility and skill when working across different cultures. Employing Pedersen's (1997) broad definition of culture allows for a more inclusive frame that respects multiple social identities and a wide range of family types. Pedersen proposes that the term "multicultural" has historically been too limited to "multinational" or "multiethnic" characteristics and argues that the various identities that each individual carries are of at least as equal importance as so-called cultural identities. This is not to say that racial or ethnic identification does not have significant bearing. For example, one cannot ignore the effects of institutional racism, particularly how it impacts children in schools. However, a counselor who takes a broader view of culture, which includes the myriad individual characteristics that make up all people, is more likely to avoid rigid stereotypes when working with students and families and is more likely to seek out effective strategies in new situations.

Counselors or other school staff members may be just as likely to find themselves in conflict with a family because of a unique family characteristic as with a cultural characteristic. Counselors who approach all families with the desire to learn about and understand them will have more success than will counselors who lump families into cultural categories and proceed based on stereotypes about that culture. For example, a counselor who assumes a white middle-class student will have adult supervision in the evening will miss the opportunity to discover whatever unique aspects of this family are keeping the student from doing his or her homework.

Within a system's frame it could be argued that any interaction between a school counselor or a teacher and a family is cross-cultural in nature—schools and families each having their own unique culture. This presents varied challenges for the schools, especially because school staff often come from communities different from the ones in which they work. Though not all school counselors are from white middle-class backgrounds, the culture—and the hidden curriculum of most schools, as institutions—leans toward white middle-class values. These values come into conflict with students and/or families who do not fit into this mold. Assumptions about the way information is shared, about physical affection toward children, about homework, about free time for children, about adult supervision of children, about how families should be involved in schools, and about gender roles within families are some examples of potential areas of conflict between schools and families.

Counselors Working for All Families and Working for Change

Placing school counselors within a cross-cultural frame while simultaneously wedding the profession to the advocacy of family–school partnerships, is asking school counselors to work proactively as agents of social change. In addition, the non-pathologizing, nonblaming framework of systemic ideas meshes well with the focus of schools on growth and change.

The work of today's school counselor is no longer, as it was in the 1950s, to nurture the best and brightest students—generally white and middle class—toward college and careers in math and science (Gysbers and Henderson, 2000). Schools are different places, with less homogeneity, and the job market is demanding more skilled workers. The more meaningful and vital work for today's school counselor is to advocate for and reach out to *all* students *and* their families, to encourage poor students and students of color to take college preparatory classes, to counter the trend of referring disproportionate numbers of poor students and students of color to special education classes which "impedes the execution of valid [educational] strategies" (Hilliard, 1991, p. 35), and to be well versed in cross-cultural counseling and communication. School counselors have the power to act as advocates rather than gatekeepers, and to help schools become places that work *for* students and their families, not *against* them.

It is clearly important for school counselors to have good working relationships with the families of their students. In a multicultural setting, however, this work requires more intention and more sensitivity. Given the dominant culture of schools in the United States, which run largely on white, middle-class principles and assumptions such as competitiveness, independence, and a focus on academic achievement, school counselors, as representatives of those schools, must reach out further to bring many families into the school, literally and symbolically. They must create bi-directional links that honor the values and characteristics of each family as vital members of the school community.

Back to Applewood Elementary School and Kinhaven High School

The aforementioned frameworks informed the partnership work at Applewood Elementary School and Kinhaven High School on a daily basis. They grounded personnel in each project as they created mission statements and set policies, and provided standards to use to evaluate project activities.

We return now to the two opening vignettes to examine with more detail the challenges in doing this work. Partnership initiatives at the elementary level are often facilitated by how schools are organized (Henry, 1996). Because an elementary school student usually has one main teacher, there are many more chances for relationships to develop between that teacher and the students' families than there are in middle or high schools. Often a student will have the same counselor year after year in elementary grades, and the counselor typically works with fewer students than do high school counselors. There are also more informal, multiple opportunities for parents to do things in an elementary school.

Connection to the curriculum is easier to maintain at the elementary level (Rutherford and Billig, 1995). It is more familiar to parents and it is sometimes easier to see ways in which the curriculum can easily draw upon cultural resources in the school community. Geographically, elementary schools generally draw students from smaller areas than do middle or high schools. Parents are more likely to walk their child to school or drop them off. All of these elements offer possibilities to sustain and nurture family–school interactions.

Family–School Resource Project at Applewood

Applebrook Elementary School hosts a diverse community, with a "majority" population of upper middle-class Anglo families and a "minority" population of working-class Latino and African American families. While there is broad internal support at the school for the integration of cultural diversity, formal and informal assessments indicate that many parents, particularly those from the "minority" culture, do not feel a strong connection to school events and activities. Many believe that their voice is left out of internal decision making and some experience powerlessness in providing advocacy for their children, especially those with special language or learning needs. There is also frustration among the dominant culture of the school with how to most effectively reach out to include the school's "minority" populations more fully.

While there are many active parents and guardians at Applebrook, there are also many for whom involvement is remote or difficult—due to multiple factors that include language barriers, single-parent status and socioeconomic considerations. Many programs and projects initiated by the Family–School partnership program have been successful for increasing parent involvement because it has taken into account some basic constraints that limit active participation for some families: childcare, transportation, and language barriers.

Because cultural assumptions and biases can be deeply ingrained in both dominant and "minority" cultures, the partnership program has also set up activities that bring students and families from different backgrounds into contact more fully with one another. By opening up opportunities for exchanging ideas about childrearing or homework strategies, for example, parents have found that they have much more in common than they might have suspected. Being able to respect differences of beliefs has resulted from ongoing efforts to open dialogue about similarities.

The positive experience highlighted in the opening vignette about the second-grade soccer program at Applebrook School demonstrates the success that the F.S.R.P. had with bringing together families from different backgrounds to work together for their children's common interests. As parents discovered new ways to reach out to and support each other, assumptions about cultural differences were challenged and were replaced with new levels of sensitivity and respect.

To replicate the success of this program, the ongoing Recreation Fund was established by the school counselor and the family–school partnership program to provide all students with the opportunity to participate in community recreational activities. Realizing that families with language barriers or limited financial resources often have difficulty accessing school and community programs, the Recreation Fund is coordinated to raise and disseminate funds and provide assistance with enrolling children in music, drama, and sports activities.

Although this is a welcomed resource for some families that enables their children to participate in activities outside of school with their peers, it is not as widely utilized as was anticipated. We believe this may be due to the fact that it is managed by individuals who work inside the school system and is thus perceived as a "hand-out" program. To be a more effective tool for creating networks between parents and teachers with different backgrounds, it would be optimal if the Recreation Fund were maintained and promoted by parents themselves, who have the most to gain from it. Recruiting volunteers to do so has been difficult, however, because it requires time that many parents cannot readily afford to give.

Another activity organized by the F.S.R.P. that directly supported the integration of Latino and Anglo students was an after-school program that offered Latino dance lessons for fourth- through sixth-graders. The Student Support Services Coordinator at Applebrook approached the F.S.R.P. with concerns about the growing social division between Latino and Anglo fifth-grade girls. She was looking for a way to help these students identify and develop some common interests in a fun and inclusive environment. Discussions with students suggested that many of the Latino girls felt ostracized from social groupings and had begun to display defensive hostility to combat their feelings of exclusion. Many of these same girls were self-proclaimed experts in salsa and merengue dancing and jumped at the chance to help teach their peers something culturally meaningful to them.

In response, the F.S.R.P. found a local Latin dance teacher to lead the group and coordinated transportation and snacks for the weekly after-school classes. Eighteen girls and one brave boy bolstered one another's self-esteem and confidence through the teaching and learning of new dance moves. Although the program was useful in shifting the intensity of the social dynamics between the Anglo and Latino girls, many were offended by the "expert" attitude they perceived coming from the teacher. The program would have been more productive and empowering for students if they themselves had designed and taught the classes, with supervision being more peripheral. Although the F.S.R.P. tried to involve parents in the program to foster cultural exchange and receptivity, many were unavailable to attend during daytime hours and perceived it to be an enrichment program for students only.

In doing multicultural involvement work in a school setting, addressing the needs of one group does not happen in isolation; there is usually overlap with corollary needs of another group. For example, limited access to transportation has frequently been cited as a major deterrent to attending daytime and evening functions at the school for many Latino and working-class families. By linking together families with children in the same classrooms for transportation purposes, cross-cultural communication has been fostered. In addition, barriers to understanding the reasons why some families are more involved than others are beginning to break down. Instead of perceiving the absence of some members of the community at school functions through a frame of "they just aren't interested," there is a greater understanding of the underlying reasons that prohibit active involvement.

Much of the work of the F.S.R.P. has focused on conducting formal and informal needs assessments with administrators, teachers, and parents. This has meant that a lot of time is spent listening and understanding the history of relationships in the school. The program coordinators make every effort to facilitate the opening of communication between parents, between teachers, and between parents and teachers together. This has been imperative for strengthening the parents' and teachers' organic process for articulating strengths and weaknesses in the system and for designing goals to build new alliances. To make a family–school partnership program viable, parents especially need to take ownership of their own ways of making meaningful and lasting connections with their children's school.

To this end, it was a high priority from the outset to form an advisory board to the F.S.R.P., which would provide a forum for parents and teachers to work together for structuring the program's vision and direction. It is important that members of this board be committed to active participation as well as be representative of the socio-economic, racial, and cultural diversity of the school population. Securing members from single-parent and dual working-parent families has been the most difficult obstacle but providing food and fun activities for children during meeting times, and keeping meetings within designated time frames has helped.

One of the major initiatives promoted by this advisory board has been to plan regular programs at each grade level to increase family involvement. This past spring, the two kindergarten classes, with assistance from pre-practicum students, organized the "Day of Reading in Spanish." For one morning, Spanish-speaking parents were invited to come into the classrooms and share some of their favorite early-reader books with the students. Some were bilingual and read in Spanish and English, others read only in Spanish and had their children translate. A few of the parents who read aloud to the classes had never before set foot in the school and were very appreciative of the personal invitation to share something of value from their culture. One woman remarked, "You don't know how scary this was for me to come into the school. It has been so much fun that I would like to come back again." Not only do parents grow from the experience of taking an active role in their child's class, but they also convey to their children the valuable message that they are interested in their school and are members of the larger school community.

These outlined examples indicate that the complexity of building an effective family–school partnership program in a multicultural system is due not to conceptual or ideological difficulties. Most of the effective solutions to the disparity of power and access in a school system are in principle very simple in that they require opening channels of communication between individuals and groups, fostering an understanding and respect for differences, and affirming the commonalities that all cultures share. Each member of the community needs to feel warmly welcomed and integrally valued in the school setting.

The F.S.R.P.'s attempts to more fully integrate all families into the Applebrook School community have met with initial success because of its commitment to receptive listening, ongoing monitoring, and putting new and creative ideas into action. One of the most challenging obstacles presented in this work has resulted from time limitations of families, teachers and administrators who all lead busy lives with restricted schedules. But by helping parents and teachers recognize the small successes that are made in connecting with each other, building sensitivity to cultural differences becomes easier.

Parent Center at Kinhaven High School

As students move from elementary, to middle, to high school, there is typically increasingly less familial involvement and contact (Henry, 1996). At the high-school level, as Connors and Epstein (1994) have carefully articulated, the fact that each student now has a number of teachers and the schools are usually larger and more complex makes it more difficult for families and schools to connect.

> Most high school teachers define themselves as subject matter specialists, few give attention to the whole child. Few teachers and administrators have had education or special training to present them for working with families in possible ways. . . . Teachers have large numbers of students, and few work closely with their students' other teachers. Most high school teachers, counselors, and administrators have little experience communicating general information on school programs and students' options to large numbers of families, focusing instead on crisis interventions with a few families when students have serious academic or behavioral problems. (Connors and Epstein, 1994, p. 1)

When children first start school, the level of parental and familial involvement is determined primarily by the adults in the family. Developmentally, as students at the high-school level move out into the community and have more input into what their peer and other relationships are like, parents and teenagers sometimes find themselves having to negotiate the level and quality of parental involvement in schools. This, too, can impact on family–school partnerships. At the same time, as so poignantly expressed by the high-school students in *A Tribe Apart* (Hersh, 1998), teenagers are looking for and wanting adult contact and direction.

At the high-school level, parents also have a history with their children's schools which accompanies them. If they have not felt welcomed or had some continuity of interactions with the schools, it may be that "gaps in knowledge and relationships have developed that make many parents less likely to initiate contact with high school teachers, administrators, or counselors" (Connors & Epstein, 1994, p. 1).

These kinds of concerns were all in the foreground as volunteers worked to open a parent center in Kinhaven High School. Given that parents did not have a clear place in the life of Kinhaven, the focus of the parent co-chairs of the center and heads of various steering committees was on how to establish themselves as a presence. These parent volunteers did not want the parent center to be run with school staff having formal decision-making roles. Nor did the parent volunteers feel that they were clear enough on what their structure was to bring students in on a decision-making level. So when an advisory board was created to provide leadership for the center, it consisted only of parents and the school counseling intern who was the parent center coordinator.

Within the larger community, there was a lot of high interest and energy for the overall concept of having a parent center housed in the school. For example, on "Back to School Night"—when parents went from class to class on their student's schedule—volunteers, stationed throughout the high school, talked to hundreds of parents who were enthusiastic and supportive of the new center.

However, as the center evolved it became clear that unique problems were engendered by the fact that everyone working on it except the school counseling intern-coordinator were unpaid. It was hard to enforce deadlines and put into place structures with accountability inherent within them. This was in stark contrast to all of the policies, procedures, and rules in place for school staff. At the same time, the parents were trying to have an openness and lack of rigid constraints within their structure that would close out interactions with different communities that felt marginalized by all the regulations of the school.

A straightforward mission statement was written:

To act as a communication center, resource center, and a clearinghouse for all parents, stepparents, guardians, and the community at large

To contribute to the school community in a way that honors our varied backgrounds, beliefs, and values

To be a link between the school, parents, and the community

To enrich the communication between parents, students, faculty, and administration

How to operationalize this mission was another question altogether. The parent center advisory group started out with a survey of all the parents in the school. Parents were then asked to comment on the mission statement, write down what activities they would like to see the parent center be involved in, and choose from a list of items they would like to see the parent center offer. (There were twelve items on this list including: provide someone on a regular basis who speaks your native language to offer assistance/answer questions; provide information about summer jobs/camps/internships for high-school students; sponsor/organize discussions/workshops about topics of interest to parents; provide information about school meetings/events; and facilitate outreach activities between the school and the larger community.) With one mailing of this survey, responses from about 15 percent of the families in the school were received. After collating the data from the survey, the parent center advisory group picked the top six areas that emerged as those they would focus on over the year. They also decided that if particular topics of interest over the year emerged as ones of high community interest they would address those as well.

What worked was small, specific, manageable projects. For example, a list was compiled of summer job, intern, and camp possibilities for students and was made available both in the parent center office and on a website for the school. A dialogue night for different points of view was held after the musical proposed to be produced at the school was cancelled because of concerns in the Latino community that it was racist. An appreciation breakfast was held for all school staff. Parents of incoming ninth-grade students were welcomed at their orientation session and told about the parent center and its offerings over the following year. We had to continuously re-mind ourselves of what we did that worked because there was always so much more to do, or always gaps in what we could manage to do.

Projects that did not work as well often required coordination between the school, parents, and students. This was harder to get into action. For example, some parents and guardians wanted to provide a companion service where any parent who wished to could request to have another person accompany him or her to meet with a teacher, or an administrator, or help them to understand and access school resources. This required recruiting parent volunteers, having school personnel do some training with them, and getting a sense of how the companions might interact with students.

Continued areas of work include focusing more on the ninth and tenth grades so that the ethos about family–school links can be changed as new students and fam-ilies enter the school. Small ways to bring students into the planning and decision making are being explored. Key liaisons within the high school—counselors, admin-istrators, and teachers—are being identified as supporters and targeted as people with whom to consistently communicate about parent center projects. A concerted effort is being made to break out of just "improving" initiatives that are already in place such as the Back to School Night. Liaison work with the middle schools that feed into Kin-haven High School is also being instituted to ensure some continuity from their parental/familial initiatives.

Partnership initiatives mean engaging in conversations with people where roles are often unclear, new relationships are being created, and outcomes are sometimes unknown. Skills in tolerating ambiguity, reaching out again and again, and recogniz-ing and marking small changes are essential. Given what has been learned from these initiatives, the work of others, and other projects, what kind of guidelines can be use-ful for this work?

Guidelines for Building Inclusive Home–School Partnerships

1. Get a solid understanding of the existing structural framework of a school. This can help you to see where there are possibilities for change, or limits to it, and to define organizational procedures (e.g., how decisions get made, who holds power, what communities are marginalized). Each school has its own "culture" and must be understood and respected before new initiatives are tried. If a partnership project does not value the school culture, implementation of new ideas might not be perceived as desirable.

For example, at Applewood Elementary, decision making is a diffuse process that occurs slowly and involves many individuals. This means that people working on partnership activities have to do a lot more joining with a wide variety of people, slow down their own timetable, and provide clarity in many different venues (such as staff meetings, school newsletters, the parent teacher organization [PTO], and the school governance council) about project activities. It is important to see this as part of the process and not become frustrated by it.

2. Assess and define the needs of the school community for more actively involving families. What does familial involvement mean to parents, students, teachers, and administrators? Is it helping teachers construct a more inclusive curriculum or providing opportunities for school staff and families to get to know each other in new ways?

Data should be gathered on a number of different levels. Surveys and needs assessments translated into the primary languages of the school community can provide some good overview information. Creative ways need to be found to distribute them such as personally at school events, out in the community on the windshields of cars, and via religious leaders in the neighborhood. Interviews and focus groups (formal and informal) with different constituencies (e.g., families of color, school staff, single-parent families) can give a rich and honest sense of the needs for more active partnerships and address skepticisms people have about family–school connections. Assessment must be ongoing and with clear messages that the participants' evaluative expertise is necessary to keeping any initiatives receptive to the ongoing needs and resources of families and the school.

3. Identify supporters and allies of a partnership program right at the beginning. Include teachers, parents, students, counselors, administrators, and outside advocates that have a commitment to linking families and schools. Forming an advisory group will disperse decision making, encourage empowerment, and foster communication across systems. Although there can be barriers such as differing cultural beliefs and perspectives, language, and prior experiences, to ensuring representation from all parts of the community, it is imperative that organizational aspects of family–school partnerships model how to work both with and across these differences. For example, pulling in more allies at Kinhaven High School would have probably made it easier to get that project off the ground.

4. Build relationships carefully. Establishing trust with administrators, counselors, students, parents, teachers, and ancillary groups (student councils, governance boards, PTOs) is the key. Endorsement of partnership activities comes one relationship at a time. Gauge the receptivity to new ideas, as well as what may need to be done to foster them such as offering a place for parents and students or staff to congregate in culturally homogeneous groups, or providing in-service training on issues such as classism or racism. Help to build networks of trust across all the different groups involved in the school community.

5. Work to designate a space in the school for parents and families. Many schools have space constraints, but setting up a comfortable place that parents can call their own gives them ownership within the school system. If possible, have families share resources there (as in a lending library of books and tapes) and decorate and outfit the area themselves.

6. Change will most likely be slow and come in small increments. Each new connection between a family and a teacher, an administrator and a parent, or African American parent and European American parent is a step toward breaking down barriers between different groups. Don't get bogged down trying to oversee each interaction. Be receptive to listening for and acknowledging small examples of new interactions. Build upon them by continually encouraging the sharing of stories and hooking up people who have traditionally not connected.

7. Help build networks of parents and guardians by offering multiple opportunities for them to join around common issues. Parents need to communicate and bond with each other as a way to get support for the day-by-day hard work of parenting. Successful bridging can occur when students' interests are the starting point. At Applewood Elementary, parenting workshops around developmental interests (pre-teen stress, limit setting for ten- to eleven-year-olds, bullying and teasing behavior) were very useful in getting parents to create networks of support for each other. At Kinhaven High School, parents passed on to other parents information about internships, summer jobs, and work opportunities.

8. Communicate to all, especially family members from minority cultures (race, class, single/dual/step/gay families), that all have experience and expertise to contribute to how schools and families can work together. Help encourage openness to all points of view within multicultural groups by identifying and clarifying strengths of each perspective. Define boundaries for dialogue that include attentiveness to listening skills, speaking from one's own experience, not generalizing about groups, sharing airtime, not blaming or scapegoating, welcoming what others have to say, and looking for and learning about cultural variations in conversational styles.

9. Set up small, workable projects and programs with doable time frames. Acknowledge little shifts, keep your eye out for ways to appreciate both what you and others do. Projects might include ones such as establishing groups of parent advocates to help others with accessing special education resources, or for parents already in the school community to welcome and orient new families. Class-based activities, rather than an all-school activity, can bring people together in a smaller, more manageable environment. Or start programs such as the one at Applewood for soccer, which provide opportunities for students from different backgrounds to be linked to each other and to other families.

10. Regularly promote what is happening with your partnership program to the public and larger community. This can be done through media visibility for programs and events, networking with outside services and agencies, and representation on community boards and councils. If feasible, hold some family–school events in the community itself—apartment complexes, neighborhood meeting places, houses of worship—wherever it is seen as common ground for people to congregate.

Conclusion

When a school counselor puts time and effort into enhancing and developing inclusive family–school links, a framework for cross-cultural interchanges can be communicated and established for the benefit of all in the school community. This provides foundation that supports each of the daily school counseling activities. In addition, it means that the school counselor can have an impact far beyond the twenty or thirty families that she or he might be able to work with directly in any given school year.

An invitational tone for family–student–school contact is especially important for groups that have been marginalized in schools. As Henry (1996) has eloquently pointed out, because schools are more often representative of mainstream, middle-class culture, it is easier for families embedded in that part of society to connect to schools. School–family linking activities promote ongoing cross-cultural interchanges where all the cultures that make up a school community are seen as resources.

Different levels of schools—elementary, middle, or high—present unique challenges to and call upon the varied skills of a school counselor. Together, the size of a school, whether it is public or private, social class differences, and different ethic and racial groups represented within it, all have significant impact on how schools and families do or do not connect. At the elementary level or with parent cooperative schools, it is often easier to build upon family–school relationships that are already in place. Projects and programs that are happening in individual classrooms can be expanded to include other parts of the school and community.

At the middle- and high-school level, as the geographic community that the schools draw from broadens, and as the schools become more organizationally complex, it may be more complicated to find already established family–school collaborations. Also, adolescents need different kinds of familial involvement; the educational stakes become higher the older the child, and families and schools start to have a history together that can sometimes impede productive involvement. Here, skills at surveying, assessing, and joining across different parts of systems may be called more into play for school counselors.

Partnership work is rich with opportunities to further develop multicultural skills as a school counselor. Whether it is helping members of the "majority" culture to see their blind spots and learn about other groups, or setting up programs that draw upon the expertise of all the key people in children's lives, or providing continuity from an elementary to a middle school, or a middle school to a high school with parent–school initiatives, school counselors are working to create an inclusive community. If school counselors can do partnership work, there is a payoff on many levels for students, staff, and families, as well as any and all counseling work that happens in their school.

DISCUSSION QUESTIONS

1. What are essential elements to be attentive to and include when developing inclusive, cross-cultural family–school partnerships?

2. What constraints are school counselors likely to run into in doing this work?

3. Why is it important to link families and schools? What does it do for students? For school staff? For family members?

4. What does it mean to have bi-directional partnerships?

5. What goals did the U.S. Department of Education set in 1995 in regards to family–school partnerships?

6. In what ways is it useful to think of every family–school encounter as a cross-cultural one?

7. Describe the similarities and differences between a multicultural and a cross-cultural perspective.

8. What are particular issues in creating family–school partnerships at the elementary level? In high schools?

9. Think back over your own experiences with familial involvement in schools when you were a child, and an adolescent. In what ways was the involvement productive or not? How do these experiences inform you now in regard to what you see as possibilities for partnerships?

10. What are some strategies that you might use to help gather information about how people of varied backgrounds might envision family–school partnerships differently?

11. Given that schools and families are both systems that often are stretched for time and resources, how can school counselors help them to see the benefits of family–school partnerships?

12. What are several things that a school can do to set an invitational tone for parents, guardians, stepparents, and other family members?

13. Which aspects of the ten recommendations for building inclusive home–school partnerships do you think would be easiest for you to implement?

14. Which aspects of the ten recommendations for building inclusive home–school partnerships do you think would be most difficult for you to implement? Why? What kinds of support would be helpful to you?

REFERENCES

Becker, H. & Epstein, J. (1982). Parent involvement: A study of teacher practices. *Elementary School Journal, 83*, 85–102.

Connors, L. & Epstein, J. (1994). *Taking stock: Views of teachers, parents, and students on school, family, and community partnerships in high schools.* Department of Education: ERIC, Report No. 25.

Epstein, J. (1986). Parents' reactions to teacher practices of parent involvement. *Elementary School Journal, 86*(3), 277–294.

Epstein, J. & Dauber, S. (1991). School programs and teacher practices of parent involvement in inner-city elementary and middle schools. *Elementary School Journal, 91*(3), 289–305.

Gysbers, N. C. & Henderson, P. (2000). *Developing and managing your school guidance program,* 3rd ed. Alexandria, VA: American Counseling Association.

Henderson, A. (1987). *The evidence continues to grow: Parent involvement improves student achievement.* Columbia, MD: National Committee for Citizens in Education.

Henderson, A. & Berla, N. (1994). *A new generation of evidence: The family is critical to student achievement.* Washington, DC: National Committee for Citizens in Education.

Henry, M. (1996). *The cultures of schools and homes.* New York: State University of New York Press.

Hersh, P. (1998). *A tribe apart.* New York: Ballantine Publishing Group.

Hilliard, A. (1991). Do we have the will to educate all children? *Educational Leadership, 49*(1), 31–36.

Moles, O., Ed. (1996). *Reaching all families: Creating family friendly schools.* Office of Educational Research and Improvement: ERIC Document Reproduction No. 400117.

Pedersen, P. (1997). Defining culture in context. In *Culture centered counseling interventions: Striving for accuracy*. Thousand Oaks, CA: Sage Press.

Rutherford, B. & Billig, S. H. (1995). Eight lessons of parent, family, and community involvement in the middle grades. *Phi Delta Kappan*, 77(1), 64–68.

U.S. Department of Education. (1997). *Father's involvement in their children's schools*. Washington, DC: Office of Educational Research and Improvement.

U.S. Department of Education. (1994). *Strong families, strong schools: Building community partnerships for learning*. Washington, DC: Author.

AUTHORS NOTES

Norma McKenna is a Guidance Counselor at Mountain View Elementary School in East Longmeadow, Massachusetts. She received her M.Ed. and C.A.G.S. from the University of Massachusetts, Amherst in May 2000. At UMass, her primary research focus was on the meaning of family ritual to the emergent identities of pre-adolescent girls and on the critical link between family involvement in schools and the academic success of students. While at UMass, she coordinated the Family–School Resource Project at Crocker Farm Elementary School and directed the Institute for Research in English Acquisition and Development, both in Amherst. Her professional interests include constructing new models for effective collaborations between teachers, administrators, and parents to increase the relevancy of learning for students and expanding access to the educational system for under-represented families. She lives in Sunderland, MA, with her husband and two children.

Janine Roberts is a professor and coordinator of the School Counselor Education concentration at the University of Massachusetts, Amherst as well as the president-elect of AFTA (American Family Therapy Academy). She is the author of *Tales and Transformations: Stories in Families and Family Therapy* (Norton Press, 1994); co-author of *Rituals for Our Times: Celebrating, Healing, and Changing Our Lives and Our Relationships* (Jason Aronson, 1998); and co-editor of *Rituals in Families and Family Therapy* (Norton Press, 1988), as well as the author of some thirty articles, reviews, and book chapters. She is also a former board member and treasurer of AFTA and the former editor of the *Journal of Feminist Family Therapy*. She is currently on the editorial boards for *Family Process*, *Journal of Feminist Family Therapy*, and the *Journal of Marital and Family Therapy*.

Libby Woodfin is a school counselor at Brattleboro Area Middle School in Brattleboro, Vermont. She received her M.Ed. and C.A.G.S. from the University of Massachusetts, Amherst in 2001 and has worked as an elementary school teacher, a case manager for college students with learning disabilities, and a therapeutic counselor for high school students. She is also the author of *Familiar Ground: Traditions That Build School Community*.

8 School Counselors and School Psychologists as School–Home–Community Liaisons in Ethnically Diverse Schools

CINDY L. JUNTUNEN
Department of Counseling, University of North Dakota

DONALD R. ATKINSON
Education, Counseling, Clinical and Social Psychology Program, University of California, Santa Barbara

GREGORY TIERNEY
Department of Counseling, University of North Dakota

OBJECTIVES

1. To describe the role of the school–home–community liaison, and the value of this role in multicultural school settings
2. To present the rationale for school counselors and psychologists to serve as school–home–community liaisons
3. To provide suggestions for ways to implement that role within multicultural school settings

Comprehensive school counseling is becoming the standard for service provision within school counseling programs (American School Counseling Association, 1999a), and with a comprehensive school program comes the need to form partnerships with constituents in the community. Specifically, school counselors are expected to serve as consultants with parents, other school personnel, and community health professionals to best serve the needs of students. Industry and potential employers are other community constituents with whom school counselors might consult, as liaisons in school-to-work and youth workforce development programs. The various consultant roles described in ASCA (1999a) can be subsumed under the umbrella term school–home–community liaison, a role in which the school counselor brokers the comprehensive resources of the school, home, and community to serve the needs of students.

The liaison role is particularly important in ethnically diverse schools, where students are often negotiating cultural differences as well as meeting academic challenges. In an ethnically diverse school, counselors and psychologists are in a position to assist students who are encountering the well-documented barriers of discrimination and cultural conflict, as well as the substantial demands of childhood and adolescent development. By serving as a school–home–community liaison, school counselors and psychologists can bring together the various components of students' lives to foster greater school success.

In this chapter, we first describe the changing and diverse populations present today in school systems in the United States. We then discuss some of the factors that influence students and parents in the current environment, particularly as related to school involvement. This is followed by discussions of specific components of the school–home–community liaison role. We conclude the chapter by suggesting that school counselors and psychologists are ideally suited for this role by virtue of training and professional mandate.

Ethnic Diversity in the United States and Its Schools

Ethnic diversity in the United States has increased dramatically since the 1960s. In absolute numbers, the immigration wave consisting of documented immigrants, undocumented immigrants, and refugees that began in the 1960s is the largest migration in U.S. history. Although the majority of earlier immigrations originated in Europe, Asian and Latin American people accounted for 68 percent of the immigration wave between the 1960s and 1980s (Hollmann, 1990). Higher birth rates among ethnic minority populations also have helped to increase the ethnic diversity in recent years. During the 1990s, based on population estimates for 1990 and projections for the year 2000, the Asian American population has increased by 51.4 percent, the Hispanic American population by 40.2 percent, the African American population by 14.6 percent, the Native American, Eskimo, and Aleut populations by 14.4 percent, while the Caucasian American population has only increased by 4.6 percent (U.S. Census Bureau, 1999). Stated as percentage of the total population, it is estimated that members of ethnic minority groups will make up 28.2 percent of U.S. residents in the year 2000. A glimpse at the continuing diversification of the United States can be seen in population projections (U.S. Census Bureau, 1999). In the year 2025 it is projected that members of ethnic minority groups will make up 33.4 percent of the population of the United States and in the year 2050 this number is projected to increase to 39.9 percent.

However, statistics based on the total population underestimate the diversity among children and youth in the classroom. The average age of U.S. citizens in general is over 30 and is expected to rise to 42 in the near future (Kellogg, 1988). In contrast, youth is the hallmark of the racial/ethnic minority groups. The U.S. Office of Refugee Resettlement estimates that 32 percent of recent immigrants are under 18 years of age. Combined with the higher birth rates among racial/ethnic minority populations, the diversity of school-age children has increased rapidly in recent years and the trend is expected to continue in the foreseeable future (Kellogg, 1988). In the year 2000, members of ethnic minority groups are expected to make up 35.6 percent of the population of children between the ages of 5 and 17 (U.S. Census Bureau, 1999). It is projected that in the year 2025 nearly half, or 46.8 percent, of children will be of ethnic and racial backgrounds other than Caucasian.

These changing demographics raise several concerns that have important implications for school personnel, including school counselors and school psychologists. One major concern is that schools lack the resources to meet the special needs of large numbers of ethnic minority students. Ethnic minority students experience a number of obstacles and stressors that can interfere with education and lead to mental health problems. Resources above and beyond those currently available in most schools are needed to overcome the effects of these obstacles and stressors. Evidence of the effects that obstacles and stressors have on ethnic minority students can be seen in the disparate dropout rates of Caucasian American, African American, and Hispanic American students. In 1997, of high-school dropouts aged 14 to 24 21.0 percent were Hispanic American, 11.2 percent were African Americans, and only 8.8 percent were Caucasian American (U.S. Census Bureau, 1999).

A second major concern is that parents of racial or ethnic minority backgrounds might encounter barriers to involvement, resulting in less participation in education and school activities. Parental involvement is a fundamental cornerstone of American education, as evidenced by the Elementary and Secondary Education Act of 1964, which called for parents to begin "serving on policy and advisory committees, working alongside educators in making important decisions, and affecting program design and operation" (Morrow, 1989, p. 293). However, the U.S. Department of Education (1996) found that while 44.5 percent of Caucasian parents had reported serving on a school committee, only 29.5 percent of African American and 27.7 percent of Hispanic American parents had served on school committees. In the next section we examine in greater detail some of the forces that adversely affect ethnic minority student learning and parental involvement in education.

Forces Impinging on Ethnic Minority Student Learning and Parental Involvement

Ethnic minority students and their families are subject to two major types of stress that are associated with their status as ethnic minorities: (1) acculturative stress; and (2) stress that results from racial discrimination. Williams and Berry (1991) define acculturative stress as "stress . . . in which the stressors are identified as having their source in the process of acculturation, often resulting in a particular set of stress behaviors that include anxiety, depression, feelings of marginality and alienation, heightened psychosomatic symptoms, and identity confusion" (p. 634). Stress associated with racial discrimination can occur at three levels: at the individual level through interpersonal interactions, at the institutional level through institutional policies, and at the cultural level through attempts to denigrate and/or eliminate minority culture (Jones, 1997). Stress associated with cultural discrimination overlaps considerably with acculturative stress.

In studies with adults, both acculturative stress and the stress associated with discrimination have been found to negatively affect ethnic minority physical and mental health. Smart and Smart (1995) reviewed the research on acculturative stress and concluded that it negatively affects physical health, decision making, and occupational functioning. Self-reports of past racial discrimination have been linked to increased blood pressure (Clark, Anderson, Clark, & Williams, 1999), decreased sense of well-being (Jackson et al., 1996; Williams, Yu, Jackson, & Anderson, 1997), and increased psychiatric symptoms (Klonoff, Landrine, & Ullman, 1999; Landrine & Klonoff, 1996). Counselors need to be aware that parents of their ethnic minority students may be experiencing physical and mental health problems as the result of stress associated with acculturation and/or discrimination.

Although many children from recently immigrated families adjust fairly well (Fuligni, 1998), there is some evidence that acculturative stress and the stress associated with discrimination can be harmful to children as well. For example, Hovey and King (1996) surveyed male and female Hispanic high school students and found acculturative stress to be predictive of both depressive symptoms and suicidal ideation. Of particular interest is a study by Gil, Vega, and Dimas (1994), in which they found that acculturative stress apparently had complex and different relationships with self-esteem of foreign-born and U.S.-born Hispanic adolescent boys. Acculturative stress was negatively associated with self-esteem (i.e., as acculturative stress went up, self-esteem went down) for both foreign-born and U.S.-born subsamples. However, acculturative stress accounted for more of the variance in self-esteem among the U.S.-born Hispanics than among the foreign-born Hispanics. Also, the variance in self-esteem explained by acculturative stress remained the same for foreign-born Hispanics regardless of their level of acculturation, while for U.S.-born Hispanics the variance accounted for decreased as the level of acculturation increased. Thus, acculturative stress played a more important role in explaining self-esteem among U.S.-born Hispanics than among foreign-born Hispanics, and the role it played among U.S.-born Hispanics decreased as their level of acculturation increased.

Numerous factors contribute to acculturative stress. The physical act of migrating from one country to another, especially if great distances and cultural changes are involved, can be very stressful. Many of the families in the current wave of immigration come from agrarian-based countries where extended families provide an indigenous support system and a buffer against stress. Immigration disrupts the extended family support system just when it is most needed. To compound matters, refugee children are often temporarily (and sometimes permanently) separated from their parents, disrupting the support system of the nuclear family. Changes in occupational and financial situations are also stressful. By taking jobs far beneath their education and training, recent immigrants often suffer a loss of self-esteem. When one or both parents experience this loss of self-esteem it can have severe repercussions on the entire family. In many situations, work may not provide adequate income to meet the family's financial needs. While the stresses associated with migration apply most directly to foreign-born immigrants, U.S.-born ethnic minority families experiences similar stresses due to migration within the United States. For example, Native Americans living on reservations are often separated from their families when they begin attending elementary or junior high school. Also, moving from a reservation to a metropolitan area is potentially just as traumatic as moving to another country. Cultural conflict can create a barrier to learning for the racial/ethnic minority child and to parental involvement in school activities. Language differences present the biggest barriers to both student learning and parental involvement; students may not understand course assignments or teacher feedback and parents may feel frustrated with their inability to communicate with school personnel (Fennelly, Mulkeen, & Giusti, 1998). In addition to language barriers, differences in culture-bound values (e.g., attitudes, beliefs, customs, and institutions) can create stresses for the ethnic minority children and parents. For example, children from a cultural background that values cooperation may experience conflict with a school environment that emphasizes competition. Parents may experience cultural conflict if they are expected by the school or society to behave in ways that are not acceptable in their indigenous culture. These conflicts put pressure on the family as a whole as well as on individual members.

School districts undergoing rapid increases in diversity often experience a concurrent drop in parental involvement, with school officials blaming cultural values and changing family structures (Heath & McLaughlin, 1987) and parents blaming discrimination and insensitivity by school officials (Fennelly et al., 1998; National Coalition of Advocates, 1988) for this decline. It is probably more accurate to identify the problem as culture conflict than to blame it on either ethnic culture or school officials. Differences in childrearing practices, the roles of educators, the expectations for parent involvement, and other cultural differences often do create barriers to parental involvement. Olsen (1988) points out that many immigrant parents are "confused and troubled by such features of American schooling as extracurricular activities, the role of play, the lack of deference to the teacher, and the insistence on attendance" (p. 215). Morrow (1989) lists a number of factors that affect parental involvement in education by immigrants from Southeast Asia, including parental literacy level in both their native language and English, level of formal education prior to arrival, and cultural expectations that parents should not interfere with the school administration. Yao (1988) suggests that Asian immigrant parents may not initiate contact with the school and only listen attentively without much input when called on out of respect for the teacher's authority. Such parental responses are often misinterpreted by school officials as lack of interest in education. According to Lee and Simmons (1988), "Black parents are often excluded from serious participation in the educational process because of misconceptions about their [lack of] influence on adolescent development" (p. 8). Similarly, failure to involve Latino parents as partners in their children's school experience has been identified as one source of the continued challenges Latino children face in dominant culture (President's Advisory Commission on Educational Excellence for Hispanic Americans, 1996). Although all families probably experience generational conflict in one form or another, it can be particularly stressful for families where the parents may be holding on to traditional cultural values while their children or grandchildren are adopting mainstream U.S. values. Children may pick up English rather rapidly while the parents and grandparents find it difficult to adopt a new language. Communication often breaks down within the family, negating its influence as a support system. Strongly held traditional family roles are threatened through contact with U.S. culture, also contributing to generational conflict. Addressing cultural and generational conflict for Asian immigrants, Yao (1985) points out that "the Asian child's traditional place in the family is challenged by the American culture that does not value boys over girls [at least not so explicitly], authority by sibling age, or unquestioning obedience and maintaining the family's honor" (p. 223). She also suggests that when multiple members of an Asian immigrant family become breadwinners (often out of economic necessity), the father's patriarchal role is threatened, leading to generational and marital conflict. We should point out that generational conflict can affect Native Americans and ethnic minorities whose families immigrated many generations ago; the key element is an older generation that holds to traditional values and a younger generation that rejects them.

Racial tension in the community and on the school grounds can carry over into the classroom to distract all students from learning. Regardless of whether they are new immigrants or U.S.-born, ethnic minorities continue to be subjected to discrimination as long as their language, customs, or physical features distinguish them from European Americans. Racial tension can occur between and among immigrants, U.S.-born racial/ethnic minority groups, and U.S.-born European Americans. Strained intergroup relations are evidenced in ethnically diverse schools by segregated seating at athletic events and school cafeterias, racial slurs on bathroom walls, and physical intimidation on the school grounds (Sherman, 1990). Racial/ethnic gangs are not uncommon in many large city school districts and gang conflict frequently results in fighting and, in some instances, death. For the majority of immigrants and U.S.-born racial/ethnic minorities, however, racial tension manifests itself as psychological rather than physical harassment. Whether physical or psychological, racially motivated discrimination can have a devastating effect on student learning. A recent study involving interviews with Latino high-school dropouts revealed a common experience of alienation and discrimination in the school setting (Davison Aviles, Guierrero, Barajas Howarth, & Glenn, 1999).

Economic oppression is another major source of stress in a country where affluence is viewed as a measure of success. There is ample evidence that the incidence and severity of stress is inversely related to socioeconomic status (Mosley & Lex, 1990). As suggested earlier, new immigrants who may have had a trade or profession in their native countries often have to take jobs for unskilled workers in this country due to language barriers and licensing restrictions. Furthermore, the immigrating family may be expected to send money back to their extended family, adding to the financial burden of the new arrivals. U.S.-born racial/ethnic minority parents also may be limited to poor paying, low-prestige jobs due to lack of formal education and discrimination. Limited financial resources mean that for many racial/ethnic minority families both parents (and sometimes the school-age children) must work in order to contribute to the family income. For both new immigrants and U.S.-born racial/ethnic minority families, the fact that both parents may have to work, often at different times of the day to eliminate child care expenses, makes it difficult for them to be involved in their children's education. Furthermore, many U.S.-born racial/ethnic minority school children come from single-parent families in which the double responsibility of raising a family and working leaves the parent too exhausted to participate in the education of their children.

Collectively, these sources of stress can contribute to physical and mental health problems for ethnic minority students and their families. As school–home–community liaisons, school counselors and psychologists can organize resources in the school and community to reduce these sources of stress and address the problems they produce.

School–Home–Community Liaison Role

The fact that ethnic minority students and their families are subjected to high levels of stress that may interfere with the educational process suggests that additional resources are required to help reduce the stress, address the ethnic minority students' special educational needs, and encourage parental involvement. However, as First (1988) points out, "because most immigrant families settle in inner-city neighborhoods, the public schools they attend are often short on resources, poorly staffed, badly maintained, and overcrowded" (p. 207). It is an unfortunate reality that the school districts most heavily impacted by the influx of immigrant children and the growing diversity of their student populations frequently have the fewest financial resources to meet the needs of these students. In order to compensate for limited school resources, First (1988) suggests that schools make use of community-based services and should recognize and tap the unique resources available within the ethnic community. Similarly, Heath and McLaughlin (1987) propose that schools move "from the role of 'deliverer' of educational services to the role of 'broker' of the multiple services that can be used to achieve the functions previously filled by families or by families and schools acting together" (p. 579).

We agree that schools must draw upon community-based resources (both in the larger community and the ethnic minority community) in order to meet the needs of students in ethnically diverse schools and their families. We also remain committed to the concept of parental involvement and we believe that schools must make every effort to include ethnic minority parents in educational activities. In order to identify, develop, coordinate, and utilize the resources of the school, family, and community, someone within the school personnel must function as a school–home–community liaison, as an interface between school and home, school and community, and home and community. We believe that school counselors and school psychologists are in an ideal position to fulfill this role.

The concept of school counselors and school psychologists serving as liaisons between school, parents, and community is not a new one. In 1962, C. Gilbert Wrenn suggested that school counselors were responsible for performing a liaison function between school and community counseling resources (Wrenn, 1962, p. 141). Shertzer and Stone (1976) reinforced the liaison role by describing the coordination and management of school and community resources as a primary guidance function (p. 42). More recently, the American School Counselor Association (1999b) has revised a position statement that encourages school counselors to assure that students of culturally diverse backgrounds have access to appropriate services and opportunities that promote maximum development.

In many ways, the school–home–community liaison will be facilitating system changes, as new resources are brought together in an innovative fashion to serve clients. As agents of systems change, school liaisons might rely on the following strategies suggested by Kiselica (2000).

- Facilitate client access to information.
- Serve as a mediator between clients and institutions.
- Negotiate with outside institutions and agencies for better client services.
- Influence policy makers through lobbying and other political action.
- Inform funding sources about the needs of clients and concerns that those needs are met.
- Facilitate organizational change.

Although Kiselica (2000) was addressing the role of counselors and psychologists generally, these same strategies apply to the school counselor or psychologist who is engaging in the role of liaison. As a broker, the liaison will increase access to information and serve as a conduit or mediator between students, parents, the school, and other agencies. In order to meet the needs of underserved students, the resources of outside agencies will frequently need to be tapped. Further, political action may be required to adequately serve students in ethnically diverse school that are facing shortages in resources, finances, and personnel. Informing legislators and funding sources about these concerns might foster organizational changes that will result in better support for students, parents, schools, and the community.

The liaison role that we describe in this chapter is intended to supplement, not supplant, more traditional counseling and psychology roles in ethnically diverse schools. We assume that school counselors in ethnically diverse schools will continue to offer one-to-one and group counseling services designed to meet the academic, vocational, and emotional needs of all students. We assume that school psychologists will continue to provide traditional psychological assessments and consultation services. We also assume that school counselors and psychologists will make every attempt to adapt other traditional guidance and psychological services to meet the needs of racial/ethnic minority and immigrant students. Given that these traditional guidance services are provided, the liaison role can serve to marshal resources that are not usually part of traditional guidance programs in service of ethnic minority student needs. Furthermore, a small investment of time in the liaison role should pay major dividends in terms of increasing direct services to students and relieving pressures on some of the traditional guidance services (e.g., counseling, career advising, placement).

For the most part, the responsibilities and functions of the liaison role will be determined by the special needs and resources of the students, parents, and community associated with a particular school. The aforementioned system-change strategies can be used toward a wide variety of functions. However, the following responsibilities and functions are likely to be relevant to the liaison role in any ethnically diverse school.

Interpreting Culture.   One of the responsibilities of the school counselor/psychologist liaison is to interpret the ethnic minority culture of the family to the school and the larger community as well as interpreting the culture of the school and larger community to the ethnic minority student, the student's family, and the ethnic minority community. Gentemann and Whitehead (1983) refer to the person who interprets culture as the cultural broker; "the broker must be able to straddle both cultures, to take mainstream values and communicate them to the ethnic cultures, and communicate the ethnic culture to the mainstream" (p. 119). The American School Counseling Association has recently reinforced the value of this role in the following statement: "Counselors may use a variety of strategies not only to increase the sensitivity of students and parents to culturally diverse persons and enhance the total school and community environment, but also to increase awareness of culturally diverse populations" (ASCA, 1999b).

In order to interpret culture, counselors and psychologists must have a sound understanding of the various beliefs, attitudes, and behaviors that are consistent with the populations in their school and community, and also have an understanding of their own beliefs and attitudes about cultural differences. Using a multicultural competencies framework (Arriedondo et al., 1996), counselors need to first consider their own attitudes or beliefs, knowledge, and skills in terms of multicultural relationships. Attitudes, knowledge, and skills related to the client's world view must also be considered so that the counselor can then determine which interventions are most appropriate for the population. In this way, counselors will be more prepared to fill the role of culture brokers and effectively serve students, parents, schools, and communities.

The students in an ethnically diverse school will benefit directly from activities related to interpreting culture. Working within the school, counselors can help to prevent prejudices from developing by planning activities that will help students understand different cultures. Given the evidence that racial (and other) prejudice exists during elementary years (Powlishta, Serbin, Doyle, & White, 1994), school personnel can play a role in prevention and early intervention by engaging students in various types of cultural education. As one example, Reeder, Douzenis, and Bergin (1997) reported that students involved in a small group counseling activity on racial relationships demonstrated some change in racial attitude. Although only initial findings were offered in this study, it does provide some evidence that cultural education may improve student relationships.

Students who are immigrants are likely to encounter particular issues in the school setting that will require cultural interpretation. Olsen (1988) points out that activities in the school that teachers and students take for granted can be mystifying to immigrant children, like opening a school locker or moving from class to class at the sound of a bell. She cites several examples of how schools have developed programs to help immigrant students orient themselves to the new and strange environment of their school. For example, one school provides a slide show and an orientation booklet in the student's language. Another involves a "buddy" system to help students become acclimated. Still another offers clubs for immigrants from the same countries. The school counselor/psychologist could use these and other activities to interpret the culture of the school for new immigrant students.

Another need for interpretation involves interpreting the culture of an ethnic community for school personnel. The purpose of this level of interpretation is to enhance the cultural sensitivity of teachers, administrators, educational specialists, and support staff to the experiences and special needs of ethnic minority students. Referring to Black men as an endangered species, Parham and McDavis (1987) recommend that schools develop formal programs "to assist parents of Black male children in communicating to teachers and counselors their academic expectations for their sons" (p. 27). A similar call has been made regarding Latino parents, where there is often a need to consider communicating in both Spanish and English (President's Advisory Commission on Educational Excellence for Hispanic Americans, 1996). With respect to Asian Americans, an in-service workshop for teachers to acquaint them with Asian American cultural values and the effect of acculturation before a "back to school night" might enhance teacher understanding of parental behavior. By alerting teachers to the fact that recently immigrated and traditional Asian Americans show respect for authority by listening and not questioning, the counselor/psychologist can help teachers perceive parental behavior as a function of respect, not disinterest.

A counselor/psychologist can also help interpret culture for students, parents, school personnel, and the community at large by organizing cultural events. Yao (1988) suggests that the school–home–community liaison should encourage immigrant parents to participate in cultural events, perhaps as school fundraisers, where they can share food, customs, artifacts, music, dance, and art from their cultural heritage. Similarly, Omizo and Omizo (1989) recommend that parents and elders from the Hawaiian community be asked to serve as tutors and to share their culture in classes. Individuals who can interpret culture can also be very important in increasing the relevance of school activities for Native American children, who may struggle in school settings that do not recognize the symbolism and spiritual importance of animals and other things from nature (Kulas, 1996). This inclusion of cultures into the school setting not only sensitizes the people who attend to an ethnic culture, it involves the ethnic community in the process of education. In a school with a great deal of cultural diversity, the counselor/psychologist also might want to establish a cultural advisory board made up of student and/or community representatives from each ethnic group found in the school population (Keyes, 1989).

School counselors and school psychologists should have the freedom to work outside the school and to use community resources to interpret culture to members of the larger community. ASCA (1989) recommends school counselors "work within the larger community to identify cultural diversities and assist in the development of community-based programs which will propagate community acceptance of all culturally diverse populations in the larger population" (p. 323). Ethnic minority parents, particularly immigrant parents, may benefit from community awareness workshops designed to acquaint parents and other members of the ethnic community with school goals, policies, and procedures (in essence, interpreting the culture of the school). Cole, Thomas, and Lee (1988) describe a "comprehensive consultation model for promoting family and community involvement in the education process of minority youth" (p. 111) that basically involves interpreting the culture of the school to ethnic minority families through community workshops and family home visits. In "Lunch with School Counselors" (Evans & Hines, 1997), one school district in Indiana made arrangements with local employers to meet with parents during their breaks to talk about academic programs, resources available for students, and other school success issues. While not specifically designed with an emphasis on ethnic minority populations in mind, such a program could be adopted for outreach to ethnic minority parents. Another example of the interpreter function in which the mainstream culture is translated for ethnic minority parents would be an explanation of educational rights to immigrant parents, including those who are undocumented workers.

Perhaps the most effective way to interpret the school culture to ethnic parents is through media aimed specifically at them. First (1988) suggests that comprehensible information about the schools should be disseminated to immigrant parents "through print and electronic media, including native-language publications and radio and television programs that regularly reach immigrant communities; through bilingual, bicultural outreach workers; and through community-based self-help and resettlement organizations" (p. 209). One example is the handbook on education developed by the California State Department of Education (1986) that is printed in several languages, including Cambodian, Hmong, Laotian, and Vietnamese. The handbook covers parental involvement, enrollment and attendance, transportation, basic school programs, promotion policies and procedures, testing, and bilingual education as well as more general information.

Referral.   Referring ethnic minority students and their parents to community institutions and volunteer agencies is a primary function of the liaison role. ASCA (1989), in its position statement on cross-multicultural counseling, recommends that school counselors "develop a resource list of educational and community support services to meet the needs of culturally diverse students and their families" (p. 322). As a liaison, the school counselor/psychologist should be familiar with the many public and private, formal and informal organizations in both the larger community and the ethnic community that can serve as resources to the school and support services to students and their parents.

Due to the disenfranchisement of ethnic minority students and their families, referrals may be required to serve developmental needs or intervene with problems (Keys & Lockhart, 1999). In order to assess the needs of students and families, the school counselor/psychologist must establish credibility, so that a level of trust can develop. Unfortunately, such trust may be lacking in the populations that most need services. Therefore, a referral to an identifiable community leader from the children and families' own culture, one who would be willing to serve as an intermediary, may be necessary to begin the therapeutic process.

A referral can be made to either enhance the ethnic student's development or to remediate a problem. A referral to enhance student development involves a different philosophy than is traditionally applied to referral of students to an outside agency. Operating from the liaison role, the school counselor/psychologist views community agencies and volunteer organizations as extensions of the school, as "institutions sharing the common concern for the productive development of children" (Heath & McLaughlin, 1987).

> The focus is no longer on assessing deficiencies in the components of the educational delivery system . . . but on identifying and coordinating the social networks of children. The school becomes the nexus for community, business, and family collaboration that places academic learning with the nurturant ecosystem of athletic, vocational, and

service-oriented agencies and of institutions dedicated to mental and physical health. Different though their activities may be, these institutions share a common concern for the productive development of children. (Heath & McLaughlin, 1987, p. 580)

Big Brothers and Big Sisters organizations, community libraries, legal aid societies, ethnic community programs, ethnic community societies (e.g., African American fraternities and sororities), after-school tutoring programs, Little League baseball, and children's drama workshops are just a few examples of community programs to which a school counselor/psychologist might refer an ethnic minority (or any) student, if their developmental need matched the program offering (Heath & McLaughlin, 1987).

Referral of ethnic minority children and their families to community agencies for the more traditional purpose of problem remediation is also called for at times, particularly referral for mental health services. Although school counselors and school psychologists may become involved in short-term family counseling, few school districts can afford the luxury of allowing them to provide direct, extended mental health services to students and their families. Therefore, community mental health services must be used to meet family counseling needs. In the case of ethnic minority families, it is important that referral is made to an agency that can provide culturally appropriate services.

Referral in the school–home–community liaison role does not mean simply giving the student or parent a name and telephone number to call. Because ethnic minority students and their families often feel disfranchised from community support or lack the English-speaking or social skills needed to assert themselves, the school counselor/psychologist must be prepared to assist with each stage of the referral. This includes contacting the receiving agency, arranging a meeting with the agency, and possibly even arranging for transportation to the agency on behalf of the student and/or parents. In some communities, programs are being developed in which the "school as center of the community" model is used to facilitate various services. For example, counseling services are being brought into the school building, rather than students and families being referred out for mental health counseling. In such a model, the school counselor or psychologist might be coordinating services with a mental health provider who comes to the school, therefore reinforcing the role of the school as a primary force in the life of the student.

Advocacy.   When functioning as an advocate, the counselor/psychologist identifies a need that is not being met or a past injustice that is not being corrected by the school or local government and speaks for (or in support of) the student or family in requesting a needed service or the redress of a grievance. The American School Counselor Association and the National Coalition of Advocates for Students (NCAS) have collaborated on a training program for multicultural awareness, multicultural counseling skills and advocacy, entitled "Counseling in Today's Real World." This program is designed to train school counselors how to develop greater multicultural skills and learn to function as an agent of change within the school system. In this way, greater advocacy for students will be developed.

NCAS also promotes advocacy training for parents. In *Mobilization for Equity*, "members of the NCAS Board of Directors, national staff, and member organizations have joined together to implement a five-year effort to train and support parents to participate effectively in local school improvement efforts" (NCAS, 1999). This advocacy effort stresses the rights of all children to have full access to the body of educational information, a culturally supportive education, the support of parents and the community, and an integrated and equitable classroom and assessment experience. Ethnic minority parents have often been unable to advocate for their children's rights due to limited English-speaking ability, lack of education, or, in the case of undocumented workers, fear of identification by the U.S. Immigration and Naturalization Service (INS). Advocacy training, such as that proposed by NCAS, can alleviate some of these limitations. In other cases, the barriers will be too great and the school counselor/psychologist liaison must speak for the student and/or the family.

The NCAS (1988) has identified a number of recommendations for advocacy on behalf of immigrant students. These include advocating with and on behalf of schools to: (1) ensure that all school personnel understand that immigrant children have a legal right to free, appropriate public education; (2) restructure those policies and practices that sort immigrant students into programs which prepare them for inferior futures; (3) ensure that immigrant students (and all students) experience a school environment free of victimization, harassment, and intergroup conflict; and (4) ensure a more equitable allocation of resources to those (typically inner-city) schools that serve immigrant students. For a legalistic but readable discussion of immigrant students' rights of access to a free public education, the reader is referred to Appendix D of *New Voices* (National Coalition of Advocates, 1988). Additional readings on advocacy are available at http://www.ncas1.org/pubs.htm.

Pushing a school district to use broadly based assessment techniques rather than standardized tests to evaluate student progress is an example of advocacy on behalf of immigrant or ethnic minority students. First (1988) proposed that school psychologists "become active advocates for the provision of appropriate educational services for immigrant children within regular classrooms, rather than assuming that all academically troubled immigrant children are best served in special education" (p. 209). The school counselor/psychologist might advocate that the school district and individual schools develop mission statements that express a strong commitment to the success of all students, regardless of racial/ethnic background or immigration history. Further, the counselor/psychologist may need to advocate that multicultural education be provided for all students, even in schools not experiencing an increase in diversity.

In the liaison role, school counselors and school psychologists can also advocate for the provision of appropriate public services for ethnic minority students and their parents. For example, the school counselor/psychologist might advocate for bilingual employees in the state and local governmental agencies, particularly those that are supposed to serve the needs of ethnic minority populations. The school counselor/psychologist might advocate with public officials on behalf of students whose parents are undocumented workers by objecting to INS harassment in schools and by arguing against the unnecessary separation of family members (NCAS, 1988). School counselors/psychologists might also become observers of political trends and critics of political initiatives that might be harmful to student welfare, or mobilize support for initiatives that would support ethnic minority students.

Program Development.   As the school official who is most knowledgeable about student needs and about existing community resources, the school counselor/psychologist is the ideal person to push for the development of new programs to meet student needs. Initially this may involve convincing educators that the support of community groups is needed, because schools often view these organizations as unprofessional and may even discourage partnerships with parents and community organizations in ethnic communities. As First (1988) suggests, however, "many community groups can provide staff training, help with the identification and recruitment of bilingual personnel, offer counseling and other mental health services for students, and provide structured social activities, resettlement services, and legal support" (p. 210) that schools cannot provide due to lack of resources.

The program-development function is particularly important in rural areas and small towns where public and private, non-profit services are often lacking. The school counselor/psychologist liaison should not wait for needed services to emerge but rather should serve as the catalyst to developing needed programs. Local service organizations, PTAs, and church groups are all potential sources of help in program development. Brotherton and Clarke (1997) describe Special Friends, a program where the talents of students from a local college were tapped to support a comprehensive school counseling program in a small rural town. In Special Friends, elementary- and middle-school students with few adult mentors or resources are matched with young adults from the university, who agree to spend about four hours per week with their matched "friend." Through this relationship, adult mentoring can contribute to both academic and emotional growth, resulting in significant change with minimal need for additional resources.

At a very basic level, the school counselor or school psychologist who identifies someone in the ethnic community who can serve as a translator for parent–teacher conferences has developed a "program" to meet the needs of ethnic minority students and their parents. Esquivel and Keitel (1990) point out that in addition to translators, people in the community who are knowledgeable about a specific culture (e.g., priests, social workers) are resources for understanding and communicating with ethnic minority students. Helping to organize these people to meet the developmental and/or remediation needs of ethnic minority students is the essence of program development in the liaison role.

At another level, school counselors and psychologists can help initiate formal programs within the ethnic community, such as a chapter of Big Brothers or Big Sisters with ethnic minority adults, an employment training program at the ethnic community center for parents of school-age children, or a mental health service similar to the Catholic Family Service (Garriott, 1986). Addressing the special needs of African American students, Lee and Simmons (1988) provide another example. They suggest that counselors develop a school–community–business network to promote student life planning. The network "is a system in which Black professionals and community representatives are included in life-planning interventions as facilitators and as role models or mentors" (Lee & Simmons, 1988, p. 8). Recent models of successful school-to-work programs (Pauly, Kopp, & Haimson, 1995) also demonstrate the efficacy of formal community program support for business and career role models.

Social Modeling. In the liaison role, the school counselor/psychologist has the opportunity to function as a model of diversity respect and appreciation for students, parents, educators, members of the ethnic communities, and members of the community at large. All too frequently cultural differences are portrayed as weaknesses rather than strengths in American society and the counselor/psychologist can help combat this bias by demonstrating personal appreciation of diversity. By promoting a social environment within the school and community that is supportive for all students and parents, the counselor/psychologist will automatically model respect for cultural and ethnic differences.

While ethnic differences may inhibit the school counselor/psychologist's effectiveness as a model, a review of the research suggests that this barrier can be overcome. Weist (1997) found that those professionals who are able to demonstrate that they "are nonprejudiced, demonstrate that they truly care about their work, and are knowledgeable and sensitive about issues of cultural diversity" (p. 344) can work effectively with ethnically different clients. The most effective means of portraying these qualities is "for the clinician to directly address issues of racial awareness" (p. 344) with those involved. It is through this quality of interaction that the school counselor/psychologist can work effectively with students, parents, and members of the community as well as model respect for and appreciation of cultural diversity.

The importance of social modeling has been demonstrated in a program at the University of Missouri–Columbia called GEAR UP, which is part of a U.S. Department of Education project entitled Raising Every African American Child Higher (REACH). The mission of the GEAR UP initiative is to accelerate the academic achievement of cohorts of low-income middle- and secondary-school students so that increasing numbers will graduate from high school, enroll and succeed in college (Mobley, Tierney, & Tan, 2000). In the GEAR UP program, counselor teams of two lead group sessions with primarily African American children. In one group, the counselors were an African American woman and a woman of European descent. The counselor of European descent described one example of modeling equitable racial relationships in the following manner: The two counselors needed to drive over an hour to get to the school, and the children asked in the initial sessions who had to do the driving. The counselors identified this as a question of whether one or the other of them was dominant in the relationship, and indicated that they shared the driving. The children asked that question at each subsequent session of the group, and the counselors, by reporting that they took turns driving, modeled an egalitarian relationship (Mobley, Tierney, & Tan, 2000).

Mediation. In some situations where the values of the student, the school, and the larger community conflict with the cultural values of the ethnic community, the counselor/psychologist can serve as a mediator rather than an advocate. Generally this would involve a situation where cultural values are in conflict but where rights are neither being denied to the student or family nor are they being harassed or discriminated against.

Mediation skills can be beneficial in dealing with a multitude of issues in the school setting, but these skills may prove particularly important when issues of ethnicity are involved. As discussed in their book, *Working Through Conflict*, Folger, Poole, and Stutman (1997) note that stereotypical interpretations of events by the parties involved increase their emotional reactions to the events. Further, such unresolved conflict will typically escalate as in-groups begin to exaggerate the actual events and differences between the groups. At this level of conflict, groups may adopt a "we–they polarization" (p. 37) attributing responsibility solely on the other party.

With this understanding it is important not to ignore the social context of conflicts involving different cultures (Folger et al., 1997). Because cultural affiliation is an important aspect of every person's identity, it is crucial to gain an understanding of, and demonstrate a respect for, diverse cultures when mediating conflicts. Resolution will be aided through serving as a mediator promoting clarification of cultural influences inherent in the conflict. For example, cultural conflict between the ethnic family and the larger community might occur in the area of disciplinary actions that are considered acceptable or unacceptable. Although school counselors and school psychologists are ethically (and legally in most states) required to report all instances of child abuse, some gray areas still remain with respect to what constitutes physical abuse and what role culture plays in making this determination. Disciplinary actions that are acceptable and effective in some cultures may be considered child abuse in the United States. For example, Morrow (1989) cites a court case in which a Laotian father "punished his son by shoving a needle through the child's ear lobe, threading it, and tying the string to a clothes closet rod so that the boy had to stand on his tiptoes" (p. 294) to avoid tearing the ear lobe. Morrow reports that although this is a common practice in Laos, the father was sentenced to one year in jail. It can be argued that jailing the father for one year is excessive punishment given traditional Laotian disciplinary practices and that his absence from the family for a year only compounds the family's difficulties. If counselors or psychologists feel that the parents' disciplinary practices are a function of cultural values and not blind cruelty, they may want to mediate discussions between the family and local child abuse enforcement agencies while interpreting the child abuse standards of the larger society to the ethnic community.

Conflicts between student ethnic groups might also require mediation. Racial tensions are likely to grow in the absence of a curriculum that incorporates multicultural appreciation courses. For example, demands that the school cafeteria serve various ethnic foods are likely to become more frequent as schools become more diversified. School counselors/psychologists can serve as mediators in these situations, although the most efficacious use of their time would be to organize programs to prevent racial tension, rather than having to mediate problems that arise due to lack of preventive programs.

Summary and Conclusion

Culturally diverse school populations present unique and diverse needs that demand novel and creative solutions. In order to meet the needs of ethnic minority students, schools will need to draw upon the resources of the students' families, their ethnic community, and the larger community. This is particularly important in a period of budgetary constraint and limited school resources; the investment of a few hours of time in the liaison role can result in many hours of services on behalf of students. School counselors and school psychologists have the appropriate training and professional mandate to serve as liaisons between the school and family, school and community, and family and community. While initially the assumption of the liaison role may appear to be another burden for overworked counselors and psychologists, we believe that in the long run the additional resources available to the school will translate into a more productive use of their time. The activities of the liaison can help to change the structure of the organization in such a way that services are more widely accessible and more efficiently delivered.

The liaison role consists of a number of different functions, each of which involves serving as an interface between two or more constituencies. When interpreting culture, referring students for developmental needs to existing community agencies, developing needed programs, and modeling cultural respect and appreciation, the counselor/psychologist is helping to promote student development as well as parent and community involvement. When advocating on behalf of a student and/or parent, referring students and/or parents to community agencies for resolution of a problem, or mediating between two constituencies, the counselor/psychologist is re-mediating an existing problem. The liaison role allows the counselor/psychologist to maximize the resources available for both prevention and remediation of student concerns, furthering the goal of providing a solid educational foundation for all children.

DISCUSSION QUESTIONS

1. What stressors might affect ethnic minority students that are unlikely to affect European American students?

2. What are some of the resource implications of the growing ethnic diversity in schools?

3. What factors contribute to the higher dropout rate among ethnic minority students than among European American students? Which of these factors is associated with the ethnic minority students in your community?

4. What coping mechanisms are used by ethnic minority students, families, and communities to help students deal with the effects of discrimination?

5. Can (and should) school counselors/psychologists help facilitate the coping mechanisms used by many ethnic minority students, parents, and communities? If you agree they can and should facilitate coping, how can they go about it?

6. How might generational conflict be more problematic among ethnic minority families than among European American families?

7. How might racial tension outside the classroom interfere with learning within the classroom? How might it affect ethnic and European American students differently?

8. What community resources might a school counselor/psychologist draw upon to help ethnic minority students in your community?

9. What could a school counselor/psychologist in your community do to increase all parent involvement, but particularly among ethnic minority parents?

10. How might a school counselor/psychologist work effectively as a system-change agent in your school and community?

11. What characteristics does a school counselor need in order to effectively interpret culture?

12. How might the role of cultural broker change when working with students who are immigrants to the United States? or whose parents are immigrants?

13. What special issues do you need to consider when referring ethnic minority students for services outside the school?

14. In what situations can you imagine yourself assuming an advocacy role as a school counselor in a school with a diverse student population?

15. What kinds of programs might you develop to foster improved relationships between ethnic minority groups in your school setting?

16. Identify ways in which you might use social modeling to have a positive effect in your school system.

17. What mediation tools would be important in your role as a school–home–community liaison? How might you develop those skills?

18. What do you see as the three most important benefits of adopting the school–home–community liaison approach in your school system?

19. In what ways can use of the strategies discussed in this chapter enrich your entire school system, including students, teachers, staff, and administration of all ethnic groups, both majority and minority?

REFERENCES

American School Counseling Association (1999a). *Role Statement* [On-line]. Available: http://www. schoolcounselor.org/role.htm.

American School Counseling Association (1999b). *The Professional School Counselor & Cross/Multicultural Counseling* [On-line]. Available: http://www. schoolcounselor.org/pubs/position1.htm.

American School Counselor Association. (1989). American School Counselor Association statement: Cross/multicultural counseling. *Elementary School Guidance and Counseling, 23,* 322–323.

Arriedondo, P., Toporek, R., Brown, S.P., Jones, J., Locke, D.C., Sanchez, J., & Stadler, II. (1996). Operationalization of the multicultural competencies. *Journal of Multicultural Counseling and Development, 24,* 42–78.

Brotherton, W. D. & Clarke, K. A. (1997). Special friends: The use of community resources in comprehensive school counseling programs. *Professional School Counseling, 1*(2), 41–44.

Clark, R., Anderson, N. B., Clark, V. R., & Williams, D. R. (1999). Racism as a stressor for African Americans. *American Psychologist, 54,* 805–816.

Cole, S. M., Thomas, A. R., & Lee, C. C. (1988). School counselor and school psychologist: Partners in minority family outreach. *Journal of Multicultural Counseling and Development, 16,* 110–116.

Davison Aviles, R. M., Guierrero, M. P., Barajas Howarth, H., & Glenn, T. (1999). Perceptions of Chicano/Latino students who have dropped out of school. *Journal of Counseling and Development, 77,* 465–473.

Esquivel, G. B. & Keitel, M. A. (1990). Counseling immigrant children in the schools. *Elementary School Guidance and Counseling, 24,* 213–221.

Evans, J. E. & Hines, P. L. (1997). Lunch with school counselors: Reaching parents through their workplace. *Professional School Counseling, 1*(2), 45–47.

Fennelly, K., Mulkeen, P., & Giusti, C. (1998). Coping with racism and discrimination: The experience of young Latino adolescents. In H. I. McCubbin & E. A. Thompson (Eds.), Resiliency in Native American and immigrant families (pp. 367–383). Thousand Oaks, CA: Sage Publications.

First, J. M. (1988). Immigrant students in U.S. public schools: Challenges with solutions. *Phi Delta Kappan, 70,* 205–209.

Folger, J. P., Poole, M. S., & Stutman, R. K. (1997). *Working through conflict: Strategies for relationships, groups, and organizations* (3rd ed.). New York: Addison-Wesley Longman, Inc.

Fuligni, A. J. (1998). The adjustment of children from immigrant families. *Current Directions in Psychological Science, 7,* 99–103.

Garriott, A. L. (1986, October). *Therapeutic services for Hispanic families in transition.* Paper presented at the Annual Conference of the American Association for Marriage and Family Therapy, Orlando, FL. (ERIC Document Reproduction Service No. 286 145).

Gentemann, K. M. & Whitehead, T. L. (1983). The cultural broker concept in bicultural education. *Journal of Negro Education, 52,* 118–129.

Gil, A. G., Vega, W. A., & Dimas, J. M. (1994). Acculturative stress and personal adjustment among

Hispanic adolescent boys. *Journal of Community Psychology, 22,* 43–54.

Heath, S. B. & McLaughlin, M. W. (1987). A child resource policy: Moving beyond dependence on school and family. *Phi Delta Kappan, 68,* 576–580.

Hollmann, F. W. (1990). *U.S. population estimates by age, sex, race, and Hispanic origin: 1989.* (Report No. 1057). Washington, DC: U.S. Department of Commerce, Bureau of the Census. (Current Population Reports Population Estimates and Projectives Series P-25).

Hovey, J. D. & King, C. A. (1996). Acculturative stress, depression, and suicidal ideation among immigrant and second-generation Latino adolescents. *Journal of the American Academy of Child and Adolescent Psychiatry, 55,* 1183–1192.

Jackson, J. S., Brown, T. N., Williams, D. R., Torres, M., Sellers, S. L., & Brown, K. (1996). Racism and the physical and mental health status of African Americans: A thirteen-year national panel study. *Ethnicity and Disease, 6,* 132–147.

Jones, J. M. (1997). *Prejudice and racism* (2nd ed.). New York: McGraw-Hill.

Kellogg, J. B. (1988). Forces of change. *Phi Delta Kappan, 70,* 199–204.

Keyes, K. L. (1989). The counselor's role in helping students with limited English proficiency. *The School Counselor, 37,* 144–148.

Keys, S. G. & Lockhart, E. J. (1999). The school counselor's role in facilitating multisystemic change. *Professional School Counseling, 3*(2), 101–107.

Kiselica, M. (2000, April). *The mental health professional as advocate: Matters of the heart, matters of the mind.* Keynote address to the Great Lakes Regional Conference of Division 17 of the American Psychological Association, Muncie, Indiana.

Klonoff, E. A., Landrine, H., & Ullman, J. B. (1999). Racial discrimination and psychiatric symptoms among Blacks. *Cultural Diversity and Ethnic Minority Psychology, 5,* 329–339.

Kulas, C. (1996). The importance of integrating culture into the curriculum. In K. Greenwood (Ed.), *The Circle of Life Curriculum.* (Product of an Experimental Project funded by the National Science Foundation, No. #HRD-94-50071). Grand Forks, ND: University of North Dakota, DREAMS.

Landrine, H. & Klonoff, E. A. (1996). The schedule of racist events: A measure of racial discrimination and a study of its negative physical and mental health consequences. *Journal of Black Psychology, 22,* 144–168.

Lee, C. C. & Simmons, S. (1988). A comprehensive life-planning model for Black adolescents. *The School Counselor, 36,* 5–10.

Mobley, M., Tierney, C. G., & Tan, J. A. (2000, April). *GEAR UP: Promoting Personal and Academic Growth via Group Counseling.* Paper presented at the Great Lakes Regional Conference of Division 17 of the American Psychological Association, Muncie, Indiana.

Morrow, R. D. (1989). Southeast-Asian parental involvement: Can it be a reality? *Elementary School Guidance & Counseling, 23,* 289–297.

Mosley, J. C. & Lex, A. (1990). Identification of potentially stressful life events experienced by a population of urban minority youth. *Journal of Multicultural Counseling and Development, 18,* 118–125.

National Coalition of Advocates for Students. (1988). *New voices: Immigrant students in U. S. public schools.* Boston, MA: Author. (ERIC Document Reproduction Service No. ED 297 063).

National Coalition of Advocates for Students. (1999). *National Projects* [On-line]. Available: http://www.ncas1.org/projects.htm.

Olsen, L. (1988). Crossing the schoolhouse border: Immigrant children in California. *Phi Delta Kappan, 70,* 211–218.

Omizo, M. M. & Omizo, S. A. (1989). Counseling Hawaiian children. *Elementary School Guidance and Counseling, 23,* 282–288.

Parham, T. A. & McDavis, R. J. (1987). Black men, an endangered species: Who's really pulling the trigger? *Journal of Counseling and Development, 66,* 24–27.

Pauly, E., Kopp, H., & Haimson, J. (1995). *Homegrown lessons: Innovative programs linking school and work.* San Francisco, CA: Jossey-Bass.

Powlishta, K. K., Serbin, L. A., Doyle, A. B., & White, D. R. (1994). Gender, ethnic, and body type biases: The generality of prejudice in childhood. *Developmental Psychology, 30,* 526–536.

President's Advisory Commission on Educational Excellence for Hispanic Americans. (September, 1996). *Our Nation on the Fault Line: Hispanic American Education* [On-line]. Available: http://www.ed.gov/pubs/FaultLine/.

Reeder, J., Douzenis, C., & Bergin, J. J. (1997). The effects of small group counseling on the racial attitudes of second grade students. *Professional School Counseling, 1*(2), 15–18.

Sherman, R. L. (1990). Intergroup conflict on high school campuses. *Journal of Multicultural Counseling and Development, 18,* 11–18.

Shertzer, B. & Stone, S. C. (1976). *Fundamentals of Guidance* (3rd ed.). Boston: Houghton Mifflin Company.

Smart, J. F. & Smart, D. W. (1995). Acculturative stress: The experience of the Hispanic immigrant. *The Counseling Psychologist, 23,* 25–42.

State Department of Education. (1986). *A handbook on California education for language minority parents.* Sacramento, CA: Author.

U.S. Census Bureau (1999). *Statistical Abstract of the United States* [On-line]. Available: http://www.census.gov/

U.S. Department of Education (1996). *National household education survey (NHES)* [On-line]. Available: http://nces.ed.gov/

Weist, M. D. (1997). Expanded school mental health services: A national movement in progress. In T. H. Ollendick & R. J. Prinz (Eds.), *Advances in clinical child psychology: Vol. 19* (pp. 319–352). New York: Plenum Press.

Williams, C. L. & Berry, J. W. (1991). Primary prevention of acculturative stress among refugees: Application of psychological theory and practice. *American Psychologist, 46,* 632–641.

Williams, D. R., Yu, Y., Jackson, J., & Anderson, N. (1997). Racial differences in physical and mental health: Socioeconomic status, stress, and discrimination. *Journal of Health Psychology, 2,* 335–351.

Wrenn, C. G. (1962). *The counselor in a changing world.* Washington, DC: American Personnel and Guidance Association.

Yao, E. L. (1985). Adjustment needs of Asian immigrant children. *Elementary School Guidance and Counseling, 19,* 222–227.

Yao, E. L. (1988). Working effectively with Asian immigrant parents. *Phi Delta Kappan, 70,* 223–225.

A U T H O R S '   N O T E S

Cindy L. Juntunen is associate professor and chair of the Department of Counseling at the University of North Dakota. She received her Ph.D. from the University of California, Santa Barbara in 1994. Professor Juntunen's research interests include vocational psychology, supervision, and social action. She has published in areas of career development for women and Native Americans, School-to-Work, and supervision. She is currently directing an action research project designed to increase career aspirations and enhance work satisfaction for people moving from welfare to self-sufficiency.

Donald R. Atkinson is a professor of education in the combined Counseling, Clinical, and School Psychology Program at the University of California, Santa Barbara. He received his Ph.D. from the University of Wisconsin in 1970. Professor Atkinson is a fellow in the American Psychological Society and Divisions 17 and 45 of the American Psychological Association. He is a co-author of *Counseling American Minorities: A Cross-Cultural Perspective* (now in its 5th edition), *Counseling Non-Ethnic American Minorities,* and *Counseling Diverse Populations* (now in its 2nd edition), and author or coauthor of over 100 journal articles, most of which report the results of research on cultural variables in counseling.

Gregory T. Tierney is a doctoral student in the Counseling Psychology Program at the University of North Dakota. He received his M.A. in Community Counseling from Loyola University Chicago in 1999. Mr. Tierney has been involved in research and prevention programs focused on prejudice/multicultural issues and substance abuse. His current dissertation research focuses on underlying beliefs that comprise psychologists' theoretical orientation. His future goals include pursuing action-oriented research interests through prevention programs centered on issues such as prejudice, sexual assault, substance abuse, and career. He would also like to pursue research and clinical use of empirically validated treatment systems.

PART THREE

Training and Intervention Strategies

9. *Improving the Multicultural Competence of Educators* (Locke)
10. *Multicultural Training in Schools as an Expansion of the Counselor's Role* (Pedersen)
11. *Reducing Violence in Multicultural Schools* (Fontes)
12. *Cross-Cultural Career Counseling in Schools* (Leong and Tan)

The four chapters in Part Three focus on strategies the school counselor can use to bring about positive change for multicultural schools. While there is a lot written about how schools should be sensitive to culture and not violate the values or integrity of the student or the student's family culture, there is much less written about how to accomplish that goal. Positive change does not happen spontaneously but only after someone has put considerable work into creating the "favorable conditions" under which contact will have positive results. Only when the school counselors discover that making culture central rather than marginal will make their job easier, not harder, and more, not less meaningful, will lasting positive change actually occur.

Each chapter in Part Three focuses on a different approach for intervention and training by school counselors. The first theme that emerges is that of "multicultural competence" in counseling and in education. Chapter 9 by Locke begins by assuming that successful strategies for multicultural education have not already been implemented. The reason presented for this gap is a lack of competence among providers. The necessary indicators of competence are described and recent efforts to increase competence are explained. Sources of resistance to multicultural competence are also identified and a continuum of cross-cultural awareness is presented. Specific case examples are presented and discussed and the considerable recent literature on how to measure multicultural competence is identified. Chapter 10 by Pedersen continues the theme of multicultural competence by describing how multicultural training can become an extension of the school counselor's professional role. The awareness, knowledge, and skill multicultural competencies are linked to specific training strategies and techniques. The consequences of incompetence are also discussed. A self–assessment of multicultural awareness, knowledge, and skills in school counseling is provided for readers to test their own level of measured competence. Chapter 11 by Fontes describes how to reduce violence in multicultural schools. The many forms of school violence are described along with the protocol methods used to reduce violence. Conflict resolution and mediation approaches are evaluated in specific case examples.

A second important theme of Part Three is that of "career counseling." In Chapter 12 Leong and Tan discuss the need for cross-cultural career counseling in schools where the match between the student's future career and their cultural roots is profoundly important. Western models of career counseling present problems when applied to students from non-Western cultures. Fortunately, there are alternative models of cross-cultural career counseling, which are presented in this chapter. Cultural differences present both problems and opportunities for career counseling. The specific problems of Western culture bias are discussed along with the advantages of considering non-Western alternatives. A seven-step sequence is discussed to help counselors become sensitive to culture in career counseling. Other specific models are also presented, discussed, and evaluated. A multiculturally competent career counselor will value both the culture-general and culture-specific aspects.

9 Improving the Multicultural Competence of Educators

DON C. LOCKE

The Asheville Graduate Center, North Carolina State University

OBJECTIVES

1. To use culture as a framework for exploring classroom activities
2. To present a rationale for educators to consider for making their classroom instruction multiculturally relevant
3. To provide a framework for use by teachers in revising their classroom instruction methods
4. To present strategies for classroom teachers who wish to make their classrooms multiculturally relevant

The status of culturally different students in our schools has changed profoundly over the last four decades. With the Supreme Court decision in 1954 outlawing segregated schools, educators found themselves faced with new students, new roles, and new challenges. These changes were exacerbated in the 1990s as many school systems found themselves populated with a majority of students who are members of culturally diverse groups. Educators concerned with these changes have spent many hours engaging in research, identifying strategies, or participating in discussions designed to encourage culturally different students and to help them appreciate their own worth and value. These collective efforts have led to significant changes in the schools and much has been accomplished. What has not been done, however, is a consideration of the context in which these changes have taken place.

In this chapter, I use "dominant culture" as a primary referent to which members of other groups are different, while recognizing that greater differences exist *among* group members than *between* groups. With that referent in mind, I assert that change is needed in institutional structures that allows greater recognition of the accomplishments of culturally different students. These changes should be aimed at encouraging and supporting a diverse student population and should specifically include culturally different students, their parents, and their culture.

Educational systems must engage in a careful and systematic examination of the values being taught and how these values impact on the culturally different as well as on members of the dominant culture. The intent of this chapter is to call attention to the fact that successful strategies for the education of the culturally different have not been implemented. Indeed, many educational practices have worked to the disadvantage of culturally different students. The ultimate goal of this chapter is to provide insight into the problems associated with the education of culturally different students and to offer some possibilities for individual and institutional change that will lead to more effective education for all students. It is time that our educational systems become responsive to the values, ideas, beliefs, talents, hopes, dreams, and visions of all students, and especially of those who are culturally different.

I do not underestimate the magnitude of the task of reshaping our educational systems or the individuals who work in them. There have already been many studies conducted and theories introduced that focus on the education of culturally different students. The recommendations made here are designed to mobilize individuals in educational systems to rethink the way they do things relative to its culturally different members.

Although our focus will be primarily on improving the competence of individuals working in systems, there are a number of institutional (system) priorities that must be clear if the people who work directly with students are to implement changes. First, there must be a strong commitment from the leadership of educational systems to the education of culturally different students. The school board and the superintendent set the tone and establish the agenda for what goes on in the system. They must see themselves as initiators of change and become more directly involved in the process, such as increased on-site visitation or participation in classroom activities. Second, the educational system must understand that it is responsible for teaching the values of the culture. The system must be willing to openly investigate its practices in terms of which values are being promoted by which practices. Evaluation should include input from all cultural groups. For example, Brookover (1985) characterized the value issue in this way:

> Under the guise of individual differences, meeting individual needs, continuous progress, humanistic education, and now kindergarten redshirting, we have sought to justify shortchanging the children of poor and minorities in American schools. The belief in vast differences in "intelligence" or ability to learn, which are highly associated with race and socioeconomic status of the family, provide the pervasive "justification" for discriminatory educational programs within our schools. (p. 261)

Third, the system must ensure that those individuals willing to implement changes are supported in their efforts. Likewise, individuals reluctant to make changes must not be able to use the excuse of being unsure of what the administration thinks or how the administration feels about implementing strategies for culturally different students. For example, school personnel must advocate for children and not feel threatened for doing so.

Fourth, the institution must communicate that it values diversity. The institution must first decide what diversity means in the context of its community and then evaluate its practices and procedures in terms of their relationship to diversity. School administrations must communicate that they believe that there is more than one way to think, feel, believe, and act. They must communicate in an open forum that differences in these areas do not mean second-class status, a decrease in excellence, or a threat to the dominant culture.

Finally, school systems need to engage in a strategic planning and evaluation process related to the education of culturally different students. School systems need to include as a part of this planning process the numbers of school personnel who are culturally different, plans for improving the multicultural competence of all its staff, goals for educational achievement for culturally different students, and how policies will be implemented relative to culturally different students. Such a planning process would include an ongoing evaluation of program effectiveness in meeting the goals established in the planning process.

For direction in establishment of multicultural planning and setting strategic goals, school administrators can seek input from professional organizations such as the American School Counselor Association (ASCA). ASCA has identified specific strategies for school districts to employ in their attempt to increase awareness of culturally diverse populations and serves as guidance for all school personnel.

ASCA (1989) has recommended that parents from culturally diverse backgrounds be included on curriculum development planning boards, committees, and other school projects. Incorporation of culturally diverse family resources into the educational process was also recommended, as was the provision of liaison services to facilitate communication between community and school. Workshops for parents (to increase awareness of system philosophy of education) as well as faculty (to increase awareness of culturally diverse people) are specific strategies that may be of great benefit. Schoolwide activities that promote individual differences and contributions made by culturally diverse people should be promoted. Finally, classroom materials must be free of culturally biased information and teachers must be discouraged from using material of such caliber.

An example of this type of commitment is evident in the Human Dignity Policy in Ferndale, Michigan. This stands as an example of how one system has translated philosophy into policy:

> The Board of Education, recognizing that we are a multiracial, multiethnic school district, believes it is part of our mission to provide a positive harmonious environment in which respect for the diverse makeup of the school community is promoted. A major aim of education in the Ferndale School District is the development of reasoned commitment to the core values of a democratic society.
>
> In accordance with this aim, the school district will not tolerate behavior by students or staff which insults, degrades, or stereotypes any race, gender, handicap, physical condition, ethnic group, or religion.

Appropriate consequences for offending this policy will be specified in the student code of conduct of each building. Staff members offending this policy will be disciplined in accordance with provisions of the appropriate employee master agreement with the School Board. (Pine & Hilliard, 1990)

Culture Defined

A common understanding of the fundamental concept of culture is essential to a shared understanding of the ideas presented in this chapter. Therefore, a brief review of the concept is necessary before we explore ways in which behaviors of educators influence student responses.

There are more than 150 definitions of culture in the literature. The term *culture* is abstract yet is often used to explain behavior. Any attempt to make the term operational in terms of groups of people is difficult. Among the numerous definitions that have been offered (Kroeber & Kluckhohn, 1952) is the theme that culture is composed of habitual patterns of behavior that are characteristic of a group of people. These shared behavioral patterns are transmitted from one generation to the next through symbolic communication. Fairchild (1970) defined culture as "all behavioral patterns socially acquired and socially transmitted by means of symbols, including customs, techniques, beliefs, institutions and material objects" (p. 80). The primary transmitter of culture is language, which enables people to learn, experience, and share their traditions and customs. Given the behavioral heterogeneity of ethnic and racial groups in the United States, it is important to consider both the diversity and the similarities found within any particular group.

Stewart (1972) identified five areas in his summary of cultural assumptions and values. These five components of culture are:

1. *Activity*. How do people approach activity? How important are goals in life? Who makes decisions? What is the nature of problem solving?
2. *Definitions of social relations*. How are roles defined? How do people relate to those whose status is different? How are sex roles defined? What is the meaning of friendship?
3. *Motivation*. What is the achievement orientation of the culture? Is cooperation or competition emphasized?
4. *Perception of the world*. What is the predominant world view? What is the predominant view on human nature? What is the predominant view on the nature of truth? How is time defined? What is the nature of property?
5. *Perception of self and the individual*. How is self defined? Where is a person's identity determined? What is the nature of the individual? What kinds of individuals are valued and respected?

For the purposes in this chapter, African Americans, Asian Americans, Native Americans, and Mexican Americans are viewed as four cultural groups that differ from the dominant culture, and that represent the majority of people in culturally different groups in the United States. The focus of the components of culture apply to other groups as well, because I do not wish to diminish the importance of smaller groups in the United States. Although there are many within-group differences in any ethnic group, there are nonetheless within-group similarities. These similarities are often viewed as between-group differences (from the dominant culture) significant enough to qualify each of the four as a cultural group, across definitions of the term.

In this discussion, the term *cultural group* is used to describe both the dominant culture and the culture of ethnic or racial groups. Such an approach provides for ease in presenting descriptions but it does much more than provide a simple approach. What is communicated is a commitment to cultural diversity as an effective educational strategy rather than the view that the culturally different are culturally deprived. Such a commitment places all cultures on an even plane and is necessary for the implementation of many of the ideas that follow.

The Dominant Culture

There are a number of values that many sociologists and cultural anthropologists characterize as the "American culture," though the term serves to discount the people of Canada and Central and South America; it could be more accurately stated as "U.S. culture." These values, beliefs, and attitudes have deeper historical roots, are held by more people, and are believed to serve as a basis of much of what is done in the United States.

Kluckholn and Strodtbeck (1961) and Williams (1970) provided insight on value orientations as a means of identifying fundamental characteristics of the U.S. culture—what might be called the world view of the dominant culture. Some of the characteristics of the dominant culture's world view that have a major impact on the educational system include: competition (winning is valued over cooperative endeavors), adherence to rigid time schedules (learning is regulated in specific time periods), dualistic thinking (emphasizing that there is a single "right" answer), linear reasoning (cause and effect), rugged individualism (valuing the individual more than a sense of community), mastery and control of nature (humans are more worthy; nature and animals are here for human pleasure or economic good), action orientation (doing rather than being), future orientation (delayed gratification), direct eye contact (control and power), written tradition (written expression valued more than oral expression), and pragmatism (ends justify the means).

Each of these values is important and useful in our culture. They are particularly useful for persons for whom they come naturally as a way of life. These values are useful when they help people work through ordinary problems faced in their lives. However, these values are not the only values that are beneficial to problem solving. There are other important and useful values and world views. Some cultures emphasize cooperation (a sense of community), adherence to less rigid time schedules, relativistic thinking (in relation to other factors, in terms of context), circular reasoning (consideration of multiple views), collateral or linear relationships, subjugation to nature (humans in harmony with nature), being (experiencing) orientation, present orientation, avoidance of eye contact, oral tradition, and a traditional orientation to problem solving (solice through tradition).

The things we do in education are based, to some extent, on a value orientation. Educational practices, like those in business or in athletics, reflect the values of the culture in which the practices take place. Heretofore, the United States has favored the dominant culture's orientation, to the exclusion of many culturally diverse people. Educators must take care that our practices not only reflect the values of the dominant culture but the values of the culturally different as well. We must incorporate more than one world view into our theories, research, and techniques.

We begin to operationalize change when we assess and understand how we view people—as individual members of society or in terms of identification with a group. In schools, from the onset, the primary emphasis is on the individual student, individual identity, individual accomplishment, and individual reward. Examples are spelling bees that recognize the best speller in a class, special privileges that are granted to the student who finishes first or scores highest, and the prestige granted to valedictorians. For students from cultures where group or community values are primary, the use of competition and individual recognition may be educational techniques that frustrate and discourage them from attempting some task, and thus are inappropriate.

Cross-Cultural Awareness Continuum

The cross-cultural awareness continuum (Fig. 9.1) (Locke, 1996) serves to illustrate the levels of awareness through which school personnel must develop in order to provide effective and relevant educational experiences for culturally different students. The continuum is linear and arranged hierarchically with each level building upon those before it. Obtaining competence in cross-cultural relationships is best described as a life-long, ongoing process rather than a product of a knowledge base or previous experience. Thus, the process of growth from self-awareness (Level 1) to the acquisition of skills/techniques (Level 7) is flexible and accounts for the fact that individuals never achieve absolute mastery of any of the awareness levels.

Self-Awareness

The first stage that school personnel must explore is self-awareness. Self-understanding is a necessary condition before one begins the process of understanding others. Both intrapersonal and interpersonal dynamics must be considered as

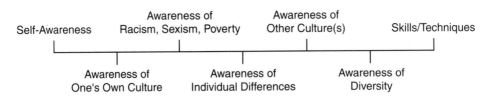

FIGURE 9.1   Cross-cultural awareness continuum.

important components in the projection of beliefs, attitudes, opinions, and values. The examination of one's own thoughts and feelings allows the educator a better understanding of the cultural "baggage" each brings to the situation. This process of introspection is a vital element of understanding one's own culture and is necessary before a framework can be created with which to explore cultural phenomena at the various levels.

Awareness of One's Own Culture

Educators bring cultural baggage to the educational situation—baggage that may cause certain things to be taken for granted or create expectations about behaviors and manners. For example, consider your own name and the meaning associated with it. Ask yourself the cultural significance of your name. Could your name have some historical significance to cultures other than the culture of your origin? There may be some relationship between your name and the order of your birth. There may have been a special ceremony conducted when you were named. Your name may have a significant relevance to your family's history.

The naming process of a child is but one of the many examples of how cultural influences are evident and varied. Language is very specific to one's cultural group, whether formal, informal, verbal, or nonverbal. Language often determines the cultural networks in which an individual participates and contributes to the values that may be culture specific.

Awareness of Racism, Sexism, and Poverty

Racism, sexism, and poverty are all aspects of a culture that must be understood from the perspective of how individuals view their effect upon themselves and upon others. The "ism" words themselves are obviously powerful terms and frequently evoke some defensiveness (Locke & Hardaway, 1980). Even when racism and sexism are denied as a part of one's personal belief system, one must nevertheless recognize existence as a part of the larger culture in which one functions. Even if the anguish of poverty is not felt personally, educators must closely examine their own beliefs regarding others who are economically less fortunate. The educator must understand the devastating effects poverty has on all facets of an individual's life and must see the role that education plays in solving the problem.

Exploration of the issues of racism, sexism, and poverty may be facilitated by a systems approach. Such an exploration may lead to examination of the differences between individual behaviors and organizational behaviors, or what might be called the difference between *personal prejudice* and *institutional prejudice*. The influence of organizational prejudice can be seen in the attitudes and beliefs of the school system in which the educator works. Similarly, the awareness that church memberships frequently exist along racial lines, or that some social organizations restrict their membership to one sex, should help school personnel come to grips with the organizational prejudice that they may be supporting solely on the basis of participation in a particular organization.

Awareness of Individual Differences

One of the greatest pitfalls of the novice educator is to overgeneralize things learned about a specific culture as applicable to all members of that culture. Stereotyping occurs when a single thread of commonality is presumed to be characteristic of all group members simply because it is observed in a few. On the contrary, cultural group membership does not mean that one must sacrifice individual differences or uniqueness. Contrary to the educator's belief that all students should be treated as "individuals" exclusively, all students must be seen as both individuals *and* members of their particular cultural group.

In the strictest sense, belief in individualism fails to take into account the collective family–community relationship that exists in many cultural groups. A real danger lies in the possibility that school personnel may unwittingly discount cultural influences and subconsciously believe they understand the culturally different when, in fact, they view others from their own culture's point of view. This belief is called ethnocentrism. In practice, what is put forth as a belief in individualism can become a disregard for any culturally specific behaviors that influence student behaviors. In sum, educators must be aware of individual differences and come to believe in the uniqueness of the individual before moving to the level of awareness of other cultures.

Awareness of Other Culture(s)

The four previously discussed levels of the continuum provide the background and foundation necessary for school personnel to explore the varied dynamics of other cultural groups. Much of cross-cultural emphasis is placed on African Americans, Native Americans, Mexican Americans or Hispanics, and Asian Americans. Language is of great significance and uniqueness to each of these cultural groups, rendering standard English less than complete in communication of ideas. Mastery of another language is indeed helpful but not required for awareness of other cultures. However, it is necessary for school personnel to be sensitive to words that are unique to a particular culture, as well as to body language and other nonverbal behaviors to which cultural significance is attached.

Hofstede (1980) researched cultural differences in forty countries and determined four criteria by which cultural groups may be said to differ: power distance, uncertainty avoidance, individualism/collectivism, and masculinity/femininity. These cultural universals carry significant implications for the student of other cultural groups. Similarly, school personnel can benefit by the use of the Kluckholn and Strodtbeck (1961) and Williams' (1970) schemes presented earlier in a study of the values or lifestyles of culturally different students.

Awareness of Diversity

The culture of the United States has often been referred to as a *melting pot*. This characterization suggests that people came to the United States from many different countries and blended into one new culture. Thus, old-world practices were altered, discarded, or maintained within the context of the new culture. Obviously, as change is a constant agent, some actual "melting" occurred. Yet, for the most part, many cultural groups did not fully participate in the melting pot process. Many African American, Native American, Mexican American, and Asian American cultural practices were not welcomed as the new culture formed. In fact, members of these culturally different groups have been encouraged to give up their cultural practices and to adopt the values, beliefs, and attitudes of the so-called melting pot, while not being fully welcomed.

Of more recent vintage is the term *salad bowl*, which implies that the culture of the United States is capable of retaining aspects from all cultures (the various ingredients). Viewed in this manner, we are seen as capable of living, working, and growing together while maintaining a unique cultural identity. *Rainbow coalition* is another term used in a recent political campaign to represent the same idea. Such concepts reflect what many have come to refer to as a multicultural or pluralistic society, where certain features of each culture are encouraged and appreciated by other cultural groups.

Skills/Techniques

Next on the continuum is implementation of what has been learned about working with culturally different groups while adding specific techniques to the repertoire of teaching skills of school personnel. Before educators can effectively work with students of diverse cultural heritage, they must have developed general competence as a teacher. Passage through the awareness continuum constitutes some degree of professional growth and will contribute to an increase in overall teaching effectiveness, but it goes much further than that. School personnel must be aware of learning theory and how theory relates to the development of psychological-cultural factors. Educators must understand the relationship between theory and classroom teaching strategies or practices. Most importantly, school personnel must have developed a sense of worth as educators in their own cultures before attaining competence in teaching culturally different students.

Developing a level of cross-cultural understanding will not substitute for demonstration of specific skills. If school personnel lack competence in the professional skills of teaching, no amount of cross-cultural awareness will compensate for this inadequacy. In fact, it appears that for effective cross-cultural educational experiences to occur, the advantage goes to the educator who has a great deal of teaching competence rather than to the educator who has little teaching competence and a great deal of cross-cultural understanding.

Language in Multicultural Contexts

If school personnel are to become competent in a multicultural context, it is necessary to examine the system of cross-cultural communication. Communication is the process of communicating, sending and receiving messages, understanding and being understood. It is accepted that words mean different things in different cultures, and abstract concepts are very difficult to communicate across cultures—especially so in the United States, where communication is linear. The content of a message is usually explicit and to the point. One is not required to interpret the meaning of a message in order to receive the full content. In other countries, particularly in African cultures, communication is circular. Less information is contained in the verbal part of the message; there is more meaning in the context.

Mehrabian (1981) characterized the content of communication in the dominant culture of the United States as 7 percent verbal, 38 percent vocal (tone, rate, pitch, and volume), and 55 percent facial (nonverbal). Thus, among members of the dominant culture of the United States, confusion in communication is likely to occur when there is inconsistency between the verbal message and either the vocal or facial message. When the speaker is from a culture other than the dominant culture, even more confusion is likely.

The vignette submitted by a practicing school counselor (Box 9.1) is an excellent example of problems that might be encountered when communicating across cultures within school settings. The barrier to effective cross-communication in this

---

BOX 9.1

Vignette

The local elementary school in which I served as a counseling intern and subsequently as an interim guidance counselor is the site of a transitional bilingual education (TBE) program for Vietnamese students residing in the local school district. A native teacher heads this program. He was hired late in the summer prior to the school year during which this program was introduced. As a result, he spent the first four to six weeks planning his curriculum and setting up his classroom, before receiving students. This delay caused confusion and resentment on the part of the school staff, who were anxious to have somewhere to send their Vietnamese students for part of the school day where they would both comprehend and be understood by an adult who was from their own culture. Some of these teachers had little patience for a colleague who was developing his curriculum during school hours while seemingly ignoring those children for whom he had the ultimate responsibility.

As the weeks wore on before the official inception of the TBE program, resentment continued to build toward this Vietnamese teacher. I understood both sides of the issue, and sympathized with everyone involved. While it would have been inappropriate to intervene directly as a facilitator, I did feel a certain obligation to do just that when the opportunity arose, as it did many times indirectly. I realized the challenge of bridging the cultural gap between this person from a culture totally foreign to my own; I wondered just how much that gap interfered with a smooth adjustment into our school community for this individual.

I became acutely aware of the distance to be bridged after spending a day outside of school helping this teacher; our ability to communicate and understand each other was quite narrow, not for lack of comprehension of the English language per se, but rather for lack of familiarity with each other's cultural worlds and consciousness.

BOX **9.1** *Continued*

Even after the TBE program had begun, stress between this Vietnamese man and many staff members continued. His style of communication was often befuddling and annoying to them; at times his behavior seemed inappropriate when judged by the standards with which the American school personnel were familiar. I often served as facilitator between the two groups; however, I myself experienced a variety of feelings toward this individual, some of which were negative. Such impressions disturbed me as I attempted to gauge how much of our relationship was defined by cultural stereotyping, and how much by difference in personalities. This question begged examination and careful analysis for without it no substantial gains would be possible in order to overcome the vast cultural distance between us.

Toward such an end, I organized a workshop for the pupil personnel staff with the purpose of offering them a brief introduction to the Vietnamese culture and some of its values, as they pertained to academic and family life. I invited a woman from the community who was quite familiar with the Vietnamese population in our town through her extensive volunteer efforts. Although she was not a native Vietnamese, but rather an American, her multicultural knowledge and experience with this particular population far outweighed my own, and her willingness to share her insights was equally impressive. The staff expressed gratitude to us both at the conclusion of this hour-long informational session. They listened attentively to her introductory remarks, participated actively in a role-playing exercise she led, and asked specific questions hand-tailored to their particular roles with the Vietnamese children under their care. They not only requested a follow-up meeting (which never took place due to a lack of commitment of the school administrator involved) but also suggested a similar workshop for the entire school staff, which similarly never occurred.

Although this workshop was in and of itself a success, as a single event it merely served to "break the ice" between the two cultures. The limitations were many, including the fact of an American communicating her secondhand knowledge of the Vietnamese culture. This reality left me with many doubts and disquieting feelings. The potential implications and interpretations were disturbing—why had we not invited the Vietnamese teacher himself to conduct such a workshop? The answer lay in the problem itself—namely, his communication style, which both alienated and perplexed so many on the school staff.

---

situation might be characterized as ethnocentrism; the Vietnamese teacher was being viewed by the standards and customs of the dominant group. The vignette serves as an example of how ethnocentrism serves only to widen the gap between people from different cultures.

The Worldview Component of Cultural Identity

One who studies other cultures seriously will soon realize that members of groups other than one's own often perceive the concepts of nature, time, and community from an entirely different point of view. As school personnel encounter students from diverse backgrounds, they must come to understand the concept and implications of a world-view approach. Jackson (1975) and Sue (1975) have conceptualized this idea and defined *world view* as how a person perceives his or her relationship with the world. World views are composed of our attitudes, values, opinions, and beliefs. World views are influenced by our cultural heritage and life experiences, and subsequently affect how we think, make decisions, behave, or define events (Sue & Sue, 1999).

Throughout the history of the United States, members of the dominant cultural group have been in the position to maintain world views indicative of a Eurocentric perspective. The result for African Americans, Native Americans, Asian Americans, Mexican Americans, and other culturally different people has been a subordinate position within society and subjection to discriminatory practices. To better understand the relevance of this practice upon different cultures, world view, as a concept, must include the interactional effects of many variables such as socioeconomic conditions, religious beliefs, and gender issues (Sue & Sue, 1999).

Interactional conditions vary within cultural groups as well as between cultural groups. Interactional conditions help explain why all members of a particular culture do not share identical views of the world. An example would be world views of an upper-class African American family residing in Silicon Valley, California, compared to the world views of a lower-class African American family residing in Bedford-Stuyvesant, New York. The educator attempting to teach children of these two families would be advised to approach the task of cross-cultural understanding and effective communication through the use of a world-view matrix based on Sue and Sue's (1999) model. Without such effort, educators would probably interact and respond in accordance with their own conditioned values, assumptions, and perspectives of reality.

The Dimensions of Locus of Control

Control is a pivotal issue when looking at relationships between individuals and between groups. Indeed, racism (prejudice plus power to implement prejudices) can exist only in the group that has control. Internal control (IC) and external control (EC) are dimensional concepts derived from the work of Rotter (1966) and are applicable as a framework for cross-cultural understanding. *Internal control* refers to the belief that people can determine or shape their fate, that their actions are reinforcements to catalysts of events. *External control*, on the other hand, refers to the belief that the future is determined more by luck or chance, that the actions of people are independent of rather than the precipitator of events.

Rotter (1966) further stated that people tend to learn one of two world views: the locus of control rests either with themselves or with some external force. Individuals found to be high on a scale of internal control (Lefcourt, 1966; Rotter, 1975) exhibited: (1) greater attempts at mastering the environment, (2) superior coping strategies, (3) better cognitive processing of information, (4) higher achievement motivation, (5) greater social action involvement, and (6) greater value placement on skill-determined rewards. Additional research (Sanger & Alker, 1972; Strickland, 1973) found that culturally different groups and women are overrepresented on the external end of the IC–EC continuum. The implication for school personnel is that culturally different students may exhibit a high external orientation ("There is nothing I can do about it," and "It's no use fighting the system") and be misread as apathetic, lazy, unwilling, or uncooperative.

Although the internal–external dimension is a useful starting point in developing cross-cultural understanding, it places little consideration on specific cultural differences or life experiences. For that reason, Sue and Sue (1999) modified the IC–EC dimension for use with cross-cultural groups. The implication for school personnel is that they should not assume high externality as an indicator of motivation when working with culturally different groups. In fact, high externality may be due to chance, cultural dictates that are viewed as benevolent, or the influence of prejudice and discrimination. An example would be an educator who works with a Native American student whose cultural values dictate an external orientation and who faces an historical experience of oppression in the United States. To view the Native American student as high in external control, with all the assumptions of that trait attached, discounts the potential influence of realistic obstacles.

The Dimensions of Locus of Responsibility

Attribution theory is a collection of ideas about when and how people form causal inferences; it examines how individuals combine and use information to reach causal judgments (Fiske & Taylor, 1984). Research concerned with how people go about making sense of other people and themselves was being conducted during the same period that Rotter drew his conclusions about individual orientation toward environment (externals) or toward self (internals).

When considered as a dimension, locus of responsibility is a measure of degree of blame or acceptance of responsibility placed on the individual or placed on the environment. An example would be the overrepresentation of African Americans who live at or below the poverty level in the United States; their lower standard of living could be attributed to personal inadequacies or attributed to discrimination and lack of opportunities. Envision locus of responsibility as a continuum where at one end we place blame on the individual and at the other end we place blame on the system. Is blame placed only at either end of the continuum adequate as an explanation for poverty? Is blame placed only at either end of the continuum adequate for use with culturally different groups?

Rather than operationalize a simplistic view of locus of responsibility, Sue and Sue (1999) suggested that we refrain from perpetuating the myth about people's ability to control their own fates. Educators must come to understand that a young African American male may be quite realistic when he reports that institutional racism prevented his employment. It has simply not been a part of the history of this country for all people to be able to "make it on their own."

Sue and Sue's Formation of Worldviews

The two psychological dimensions of locus of control and locus of responsibility have been discussed as background for a discussion of world views. Sue and Sue's (1999) matrix of locus of control (Fig. 9.2) shows how both dimensions may be placed to intersect and thus form four quadrants:

1. **Internal locus of control–internal locus of responsibility (IC–IR) (quadrant I)** is a view typical of Western culture. There are feelings of high internal personal control combined with personal attributions for success or failure ("I made it happen," "I am successful"). Value is placed on self-reliance, pragmatism, individualism, status through achievement, and control over nature and others. The individual is held accountable for all that transpires.
2. **External locus of control–internal locus of responsibility (EC–IR) (quadrant II)** individuals are most likely to accept the dominant culture's definition of self-responsibility yet exhibit very little real control over how each individual's role is defined by others. EC–IR individuals work hard at not being different but do not really participate in the majority culture.
3. **External locus of control–external locus of responsibility (EC–ER) (quadrant III)** individuals feel very little can be done about prejudice and discrimination. Injustice is out of their control and not their responsibility. They likely will either "give up" or try to placate those in power.
4. **Internal locus of control–external locus of responsibility (IC–ER) (quadrant IV)** individuals are culturally different people who do not accept their difference as due to their inherent weakness. They believe they can shape their future if given the chance; however, they are realistic about the barriers (prejudice and discrimination) to be faced and overcome. Racial pride, close identity with their cultural group, and perhaps some degree of militancy may be seen in the IC–ER position.

If school personnel knew a student's degree of internality or externality on the two dimensions, it would be theoretically possible to place the student into a quadrant. However, Sue and Sue (1999) speculated that various culturally different groups would not be randomly distributed throughout the four quadrants. Education in this country tends to fall in the IC–IR quadrant. Students are seen as able to take

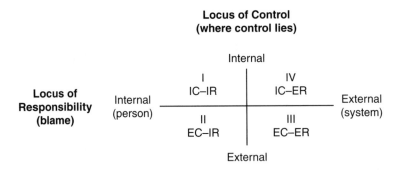

FIGURE 9.2   Graphic representation of worldviews.

action and be responsible for their behaviors (both success and failure). School personnel need to recognize the quadrant most reflective of their teaching style and to recognize and legitimize the quadrant in which others' world views may fall.

Students in the IC–ER position may be very difficult to work with in the school setting. They may require action in the community such as setting up job interviews or helping fill out job applications. IC–IR students from culturally different groups may not be self-assertive. EC–IR students may feel self-hatred, and re-education becomes necessary to get students to become aware of the wider sociopolitical forces at work. EC–ER students must be taught new coping skills to deal with people. Educators must skillfully plan and guide success experiences for students in this quadrant.

The culturally effective educator is the one most able to generate the widest repertoire of teaching skills consistent with the lifestyles and values of culturally different students. A balance must be reached between questioning and giving suggestions. School personnel need to come to understand that each world view has positive aspects. The role of the educator is to help culturally different students integrate aspects of each world view in order to maximize effectiveness and well being (Sue & Sue, 1999).

Strategies for Improved Competence

Concerned educators have long wrestled with issues of professional development. Issues of multicultural competence are important to the professional development of all educators. The recognition of this need implies acceptance by educators of the need to bring educational experiences into harmony with the cultural experiences of students from diverse cultural backgrounds. And, such harmony is not easily obtained because it requires a focus on both content and process. The change in content begins as educators ensure that curriculum materials are reflective of and relevant to various groups in the culture. Changing the process involves deep examination of beliefs, values, and attitudes of each educator, individually.

The strategies that follow are divided by content and process. With them we can increase our capacity to educate students where they are and thus make the most of their capabilities and talents in the classroom. Strategies for improvement of multicultural content include the following:

1. Develop attitudes, skills, and techniques so that knowledge of human relations, including racial and ethnic relations, can be translated into learning experiences for students.
2. Conduct surveys of present curricula materials being used to ensure accurate representation of racial and ethnic groups.
3. Identify and use supplemental materials that provide additional information on varying racial and ethnic groups. Include curriculum materials and information on all cultural groups present in the classroom, the school, or the school district.
4. Select subject matter content and materials that foster cultural pluralism. Use diverse individual and community characteristics and resources to supplement

text material so that students see a connection between the subjects they are studying and their lives.

5. Evaluate ways in which topics related to racism, prejudice, and discrimination can be reflected in instructional materials.
6. Increase personal knowledge of other group customs, values, language, contributions to society, social structure, and other factors of racial and ethnic identity.
7. Collect materials that portray culturally diverse groups in positive ways and request that these materials be added to school libraries.

Multicultural competence is much more than a curriculum whose course content is reflective of various racial and ethnic groups. Earlier, some suggestions based on the ASCA (1989) strategies and the cross-cultural awareness continuum (Locke, 1996) were presented. The process strategies that follow (Locke, 1989) are aimed at providing educators with additional ways to improve multicultural competence.

1. Be open and honest in relationships with culturally different students. Leave yourself open to culturally different attitudes and encourage culturally different students to be open and honest with you about issues related to their cultures. Talk positively with students about their physical characteristics and cultural heritage. Make it clear that a person's identity is never an acceptable reason for rejection by others.
2. Learn as much as possible about your own culture. One can appreciate another culture much more if there is first an appreciation of one's own. Understand, honestly face, and improve the knowledge of yourself and this will lead to positive reactions to others.
3. Seek to genuinely respect and appreciate culturally different attitudes and behaviors. Demonstrate that you both recognize and value different cultures. Provide opportunities for students to interact with other students who are racially or culturally different from themselves. Help students learn the difference between feelings of superiority and feelings of self-esteem and pride in one's heritage.
4. Take advantage of all available opportunities to participate in activities of cultural groups in the communities of the cultural groups. Invite persons from the various communities to your classroom or school throughout the school year. Work to understand and analyze the development of students' social, home, and community relationships. Try to obtain direct involvement with members of racial and cultural groups and/or with organizations working to improve human relationships, including intergroup relations.
5. Keep in mind that culturally different students are both unique individuals and members of their cultural group as well. Strive to keep a reasonable balance between your views of students as unique beings and cultural group members.
6. Eliminate all your behaviors that suggest prejudice, racism, or discrimination against culturally different populations and work toward elimination of such behaviors from your students and colleagues. Teach your students how to

recognize stereotypes and how to challenge biases. Involve students in taking relevant action on issues important in their lives.

7. Encourage teachers and administrators to institutionalize practices in each school that acknowledge the contributions of various racial and ethnic groups. Strive to work together toward agreed-upon solutions and interactions with respect for differences.

8. Hold high expectations of all students and encourage all who work with culturally diverse students to do likewise. Initiate activities to build self-identity and teach the value of differences among people.

9. Ask questions about the culturally diverse. Learn as much as you can about the various cultural groups and share what you learn with your classes and your colleagues. Recognize that the cultural heritage of students is as much a part of their make-up as their physical characteristics.

10. Develop culturally specific programs to foster the psychological development of culturally different children. Be sensitive to classroom grouping procedures that result in racially or ethnically identifiable groups.

School systems that increase their strategy competence become empowered to make the educational experience of diverse populations more relevant, meaningful, and beneficial. We have long held the view that all children can learn. The question becomes "Can we, as educators, teach?" When a child fails in school, it is not a failure in isolation, for the school has also failed. The effect on society in terms of loss of human potential is incalculable. We, as educators, therefore must hold ourselves accountable and continually examine ourselves and evaluate the appropriateness of our teaching methods, materials, and experiences. Truly, if *we* can teach it, *they* can learn it.

Summary

Educators have struggled long and hard with a variety of approaches related to education of the culturally different. Issues of culturally sensitive education have been explored from the perspective of a need for educational systems to examine the values being taught and how these values affect the dominant culture and members of culturally different groups. Needed changes have been explored from the perspective of both content and process, while recognizing that many attempts at altering educational systems to educate all students have failed and some have even worked to the disadvantage of culturally different students.

Any successful strategies must begin with a system focus on issues of cultural diversity. System priorities must serve as the foundation for any efforts by individual educators. The commitment of the system, a belief that students can and want to learn (If you can teach it, I can learn it), and a teacher who values the worth and dignity of all students will together result in successful experiences for all. The picture that emerges is one of a school where teachers are interested in students, students are interested in learning, cultural diversity is valued, and educational goals are achieved.

DISCUSSION QUESTIONS

1. Discuss the importance of "within group" and "between group" variations in cultural groups in the United States.

2. Identify the principles and a rationale for including them in a diversity policy for a school system.

3. Define culture. Defend your definition in terms of why elements are either included or excluded from your definition.

4. Describe the "dominant culture" of the United States.

5. Why is self-awareness identified as an early step in cross-cultural awareness?

6. Identify and discuss elements of your own cultural identity that you believe impact how you relate to others.

7. Why are racism, sexism, and poverty important elements in cross-cultural understanding?

8. Why is it important for one to focus on both individual differences and cultural group characteristics at the same time?

9. What do you see as the most important elements that distinguish one cultural group from another and why are these elements important?

10. How does one focus on cultural group characteristics without stereotyping the individuals under study?

11. Compare and contrast the phrases "melting pot" and "salad bowl" as manifestations of culture in the United States.

12. Why is language so important in cross-cultural understanding?

13. Provide two concrete examples of the Mehrabian characterization of communication content.

14. Using the Sue and Sue world view model, identify where you place yourself, and explain what personal characteristics you identify which are consistent with placement in this quadrant.

15. Using the Sue and Sue world view model, identify where you might place a student with whom you might have the greatest difficulty teaching. How might you reconcile the difficulties you might experience in such a situation?

16. Why are personal attitudes so important in cross-cultural understanding?

17. What objectives would you have for yourself for participating in a cross-cultural activity in your community?

18. Which is more important in cross-cultural education—content or process? Why?

19. How can you concretely demonstrate that you genuinely respect and appreciate culturally different students?

20. Identify at least ten questions you might ask about culturally different students and their culture which would help you understand them and their learning style in your classroom.

REFERENCES

American School Counselor Association. (1989). American School Counselor Association position statement: Cross/multi-cultural counseling. *Elementary School Guidance and Counseling, 23*, 322–323.

Brookover, W. B. (1985). Can we make schools effective for minority students? *Journal of Negro Education, 54*, 257–268.

Fairchild, H. P. (Ed.). (1970). *Dictionary of sociology and related sciences*. Totowa, NJ: Rowan and Allanheld.

Fiske, S. T. & Taylor, S. E. (1994). *Social cognition*. New York: Random House.

Hofstede, G. (1980). Motivation, leadership and organization: Do American theories apply abroad? *Organizational Dynamics, 9*, 42–63.

Jackson, B. (1975). Black identity development. *Journal of Education Diversity, 2*, 19–25.

Kluckholn, F. & Strodtbeck, F. (1991). *Variations in value orientations*. Evanston, IL: Row, Peterson.

Kroeber, A. L. & Kluckhohn, C. (1952). *Culture: A critical review of concepts and definitions*. New York: Vintage Books.

Leftcourt, H. (1966). Internal versus control of reinforcement: A review. *Psychological Bulletin, 65*, 206–220.

Locke, D. C. (1989). Fostering the self-esteem of African-American children. *Elementary School Guidance and Counseling, 23*, 254–259.

Locke, D. C. (1996). Multicultural counseling issues. In A. J. Palmo & W. J. Weikel (Eds.), *Foundations of mental health counseling* (2nd ed.) (pp. 137–156). Springfield, IL: Charles C Thomas.

Locke, D. C. & Hardaway, Y. V. (1980). Moral perspectives in interracial settings. In D. Cochrane & M. Manley-Casimir (Eds.), *Moral education: Practical approaches* (pp. 269–285). New York: Praeger.

Mehrabian, A. (1981). *Silent messages*. Belmont, CA: Wadsworth.

Pine, G. J. & Hilliard, A. G. (1990). Rx for racism: Imperatives for America's schools. *Phi Delta Kappa, 71*, 593–599.

Rotter, J. (1966). Generalized expectancies for internal versus external control of reinforcement. *Psychological Monographs, 80*, 1–28.

Rotter, J. (1975). Some problems and misconceptions related to the construct of internal versus external control of reinforcement. *Journal of Consulting and Clinical Psychology, 43*, 56–67.

Sanger, S. P. & Alker, H. A. (1972). Dimensions of internal–external locus of control and the women's liberation movement. *Journal of Social Issues, 28*, 115–129.

Stewart, E. C. (1972). *American cultural patterns*. La-Grange Park, IL: Intercultural Network.

Strickland, B. (1973). Delay of gratification and internal locus of control in children. *Journal of Consulting and Clinical Psychology, 40*, 338.

Sue, D. W. (1975). Asian Americans: Social-psychological forces affecting their life styles. In S. Picou & R. Campbell (Eds.), *Career behavior of special groups* (pp. 97–121). Columbus, OH: Charles E. Merrill.

Sue, D. W. & Sue, D. (1999). *Counseling the culturally different: Theory and practice*. New York: John Wiley & Sons.

Williams, R. M. (1970). *American society: A sociological interpretation*. New York: Alfred Knopf.

AUTHOR NOTE

Don C. Locke is Director of the Asheville Graduate Center of the University of North Carolina. He has served as Head of the Department of Counselor Education at North Carolina State University in Raleigh; president of Chi Sigma Iota International; and president of the Association for Counselor Education and Supervision. He is the recipient of the Professional Development Award from the American Counseling Association (1996). He is the author or coauthor of more than 60 publications, with a current focus on multicultural issues. Books include *Increasing Multicultural Understanding, Psychological Techniques for Teachers*, and *Culture and Diversity Issues in Counseling*.

10 Multicultural Training in Schools as an Expansion of the Counselor's Role

PAUL B. PEDERSEN

Professor Emeritus, Syracuse University
Visiting Professor, University of Hawaii

OBJECTIVES

1. To demonstrate how multicultural training can be included in the professional role of school counselors
2. To describe the importance of multicultural training outcomes in schools
3. To describe multicultural competencies in training designs
4. To develop a multicultural training plan of awareness, knowledge, and skill objectives suitable for schools
5. To review constructive conflict management training in schools

With the widely documented recent demographic shift toward increasing student diversity, especially in urban schools, the need for multicultural training has become more urgent. This chapter will provide some guidelines, identify some examples, describe some competencies, and present some models of multicultural training in schools. These materials show how training is an expansion of the school counselor's role as it relates to teachers, administrators, parents, students, and other counselors in the school system. Colbert and Colbert (2003) present a taxonomy of interventions integrating the perspectives of the individual student, the school, and the community which highlights the broad context in which multicultural training must take place.

The Multicultural Mandate

The American School Counselor Association (ASCA) has targeted the need to provide appropriate multicultural services in schools to promote maximum development since 1988 (ASCA, 1988). In 1992 (ASCA, 1992) they declared a competency in multicultural counseling to be an ethical obligation of school counselors. While this mandate targets the conventional school counselor functions such as pedagogical services, referral, services, accountability services, family consultation, career development and placement, and assessment services (Baker, 1992) it applies equally well to the training functions highlighted in this chapter. Among both the formal and traditional roles of the counselor the multicultural emphasis has usually highlighted those that involve family consultation, career guidance or placement services, and assessment services (Kisellica, Changizi, Cureton, & Gridley, 1995). This chapter will go beyond the scope of such roles to explore nonformal and nontraditional expansions of the school counselor's role through training.

Herring (1997) highlights the importance of counselor-led support groups, assessing the knowledge of school counselors and performance assessment as three important preservice areas of school counselor training programs. These examples of training just as easily apply to the in-service training that school counselors provide for themselves, one another, and their clients in the school context. Just as with teachers, there is a new emphasis on continued in-service training of counselors in a rapidly changing field of counseling so they stay current in their field. Their knowledge and expertise can be evaluated through performance appraisals.

In addition to the personal mandate and professional mandate for counselors to stay current there is also an increased interest by U.S. state legislatures to mandate increased training in multicultural issues. Pedersen (1994) describes state mandates for New York, California, Pennsylvania, Minnesota, and North Carolina as examples. These programs have emphasized competencies aimed at: (1) understanding the contributions and lifestyles of various cultural groups; (2) the recognition of dehumanizing biases, discrimination or prejudices, and the skills needed to change them in the trainee; (3) the need to create learning environments that contribute to the self-esteem of all persons and to positive interpersonal relations; and (4) skills that teach respect for human diversity and personal rights. Since that time other states have followed these models and established government mandates of their own.

Brislin and Horvath (1997) describe the research literature on training program outcomes focused on changes in participants' thinking, affective reactions, and actual behaviors. Training can change how people think by increasing their awareness, knowledge, and skill in working with other cultures, by increasing the complexity of their thinking to take multiple viewpoints, and to identify new alternative solutions for familiar problems. Culture assimilators are one well-documented approach: changing people's thinking by offering multiple interpretations of the same situation and discussing the consequence of each response. Training can also change how people feel about a situation or a group, focusing on emotional aspects of "culture shock" (Pedersen, 1995). Culture shock occurs when: (1) one has to adapt to an unfamiliar situation; (2) there exists a sense of loss or deprivation; (3) there is rejection by or of a new culture; (4) there is confusion in what can be expected of others or of self; (5) unexpected anxiety and disgust surface; and (6) feelings of helplessness pervade. Changing people's behavior is perhaps the easiest and most frequently oversimplified outcome of training, especially if the behavior is changed by force. Interpreting or changing behaviors without regard to the cultural context in which that behavior was learned and is displayed is dangerous. Good training is defined by positive goals and by long-term outcomes.

The four goals of most multicultural training approaches cited by Cushner and Brislin (1997) are: (1) assisting people to overcome obstacles that could interfere with the enjoyment they experience or their sense of well being; (2) developing positive and respectful relationships with members of the host culture—an important but difficult goal to attain; (3) assisting people to accomplish the tasks associated with their work or studies; and (4) helping people deal with the inevitable stress that results from adapting to an unfamiliar culture.

The three outcomes by which most multicultural educational training programs are typically evaluated are student mastery, increase in knowledge, and student empowerment. Student mastery relates to the degree by which individuals can control events in an environment resulting in self control or "internal" locus of control. Learning a language would be an example of mastery. Increasing knowledge might be especially appropriate when working with immigrants, sojourners, and refugees learning about a new environment. Here the goal is to understand the consequences for the decisions made with regard to another cultural group. Critical incidents are particularly helpful, for example, to increase one's knowledge about another group. Student empowerment is directed toward feelings of alienation and powerlessness when there is not a good fit between students and the educational system. Training for empowerment usually makes a change in the social system of the educational context and involves advocacy for social change.

Most training can be classified as didactic, with topics being lectured about rather than experienced. Training can also be either culture specific or focused on a particular defined group as opposed to focused on culture in general and applied to all cross-cultural relationships. Thus training programs can be classified as culture general didactic, culture general experiential, culture specific didactic, and culture specific experiential. There are advantages and disadvantages to each of these classifications, so the trainer needs to carefully match each specific training activity to the local situation and its needs.

While there is much support for increased multicultural emphasis Sue (1999) points out there is also a strong group opposing multiculturalism. Some see multiculturalism as competing with established theories. Others associate multiculturalism with affirmative action, quotas, and emotional controversy. Some universalists see multiculturalism as heresy. Opponents argue that there is no accepted standard for describing or measuring competencies of multiculturalism, that multicultural goals are too unrealistic and complicated, that more research on multiculturalism is needed, that multicultural standards cannot include all possible groups, and that multiculturalism is "anti-White." This hostility toward multicultural education and counseling has led the Massachusetts Department of Education, for example, to drop all multicultural competence requirements for certification. The role of professional organizations, higher education institutions, and a commitment to understanding multicultural education is even more important in the face of this political hostility.

Just as multicultural schools are complex but not chaotic, so should multicultural training in schools be guided by a sequence of learning objectives that reflect the needs of both the student and the multicultural context. Training for multicultural competency rightly includes any and all methods relevant to the multicultural context from that culture's viewpoint. Training designs need to be comprehensive enough to include both culture-general and culture-specific perspectives, as well as experiential and didactic methods. The developmental sequence from awareness to knowledge to skill provides an eclectic framework for organizing the content of multicultural training in schools and a rationale for educational development in all multicultural settings.

Multicultural Competencies

A framework of multicultural competencies was first developed by a group responding to the APA Division 17 Education Committee mandate to establish clear guidelines for multicultural training. A three-stage developmental sequence was presented (Sue et al., 1982) that has become the basis for identifying multicultural competencies among counselors. Other publications have come out since that time elaborating the original competency statements (Arredondo et al., 1996; Pope-Davis & Coleman, 1997; Sue, Arredondo, & McDavis, 1992; Sue et al., 1998). As a result both the American Counseling Association and the American Psychological Association have adopted these competencies as standards for training.

The first stage—awareness provides the basis for accurate opinions, attitudes, and assumptions. It is essential to first become aware of implicit priorities given to selected attitudes, opinions, and values. Awareness presumes an ability to accurately compare and contrast alternative viewpoints, relate or translate priorities in a variety of cultural settings, identify constraints and opportunities in each cultural context, and have a clear understanding of one's own limitations. A well-defined awareness becomes essential for teaching, research, training, direct service, and consultation. If the awareness stage is overlooked in multicultural training, then the knowledge and skills may be based on false assumptions. If, however, training does not go beyond awareness objectives, the trainees will be frustrated by seeing the problems but not being able to do anything to change things.

As the second stage, knowledge provides the documentation and factual information necessary to move beyond awareness toward effective and appropriate change in multicultural settings. Through accumulated facts and information based on appropriate assumptions, it is possible to understand or comprehend other cultures from their own viewpoint. The facts and information about other cultures are available in the people, the literature, and the products of each culture at the local, national, and regional levels. The knowledge stage helps people access those facts and information, directs people to where the knowledge can be found, and identifies reliable sources of information with which to better understand the unfamiliar culture. If the knowledge stage is overlooked in training, then the cultural awareness and skill, however appropriate and effective, will lack grounding in essential facts and information about the multicultural context, and the resulting changes may be inappropriate. If, however, training does not go beyond the collection of facts and information about other cultures the clients will be overwhelmed by abstractions that may be true but will be impossible to apply in practice.

The third stage, skill, provides the ability to build on awareness and apply knowledge toward effective change in multicultural settings. Trained people will become skilled in planning, conducting, and evaluating the multicultural contexts in which they work. They will assess needs of other cultures accurately. They will work with interpreters and cultural informants from the other cultures. They will observe and understand behaviors of culturally different people. They will interact, counsel, interview, advise, and manage their tasks effectively in multicultural settings.

Pope-Davis and Dings (1995) provide the best discussion of the research attempting to measure and validate the multicultural competencies. Four different measures have been developed to assess multicultural awareness, knowledge, and skill. The Cross-Cultural Counseling Inventory-Revised (CCCI-R) by LaFromboise, Coleman, and Hernandez (1991) directs a supervisor to rate the counselor on twenty Likert-scale items. Ponterotto, Reiger, Barrett, and Sparks (1994) suggested that the CCI-R measures knowledge more than awareness. The Multicultural Aware-ness–Knowledge–Skill Survey (MAKSS) by D'Andrea, Daniels, and Heck (1991) includes 3 twenty-item scales to measure awareness, knowledge, and skills useful for examining student performance in relation to coursework for multicultural courses organized around the awareness–knowledge–skill structure. The Multicultural Coun-seling Awareness Scale-B described by Ponterotto et al. (1994) includes two subscales: a fourteen-item awareness scale and a twenty-eight-item knowledge/skills scale with some evidence that the subscales measure different factors. The Multicultural Coun-seling Inventory (MCI) by Sodowsky, Taffe, Gutkin, and Wise (1994) contains four factors: skills (eleven items), awareness (ten items), knowledge (eleven items), and counseling relationship (eight items). The advantage of the MCI is that it includes the relationship factor and the items describe behaviors rather than attitudes (Lee, 1999). Ponterotto et al. (1994) and Sue (1998) suggested that more study is needed and that the awareness–knowledge–skill measures of competency have not yet been satisfacto-rily validated.

Developing a Multicultural Training Plan

Whether you are preparing an individualized training plan for your own self-development or preparing a program for an audience of participants it is important to develop a plan that approaches training in a series of sequential tasks. Pedersen (2000a) provides a five-stage structure for planning a training activity with specific items for awareness, knowledge, and skill at all five task levels of developing the training plan. In describing this training plan the participants will be in many dif-ferent roles so "trainee" can mean student, teacher, or other school-related persons.

Awareness Needs

The first step in training is a "needs assessment" to determine which priorities are most needed among those persons being trained. Assessing awareness will look at whether participants can accurately judge a cultural situation from each's own as well as the other's cultural viewpoint. The trainee should be able to describe a situation in the target culture in such a way that a member of that culture will agree with the trainee's perception. The competencies for an assessment of awareness needs might include whether the trainee has:

- the ability to recognize direct and indirect communication styles
- sensitivity to nonverbal cues
- awareness of cultural and linguistic differences
- an interest in the culture
- sensitivity to the myths and stereotypes of the culture
- concern for the welfare of persons from another culture
- the ability to articulate elements of the trainee's own culture
- an appreciation of the importance of multicultural training
- awareness of the relationships between cultural groups
- the ability to define what is good and bad from the other culture's viewpoint

Knowledge Needs

Assessing the level of a trainee's knowledge become the next task. If awareness helps the trainee to ask the right questions then knowledge provides access to the right answers. An adequate level of knowledge should clarify the alternatives and reduce the ambiguity in the trainee's understanding the target culture. Learning the language of another culture is an effective way, for example, to increase one's information. Anticipating preconceptions and stereotypes from another culture's viewpoint requires knowledge about that culture's myths and perceptions. Examples of specific criteria of knowledge needs include whether the trainee:

- has specific knowledge about the culture
- knows the history, adjustment styles, values, and attitudes of the culture
- has information about resources for teaching and learning about the culture
- knows about her or his own culture in relation to other cultures
- has professional expertise relevant to the other culture
- has information the other culture will regard as valuable

Skill Needs

Assessing the level of a trainee's skill is the most important task of all and therefore re-quires a great deal of preparation regarding awareness and knowledge. The skilled trainee should be able to teach awareness and knowledge to others. Skill presumes the ability to do the right thing at the right time in the right way and provides the final test of whether there are unmet needs that will require more training. Examples of specific skill-needs questions might include whether the trainee:

- has an appropriate teaching/learning style
- has appropriate training techniques
- has the ability to establish empathic rapport with persons from the other culture
- is able to receive and accurately analyze feedback from persons of the other culture
- has the creative ability to develop new methods for work in the other culture

Awareness Objectives

The second step is to design appropriate objectives for a training plan. The relative emphasis on awareness, knowledge, or skills will depend on the results of the needs assessment. An awareness objective will change the person's attitudes, opinions, and personal perspectives about a topic. The primary need may be to help groups discover their own stereotyped attitudes and opinions. Usually the awareness objectives focus on a person's unstated assumptions about another culture or about the person in relation to the other culture. The awareness objectives for multicultural training will focus on changing the trainee's attitudes, opinions, and personal perspectives about themselves and/or the target culture so that these elements will be in harmony. Some examples of awareness objectives include whether the trainee:

- is aware of differences in cultural institutions and systems
- is aware of the stress resulting from functioning in a multicultural situation
- knows how rights or responsibilities are defined differently in different cultures
- is aware of differences in verbal and nonverbal communication styles
- is aware of significant differences and similarities of practices across different cultures

Knowledge Objectives

The knowledge component for developing multicultural objectives focuses on increasing the amount of accurate information available to the trainee. Having developed a correct and accurate awareness of the other culture, trainees enrich that awareness by testing attitudes, opinions, and assumptions against the body of factual information they now control. The trainee's level of awareness is certain to increase in direct proportion to the extent of his or her knowledge about the other culture. Some examples of knowledge objectives might include whether the trainee:

- knows about social services available to the other culture
- knows about the theory of culture shock

- knows how the other culture interprets its own rules
- knows patterns of nonverbal communication and language when communicating with the other culture
- knows how differences and similarities are patterned in the other culture and how priorities are set

Skill Objectives

The skill objectives focus on what the trainee can now do. If any of the previous training about awareness or knowledge is missing or inadequate the trainees will have difficulty making the right decisions in their multicultural communication. If awareness has been neglected they will build their plan on wrong assumptions. If knowledge has been neglected, they will describe the cultural situation inaccurately. If skill has been neglected, they may well change a situation in counterproductive directions. Some examples of skill objectives include whether the trainee:

- is able to gain access to social services and resources
- is able to cope with stress and manage difficulties in the new culture
- understands the consequences of a couselor's behavior in the multicultural setting
- uses the other culture's language appropriately
- functions comfortably in the new environment without losing the counselor's own identity

Awareness-Based Designs

The third step in developing a training program is to design a plan that shows how the identified objectives and previously identified needs will be met. Teaching-increased awareness frequently relies on experiential exercises such as role plays, role reversals, or simulations of multicultural interaction. Other approaches include field trips to areas where the target culture lives. Sometimes critical incidents or brief case studies from the culture can be analyzed to increase a trainee's awareness of the culture. A resource person or informant from the culture enables effective bicultural observation whereby both the resource person and trainees can exchange questions and answers in a discussion.

Knowledge-Based Designs

The increase of multicultural knowledge frequently relies on books, lectures, and classroom techniques. Guided self-study with a reading list also is an effective way to help trainees increase their knowledge. Panel discussions about the other cultures help trainees absorb more information relevant to their particular situation. Audiovisual presentations, when available, are valuable, and interviews with resource persons and experts knowledgeable about the other culture will help trainees fill in gaps where accurate information might otherwise be difficult to secure.

Skill-Based Designs

Modeling and demonstrating a skill is an effective skill-based learning design. When available, audiovisual models provide important examples to trainees about how the skill is performed in the other culture and about how well they can replicate that skill by themselves. Supervising trainees' work in the other culture provides a valuable resource for assessing the increased levels of skill. The increase of multi-cultural skills is often premature before the trainee has acquired competence in awareness and knowledge.

Awareness-Based Training Approaches

The fourth stage in developing a training package is the actual implementation of a training design. Most training approaches begin in more or less the same way. There is an introduction with some attempt to break the ice. This might include a formal welcome, a discussion of the training objectives and expectations, and a review of the agenda. In training for awareness, you should help trainees to become aware of the contrast and conflict between their background and that of the target population. In training for knowledge, you should help trainees to have accurate information and comprehension of the target population institutions at the national, regional, and local levels. In training for skill you should help trainees to bring about appropriate change by working with interpreters and cultural informants. Goldstein (2000) provides an entertaining and insightful guidebook for designing training.

Awareness-Based Evaluation

The fifth and last step of a training sequence is evaluating whether the persons you trained have met your objectives in awareness, knowledge, and skill. This is called formative evaluation. Another kind of evaluation is long term and is a much more complicated evaluation that verifies whether or not the trainee's objectives were appropriate for meeting the long-term needs of the target group. This second type of evaluation is called summative evaluation, and its methods range from an informal discussion over wine and cheese to formal written evaluations of long-term changes in productivity determined by random work samples. However you proceed, you should allow room for evaluation in your training activities. These data will be valuable to your trainees in giving them feedback on their accomplishment, valuable to you in demonstrating the strength or weakness of your design, and valuable to those sponsoring the training activity as a basis for making decisions.

Awareness outcomes can be evaluated according to whether the trainee:

- appropriately recognizes the valued priority given to the trainee's own basic attitudes, opinions, and assumptions
- accurately compares the trainee's own cultural perspective with that of others
- is sensitive to the trainee's role in relation to the other culture
- appropriately estimates the constraints of time, setting, and resources in the other culture
- is realistic in estimating resources available to the other culture

Knowledge outcomes can be evaluated according to whether the trainee:

- understands the process of institutional change in the other culture
- can cite the relevant literature about the other culture
- can identify similarities and differences between the trainee's own home culture and the other culture
- can identify referral resources relevant to the other culture
- can identify key resource persons from the other culture

Skill outcomes can be evaluated according to whether the trainee:

- can efficiently plan, conduct, and evaluate training about the other culture
- can accurately assess the needs of persons from the other culture
- can utilize the talents of interprets and cultural informants from the other culture
- observes, understands, and articulates what the trainee learned in the other culture
- can interact, advise, and appropriately manage the work in the other culture

When multicultural training programs fail, they fail in three ways. Some of the programs emphasize awareness objectives almost exclusively. As a result the participants become painfully aware of their own inadequacies or the inadequacies of their environment and the hopelessly overwhelming problems they face. Trainees who overdose on awareness are frustrated because they do not know what to do with the awareness they have gained in terms of increasing their knowledge and skill.

Some of the programs fail by overdosing on knowledge. Teaching programs that overemphasize knowledge about a culture exclusively through lectures, readings, and information fail unless the student is already aware of why these data are important. The participants who lack awareness are frustrated because they do not see the need for all this information and because they are not sure how to use it once it has been gathered.

Training programs that overemphasize skill without providing appropriate awareness and knowledge about the cultural context may be implementing change in the wrong or culturally inappropriate direction. Participants in these programs emerge with the capability of changing other people's lives but—in the absence of knowledge and skill—they are never sure whether they are making things better or worse.

Constructive Conflict Management Training

Until recently little attention was given to the cultural context in training people for constructive conflict management (Kramer & Messick, 1995). Conflict and violence in the school setting often involves people from different cultural backgrounds.

These cultural backgrounds occur not only in terms of ethnic differences but also in the broadly defined cultural categories of demographics (gender, age, place of residence), status factors (social, economic, educational), or formal/informal affiliations with gangs, groups, schools, and other potentially salient memberships of students, administrators, and faculty of schools. With the increase in minority groups in schools, the understanding of cultures is likely to become even more important (Jandt & Pedersen, 1997; Kruger, 1992).

The unique contribution of "multicultural" conflict management training is that by thinking of the roles of those persons or groups in conflict as "cultural" identities, it becomes possible for both persons and/or groups to disagree without either one being "wrong." Two groups or individuals may share the same positive expectation of respect even though their behaviors attached to that expectation are quite different. Reframing the conflict in cultural terms allows both sides to find common ground and to interpret behaviors in the cultural context where those behaviors were learned and are displayed.

Conflict is a natural part of any relationship and has the potential to be either a positive experience, as when the conflict results in learning and growth, or a negative experience, when one or both groups/individuals in conflict are seriously hurt in the process. Negative conflict threatens to erode the consensus needed for growth and development while positive conflict takes place within the context of a general consensus, as it does between good friends. Positive conflict can actually strengthen group relations and help people define their common ground.

The ways that conflict is managed reflects the culturally learned attitudes and beliefs of the participants. These patterns may involve punishing wrongdoers, repairing strained or broken relationships, or some forms of exploitation. Making culture central to constructive conflict management has many implications. First, groups in conflict might be limiting their alternatives to those within their own specific culture. Second, given an appreciation of cultural complexity they are discouraged from quick and easy answers or from forcing one cultural perspective on another. Third, by understanding a range of culturally different approaches to conflict management, groups increase their practical and theoretical options for managing conflict. Cultural systems are not abstract models of reality but are guidelines for action through culturally learned patterns of behavior that create our reality.

The source of conflict lies in the minds of people, reflecting conflict inside the person (Bjorkqvist & Fry, 1997). Imagine that there are one thousand people sitting in your seat with you now as you read this book. They include family, friends, enemies, and significant mentors, as well as individuals, you perhaps fantasize about becoming. You have collected these alternative identities over a lifetime and they speak to one another as they each patiently wait their turn to speak with you and give you advice. These thousand people are a visual image of your "culture." By understanding each conflict according to culturally constructed similarities and differences we can discover a unified platform for understanding the persistence and intensity of the conflict. A culture-centered model of conflict management interprets the conflict in a cultural context that makes the conflict meaningful in terms of causes, processes, and effects among your thousand different cultural identities.

Culture-centered training in conflict management seeks win–win solutions to conflicts by seeking out the shared positive expectations—such as respect, safety, success, and efficiency—that both sides of the conflict share, in spite of their culturally different behaviors. By jointly constructing cultural meaning, the cultural differences are not erased, the cultural integrity of all parties is preserved, and a new basis for intercultural cooperation and coordination is constructed as a metaphoric bridge to the island of common ground for both sides of the dispute. By reframing conflict between people into cultural categories, it becomes possible for two people to disagree without either of them being wrong, based on their different culturally learned assumptions.

The best review of conflict resolution and peer mediation programs in elementary and secondary schools is that by Johnson and Johnson (1996). They point out that programs in training peer mediators are doubling in number every year in response to the needs of schools. The conflict resolution and peer mediation programs often involve the total student body, are built into the curriculum or formal programs, and offer skills-oriented training. When we talk about conflict in the schools we are not talking about competition, influence, dominance, or even aggression, which are managed differently. There are two different perspectives on how conflict is perceived in the school. First, there is the perception that schools are a microcosm of society's violence. Second, there is the perception that schools should be safe havens from violence in society. Proponents of either perspective will disagree on how to train conflict managers.

Conflict in schools can be classified into three perspectives. First, social interdependence theory requires an outcome that satisfies everyone, improves relationships, and increases the ability to resolve future conflicts. Second, structure–process–attitude theory links the conflict to role definitions, expectations, and situational influences, and discusses how changing any one factor causes changes throughout the system. Third, the dual-concerns theory emphasizes the importance of reaching one's goals while also maintaining appropriate relationships. Dual-concerns approaches depend on integrative negotiations, compromise, smoothing, withdrawing, or forcing. Dual-concerns approaches depend on cooperation.

Interpersonal and culture group cooperation is the key factor to constructive conflict management at two levels. First, conflict management seeks to restore cooperation between parties. Second, cooperation provides a favorable context that influences conflict management. The more cooperative the relationship the more frequently conflicts occur; however this increase in volume results in fewer negative effects or explanations, in criticisms that are more detailed, and a greater change in position and reasoning by both sides. In cooperative situations, generally: (1) communication of relevant information is open and honest; (2) perceptions of the other are accurate and constructive; (3) relationships are characterized by trust and responsiveness; and (4) individuals recognize the legitimacy of others' interests. By contrast, in competitive situations, generally: (1) communication is avoided or misleading; (2) frequent misperceptions and distortions exist; (3) relationships are characterized by distrust and exploitation; (4) legitimacy of the other's wants and needs are denied.

Training students for constructive conflict management has a significant positive effect. Strategies used by untrained students include withdrawal, suppression, force/coercion, intimidation or win–lose negotiations. Strategies used by trained students include facing the conflict, learning a set of procedures, applying those procedures, transferring those conflict resolution procedures to nonschool conflicts, problem solving, and integrative negotiations for win–win outcomes. Most of the training being done has focused on the "Teaching Students to be Peacemakers Program" (Johnson & Johnson 1996). However we still know little about how conflicts unfold in schools and what the natural patterns of interaction are among students as they resolve their conflicts, and we know little about the emotional parts of school conflicts.

Johnson and Johnson (1996) point out the advantages of training programs. Outcome data of programs where students were not trained resulted in a lack of agreement, emergence of a winner and a loser, decreased achievement, negative attitudes toward conflict, negative school climate, psychological maladjustment, discipline problems such as suspensions, negative feelings, and discontinued interaction between groups. The outcome data of programs where students were trained indicate increased agreement, maximizing of joint gain, increased achievement, positive attitudes toward conflict, a positive school climate, psychological health, students resolving their own conflicts, positive feelings, and continued ongoing interaction across groups.

Training to reframe conflict into cultural categories, even when that conflict is not normally perceived as cultural, increases the possibility of win–win outcomes. For example, when a conflict with someone from the other side of the world takes place, it is more likely to be considered a "cultural misunderstanding" than if the conflict is with someone from across the street. However, cultural conflicts can occur between a parent and child, brother and sister, or any two people or groups when culture is defined broadly.

Training Peer Helpers

One of the few things we know about how students manage conflict is that they are more likely to go to peers for help than to counselors or even their own parents. Peer pressure is very powerful as a natural stage of identity development among school-aged youth so it makes good sense to train students to help other students. The Peer Helpers Association has a national network of teachers, counselors, parents, and other school-related persons who work together on a regular basis in developing training programs. Most schools have someone on staff who is connected to the network of training resources offered by this association. Many of the previously described goals of win–win conflict management, the importance of common ground, and the importance of context are highlighted in the materials produced by groups affiliated with the Peer Helpers Association such as Win–Win and Associates (2222 Greenway Ave., Charlotte, NY, 28204) who invite school-related persons to contact them for a training kit and manual. What follows are some of their conflict management suggestions.

1. Do LISTEN. Don't do most of the talking.
2. Do help disputants come up with their own solutions. Don't say what YOU would do.
3. Do ask how each person feels. Don't tell them how they should feel.
4. Do let each person tell what happened. Don't focus on blame.
5. Do treat each person with respect. Don't ask, "Why did you do it?" or "Who started it?"
6. Do keep all that is said confidential. Don't take sides.
7. Limit mediation to two people only. Don't bring witnesses to the mediation session.

Their training kit includes a great variety of successful peer mediation training exercises for use in the classroom. The advantage of the peer mediation materials is that they provide a clear structure with which any teacher, student, or school personnel can organize a training program. By providing a clear and detailed structure these materials engender safety both for the persons in conflict and for those attempting to mediate that conflict. In some cases what mediators are to say is literally scripted. It is suggested, too, that the persons in conflict make a contract following seven ground rules where they agree to: (1) try to solve the problem; (2) tell the truth; (3) respect each other with no put-downs, name calling, or fighting; (4) listen to each other without interrupting; (5) carry out what is agreed to; (6) keep everything that is said in mediation confidential; and (7) begin the mediation session by speaking directly to the mediators.

An exercise entitled "Fighting Clean, Fighting Dirty" divides the students into two-person teams to role-play a conflict situation where each team takes a separate side of the dispute and argues with the other team. Both teams are provided with the rules for fighting fairly, which are: (1) be respectful; (2) be direct and honest; (3) stay calm and in control; (4) take responsibility for your part of the problem; (5) focus on solutions and not blame; (6) listen with an open mind; (7) stay in the present; (8) acknowledge the other person's feelings and point of view; and (9) be flexible and willing to work with—instead of against—the other person.

Both teams will also be provided with the rules for fighting "dirty" that are to be avoided such as: (1) be disrespectful; (2) don't take responsibility for your part of the problem; (3) ignore the other person's concerns; (4) blame, judge, and criticize; (5) bring up the past; (6) interrupt and try to get in the last word; (7) bump, shove, hit, or threaten to do so; (8) generalize by saying, "You always . . . ." or "You never . . . .";
(9) avoid or ignore the problem and stuff the angry feelings deep inside; and (10) don't budge, and act as if winning is more important than the relationship.

Prior to implementing a program for peer mediation training careful planning is needed.

1. There needs to be a clear and compelling rationale for the development of the program through a formal or informal needs assessment.
2. The purpose of the program needs to be formalized in a mission statement.
3. Program goals and objectives need to fit with the rationale and purpose, be realistic, and be clearly stated.

4. The procedures and activities of the program need to be organized in a clear and systematic format.
5. The program needs to fit with the local, state, and national guidelines for professional and ethical training.

There needs to be evidence of commitment to involvement from those providing and using the peer helper services. Evidence of this commitment includes the support of high-level administrative staff and faculty, the organization of a program advisory committee, and sufficient financial or logistical support. Program staff needs the appropriate background, training, and ability to carry out their responsibilities. This includes:

1. Strong positive rapport with the target population.
2. Appropriate educational and/or practical experience.
3. Understanding and commitment to the fundamental principles of peer helping.
4. Close familiarity with the target setting.
5. Clear grasp of the program needs and goals and the ability to articulate those.
6. Recognition of the importance of their being a role model.
7. Familiarity with different learning styles and teaching strategies.
8. The ability to work effectively with groups.
9. Mastery of relevant concepts and skills.
10. Sufficient time and energy to carry through.

These criteria are used for screening, selection, and training of peer helpers and their supervisors. Program maintenance includes a constant evaluation of both a formative (were goals met?) and summative (were those goals the right ones?) nature. A code of ethics for peer-helping professionals and for the peer helpers themselves is also provided, modeled on the ethical standards of other professional helping associations.

The peer-helping approach is a tried and true approach that involves little financial investment or outside expertise. The focus of the training is on local and immediate problems. The people doing the training are available for follow-up later and the success rate of peer helping is impressive.

Additional Training Materials

Other peer-helper training materials are available, such as the Rehearsal Demonstration Model (Pedersen, 2000b). The Rehearsal Demonstration Model (RDM) is designed to match each spoken and explicit communication with a parallel message, indicting what the person is thinking but not saying, by a coached alter-ego peer (Pedersen, 2000b). Initially the RDM is fully scripted, and the participants read their scripted role messages. If for example the teacher says, "Wan Lee-Ho, why can't you do better work in school?" the student might respond, "I'm sorry."

The teacher's unspoken message might be, "I keep getting after you to do better work, and you never do better work! Why is that? Why is it that you can't work harder?" And, the student's unspoken message might be, "No matter what I do, it isn't appreciated, so why should I do more work?"

If we focus only on the verbal explicit message, we only get the messages the student is saying and not what they are thinking. To work effectively we need to know not just what is being said but what is being thought from the other person's cultural perspective. The RDM script to get the interaction started might resemble the following:

TEACHER: Look at me! What happened?

TEACHER UNSPOKEN: You must be guilty or you would look me in the eye. Your kind never look others straight in the eye.

STUDENT: I dunno . . . .

STUDENT UNSPOKEN: What's the use? You won't believe me anyway. I am not comfortable looking back at you.

Other scripts can be generated to fit specific and typical conflict situations in the school where students teach one another to hear one another's internal dialogue more accurately. One approach suggests that when two people are talking there are three conversations going on. The first conversation is the verbal exchange. The second conversation is the helper's internal dialogue. The third conversation is the other person's internal dialogue. The speaker doesn't know what exactly the other person is thinking but does know two things *about* what they are thinking: that part of what the other is thinking is positive and part is negative. Another training model in Pedersen (2000b) matches the student with two other persons from that student's "culture," one as a "pro" to articulate the positive things the student is thinking but not saying and the other as an "anti" to articulate the negative things the student is thinking but not saying. The "pro" is like an angel sitting on the student's shoulder while the "anti" is like a devil sitting on the other shoulder. This Triad Training Model has been used successfully in a variety of settings.

Pedersen and Hernandez (1997) provide a variety of multicultural exercises and structured activities that are useful in training. A variety of exercises for looking at the different cultural perspectives of education, training elementary school children about multiculturalism, and demonstrating how culturally learned roles divide and unite in the school context are provided. A longer section of this book deals with collecting and using critical incidents in a variety of settings. The critical incidents help us turn problems into solutions and provide some excellent teaching/training materials.

Another very useful resource for peer training is the Tyson and Pedersen (2000) book with thirty-two critical incidents that have occurred in the school setting. Each incident was reported by a school counselor and is accompanied by comments from two other highly qualified helpers familiar with the school setting. The critical incident technique is closely related to the case study method, which evaluates the behavior of a person in a clinical or decision-making setting, examining background, behavior, and changes of behavior. Case data describe and interpret impressions from a qualitative and subjective viewpoint. The critical incident method is frequently used in law schools and schools of management.

The incidents or situations encountered by school counselors can be reframed as learning opportunities. Each problem or crisis school counselors encounter has something to teach them in preparation for the next crisis. If counselors teach themselves to learn from these incidents, they may better learn from future problems they encounter. The incidents blur the boundaries between the classroom and the community in which school counselors work, focusing on the community–school connection.

The critical incidents technique highlights five areas of influence working on the school counselor.

1. The school counselor's need to lease individuals in positions of power and influence for reasons of self-interest
2. The school counselor's theoretical–philosophical orientation
3. The expectations and demands of faculty and colleagues
4. The wants and needs of the student
5. The demands of parents and others outside the school system

A variety of simulations are available such as the three-hour Synthetic Culture Laboratory (Hofstede & Pedersen, 1999; Hofstede, Pedersen, & Hofstede, 2002; Pedersen & Ivey, 1994) that divides the group into four synthetic cultures called Alpha (high power, distance), Beta (strong uncertainty, avoidance), Gamma (high individualism), and Delta (strong, masculine). Each synthetic culture interacts in turn with other synthetic cultures regarding problems caused by "outsiders" to find common ground without losing each synthetic culture's integrity. The Lab provides a safe environment in which to rehearse interacting with different cultural groups.

In addition, Ivey, Pedersen, and Ivey (2001) wrote a book on training group leaders to be more intentional through the use of micro-skills as applied to the cultural context. These micro-skills include listening and processing information, focusing, pacing, questioning, and other basic influencing skills. Ivey and Ivey (1999) provide another excellent textbook on intentional counseling micro-skills using the micro-skills approach for one-on-one interaction as well.

REFERENCES

American School Counselors Association. (1988). *Position statements of the American School Counselor Association*. Alexandria, VA: Author.

American School Counselor Association. (1992). *American School Counselor Association Ethical Standards for School Counselors*. Alexandria, VA: Author.

Arredondo, P., Toporek, R., Brown, S. P., Jones, J., Locke, D. C., & Sanchez, H. (1996). Operationalization of the multicultural counseling competencies. *Journal of Multicultural Counseling and Development, 24*, 42–78.

Baker, S. (1992). *School counseling for the twenty-first century*. New York: Macmillan.

Bjorkqvist, K. & Fry, D. P. (1997). Conclusions: Alternatives to violence. In D. P. Fry & K. Bjorkqvist (Eds.), *Cultural variations in conflict resolution*, 243–254. Mahwah, NJ: Erlbaum.

Brislin, R. & Horvath, A. M. (1997). In J. W. Berry, M. H. Segall, & C. Kagitcibasi (Eds.), *Handbook of cross-cultural psychology: Volume 3, social behavior and applications*, 327–370. Boston: Allyn & Bacon.

Colbert, R. D. & Colbert, M. M. (2002). Conceptualizing school counselor involvement in Educational Reform. In P. Pedersen & J. Carey (Eds.), *Multicultural counseling in schools* (2nd ed.). Boston: Allyn & Bacon.

Cushner, K. & Brislin, R. (1996). *Intercultural interactions: A practical guide* (2nd ed.). Thousand Oaks, CA: Sage.

D'Andrea, M., Daniels, J., & Heck, R. (1991). Exploring the different levels of multicultural counseling training in counselor education. *Journal of Counseling and Development, 70,* 143–150.

Goldstein, A. (2000). *The workshop: An irreverent guide,* Sebastopol, CA: National Training Associates.

Herring, R. D. (1997). *Multicultural counseling in schools: A synertetic approach.* Alexandria, VA: American Counseling Association.

Hofstede, G. J. & Pedersen, P. (1999). Synthetic cultures: Intercultural learning through simulation games. *Simulation & Gaming, 30*(4), 415–440.

Hofstede, G. J., Pedersen, P., & Hofstede, G. (2002). *The Synthetic Cultures Model.* Yarmouth, ME: Intercultural Press.

Ivey, A. & Ivey, M. (1999). *Intentional interviewing and counseling.* Belmont, CA: Wadsworth.

Ivey, A., Pedersen, P., & Ivey, M. (2001). *Intentional group counseling: A microskills approach.* Belmont, CA: Wadsworth.

Jandt, F. E. & Pedersen, P. B. (1996). *Constructive conflict management: Asia–Pacific cases.* Thousand Oaks, CA: Sage.

Johnson, D. W., & Johnson, R. T. (1996). Conflict resolution and mediation programs in elementary and secondary schools: A review of the research. *Review of Educational Research, 66*(4), 459–506.

Kisellica, M. S., Changizi, J. C., Cureton, V. L., & Gridley, B. E. (1995). Counseling children and adolescents in schools: Salient multicultural issues. In J. Ponterotto, J. M. Casas, L. A. Suzuki, & C. M. Alexander (Eds.), *Handbook of multicultural counseling,* 516–532. Thousand Oaks, CA: Sage.

Kramer, R. A. & Messick, D. M. (1995). *Negotiation as a social process.* Thousand Oaks, CA: Sage.

Kruger, J. A. (1992). Racial ethnic intergroup disputing and dispute resolution in the United States: A bibliography and resource guide. (Available from Judith A. Kruger, P.O. Box 3, Collingswood, NJ 08108).

LaFromboise, T. D., Coleman, H. L. K., & Hernandez, A. (1991). Development and factor structure of the Cross-Cultural Inventory–Revised. *Professional Psychology Research and Practice, 22,* 263–271.

Lee, W. M. L. (1999). *An introduction to multicultural counseling.* Philadelphia: Accelerated Development (Taylor & Francis).

Pedersen, P. (1994). Multicultural training in schools. In P. Pedersen & J. C. Carey (Eds.), *Multicultural counseling in schools,* 225–238. Boston: Allyn & Bacon.

Pedersen, P. (1995). *The five stages of culture shock: Critical incidents around the world.* Westport, CT: Greenwood Press.

Pedersen, P. (2000a). *A handbook for developing multicultural awareness* (3rd ed.). Alexandria, VA: American Counseling Association.

Pedersen, P. (2000b). *Hidden messages in culture-centered counseling: A triad training model.* Alexandria, VA: American Counseling Association.

Pedersen, P. & Hernandez, D. (1997). *Decisional dialogues in a cultural context: Structured exercises.* Thousand Oaks, CA: Sage.

Pedersen, P. & Ivey, A. E. (1994). *Culture-centered counseling and interviewing skills.* Westport, CT: Greenwood Press.

Ponterotto, J. G., Reiger, B. P., Barrett, A., & Sparks, R. (1994). Assessing multicultural counseling competence: A review of instrumentation. *Journal of Counseling and Development 72,* 316–322.

Pope-Davis, D. & Coleman, H. (1997). *Multicultural counseling competencies.* Thousand Oaks, CA: Sage.

Pope-Davis, D. B. & Dings, J. G. (1995). The assessment of multicultural counseling competencies. In J. G. Ponterotto, J. M. Casas, L. A. Suzuki, & C. M. Alexander (Eds.), *Handbook of multicultural counseling,* 287–311. Thousand Oaks, CA: Sage.

Rabie, M. (1994). *Conflict resolution and ethnicity.* Westport, CT: Praeger.

Sodowsky, G. R., Taffe, R. C., Gutkin, T. B., & Wise, L. I. (1994). Development of the Multicultural Counseling Inventory: A self-report measure of multicultural competencies. *Journal of Counseling Psychology, 41,* 137–148.

Sue, S. (1998). In search of cultural competencies in psychology and counseling. *American Psychologist, 53,* 440–448.

Sue, S. (1999). Science, ethnicity and bias: Where have we gone wrong? *American Psychologist, 54*(12), 1070–1077.

Sue, D. W., Arredondo, P., & McDavis, R. J. (1992). Multicultural counseling competencies and standards: A call to the profession. *Journal of Counseling and Development, 70,* 477–486.

Sue, D. W., Bernier, J. E., Durran, A., Feinberg, L., Pedersen, P., Smith, C. J., & Vasquez-Nuttall, G. (1982). Cross-cultural counseling competencies. *The Counseling Psychologist, 19*(2), 45–52.

Sue, D. W., Carter, R. T., Casas, J. M., Fouad, N. A., Ivey, A. E., Jensen, M., LaFromboise, T., Manese, J. E., Ponterotto, J. G., & Vasquez-

Nuttall, E. (1998). *Multicultural counseling competencies*. Thousand Oaks, CA: Sage.

Sue, D. W. & Sue, D. (1999). *Counseling the culturally different: Theory and practice* (3rd ed.). New York: Wiley.

Tyson, L. E. & Pedersen, P. B. (2000). *Critical incidents in school counseling*. Alexandria, VA: American Counseling Association.

AUTHOR NOTE

Paul B. Pedersen is Professor Emeritus, Syracuse University. He is also a visiting professor in the Department of Psychology, University of Hawaii. He has authored, coauthored, or edited 39 books, 67 chapters, and 93 articles on multicultural counseling and communication. He is a fellow in Divisions 9 (Social Issues), 17 (Counseling), 45 (Ethnic Minorities), and 52 (International) of the American Psychological Association. He has taught at universities, in Indonesia, Malaysia, and Taiwan for eight years and was in Taiwan on a Senior Fulbright for a year.

APPENDIX A

A Self-Assessment of Multicultural Awareness, Knowledge, and Skills in School Counseling

The first person you need to train is yourself. The following questions were adapted from Sue et al. (1982), Sue et al. (1992), Arredondo et al. (1996), and Sue et al. (1998), and summarize many of the points made in this chapter as they apply to your own counseling in multicultural schools. In addition, each chapter author of this book was asked to submit one "awareness," one "knowledge," and one "skill" criteria to add to this list of indicators. These items are useful criteria for self-assessment of your understanding multicultural counseling in schools.

Read the following questions and indicate how well you think you would be able to answer it using your own criteria. If you think you would provide an excellent answer give yourself an "A," if you think your answer would be generally good give yourself a "B," if you think your answer would be acceptable but not as good as you would like, give yourself a "C," and if you feel unable to answer the question give yourself an "F." An "A" counts for 3 points, a "B" for 2 points, a "C" for 1 point, and an "F" for 0 points. Divide the number of points you awarded yourself by the number of questions to get your GPA.

AWARENESS QUESTIONS

1. Can you construct a genogram of your family for the last three generations on both your mother's and father's side?

2. What does your cultural heritage mean to you?

3. How well do you value, respect, and model "harmony" when working with persons from other cultures in your school?

4. Which cultures do you least understand in your school?

5. What do you do to seek out students who are different from you?

6. What culturally learned assumptions do you have that are different from other school counselors or teachers?

7. How do issues of oppression, racism, discrimination, and stereotype influence your school counseling?

8. Can you identify examples of racist attitudes, beliefs, and feelings in your school?

9. What have you done to increase multicultural harmony in your school?

10. Can you provide counseling in a variety of different styles that fit the different cultures of your students?

11. Do you know how your culturally different students feel about your way of doing counseling in the school?

12. How do you evaluate your counseling with culturally different students?

13. When have you sought consultation from outside resource persons for working with culturally different clients?

14. Do you have a plan for increasing your multicultural awareness for the future?

15. Do you consider yourself to have achieved multicultural awareness?

KNOWLEDGE QUESTIONS

1. Can you describe the social, political, and economic background of negative emotional reactions toward specific racial and ethnic groups in your school or community?

2. How well do you know the beliefs and attitudes of culturally different students in your school?

3. Are you aware of the life experiences, cultural heritages, and family backgrounds of your culturally different students?

4. Are you aware of the similarities and differences between yourself and the students or teachers in your school?

5. Are you able to explain how your students' backgrounds influence their behavior?;

6. Their vocational choices?;

7. Their help-seeking behaviors?; and

8. Their evaluation of your school culture?

9. Can you discuss issues of race, poverty, stereotyping, and power with your culturally different students?

10. In the last month have you read books or articles regarding culture and counseling in schools?

11. In the last month have you been involved with culturally different groups outside your role as a school counselor?

12. Do you attend community events, political functions, or celebrations with groups from other cultures?

13. Have you had training in multicultural counseling?

14. Are you familiar with at least ten different publications about multicultural counseling?

15. Are you able to articulate questions about multiculturalism in your school for which you do not yet know the answer?

SKILLS QUESTIONS

1. Do you refer in counseling to your students' religious and/or spiritual beliefs and values?

2. Are you able to manage a dual relationship of being both friend and counselor with culturally different students when necessary?

3. Do you understand how your students' beliefs and attitudes influence your work as a school counselor?

4. Are you aware of indigenous and alternative therapies being used by the students and teachers in your school?

5. Are you able to defend the positive value of bilingualism or multilingualism in schools and/or the community?

6. Can you identify examples of cultural encapsulation in the textbooks about school counseling?

7. Can you interpret scores from a culturally biased test to your culturally different students in a helpful way?

8. Do you get defensive when culturally different students or teachers in the school get angry at you?

9. Are you able to articulate the argument for affirmative action in schools?

10. Do you have contact with the families of your culturally different students when appropriate for your counseling?

11. Are you able to reduce discrimination in your school?

12. Have you taught a course or training workshop on multicultural counseling in schools?

13. Do you have a network of resource persons from different cultures to whom you can go with your questions?

14. Are you able to do school counseling in languages other than English?

15. Do you have a plan for increasing your multicultural skill as a school counselor?

11 Reducing Violence in Multicultural Schools

LISA ARONSON FONTES
Springfield College

OBJECTIVES

1. Understand ways to prevent and resolve various forms of violence that can occur in multicultural schools
2. Understand the relationship of violence that occurs in schools to community and societal conditions
3. Take steps to prevent violence without relying on stereotypes or discriminatory practices
4. Understand a variety of ways to make schools safer for all students

On her first day of kindergarten in a new school, Marta is surprised when a group of boys chase her and knock her to the ground. While many of the other girls seem to enjoy this form of attention, Marta does not and asks the boys to stop. The boys persist and Marta complains to the playground supervisors, who tell her to "lighten up." After several days of similar interactions, Marta's mother informs the school principal. He replies that "boys will be boys" and there is not much he can do. He suggests that there may be something wrong with Marta for not wanting to play along, and that it would be helpful for her socially to avoid "making a fuss."

Twelve-year-old Antonio's parents step into the school counselor's office reluctantly, embarrassed to have been called in because of their son's frequent tardiness. The counselor soon realizes that Antonio's parents speak only limited English, and Antonio interprets during the meeting. After some inquiry, Antonio explains that he has been walking the two miles to school every morning. He says that when he did ride the school bus, the other boys would grab his hat and backpack and toss them around. They would trip him and steal his lunch. Once, they even tore off and broke his eyeglasses. Antonio's parents explain apologetically that they have taught him not to fight, because they don't want him to get into trouble, but they don't know how to help him. When the counselor asks the family why they think Antonio is being teased, they shrug their shoulders. When the counselor asks if they believe he is being picked on because he is Mexican, his mother bursts into tears and grabs the counselor's hand, saying "Yes, yes, please help my son feel better in school."

What do these vignettes have in common? In each, a student is singled out for verbal or physical violence because of identity group membership. In each, the adults charged with their care have failed to provide a safe environment for all the various groups in the school.

Violence in schools leapt into the national consciousness with a string of school and schoolyard shootings in the late 1990s. Some believe that the seemingly random nature of these shootings and the fact that they largely occurred in rural and suburban schools with majority White student bodies indicates that school violence has reached new heights. Others resent the increased national attention paid to these middle-class White victims, claiming that school shootings had already cost the lives of hundreds of children in poor and minority school districts, with scant media or political attention.

 In fact, the numbers of deaths on school grounds decreased steadily from fifty-four in the 1992–93 school year, to fifteen in 1999–2000 (SAVD Report, 2000). In fact, youth are much more likely to be victims of serious violent crimes outside school than in school. However, violence in schools remains a large problem, with 202,000 serious violent incidents (sexual assault, rape, robbery, and aggravated assault) a year occurring on school grounds (Donahue, Schiraldi, & Macallais, 1998), and far greater numbers of crimes that are not officially considered "serious crimes," but which can severely impact a child's success and feeling of well-being in school (e.g., nonphysical racial harassment).

For the most part, "school violence" does not originate in schools, but rather in communities, the nation, and perhaps even the global environment, which is rife with ethnic and racial tension and violence. The solutions to violence in schools, therefore, cannot lie entirely within schools themselves, but rather must be integrated with violence-reduction efforts that extend beyond school buildings.

A 1995–96 study of Los Angeles diverse public high schools, supported by the American Civil Liberties Union (ACLU-SC), reported that students found their schools to be relatively safe environments—despite high rates of assault and weapons possession—compared to the streets. Additionally, the report concludes, "teens thirst for courses and other means to lessen racial tension and to provide them with better conflict resolution skills." While school counselors alone cannot eliminate violence in young people's lives, clearly they can have an important role to play through psychoeducation and supportive interventions.

In this chapter, I address the great potential of schools to serve as safe havens where children can find refuge from violence in their homes, the media, society, and the streets. Beyond being safe themselves, however, schools can also serve as centers where children learn to live in harmony, resolve conflicts peacefully, and relate to diverse people with respect and appreciation. School counselors have a unique role in assuring the safety of schools for all students, regardless of their background, and the promulgation of a culture of harmony and mutual support.

School Violence in Its Many Forms

The close relationship between violating people's rights, because of their group membership, and violence, may be seen by their origin in the same Latin root the word "violare," which means "to treat with violence." I believe that a violation of people's civil rights, of their psychological or personal integrity, is an act of violence, even when its manifestation does not take on a physical form. Preventing and interrupting non-physical rights violations leads to a decrease in other, physical forms of violence.

The violence that occurs in schools ranges from those behaviors at the milder end of the spectrum that are often considered "ordinary," such as verbal taunts, teasing, bullying, and harassment, to those that are more severe, such as hazing, physical assault, rape, and murder. Violence may be perpetrated by students individually, in loosely affiliated groups, or in school-sanctioned organizations such as athletic teams, or banned groups such as gangs.

In a book on multicultural school counseling, readers might wonder why this chapter discusses diverse forms of violence and diverse solutions, rather than limiting itself to forms of racial or ethnic violence across groups. There are three main reasons: (1) because forms of violence that exist in many schools, such as sexual harassment, can be expressions of intergroup conflict in multicultural schools; (2) because eliminating the harassment of one group (such as gay students) helps everyone feel safer; and (3) because the strategies that counselors implement in one area often reduce additional forms of conflict.

The literature on school violence is remarkably silent about issues of culture, race, sexual orientation, and gender. The professional literature and the media discuss the problem of "youth crime" or "gangs" or the "war on drugs" without noting the racially imbalanced ways in which youth crime is prosecuted in this country (for example, although Black and White youth use drugs to similar degrees, Black youth are much more likely to end up incarcerated for drug-related crimes). Avoiding the mention of race in these discussions allows the racism of the law enforcement and justice systems to remain invisible, and allows White youth to remain free from the stigma of drug use and related crimes. By not mentioning the homophobia that undergirds many school assaults, theorists and practitioners alike can avoid confronting this wide social ill. By rendering invisible the fact that males are most commonly both the perpetrators and victims of violence in schools, social commentators remain free to ignore the role of male socialization. The absurdity of this position becomes clear when we review the June, 2000, special issue of the American School Counseling Association flagship journal, *Professional School Counseling*, dedicated to "collaborating for safe schools and safe communities," and find not a single article dedicated to gender, racial, cultural, or sexual orientation issues in school safety, and scant mention of these topics in any of the articles.

Just how bad is the problem of violence in schools? The Department of Education (1998) reports that in the 1996–97 academic year, 43 percent of schools reported crimes committed on school grounds; 10 percent reported violent crimes; 16 percent of high-school students reported being involved in one or more fights in school; 3 percent of high-school seniors reported carrying a gun to school at least once a month; 29 percent of eighth-graders reported being threatened; and one out of four high-school students say their most serious concern is a fear of bullies. These numbers do not even begin to tell the story, however, because many of the incidents of violence are not reported and may not rise to the level of reportable crimes. For instance, a boy who is humiliated in the locker room and a girl who finds racial epithets scrawled in her notebook may well keep these incidents to themselves. The impact of such encounters is often great, however, and may affect how these students feel in their schools, and how likely they are to succeed academically.

Currently, in most schools problems of real or threatened violence are handled through brief punitive interventions such as detentions or suspensions, with little lasting change. In this chapter, I examine approaches to reducing violence in multicultural schools in three sections: protocols for handling violent incidents, conflict resolution strategies, and initiatives addressing specific forms of violence. Counselors are key players in designing and implementing each strategy. The important issue of transforming the school climate through diversity education is discussed in Chapter 10 of this book.

Protocols

After hearing reports of school violence in the media, counselors often wonder how they can prevent similar incidents in their schools. They wonder how they can identify the young people who are sufficiently troubled to engage in violent behavior, and may wonder which of the myriad conflicts that appear in school on any given day could explode into violence.

In schools with high levels of customary violence, or when a violent incident has occurred, school personnel often sense with dread that they are waiting for the next incident. Teachers may approach counselors, asking them to "please do something" about a specific student, and counselors often feel that their hands are tied "until something happens." Counselors are rightly concerned about labeling children and youth unnecessarily, and most school counselors are not trained to evaluate students' potential for violence.

To complicate matters, school personnel including counselors often fear retaliation by violent students and their defenders. Counselors wonder how they can respond appropriately to signs of potential violence while avoiding stereotyping. Counselors may wonder how to get appropriate help for the students who worry them, especially when they are overwhelmed with responsibility for hundreds of students, and when parents refuse to cooperate or deny that their child may be troubled or at risk. School counselors often have few options for speedy community mental health intervention, where children have inadequate health insurance or belong to health maintenance organizations with cumbersome referral processes. Schools are usually uncertain of how to involve law enforcement in all but the most violent incidents, *after* a crime has been committed. Members of minority communities often fear the police, and the mere presence of police officers in a building can be perceived as a sign that something is deeply wrong in a school.

Using a protocol approach for assessing and averting violence ameliorates some of these problems. The protocols standardize school personnel behaviors, and take "the burden of assessing the language and behavior of a student off the shoulders of teachers, administrators and other students" (Moriarty & Kalill, 1999, p. 2), moving it to the sphere of counselors, adjustment counselors, or school psychologists, depending on each school's preference. (I will use the term "school counselors" to refer to this group.) The protocol approach described next is drawn from Moriarty, Kalill, and Benander's, *A Protocol Approach to Violence* (2001), which has been implemented successfully in culturally diverse Springfield, Massachusetts, middle and high schools.

Advocates of protocols suggest that they serve a preventive function, providing a standard format for identifying students who are showing signs of problems, before violence erupts. The protocols are deliberately designed to cast a wide net, identifying a variety of youth in need of help—not just those who may later become violent. The protocol approach is designed to lead to early intervention and support from family, school, and community.

In the protocol approach, specific kinds of student statements or behaviors trigger the implementation of a protocol, which push the incident into the realm of the school counselor. The school counselor then seeks specific information and—based on this information—can either terminate the protocol at any point, believing there is little or no risk, or proceed with specific interventions as indicated in the protocol. When a protocol has been triggered, the school counselor and others must follow a specified procedure in chronological order, including filling out brief paperwork. This assures standardization, and reduces liability, guesswork, individual variability, and room for bias.

The protocol provides accountability, clear definition of roles and procedures, and a strict timeline for involving all the necessary members of the student's world. The interventions needed may be as minor as peer support or a conversation with a guidance counselor, or as significant as a full-fledged crisis response involving multiple professionals and agencies. Protocols can be modified to meet the needs of specific schools systems, student bodies, and local statutes.

Moriarty and Kalill (1999) suggest that there are six phases to implementing a protocol approach to school violence. The first consists of separate educational workshops for students, parents, teachers, administrators, and law enforcement about the language and behavior that could be defined as a trigger; the reporting process; interventions that may occur; and expected results. When conducted properly, the education sessions themselves are an intervention that should lead to an increased sense of community.

In the second step, the school counselors are trained in implementing the protocol. The counselors are primarily responsible for most phases of the assessment, and for coordinating the response and follow-up. As the school personnel with the most mental health training, the school counselors need to learn how to respond to some of the more subtle questions in the protocol forms, including being able to describe the affect of a person who has made a threat, or being able to assess a person's intent.

The third phase involves establishing two committees. The first committee facilitates communication among the various groups involved in the protocols and monitors and reviews all interventions. This committee should include representatives from each constituency. The second committee is a group of students willing to facilitate peer support and antiviolence measures with their schoolmates.

After the three previous phases have been completed, schools are ready to implement the protocols. That is, from this point forward, whenever student speech or behavior falls within the guidelines, the appropriate protocol is triggered.

In the fifth phase, after a specific period of time has passed, the protocol system is evaluated. In the sixth and final phase, the protocol implementation is adjusted to meet the school's particular needs.

Moriarty and Kalill recommend the following five protocols: (1) verbal threat of harm to self or other (with affect congruent with idea of self-harm or harm to others); (2) act of physical violence with intent to cause harm; (3) bringing a weapon to school (without intent to use it); (4) bringing a weapon to school (with intent to cause harm); and (5) aggregate warning signs (to trigger a response based on multiple indicators over time that do not meet the criteria of the other protocols).

Moriarty (personal communication, September 2000) reports that schools using these five protocols have not only reported a decrease in incidents of violence, but have also seen a decrease in disciplinary referrals. Apparently, help is reaching troubled students earlier than prior to the implementation of the protocol. This creates a safer and more responsive school community for all students.

Conflict Resolution Strategies

In recent years, many schools with multicultural student bodies have begun to promote formal alternative strategies for resolving conflict as ways to reduce violence and increase harmony and cooperation (Aber, Jones, Brown, Chadry, & Samples, 1998). In general, these strategies run along a continuum from those that favor a top-down process of adjudication to those that favor a process of negotiation. In the adjudication end of the spectrum, an aggrieved party and an accused party present their claims to a judge or jury (usually a school administrator, but sometimes a trained pre-selected team composed of students, faculty, and administrators). The parties follow strict guidelines around who can speak when, and decisions are made based on a standard set of rules (for example, "did the student behavior violate the school rules as outlined in the student handbook?"). The adjudicators then render a decision. This is an authoritarian, top-down approach, which can be fair or unfair depending on the governing style, wisdom, and compassion of the adjudicators. In multicultural schools, it is important that those who adjudicate disputes are not seen as biased toward or against any of the different groups in the school. Even the appearance of bias can mean that the decisions will increase rather than diminish conflict and resentment in the school community.

Moving along the spectrum, some schools have set up procedures for arbitration. With this approach, the arbitrator determines the rules and decides the outcome. In *most* schools, teachers and administrators serve as informal arbitrators. A student with a complaint will approach a teacher who has the authority to resolve it. When there is a conflict between a student and a teacher, or among teachers, typically one of the school principals will listen to the complaints and decide the outcome. The arbitrator or team of arbitrators in a school may be seen as biased or unbiased, depending in part on their identity group membership (e.g., race, sex), and their ability to be flexible and listen to everyone's side. An arbitrator who takes the position that "the teacher is always right" is not apt to be perceived as fair by the students, and therefore students will avoid bringing issues before the arbitrator. Similarly, an arbitrator who is seen as always favoring one group over another (for example, the African American over the Korean American students, or the "preppies" over the "jocks") will not be perceived as fair, and therefore will be less effective.

The next area along the spectrum that I will describe is mediation. The basic goal of mediation is to get the parties to agree. The mediators are usually a group of trained students, but may also include other members of the community (e.g., teachers, parents) who ideally make decisions based on the needs of the parties, rather than a set of externally imposed rules. (I will discuss mediation in more detail.)

The final area in the spectrum is negotiation, in which parties are asked to communicate directly about the problem at hand, without intervention by an external authority or a peer. Most teachers and counselors advocate informally for negotiation, telling students to work it out by themselves. More recently, some schools have begun teaching negotiation skills as early as kindergarten (Lantieri & Patti, 1996). Next, I will discuss mediation and negotiation in greater depth, as two approaches to resolving conflicts in multicultural schools.

Mediation

School counselors implement and monitor mediation programs, which have grown exponentially in recent years. Mediation programs may be implemented by educating the faculty through in-service training, educating a small group of students who serve as mediators, and/or infusing information and training in peer mediation into the school curriculum in a variety of disciplinary classes. For instance, in a science class, faculty could discuss how scientists resolve ethical disputes; in a language class, the teacher could compare the Spanish concept *derecho* with the English concept of law or rights; in social studies, a teacher could discuss how differing forms of government resolve disputes. Schools have experienced great success by adapting the whole-school approach, engaging in all the strategies just described, and training parents and teachers as peer mediators, too. While the whole-school approach is probably the most effective for educating all parties in a school about mediation and maximizing the number of conflicts resolved through mediation, most schools opt for the easiest approach, which is to train a small group of students. Unfortunately, when only a small group of students receive training as mediators and learn about its usefulness, the number of referrals is apt to be low, and conflicts in the school will generally continue to be decided by more conflictual and authoritarian means, such as "might makes right" in the lunchroom, or a teacher or administrator "lays down the law." For mediation to be effective, school counselors are advised to enlist the help of diverse students and staff in designing the mediation program. Additionally, counselors should select a diverse group of mediators for intensive training (*not* just the students who would be perceived as "geeks" or "kiss-ups" or "brains") (Campbell, 2000). Support from the senior administration is considered essential for the success of mediation programs. Counselors are advised not to invest major effort in establishing peer mediation programs before securing not only the approval of the principal, but also, ideally, also the principal's whole-hearted and enthusiastic support.

In schools with successful mediation programs, not only are student–student and student–teacher conflicts frequently resolved through student mediation, but occasionally teachers will approach student mediators for help with teacher–teacher conflicts as well.

Success in peer mediation programs is usually measured by the number of referrals, the number of mediations attempted, and the number of agreements reached and kept. However, these numbers may not adequately assess the impact of such a program on a school. For instance, an active peer mediation program in a school may actually encourage students to resolve more conflicts among themselves, rather than letting them fester, because peers or school staff might say, "If you don't have some kind of agreement by the end of the week, you're going to need to bring this to mediation." The desire to avoid peer mediation—which can be an arduous process—may serve as an impetus for compromise and understanding. Additionally, training diverse students in peer mediation means that their skills are sprinkled throughout the student body, and used informally to resolve conflict at different times. Finally, when diverse students are brought together to train as peer mediators, they learn about each other, understand each other, and learn to work toward common goals. In and of itself, this can reduce intergroup conflict. (For more information about peer mediation, contact the Conflict Resolution Education Network–CREnet, 1527 New Hampshire Ave, NW, Washington, DC, 20036; (202)667-9700, www.crenet.org.)

As they are usually implemented, mediation programs are not culturally competent and may actually serve to further marginalize students from diverse communities within a school (Baker, French, Trujillo, & Wing, 2000). For instance, mediation programs usually try to reduce the number of people involved, distilling the problem to a conflict between individuals, whereas people from minority cultures often view conflict as tied in with community concerns, and therefore requiring a community rather than an individual approach. Further, students who feel disempowered in a school may especially need to bring allies with them to the mediation setting. By conceiving of a conflict as a problem between individuals, mediators may inadvertently ignore the oppression issues and structural problems that undergird the conflict.

Conflict resolution can be approached from either an exchange or a transformative perspective (Wing, personal communication, April 2000). The exchange perspective is by far the more common approach, whether it is reached through adjudication, arbitration, mediation, or negotiation. Its basic tenet is, "give a little, get a little." The following vignette will illustrate the resolution of conflict from this perspective:

> One day, a group of sixth-grade girls marches into the office of Ms. Brice, the counselor at Maplewood Elementary School. They complain that at recess each day, they are excluded from soccer games. The soccer field is relatively small and the recess monitors will only allow eight players on a team. Boys are always voted as captains, they choose other boys to be on their teams first, and most girls are relegated to the sidelines, to watch soccer, play four square, or jump rope.

Working from an exchange perspective, the counselor can serve as an arbitrator, bringing a group of boys and girls together, listening to the concerns first of one group and then the other. The boys insist that the students should be able to vote for the captains each day, and that the captains should be able to choose teams based on how good they think the players are. The girls insist that they should be allowed to play and that the teams should be assigned in advance, to avoid the conflict each day. The counselor might lay down the law, for instance, by insisting that the captains have to alternate in their choice of players, choosing a boy and then a girl, and so on. This is an exchange because the boys are giving up some of their autonomy in choosing teams but maintaining the ability to elect the captain, whereas the girls are gaining the right to play but having to put up with the team selection process each day. While this decision might seem like a fair exchange, it does nothing to transform the gender conflict and hierarchy that led to the polarization on the soccer field in the first place. In all likelihood, if Ms. Brice observes future recesses, she will note that while the teams might be mixed in terms of gender, the girls may remain equally frustrated in their desire to play, because their male teammates may refuse to pass them the ball. The gender conflict may manifest itself in boys holding their noses while obligatorily choosing girls for their teams. Alternatively, the girls may simply decide not to play soccer, thinking it is not worth the hassle of the selection process each day.

If Ms. Brice took a transformative approach to the conflict, she would allow each side to tell their story of what happened—first one and then the other. She would listen carefully to each side and help each side bring out its story. Usually, each party believes it is a victim (Wing, personal communication, April 2000). Ms. Brice would then help each side understand the other's story. At the same time, she would acknowledge a power differential—that the boys have been setting the terms of the play, that many of them have been playing soccer intensively for years and therefore are more familiar with the rules, and that some of the boys have been intimidating the girls into complying with their wishes on the field. She would teach principles of gender equity in this specific situation while noting the need for further training around these issues in the school at other times. She would help the students agree on a mutually satisfactory future, perhaps by alternating the ways the teams are chosen, allowing the girls to play one day and the boys the next, having girl captains, or devising another solution. The basic notion is that the conflict would be seized upon as an opportunity to transform the sixth-grade class, moving it in the direction of greater harmony and social justice, rather than simply resolving a particular dispute.

Peaceful Schools

A number of theorists call for schools to broaden their notion of what it means to be an educated person, to include teaching children how to get along with others in addition to academic skills. This is variously termed emotional education (Goleman, 1995), character education, moral education, social problem skills (Elias & Clabby, 1992), and conflict resolution (Kriedler, 1994). Two subsets of this movement are violence prevention and diversity education. Advocates assert that teaching these skills will not only lead to more peaceful and successful learning environments, they will also shape youth into adults who will be more successful in their workplaces and families, and—ultimately—create a more harmonious society. Kriedler (1994) stresses the importance of six principles: cooperation, caring communication, appreciation of diversity, expression of feelings, responsible decision making, and conflict resolution. Physical conflict is not tolerated, nor are hurtful, discriminatory words or "put-downs." Students are taught a variety of ways to de-escalate conflictual situations. Typically, a variety of routes are used to communicate to students about the various "isms," for instance sexism, racism, ableism, classism, and heterosexism, and students invest in the project of creating a harmonious community. Lantieri and Patti (1996) emphasize that learning the skills of a peaceable classroom is a slow process, and educators cannot expect to achieve their goals without some resistance on the part of students who may feel "foolish, phony, or insincere" (p. 28) trying out new behaviors.

Counselors alone cannot create a peaceable school or even a peaceable classroom. Sometimes—usually in the aftermath of a change of administration, a flare up of conflict, or a tragedy—schools try to transform their culture overnight. More commonly, counselors need to work incrementally, carefully building alliances among the administrators and faculty. Counselors can seek out opportunities to inform their colleagues about the principles of peaceable schools through in-service trainings, and perhaps work closely with the teachers in a single classroom to create a peaceable classroom, which can then serve as a lab or model for the entire school.

Addressing Specific Forms of Violence

Racial Harassment and School Climate Issues

Ever since the 1960s schools have engaged in myriad efforts to improve their racial climate, ranging from changing the student body through bussing and redrawing school district lines, hiring more personnel from minority groups, changing the curriculum (by including minority authors in English classes, for example), and instituting curriculum designed specifically to improve the climate for diverse students. Three large classes of programs fall into this last category: (1) multicultural or diversity education designed to teach students about cultural differences among groups of people, (2) antiracist education that includes an analysis of social power, and (3) social justice education, which includes antiracism education along with material about other forms of oppression (e.g., sexism and ableism), and considers social justice as the desired outcome.

Despite these efforts, few multicultural schools evidence racially and ethnically harmonious environments. Discrimination, racism, and cultural bias have been defined as forms of psychological abuse, and therefore as a form of violence (Reschly & Graham-Clay, 1987). The effects of prejudice and bias in schools can be seen in curricula, the application of disciplinary procedures, the differential placement of children into honors or college-bound classes, and the differential treatment of children by race or culture. Some scholars define "institutional racism" as "unequal results," a definition that should lead any school that evidences a difference in graduation rates, test scores, grades, or club participation by race or ethnic culture into intense self-examination. A definition which mandates equal results rather than equal treatment pushes schools to support special programs to boost the achievement of those students who may have entered with disadvantages.

Racial harassment usually involves the existence of a hostile environment for people from certain racial groups. A hostile environment may be created by school personnel, students, or visitors to the school community. Behaviors that create a hostile environment include racial graffiti, racially based assaults, the presence of a confederate flag or other symbol that offends members of specific racial groups, the school's use of a mascot that demeans people of a particular racial or ethnic group, racial taunting, displaying or distributing racist materials, gestures that mock people of a particular racial group, and racist jokes.

Some people are concerned about the First Amendment implications of restricting racist speech, seeing it as a prohibitive form of censorship. However, schools routinely restrict behaviors that might be protected as free speech in other settings. For instance, dress codes frequently restrict the kinds of clothes that students may wear, and school committees frequently restrict the contents of library books, plays, school newspapers, and classroom reading lists. Given this environment, forbidding "hate speech" or harassment of all kinds does not seem so extreme. Schools should be aware that the existence of a hostile environment for members of a racial group constitutes discrimination, and school personnel who become aware of such an environment and do not try to ameliorate it can be held liable.

Children who are subjected to a hostile environment or discriminated against by school personnel may evidence lowered self-esteem, lower levels of achievement, and higher levels of acting-out behavior. Counselors who are committed to the achievement of all students must facilitate prejudice reduction and diversity education for all members of the school community.

School Shootings

School shootings are nothing new, and, as noted earlier, they are less common than they were a decade ago, perhaps due to the installation of metal detectors in urban schools and lower rates of crime in general. However, the nature of school shootings has changed somewhat. "Interpersonal school shootings" have existed for years, where the youngster yielding the gun is more likely to be from a low-income family, and be African American (Katz, 2000), and where there is rarely more than one victim in addition to the perpetrator, who sometimes kills himself. These are young people with access to guns who settle a personal score—often a perceived slight to the dignity of the killer—using fatal means in a public situation. Usually the killer targets a specific person. The murder may be seen as the killer's attempt to recover his dignity, and may be carried out impulsively. (These murders, like those of the mass killers that will be profiled here, are perpetrated almost exclusively by males.)

The "mass school killer" fits a somewhat different profile. He is more likely to be a young White teenager who has been marginalized or bullied by the more popular students as a "nerd" or "weirdo." Mass school killers often plan their attacks, work with other students, and give out clear signals that they are planning to seek revenge. They are more likely to shoot at random, or to target teachers and administrators, as well as their peers (Katz, 2000).

Organizations such as the National School Safety Center (see its website) recommend essentially a law-and-order approach to school safety, including installing video cameras to monitor areas of the school, putting elaborate locks on the doors, and cutting bushes that may obstruct a full view of school entryways. Schools are hiring security guards and installing spiked fences and emergency alert systems. Before they enter school each day, some students are required to pass through metal detectors or allow their bags to be searched at the door. Some schools are informing students that their lockers may be searched on any day for any or no reason. And some schools are adding "lock down drills" to their emergency preparedness program (Easterbrook, 1999).

Some school communities—and particularly those that have experienced repeated incidents of students bringing knives and other weapons to school, and those in neighborhoods where young people are often armed—may find such an approach helpful. In fact, assuring that schools are weapons-free zones can help make schools oases of safety in dangerous neighborhoods. Clearly, however, such an approach is not sufficient, because students who experience conflict and are determined to hurt each other can do so with weapons readily available at school, such as a chair or a fist, or conflicts can be "saved" until the end of the school day when students step outside. Additionally, members of diverse cultural groups may experience this law-and-order approach differently.

The police are an increasingly visible presence in many schools. While judicious use of law enforcement can make schools feel safer to some members of the school community, seeing police in school halls and at their doors may make youth and families of color feel *less* safe. Some parents believe that the presence of police in schools adds to the criminalization of children, and particularly children of color. Throughout the country, diverse parents are objecting to the presence of law enforcement officers in schools. According to Davis (1999–2000), "In Drew, Mississippi, a rural town of 8,000 people, of whom 80 percent are black, there are reports of 10-year-old children being taken from school to the State Department of Corrections for such 'crimes' as talking back to teachers" (p. 15).

School counselors alone cannot solve the problems of school shootings. At the same time, school counselors need to make sure they are part of a concerted plan—which draws on various members of the community—to address both potential forms of school shootings. Additionally, counselors may have a key role in helping schools explore alternatives to a police presence, and helping administrators understand the potential impact of a police presence on different segments of the school community.

Gender-Based Violence

Sexual Harassment.   Sexual harassment is considered a form of discrimination because it interferes with the target's ability to succeed in school. Sexual harassment can threaten students' physical or emotional well-being, influence their attitudes toward school, and impede their achievement. Sexual harassment can lead students to lose self-esteem, feel unsafe, drop classes, skip school, and even drop out. Additionally, sexual harassment is illegal. Title IX of the Education Amendments of 1972 prohibits sex discrimination, including sexual harassment. Preventing and remedying sexual harassment in schools is essential to ensure nondiscriminatory, safe environments in which all students can learn (U.S. Department of Education, 1997).

The problem of sexual harassment is pervasive for boys and especially girls. For instance, in many high schools, girls routinely endure catcalls, sexualized comments, and even groping as they walk down the hallway between classes. In elementary and middle schools, distinct forms of sexual harassment sometimes acquire their own descriptors, such as "grading" (rating girls' sexual attractiveness), "drooping" (boys pulling down girls' gym shorts), flip-flopping (boys pulling up girls' skirts as often as possible on designated flip-flop days), and of course mooning (kids deliberately exposing themselves to each other). School faculty and staff are often aware of these public forms of harassment and do little to intervene (Stein, 1993). Ignoring these systematic harassing behaviors would be unthinkable if another group of people—defined by race or ethnic origin, for instance—was routinely subject to degrading or abusive treatment by their peers. Unfortunately, ignoring harassing behavior often leads to an increase in its frequency and intensity—it does not go away and the perpetrators do not cease their behaviors unless motivated to do so.

There are two kinds of sexual harassment: quid pro quo and hostile environment. In the first, a person in a position of power (such as a teacher, counselor, administrator, team captain, or athletics coach) requests sexual favors in exchange for special treatment (such as a higher grade or a spot on a team). Sexualized attention by adults directed toward minors is sexual harassment and may also constitute prosecutable child sexual abuse.

Hostile environment sexual harassment can be inflicted by anyone on school grounds including students, faculty, staff, or visitors. Adults (usually men) create a hostile environment when they make sexualized comments to children (e.g., "I think you're the sexiest girl in the sixth grade," or "Stay after swim class, girls, and I'll work with you on strokes"), or when they are aware of peer sexual harassment and allow it to persist. Peer sexual harassment is often seen as bullying that has taken a sexual form. Stein (1993) refers to it as "gendered terrorism" (p. 3). A hostile environment exists when unwelcome sexual conduct is so severe, persistent, or pervasive that it affects a student's ability to participate in or benefit from an education program or activity, or creates an intimidating, threatening or abusive educational environment.

Examples of behavior that could be considered sexual harassment include unwanted sexual advances, sexual touching, sexualized graffiti, displaying or distributing sexually explicit materials, sexual gestures, sexual or "dirty" jokes, pressure for sexual favors, touching oneself sexually or talking about one's sexual activity in front of others, and spreading rumors about or rating other students as to sexual activity, attractiveness, or performance. Explicit Department of Education guidelines (1997) indicate that not all sexualized behavior constitutes sexual harassment, and school personnel are encouraged to use their judgment and common sense in determining whether a behavior should be handled under the sexual harassment policy and when it should be handled according to other disciplinary procedures, taking the child's age into account. For example, consider each of the following incidents, which may seem similar on their surface:

> Four-year-old Samuel frequently rubs and touches his genitals in his pre-school classroom, particularly when stressed.
>
> Six-year-old Elena frequently rubs and touches her genitals in her first-grade classroom, and follows specific boys, asking them to touch her, too.
>
> One day twelve-year-old Joshua, who is known as something of a joker and a "wise guy," pulls out his penis while on the school bus to "freak out" the kid sitting across from him.
>
> Fourteen-year-old Matt rubs his genitals whenever he sees his classmate, Cindy, and sends her notes telling her what he'd like to do to her. She has asked him to stop but he persists.

While each of these incidents seems similar, there are important differences. In the first example, there is no indication of the behaviors being directed toward other children or even being noticed by them. Sam may be suffering from an infection, may be self-soothing, or may be acting out experiences of sexual molestation. Samuel is in need of empathic intervention because masturbating at school is not appropriate, but this situation could be termed neither sexual harassment nor a disciplinary problem. Elena's behavior is directed toward other children and could certainly constitute sexual harassment. However, given her young age, Elena is in need of supportive interventions aimed at understanding the root of her behavior (sexual acting out of this kind may be due to experience of molestation or exposure to inappropriate stimulus), and helping her stop these behaviors. In the third instance, Joshua has engaged in an inappropriate behavior directed at a specific child. Because it is a one-time instance and fits into Joshua's behavioral pattern, it is probably more productive to handle this as a routine disciplinary incident than a situation of sexual harassment. However, as in the other cases, it would be wise to explore with Joshua why he chose to act out in the sexual way at this time. In the final situation, Matt is clearly sexually harassing Cindy. Cindy needs immediate protection and Matt's behavior should be handled according to the disciplinary procedures in place for sexual harassment. At the same time, sexual acting out by someone Matt's age may still indicate a history of sexual victimization, and this needs to be investigated compassionately.

Court rulings in the 1990s have made it clear that school personnel who ignore instances of sexual harassment that have been called to their attention do so at their own peril (Schimmel, 2000). Schools need to respond to notice of possible sexual harassment by taking immediate and appropriate steps to determine what occurred, and take reasonable steps to end any harassment, eliminate a hostile environment if one has been created, and prevent harassment from occurring again. By federal law, schools are required to have a written policy on sexual harassment including procedures for filing grievances. This policy needs to be made known throughout the school community. School counselors are often selected to make members of the school community aware of the procedures for reporting sexual harassment, and school counselors are frequently the first school personnel to learn about instances of sexual harassment. School counselors can also help the targeted students recover their faith in the school, their feelings of safety, and their ability to succeed.

Policing the Gender Polarities

> Earl is shorter and slighter than many of the other boys in his high school sophomore class. He runs on the cross-country team, but he is most passionate about books and theater. He loves reading alone in his room. His grades have always been outstanding. Over the years, he has been teased for his academic prowess, small size, and gestures that others perceive as effeminate. One day, while he is standing in line at the cafeteria, a student sneaks up behind him and ties his shoes together. He stumbles when he tries to walk forward, and blushes as a ring of boys forms around him, mocking him as he unknots his laces. He breathes a sigh of relief as an English teacher approaches, expecting the teacher to come to his aid. The teacher laughs when he sees what has happened and tells Earl that if he would just stop being such a "wuss," the other kids wouldn't pick on him.

Much of the gender-based violence in school involves students (and sometimes educators) oppressing students who are not seen as conforming sufficiently to gender stereotypes. For instance, boys who are seen as not manly or macho enough, perhaps because they are studious, artistic, or not athletic, may be called "fag," hung up by their underwear in the locker room, and generally tormented as "sissies." Girls who are seen as insufficiently feminine in looks and behavior, perhaps because they are strong and athletic, or choose not to be flirtatious or subservient to boys, may suffer similar attacks. The frequent pejorative use of homophobic names (e.g., queer, fag, dyke) keeps these students and others in line, forcing them to either conform to traditional gender stereotyping or risk physical and verbal assaults by their peers. Obviously, this kind of forced conformity inhibits children's ability to express their inner selves.

The marginalization and oppression of children who deviate from standard gender-role expectations has special implications for multicultural schools because of the ways gender is expressed in various cultures. For example, often boys from the Indian subcontinent are raised to be more contemplative, studious, and less athletic than boys from Anglo American families. Boys from many immigrant families are expected to nurture and care for their younger siblings. These boys are apt to be especially targeted for not conforming to narrow definitions of gender roles. Additionally, Jewish and African American girls may be raised to be self-sufficient and speak their minds in a way that is less common for girls from other cultures. These children—and others who do not conform to traditional gender stereotypes—should not be oppressed for "being themselves."

Assuring Safety for Gay, Lesbian, Bisexual, and Questioning Students

> "I just began hating myself more and more, as each year the hatred towards me grew and escalated from just simple name-calling in elementary school to having persons in

high school threaten to beat me up, being pushed and dragged around on the ground, having hands slammed in lockers, and a number of other daily tortures"—a gay male high school student. (Gay, Lesbian & Straight Education Network, 1999)

A year-long, student-generated survey in Iowa found that young people heard antigay comments once every 7 minutes while at school, which totals more than 26 times each day, and that educators who heard those comments failed to intervene 97 percent of the time (Bowman, 1999). Schools are required to treat all students equally, regardless of their perceived sexual orientation. This includes protecting students from antigay harassment, just as they are required to protect students from other kinds of harassment. In 1996 a Wisconsin jury awarded a student nearly one million dollars after it found that his school had failed to stop repeated antigay harassment directed at him (Just the Facts Coalition, 1999).

Through diversity education and fostering an atmosphere of mutual acceptance, school counselors can work to create a school climate where girls and boys express themselves freely, without fearing condemnation for stepping outside gender stereotyped behavior, or expressing a gay, lesbian, or bisexual orientation. Clearly, homophobic terms like "fag" and "dyke" have no more place in a school than pejorative racist terms. Several schools have instituted programs to make their communities "put-down-free zones" (see Fogg, 1999). Additionally, gay–straight alliances have sprung up in recent years in schools throughout the United States. Gay–straight alliances provide opportunities for students of all sexual orientations to get together in a safe environment for social events and school-based education and intervention about issues of sexual orientation. The Safe Schools movement emerged in response to high rates of antigay harassment in schools, and high rates of suicide among lesbian, gay, bisexual, transsexual, and questioning (LGBTQ) youth. Local and state Safe Schools coalitions work to help schools and school districts create, support, and enhance learning environments that are free from antigay harassment, intimidation, and violence. The Sexual Minority Youth Assistance League makes the following suggestions (Bowman, 1999, p. 18):

- Enact antiharassment policies to protect LGBTQ youth from verbal and physical abuse.
- Include sexual orientation in student and staff nondiscrimination policies.
- Mandate LGBTQ support groups and gay–straight alliances in all secondary schools.
- Integrate positive LGBTQ images and issues into existing courses across school curriculum.
- Discuss sexual orientation and safe sexual behavior for LGBTQ youth in health and sex education classes.
- Purchase LGBTQ books and resources for school libraries.
- Create an anonymous system for reporting LGBTQ harassment and violence in schools.
- Provide referrals to support organizations for LGBTQ youth and their parents and friends.

■ Hire openly LGBTQ faculty, staff, and administrators to provide role models for all students.

Gangs

Gangs are often hard to pin down, with membership frequently informal and unstable. In the late 1980s, as part of the "war on drugs," states began efforts to enhance punishments of gang-related offenses, created new categories of crimes specific to gang activity, and even criminalized gang membership itself (Pintado-Vertner & Chang, 1999–2000). As part of this effort, state and federal law enforcement agencies began developing large databases containing the names of hundreds of thousands of suspected gang members—in their great majority, youth of color. The American Civil Liberties Union has filed suits challenging local authorities' definitions of gang membership, and asserting that such practices serve to criminalize youth before crimes have been committed. In some areas, employers have been able to contact local police and ask if given individuals were on "the list." In Denver in 1993, an investigation revealed that eight of every ten young persons of color were on the list. In response to public outcry, protocols were changed in Denver, but clearly remain discriminatory there and elsewhere, by holding certain kinds of jewelry, tattoos, and clothing styles as "evidence" of gang membership.

The notion of "gangs" is clearly racially based. When members of a mostly White athletic team or a group of White friends commits a crime or a series of crimes, they are not likely to be prosecuted as gang members, although they may wear distinctive clothing, congregate in groups, and so on. Similar groups of youth of color are apt to be perceived as members of a gang, and face harsher criminal punishment because of it. A thorough discussion of combating gang violence in multicultural schools is beyond the scope of this chapter. However, counselors are urged to be cautious in applying the label "gang" to a group of young people of color.

Child Abuse Intervention in Multicultural Schools

Counselors who work in multicultural schools have the same obligations to report suspected child abuse and neglect as do professionals who work in less diverse settings. This reporting may be complicated, however, by counselors' concerns that well-meaning parents will be punished due to their lack of knowledge of United States laws or for cultural differences in disciplinary practices (Bradley, 1998; Fontes, 2000c). Research on whether professionals are more or less likely to report child abuse suspected in minority families is inconclusive (Ards, Chung, & Myers, 1998). It may be that professionals are more apt to report child abuse in minority families because their biases lead them to be more likely to suspect inadequate parenting, or to confuse cultural practices with inadequate parenting. In his research on teachers' reporting practices in schools, however, R. Wilson (1999, personal communication) found that White teachers regularly overlooked clear evidence of neglect and abuse presented by

African American children in poor neighborhoods. He hypothesized that the teachers were hesitant to report for three main reasons: (1) they had grown accustomed to the high levels of poverty in the neighborhood and failed to notice when children were neglected; (2) they were afraid of being perceived as racist; and (3) they felt genuinely confused about child discipline techniques that appeared to have a cultural foundation but crossed the line into abuse. Because of their cultural and social class differences from the children they were teaching, they repeatedly overlooked signs of "reportable" problems such as children complaining that they were hungry, or showing bruises.

Counselors should remember that children from all cultural groups can be vulnerable to child abuse and neglect, and all children deserve the same level of protection and safety (Fontes, 2000a). Therefore, it behooves counselors to attend equally to the needs of all maltreated children regardless of their cultural background (Fontes, 2000b). Immigrant, minority, and low-income families are apt to be less familiar with the potential benefits of social services and may view them with caution or downright suspicion. However, this should not cause counselors to neglect their legal (and moral) obligation to report suspected child abuse and neglect. Rather, the reporting and accompanying interventions should be conducted in culturally competent ways (see Fontes, 1995, 2000b, 2002).

Beyond reporting, school counselors can help children succeed in school through counseling and classroom interventions, and reaching out to nonoffending parents (Barrett-Kruse, Martinez, & Carll, 1998; Fontes, 2000a). A number of authors have suggested that children's victimization in the home increases their response to trauma exposure in other situations, such as the trauma of racism (Sanchez-Hucles, 1998), community chaos and instability (Duckworth, Hale, Clair, & Adams, 2000), and community violence (Garbarino, Dubrow, Kostelny, & Pardo, 1992). The effects of trauma appear to be additive and increase greatly with each additional risk factor (Garbarino et al., 1992). In other words, when children who live in a generally sound environment are exposed to a single trauma (e.g., a single episode of school violence), they recover more easily than do those who are exposed to multiple traumas (e.g., victimization at home, street violence, the loss of a parent, and an episode of school violence). Counselors who work in schools where children suffer multiple traumas need to do their best to reduce children's *vulnerability* to violence at school and at home, and create supportive and healing environments in school. Reducing home-based trauma in children's lives is also apt to contribute to a more orderly school environment, because children with a history of traumatic exposure are more likely to act out in school in a variety of ways.

Suicide

Suicide is a form of violence against the self, family, and community. Suicide is currently the third leading cause of death among children, and the second among older teenagers (Brody, 1992). When a student—usually an adolescent—commits suicide, sorrow, anger, and confusion ripple through the school community for years to come. While girls make more suicide gestures and attempts than boys, more boys actually kill themselves than girls, because boys usually choose more lethal and irreversible means. For example, girls are more likely to cut their wrists or attempt to overdose on pills, whereas boys are more likely to shoot themselves with a gun or hang themselves. Additionally, there is no way of knowing what proportion of adolescent deaths by "accidental" means—such as automobile accidents, fatally reckless behavior, and gang-related shootings—are actually a masked form of suicide. Anxiety, depression, access to a firearm, and use of drugs and alcohol emerge as potent risk factors. Currently, little information is available about whether risk factors vary among different ethnic groups.

Some suicidal teens suffer greatly from anxiety. These include successful students who are anxious about their ability to meet parents', teachers', and their own expectations, as well as students who experience fear and dread from other causes, such as violence at home or at school, a recent arrest, breaking up with a romantic interest, or dread about taking an important test or moving to a new school. These students may be pathologically focused on a single event, believing that its outcome will determine their future (Brody, 1992).

Youngsters who are depressed are thirty times more likely to commit suicide than other youth (Brody, 1992). The depression may manifest itself in suicidal male teens with symptoms of irritability, difficulty concentrating, racing thoughts, and impulsivity. This is different from the numbness or weepy hopelessness that is common in adult women.

Many depressed teenagers try to overcome their depression through using drugs and alcohol, which serve to deepen the depression and reduce inhibitions, and is a potent risk factor. Additionally, those students who are frequently referred to the counselor for their behavior problems, such as getting into fights, disrupting classes, vandalism, running away from home or truancy, are also at increased risk for suicide.

Below are some concrete steps counselors can take to reduce the risk of suicide in schools.

1. In the beginning of the year, in a letter introducing yourself to parents, advise them to make sure children do not have access to firearms.
2. Seek out information and conduct information sessions for teachers, parents, and/or students. These trainings do not have to contain "suicide" in the title, and instead can focus on depression, anxiety, drug, or alcohol use. For example, a workshop for parents might be called "Surviving and Thriving: Your Child's Teen Years," and include a section on suicidality (see Poland, 1989, for suggestions).
3. Provide teachers with an "alert" form so they can provide you with information about students whom they feel may be suffering from depression, anxiety, or other mental health problems. Encourage teachers to discuss with you any student writing (in an English class, for instance) that makes the teacher believe the student may be at risk. (If the protocol approach described earlier were implemented in a school, it would automatically be triggered by the earliest expressions of suicidal ideation).

4. Be alert to signs that youth are in trouble. Whenever working with a student who shows behavioral problems, remember that the problems may be a cry for help, and be sure not to restrict your response only to punishment.

5. Remember that experiences of sexual assault are risk factors for girls, in particular, but also for boys. Be alert to signs that children may be abused sexually in their families, or assaulted by others (including boyfriends). Train yourself to handle issues of sexual abuse and assault, and make it known to students that you—or another professional—are available to provide counseling and other forms of assistance on this issue.

6. Make sure your school has a protocol in place to handle suicide and minimize the subsequent trauma and the likelihood of "copycat" attempts (see Poland, 1989).

Reducing Violence in Multicultural Schools

It would be wonderful if all societal violence could be overcome through school interventions. Unfortunately, as long as children are exposed to violence in the media, their homes, and their communities, schools are apt to make only a modest difference. However, this should not prompt us to throw up our hands in despair. Rather, we should make efforts to widen our sphere of influence to address the societal roots of violence, even as we attempt to address violence in schools.

What improvements are realistically within the reach of an individual school counselor? I have no doubt that schools can have an impact on individual children, on cohorts of children, and on communities. Schools can help children understand and relate to others, even people who are different from them. Schools can help children learn "the fourth R"—resolution of conflicts—along with reading, writing, and 'rithmetic. Working alone, individual counselors have limited impact. But counselors who form meaningful alliances with other counselors, teachers, administrators, students, parents, and community members, will see their violence reduction efforts bear fruit. Such alliances are especially necessary—and can be especially successful—in schools with multicultural student populations.

DISCUSSION QUESTIONS

1. Compare and contrast two forms of violence that may exist in a multicultural school. Be sure to refer to similarities and differences in the ways that the violence manifests and can be resolved.

2. Describe the relationship between physical and nonphysical forms of violence.

3. Describe the relationship between violence in school and violence in other areas of a child's life.

4. Describe the protocol approach to school violence, and why it might be especially useful in a multicultural school.

5. Compare and contrast protocol approaches and conflict resolution strategies as ways to handle interethnic conflict.

6. Compare and contrast the exchange and transformative approaches to mediation of violence in multicultural schools. If you favor one, say why.

7. Do you think the peaceful schools approach could be implemented in one of the schools you attended (or where you work)? Describe why or why not.

8. Imagine you are a school counselor, about to implement the peaceful schools approach in a multicultural middle school. Describe four steps you would take to assure the program's success.

9. Compare and contrast the three major classes of programs for improving the racial climate in multicultural schools.

10. How could a hostile racial environment in a school impact student achievement?

11. Do you think it is a counselor's job to work at eliminating racial and sexual harassment? Why or why not?

12. Compare and contrast "interpersonal school killings" and "mass school killings."

13. Why do you think school shootings have gained such attention in recent years, despite the fact that the numbers of children shot in schools has decreased?

14. Describe potential problems of the "law and order" approach to school violence, including lockdown drills, inspection of backpacks and lockers, and police presence.

15. Why might certain children and families feel uncomfortable with police in their schools? How might this affect their learning?

16. Is sexual harassment just an issue of kids kissing kids? Should school counselors intervene?

17. Should school counselors intervene in instances of homophobic harassment, or work to create a safe environment for gay, lesbian, bisexual, and questioning youth? Why or why not?

18. Do you think school counselors can have an important role in reducing violence in multicultural schools? Why or why not?

19. Why is it sometimes hard for school counselors to know what to do when they suspect that a child from a different culture has been abused or neglected at home? What should they do?

20. Describe four steps school counselors can take to reduce the likelihood of students committing suicide.

REFERENCES

Aber, J., Jones, S., Brown, J., Chadry, N., & Samples, F. (1998). Resolving conflict creatively: Evaluating the developmental effects of a school-based violence prevention program in neighborhood and classroom context. *Development and Psychopathology, 10,* 187–213.

ACLU-SC (American Civil Liberties Union of Southern California) (1997). From words to weapons: The violence surrounding our schools, http://www.aclu_sc.org/school.html.

Ards, S., Chung, C., & Myers, S. L. (1998). The effects of sample selection bias on racial differences in child abuse reporting. *Child Abuse and Neglect, 22,* 103–115.

Baker, M., French, V., Trujillo, M., & Wing, L. (2000). How CRE has not addressed the needs of diverse populations. In T. S. Jones & D. Knitta (Eds.). *Does it work: The case for conflict resolution education in our nation's schools* (pp. 61–78). Washington, DC: CREnet.

Barrett-Kruse, C., Martinez, E., & Carll, N. (1998). Beyond reporting suspected abuse: Positively influencing the development of the students within the classroom. *Professional School Counseling 1*, 57–60.

Bowman, C. (September & October, 1999). Washington, DC: SMYAL serving LGBTQ Youth. *The Fourth R*, *88*, 17–18.

Bradley, C. R. (1998). Cultural interpretations of child discipline: Voices of African American scholars. *The Family Journal*, *6*, 272–278.

Brody, J. (June 16, 1992). Suicide myths cloud efforts to save children. *The New York Times*, C12.

Campbell, C. (2000). K–12 Peer Helper Programs. In J. Wittmer (Ed.), *Managing your school counseling program: K–12 developmental strategies* (pp. 229–242). Minneapolis, MN: Educational Media Corporation.

Davis, N. (Winter, 1999–2000). Schoolground or police state. *ColorLines*, p. 15.

Donahue, E., Schiraldi, V., & Macallais, D. (1998). *School house hype: The school shootings and the real risk kids face in America.* San Francisco, CA: Justice Policy Institute.

Duckworth, M. P., Hale, D. D., Clair, S. C., & Adams, H. E. (2000). Influence of interpersonal violence and community chaos on stress reactions in children. *Journal of Interpersonal Violence, 15*, 806–826.

Easterbrook, M. (July/August 1999). Taking aim at violence. *Psychology Today*, 52–56.

Elias, M. & Clabby, J. F. (1992). *Building social problem skills: Guidelines from a school-based program.* San Francisco: Jossey-Bass.

Fogg, R. W. (September & October, 1999). Schools stop put-downs. *The Fourth R*, *88*, 8–9.

Fontes, L. A. (1995). *Sexual abuse in nine North American cultures: Treatment and prevention.* Newbury Park, CA: Sage.

Fontes, L. A. (2000a). Children exposed to marital violence: How school counselors can help. *Professional School Counseling, 3*, 231–237.

Fontes, L. A. (2000b). *Interviewing immigrant children about child maltreatment* (Audiotape). Newbury Park, CA: Sage.

Fontes, L. A. (2000c). Working with Latino families on issues of child abuse and neglect. *The National Child Advocate*, *3*(1), 4–7.

Fontes, L. (2002). Child discipline and physical abuse in immigrant Latino families: Reducing violence and misunderstandings. *Journal of Counseling and Development, 80*, in press.

Garbarino, J., Dubrow, N., Kostelny, K., & Pardo, C. (1992). *Children in danger.* New York: Jossey-Bass.

Gay, Lesbian & Straight Education Network (September & October, 1999). Just the facts. *The Fourth R*, *88*, 10–11.

Goleman, D. (1995). *Emotional intelligence.* New York: Bantam Books.

Just the Facts Coalition (1999). *Just the facts about sexual orientation & youth: A primer for principals, educators & school personnel.* Available from the American Counseling Association.

Katz, D. M. (June 19, 2000). Profile seen emerging in school shootings. *The National Underwriter*, pp. 9 & 14.

Kriedler, W. J. (1994). *Conflict resolution in the middle school.* Cambridge, MA: Educators for Social Responsibility.

Moriarty, A. L. & Kalill, P. M. (1999). *Mental health and children: A protocol approach to school violence.* Springfield, MA: Kalill, Moriarty & Associates.

Moriarty, A. L., Kalill, P. M., & Benander, M. (2001). The protocol approach to school violence. *Smith College Studies in Social Work, 71*, 279–296.

Pintago-Vertner, R. & Chang, J. (Winter, 1999–2000). The war on youth. *ColorLines.*

Poland, S. (1989). *Suicide intervention in the schools.* New York: Guilford.

Reschly, D. J. & Graham-Clay, S. (1987). Psychological abuse from prejudice and cultural bias. In M. R. Brassard, R. Germain, & S. N. Hart (Eds.), *Psychological maltreatment of children and youth.* New York: Pergamon.

Sanchez-Hucles, J. (1998). Racism: Emotional abusiveness and psychological trauma for ethnic minorities. *Journal of Emotional Abuse, 1*(2), 69–87.

Schimmel, D. (2000). When schools are liable for peer sexual harassment: an analysis of Davis v. Monroe. *Education Law Reports, 141*, 437–452.

Stein, N. (1993). Secrets in public: Sexual harassment in public (and private) schools. Working paper #256. Wellesley, MA: Wellesley College Centers for Research on Women.

U.S. Department of Education, Office of Civil Rights. (1997). Sexual harassment guidance (electronic version). Available at http://www.ed.gov/offices/OCR/OCRpubs.html.

U.S. Department of Education. (1998). *Early warning, timely response: A guide to safe schools.*

AUTHOR NOTE

Lisa Aronson Fontes is a psychologist dedicated to making the social service, mental health, and education systems meet the needs of diverse people. She edited the book, *Sexual Abuse in Nine North American Cultures: Treatment and Prevention*, and has written numerous articles and chapters on school and family violence. She has conducted research in Chile and with people from various ethnic groups in the United States. Dr. Fontes frequently conducts training sessions on cultural issues for diverse professionals, and serves as an ethics and cultural competency consultant on research projects. She is fluent in Spanish and Portuguese.

12 Cross-Cultural Career Counseling in Schools

FREDERICK T. L. LEONG
Ohio State University

VICKY L. M. TAN
National University of Singapore

OBJECTIVES

1. To present several current models of cross-cultural career counseling
2. To discuss the need for cross-cultural career counseling in schools in relation to culturally different students
3. To discuss the problems associated with Western models of career counseling

In this chapter, we will provide school counselors with several current models of cross-cultural career counseling. To provide a context for the discussion of those models, we begin by describing culturally different students and their unique backgrounds and experiences. Next, we discuss why cross-cultural career counseling models are needed. A major reason for the need for cross-cultural counseling approaches that are distinct and different is due to the problems inherent in Western models of career counseling. These problems are also presented in the chapter. Finally, we move to a presentation of the actual models of culturally appropriate career counseling.

Culturally Different Students

In recent years the counseling of culturally different students from various ethnic and racial groups has presented both a challenge and an impetus for setting new directions in the field. Professionals are increasingly aware of the need to develop career counseling objectives and strategies that can appropriately address the needs of a culturally diverse population (Lee, 1995a; Leong, 1995). There are various groups of culturally different students in the United States but the literature primarily focuses on four: African Americans, Hispanic Americans, Asian Americans, and Native Americans

(Osipow & Littlejohn, 1995). Despite these categorizations, it is clear that diversity exists across and within each of these groups.

Census data over the last decades have shown significant changes in the number, distribution, and the ethnic group characteristics of culturally diverse populations (Aponte & Crouch, 2000). The U.S. Bureau of Census growth record of 1990 to 2000 shows a steady population increase in all the different racial ethnic groups except the White, European American group, whose population decreased. From 1990 to 2000, with a total population growth of 248 to 275 million for this period, the Hispanic American population grew from 9 to 11.8 percent of the total in these respective years, African Americans from 11.8 to 12.2 percent, Asian Americans from 2.8 to 3.8 percent. Native Americans remained the same at 0.7 percent while White, European Americans decreased from 75.7 to 71.4 percent (U.S. Census Bureau, 2000).

Some estimates are that by 2020, the majority of school-age children in the United States will be from racial/ethnic minority groups (Hodgkinson, 1985; cf., Lee, 1995a). The Western Institute Commission for Higher Education and the College Board (1988) conducted a review of the public elementary and secondary school enrollment trends by race/ethnicity for the period from 1985 to 1995. The indication then was that during this period, White students, while still a majority, would be a smaller proportion of the overall elementary and secondary school population. It was expected that White enrollments would decrease from 71 to 66 percent. Conversely, Asia/Pacific Islander enrollments in the nation's schools were increasing more rapidly than any other group, more than 70 percent between 1985 and 1995. Latino/Hispanic enrollments were also increasing rapidly, more than 54 percent, from 3.3 to 5.1 million during this period. African Americans were still expected to be the second largest racial/ethnic group among enrolled students. Finally Native Americans, although the smallest racial/ethnic group would still experience a 29 percent increase in enrollment.

These data illuminate the social and cultural pluralism of the U.S. school environment. Children representing diverse behavioral styles, attitudinal orientations, and value systems have been brought together with one goal: to maximize their potential as human beings (Lee, 1989). In the midst of such sweeping demographic changes, school counselors, educators, and professionals have various issues to consider. Apart from gaining an understanding of the situation, they have to look into providing comprehensive services that promote student development. The American School Counselor Association has established a position statement on cross-multicultural counseling that calls for the facilitation of student development through an understanding of and appreciation for cultural diversity. This position statement encourages school counselors to take the necessary action to ensure that students from culturally diverse backgrounds receive services that foster their development (Lee, 1995b). Although there are provisions for a series of strategies to develop the awareness, knowledge, and skills necessary for promoting cultural diversity within the school environment and beyond (American School Counselor Association, 1988), there is an emergent realization that current services often do not have broad applicability across the range of cultural backgrounds represented by students.

School counselors have become increasingly aware that their practices primarily reflect the values of the European and European American middle-class culture. In contrast, the cultural values of a significant portion of their student clientele represent world views whose origins are African, Asian, Mexican, Central American, Caribbean, or Middle Eastern (Lee, 1995b). Along with this awareness, counselors may become frustrated in their attempts to promote student development, as the values inherent in counseling and those of the culturally diverse students often are mismatched in the helping process (Lee, 1989). This frustration experienced by the school counseling professionals is compounded by the fact that many received little or no systematic training in cross-cultural counseling (Carey, Reinat, & Fontes, 1990). This is because in most counselor education and related training programs, training in cross-cultural work is still a relatively new curriculum dimension (Ponterotto & Casas, 1987).

Counseling professionals need a framework from which to operate if they are going to ensure that students from culturally diverse backgrounds have access to services that promote optimal development. Professionals are increasingly aware of the need to develop career counseling objectives and strategies that will help students from these various ethnic and racial groups overcome a multitude of barriers that may impede career development for this population. The barriers may include stereotypes, prejudice and discrimination, any form of bias, language differences, and cultural differences (Zunker, 1990). The need for career services to be equipped to address and help culturally different students overcome these environmental barriers cannot be overemphasized.

Omizo and D'andrea (1995) noted that the current level of interest and demand for curriculum changes reflect a respect for cultural ethnic and racial difference and this will continue to increase. Given the state of current curriculum material such as textbooks and the nature of teacher training which often lacks a multicultural perspective, it will undoubtedly take time for schools to make the transition to a cross-cultural orientation in the context and process of American education.

With the sizeable increase of the different ethnic minorities in the population of the United States, their needs cannot be ignored. This growing cultural diversity in the population and workforce in the United States has led to an increasing awareness of the need to improve current understanding of racial and ethnic minorities in the workforce (Jackson & Associates 1992; Triandis, Kurowski, & Gelfand, 1994).

According to Lee (1995) one main focus in developmental counseling that is a major principle for guidance and counseling is promoting human development (Myrick, 1987). This approach focuses on the needs at each life stage and the development of human potential such as life management skills. The emphasis is on growth, differentiation, and the use of resources to meet the needs of students from diverse cultural background.

If one takes the perspective that the mission of the schools is to prepare students for life (Jackson, 1987), the need is then to help students master more than academic knowledge. The education goals may entail helping students develop skills that include but are not limited to social, cognitive, emotional, psychological, and ethical competencies. The purpose of classroom education would then move away from academic centrism to meet students' social, emotional needs, and look into the development of a person's worth, sense of competence, and personal well-being (Omizo & D'andrea, 1995).

The cross-cultural perspective seeks to understand the cultural background and its impact on psychological development. This perspective takes into consideration the context of the student, including cultural tradition, family values, and language. All of these impact on the student's development (Omizo & D'andrea, 1995).

The need is for professionals and educators to grow in cross-cultural awareness and be more tolerant and respectful of individual differences. On a broader level, the need is to increase and enhance the incorporation of multicultural orientation in school materials so that the approach is more culturally sensitive and relevant in terms of content and process.

Why Do We Need Cross-Cultural Career Counseling?

An observer of the developing literature on cross-cultural counseling will surely notice that despite having a subpopulation of racial and ethnic minorities in this country since its founding in the 1700s, a significant growth in the literature did not occur until the last two decades. One way to understand this development is to adopt the neo-classical approach of economics to our current problem, namely the utilitarian view of human behavior. According to this approach, human beings (social scientists included) are motivated by self-interest and will make choices aimed at maximizing their self-interest. In this perspective, human beings are only likely to change their behaviors if and when the new behaviors will help them maximize their utility.

In previous decades, counseling of culturally different students received little attention as their numbers were too insignificant to affect counselors' functioning and performance. In other words, being able to work with these small numbers of racial and ethnic minority group clients did not much affect the day-to-day functioning and performance of counselors. However this is fast changing. The Workforce 2000 Report (Johnson & Packer, 1987) confirmed that an increasingly culturally diverse population has transformed the demographics in the United States. With this, more and more social scientists and counseling practitioners realize that it is essential for them to be more knowledgeable about these culturally different clients. With an increasingly culturally diverse population, lacking such cross-cultural competence is a significant problem for counselors. Therefore the changing demographics within the United States is the major impetus for the current movement toward greater cross-cultural competence in health and mental health services.

Koss-Chioino and Vargas (1992) suggested that social environmental factors play an important role in a student's psychosocial development. In the complex cultural context of the American society, the major factors identified are racism, economic disadvantage, and acculturation.

Pinderhughes (1973) defined racism as a pattern of discrimination and prejudice between one group who is idealized and favored and another group who is devalued and exploited solely on the basis of race. The racial/ethnic group that an individual belongs to and whether that group is in the majority or minority would determine the extent and impact of racism. Racism can adversely affect the cultural dynamics associated with the ethnic identity development of both ethnic minority and majority youths.

According to Koss-Chioino and Vargas (1992), poverty affects racial/ethnic groups disproportionately. Economic disadvantage in the form of poor housing, inadequate schooling, and low-quality health care negatively impact most aspects of family and community life and in turn adversely affect the psychosocial development of children and adolescents.

Lee (1991) asserts that in the context of U.S. society, acculturation refers to the degree to which an individual identifies with the attitudes, behaviors, and values of the predominant macroculture, which is primarily rooted in the culture and traditions of middle-class Americans of European origin.

The extent to which a young person is successfully acculturated depends on the person's racial/ethnic group and whether that group has majority or minority status in society (Lee, 1995). Acculturation can be a major developmental challenge for young people from ethnic minority groups. Young people from ethnic minority backgrounds often find themselves trying to straddle the two cultures. They must be able to master the tasks of balancing their own ethnic identity with that which will ensure social and economic success in the macroculture.

The social environmental factors described here are not exhaustive but they play an important role in the students' psychosocial development (Lee, 1995). To effectively meet the academic, career, and social needs of students from diverse racial/ethnic backgrounds, school counseling professionals must understand and consider such dimensions in the helping process. This would help facilitate the students' developmental process within myriad of cultural contexts.

As the cultural diversity within our schools, workforce, and communities increases (Fitzgerald & Betz, 1994; Fouad, 1995; Savickas, 1995), scholars and practitioners have begun reflecting on the extent to which existing career choice and development theories explain, predict, and describe the career development and vocational behavior of racial and ethnic minority group students (see for example, Fitzgerald & Betz, 1994; Leong, 1995; Savickas, 1995). Some have argued that extant career development theories and career counseling models are of limited utility for the racial and ethnic minority students. These models are primarily applicable to college-educated, White, male, middle-class individuals. Such a claim derives support from those who quickly note that most research in psychology and on career theories generally involve White, European American, college undergraduate students (Fitzgerald & Betz, 1994; Triandis, 1994).

We need cross-cultural career counseling models because most, if not all, of the major career development theories that guide the work of career counselors have been developed for the majority population, namely White European Americans. And because culture is such a major influence on human behavior, there are strong suspicions that these Western-based models may not be relevant for racial and ethnic minorities (see Leong, 1995). More accurately, we do not know if these models will work with racial and ethnic minority students. As will be discussed, we need to evaluate the cultural validity of these Western-based models. At the same time, we also need to develop models that more closely approximate the cultural realities of racial and ethnic minorities.

Problems with Western Models of Career Counseling

In a review of the literature, Leong and Brown (1995) summarized some of the major criticisms that have plagued Western-based career choice theories: (1) they are based upon a restricted range of persons; (2) they are based upon assumptions of limited scope; (3) they confuse or inappropriately define terms such as race, ethnicity, and minority; and (4) they tend to ignore or limitedly address the sociopolitical, socioeconomic, social psychological, and sociocultural realities of minority individuals. These problems have led some scholars either to dismiss current theories as models for understanding the career behavior of diverse groups or to call for rearticulations that would render the theories more cross-culturally relevant (cf., Brooks, 1990; Smith, 1983).

Leong and Brown (1995) also observed that most theories of career choice make five assumptions: (1) career development is continuous, uninterrupted, and progressive; (2) decision makers possess the psychological, social, and economic means of effecting their choices; (3) there is dignity in all work; (4) there exists a free and open labor market; and (5) most career choices flow essentially from internal (viz., personality) factors. However, from a cross-cultural perspective, the validity of these approaches has yet to be verified.

Leong and Brown (1995) went on to observe that the problems with existing career development theories could be summarized under the dual framework of cultural validity and cultural specificity. They also proposed that cultural validity and cultural specificity are two dimensions that can serve as components of a unifying theoretical framework for cross-cultural career development. Cultural validity considers the construct, concurrent, and predictive validity of Western-based theories and models for culturally different individuals. For example, Holland's (1985) concept of congruence has been found to be predictive of job satisfaction among White Americans in the United States, but whether this prediction would also hold for culturally different minority students is yet to be confirmed.

Cultural specificity examines the concepts, constructs, and models that are specific to certain cultural groups in terms of its role in explaining and predicting behavior. An example is the concept of colorism or the level of melanin in the skin tone of African Americans as a variable in vocational behavior (Hughes & Hertel, 1990; Keith & Herring, 1991).

According to Leong and Brown (1995), we need to continue to study the cultural validity of Western-based models of career counseling and development with culturally different populations. We should not automatically assume that Western-based models would not work with racial and ethnic minorities or that they would work for all populations without empirical testing. However, testing for cultural validity will only solve half of the problem. To solve the other half, we need to develop and measure culture-specific variables that are likely to influence the career and vocational behavior of racial and ethnic minorities.

Culturally Appropriate Models of Career Counseling

In recent years, given the problems associated with applying Western-based models of career counseling to culturally different clients (see Leong, 1995), more and more scholars have begun to reformulate existing career theories with greater attention to issues of culture and context in career development and counseling. For example, Super, Savickas, and Super (1996) described how the constructs of roles and values make life-span, life-space theory more relevant to women and diverse cultural and ethnic groups. Similarly, Young, Valach, and Collin (1996) embedded issues of culture within the fabric of their contextual explanation of career. Much scholarship has also focused on examining the relevance and usefulness of career counseling models and interventions for individuals representing diverse racial and ethnic minority groups (see for example, Betz & Fitzgerald, 1995; Bowman, 1993; Subich, 1996).

Another trend has been for scholars and practitioners within the fields of vocational psychology and career development to propose more culturally appropriate models for racial and ethnic minorities. Following upon the revision and expansion of existing career theories has been the development or adaptation of several distinct models of cross-cultural career counseling. These models have been advanced in efforts to improve the process and outcome of career counseling and career intervention for clients of diverse racial and ethnic minority backgrounds by situating counseling in a cultural context (Fouad & Bingham, 1995; Leong, 1993; Leong & Brown, 1995; Leong & Hartung, 1997).

In this section, we would like to share several recently developed models useful for conducting cross-cultural career counseling. We decided that a review of these new models would be much more useful to career counselors in the schools than would a review of disparate empirical studies of career development among racial and ethnic minority students. These models were chosen for review here because they embed cultural variables and issues throughout the career counseling process. The first model was developed specifically for cross-cultural career counseling drawing primarily from the cross-cultural and multicultural counseling literature (e.g., Sue & Sue, 1990). The second model represents an elaboration of an existing developmental career assessment and counseling approach designed to increase its relevance for use in cross-cultural career counseling contexts. The third and final model is an integrative one that was developed for cross-cultural counseling in general but can be readily adapted to career counseling clients.

A Culturally Appropriate Career Counseling Model

Fouad and Bingham (1995) articulated the centrality of culture in effective career counseling in their Culturally Appropriate Career Counseling Model. The seven-step model extends prior work by Ward and Bingham (1993) who sought to develop a culturally sensitive model for use in career assessment with ethnic minority women. The model rests on the fundamental assumption that counselors must consider and attend to a wide array of important cultural variables in the career counseling process and when designing career interventions with racial and ethnic minorities. These cultural variables include, for example, racial identity development, discrimination, family and gender-role expectations, and various world view dimensions. Let us consider each of the model's steps in turn.

Step 1. Establish a Culturally Appropriate Relationship. Issues of culture are considered throughout each step of the counseling process which begins in Step 1 with the counselor establishing a culturally appropriate relationship. For many ethnic minority individuals who may prize the relationship more than any other component of counseling, this step may be the most crucial (Bingham & Ward, 1996). As in any client–counselor relationship, establishing rapport is important to successful engagement of the client in the counseling process. With racial and ethnic minorities it becomes particularly important for the counselor to attend to issues of culture that may influence the client's perception of the counseling process and their expectations for its outcome. Different clients will likely approach the relationship with a counselor differently as a function of their cultural values and beliefs. These differences may surface during counseling in verbal and nonverbal behaviors, such as level of self-disclosure and degree of eye contact, and in the client's expectations of the counselor. Fouad and Bingham (1995) noted, for example, that Asian American clients may expect the counselor to take an authoritative or expert role, whereas Hispanic clients may expect the counselor to self-disclose and share personal information. In this opening phase of cross-cultural career counseling, counselors must demonstrate flexibility in adjusting their styles to appropriately connect with the client, suspend their own stereotypes and biases, and accommodate the needs and expectations of the client relative to the role the client desires the counselor to assume in the relationship.

Step 2. Identify Career Issues. Step 2 of the Culturally Appropriate Career Counseling Model involves identifying career issues with which clients present. This step centers on determining what the client defines as a "career issue" and therefore it is important for the counselor to conceive career issues in the broadest sense. Clients must be allowed and encouraged to explore whatever problems and concerns they are experiencing across a broad range of cognitive, emotional, behavioral, environmental, and other domains. The counselor facilitates this process through open-ended questions and prompts aimed to help the client broadly examine and then specify what the client perceives and defines as career issues. To further assist in this process, Bingham and Ward (1997) described the Career Counseling Checklist and the Decision Tree as career assessments to help clients broaden their cultural perspectives on the world of work and to assist counselors to determine the need for counseling and when to address racial and ethnic issues. Fouad and Bingham (1995) also strongly advised that in this step of the counseling process, counselors help clients to explicitly define any external barriers to their career choice and development such as employer, co-worker, or institutional prejudice, racism, and discrimination.

Step 3. Assess the Effects of Cultural Variables.   Having established a culturally appropriate relationship and identified the client's career concerns and perceived barriers in steps 1 and 2, step 3 moves to assessing the effects of cultural variables on the client's career issues and decisions. The outcome of this step should be a clear understanding of how cultural variables influence the client's career decision making and development. Fouad and Bingham (1995) depicted various spheres of influence of cultural variables using a concentric circles diagram. The individual self, including biological and genetic factors, occupies the core circle with gender, family, racial, or ethnic group, and with the dominant (majority) group emanating outward from and exerting an influence on this core of the person. In counseling, the model asserts the importance of examining the full range of these variables to determine what particular spheres may be affecting the client. For example, gender-role expectations may inhibit some women from exploring traditionally male-dominated occupations. Family-based norms of duty, obligation, and deference to parents may affect the career decision-making process for various ethnic minorities. On another level, structural factors such as stereotyping, racism, and discrimination that limit racial and ethnic minority group members' participation in particular occupations can and do significantly affect and inhibit career development and work adjustment for these individuals. By working with clients to assess and pinpoint the particular cultural issues that affect their career development, appropriate treatment goals and interventions can be designed.

Step 4. Set Counseling Goals.   In a 1993 article, Leong described the importance of setting culturally appropriate goals in cross-cultural career counseling. Leong cautioned counselors against directing clients toward culturally inappropriate goals due to their own prejudices and stereotyping. For example, a counselor may become frustrated with a racial or ethnic minority client's lack of English language proficiency which may in turn dilute the career counseling services the client receives as the counselor believes the client cannot benefit from counseling. Counselors might also steer racial and ethnic minority clients toward occupations based on stereotypical beliefs about what those clients might be best suited for (e.g., Asian Americans in science occupations or Hispanic Americans in service-oriented occupations). Fouad and Bingham (1995) concurred with Leong's assessment and therefore included as step 4 of their model the importance of establishing counseling goals consistent with the client's world view, cultural value orientation, and cultural practices. Vital to this step of the process is the counselor underscoring the collaborative nature of the counseling relationship. This translates into the counselor actively working in partnership with the client to set goals that the client wants, that the client can realistically achieve, and that respect the client's cultural background.

Step 5. Design Culturally Appropriate Counseling Interventions.   In step 5 the focus of counseling centers squarely on interventions. With a trusting relationship and appropriate goals established, client and counselor work in tandem to se-lect and implement culturally relevant counseling interventions designed to promote attainment of the mutually agreed-upon goals set in the previous step. Reviewing the scant literature on career interventions with racial and ethnic minorities up to 1993, Bowman delineated several areas and types of interventions for counselors to consider using with racial and ethnic minority clients. Among her recommenda-tions, she suggested that counselors: (1) use group rather than individual interven-tions for clients with more collectivistic and relational cultural value orientations; (2) incorporate the family in the counseling and decision-making process; (3) use role models working in nontraditional occupations that appropriately reflect the racial and ethnic identity of the client and that promote the client's awareness of previously unconsidered options; (4) use career information materials in ways ap-propriate to the client's language and cultural background (see Hartung, 1996 for more discussion of this point); and (5) enlist counselors of the same ethnicity as the client to deliver the intervention.

Step 6. Make a Decision. Readiness to make a career-related decision in step 6 oc-curs only after client and counselor have successfully completed the previous 5 steps (Bingham & Ward, 1996; Fouad & Bingham, 1995). Upon reaching step 6, the client would be expected to be involved in decision making related to their specific career concerns and goals, initially implementing their plans, and moving toward closure of the counseling process. There may arise at this point a need to revisit earlier steps to reconsider or reappraise the client–counselor relationship, revise and reestablish counseling goals, or redesign intervention strategies. The model suggests here that it is incumbent upon the counselor to remain sensitive and open to the possibility of again working through previously "completed" steps.

Step 7. Implement and Follow Up. Counseling draws to a close in step 7 with the client becoming more highly involved in implementing decisions and plans toward ultimate goal attainment. Fouad and Bingham (1995) discussed how, at this step, the counselor may need to encourage the client to seek further counseling despite any feelings on the part of the client that doing so would somehow indicate that the client failed and possibly result in the client's "loss of face." The counselor must when necessary convey clearly to the client that returning to counseling occurs frequently among clients and represents an opportunity to reevaluate and improve upon the gains already made.

A Developmental Approach to Cross-Cultural Career Counseling

Taking a different approach to conceptualizing the cross-cultural career counseling process, Hartung, Vandiver, Leong, Pope, Niles, and Farrow (1998) elaborated the Career-Development Assessment and Counseling (C-DAC; Super, 1983) Model for use in career counseling with racial and ethnic minorities. Rather than developing an entirely new model, Hartung et al. decided to extend the C-DAC model as an exist-ing conceptual scheme with the goal of making it more relevant in cross-cultural counseling contexts. They argued that counselors who take a developmental career assessment and counseling approach would benefit from using this elaborated framework by increasing their awareness, knowledge, and skills relative to the influence of cultural factors on racial and ethnic minority career development and vocational behavior throughout the counseling process.

The C-DAC Model.   The four-step C-DAC approach begins in step 1 with a *preview* of the client's record and an initial interview to assess role salience. step 2, *depth-view*, comprises a formal assessment of career choice readiness and adaptability, interests, and values. *Data assessment* in step 3 reviews all information gathered, and *counseling* in step 4 explores what the data mean for the client. These four steps incorporate the following five dimensions of career assessment and counseling interventions designed to promote successful career decision making:

- role salience: the relative importance of work and non-work roles;
- career development: assessing developmental stages and tasks;
- career choice readiness: career planning attitudes and knowledge;
- values and interests; and
- tentative decision making, plan formation, and initial implementation.

Hartung et al. recommended extending the C-DAC model to infuse assessments and interventions that address the following sixth dimension: cultural identity development. Incorporating this sixth dimension was designed to make cultural identity a core component of the C-DAC model, foster cultural relevance in implementing each step of the model, and specify culturally sensitive assessments and counseling interventions as part of the assessment and counseling process. They recommended including in the assessment and counseling process culture-sensitive assessments such as the Multicultural Career Counseling Checklist (MCCC; Bingham & Ward, 1996; Ward & Bingham, 1993) and the Career Counseling Checklist (CCC, Bingham & Ward, 1996; Ward & Bingham, 1993).

Hartung et al. (1998) thus elaborated the model to formally appraise cultural identity in step 1 and to consider cultural identity concerns throughout the counseling and assessment process. They recommended adding to the model assessments and interventions that address cultural identity development as a significant variable affecting career exploration, choice, development, and adjustment. In so doing, counselors might take better account of cultural factors, such as those described in step 3 of Fouad and Bingham's (1995) model, that influence each C-DAC step and attend to how those factors promote or inhibit racial and ethnic minority career development. The elaboration further recognizes the influence of such factors as acculturation, cultural value orientations (individualism and collectivism), and external career barriers (e.g., stereotypes, prejudice, and discrimination) on racial and ethnic minority career development and vocational behavior.

Including cultural identity as a core C-DAC element should prompt career counselors to be aware of their own attitudes about clients who are culturally different from themselves. For example, Hartung et al. (1998) suggested that counselors might examine their own career development and take a C-DAC battery of instruments. This would effectively create a parallel process that might enhance a counselor's empathy for the career process of the client.

An Integrative and Multidimensional Model of Career Counseling

Although cross-cultural studies of psychology and vocational behavior have made commendable progress in recent decades, comprehensive and integrative theoretical models for cross-cultural counseling are still underdeveloped. The limits of the unidimensional nature of the career development theories confine the benefits of the counseling services for minority members, including Asian Americans. The following discussion focuses on using a cultural accommodation approach in expanding current theories to make them more culturally relevant for racial and ethnic minorities in general, and Asian Americans in particular.

Leong's (1996) recent multidimensional and integrative model of cross-cultural counseling and psychotherapy used Kluckhohn and Murray's (1950) tripartite framework. Leong (1996) proposed that cross-cultural counselors and therapists need to attend to all three major dimensions of human personality and identity, namely the Universal, the Group, and the Individual dimensions. The Universal dimension is based on the knowledge base generated by mainstream psychology and the "universal laws" of human behavior that have been identified (e.g., the universal "fight or flight" response in humans to physical threat). The Group dimension has been the domain of cross-cultural psychology as well as of ethnic minority psychology and the study of gender differences. The third and final dimension concerns unique Individual differences and characteristics. The Individual dimension is more often covered by behavioral and existential theories where Individual learning histories and personal phenomenology are proposed as critical elements in the understanding of human behavior. Leong's (1996) integrative model proposes that all three dimensions are equally important in understanding human experiences and should be attended to by the counselor in an integrative fashion.

Leong (1996, p. 35) used a famous quote from Kluckhohn and Murray's (1950) influential article, "The Determinants of Personality Formation," published in their book *Personality in Nature, Society, and Culture*, as the beginning point for his integrative model. With "Every man is in certain respects: a) like all other men, b) like some other men, and c) like no other man (p. 35)" Kluckhohn and Murray are pointing out that some of the determinants of personality are common features found in the genetic makeup of all people. This addresses the biological aspect of the biopsychosocial model generally used in today's medical sciences. For certain other features of personality, however, Kluckhohn and Murray (1950) state that most men are like some other men, showing the importance of social grouping, whether that grouping is based on culture, race, ethnicity, gender, or social class. Lastly, they said that "Each individual's modes of perceiving, feeling, needing, and behaving have characteristic patterns which are not precisely duplicated by those of any other individual" (p. 37). Each person's individuality, often the focus of social learning theories and models, is thus expressed in the last part of the quote. It accentuates the fact that all persons have distinct social learning experiences that can influence their values, beliefs, and cognitive schemas.

According to Leong (1996), the Universal component of personality is reflected in Kluckhohn and Murray's (1950) observation that "all persons are like all other persons" in some respects. This statement accentuates the idea that all human beings share some characteristics, whether they are physical or psychological. There is much evidence to support this notion, as all humans develop physically in similar fashions, learn to talk in similar fashions, and learn to think in similar fashions (e.g., Piaget's conservation experiments [1929]). This notion has been thoroughly accepted by the medical community, whereas Group and Individual differences are often not seen as important in medical treatment. This Universal component of human personality has also been accepted by many in the psychological community, as exemplified by the common factors model (Frank, 1961) which points out that the effective aspects of counseling and psychotherapy are shared by many cultures.

In their search for universal laws of human behavior, psychologists are looking for these universal elements of human personality. The concept of cultural validity as articulated by Leong and Brown (1995) is concerned with these universal principles. Each psychological construct or model needs to be examined in regard to its cultural validity. Until its cultural validity is evaluated, cross-cultural extensions and applications of a construct or model beyond the cultural population upon which it has been developed need to proceed cautiously. As pointed out by Leong and Brown (1995), much of the work of cross-cultural psychology is concerned with the assessment of the cultural validity of psychological constructs and models that have been developed primarily within the Western cultural context.

On the other hand, simply focusing on the Universal dimension completely ignores the Group and Individual components that are absolutely necessary for a complete understanding of human behavior. While the Universal dimension in counseling is very important to the integrative model, it is necessary but not sufficient (Leong, 1996). According to Leong (1996), the Group component of human personality is equally as important as the Universal component. These groupings may be based on culture, race, ethnicity, social class, occupation, or gender. All persons in one group share some type of bond with other members of the group, and this bond will distinguish the group members from members of other groups. It is further believed that belonging to a group will be a major determinant of a person's personality.

Membership in a group can affect an individual in many ways, and these ways can become the focus of counseling and psychotherapy. For example, persons who have suffered from oppression because of their religion or race will need to address these feelings. They will no longer be speaking from a Universal perspective, as their experiences have not been shared by all persons. A therapist who tries to relate to these clients on a Universal level will be doing them a disservice, and this will most likely lead to premature termination of the therapeutic relationship.

The Group component of personality is especially important when discussing cross-cultural counseling and psychotherapy. There have been many models of racial identity that focus on the Group component. Other important constructs related to the Group dimension include racial/ethnic identity, acculturation, and value preferences. A competent counselor must be able to look at all these variables from the standpoint of his or her client, especially if the client is a member of a different group. Not doing so would make it impossible to accurately conceptualize the client's psychological state, which in turn would make effective therapy impossible.

There has been much research looking at the experiences of different groups. There are many dynamics that must be taken into consideration in counseling situations involving a client and therapist of different cultural backgrounds. Each person must have some awareness of the experiences of the other in order to be able to form a relationship. This is especially true for the therapist. A therapist operating only at the Universal level may alienate the client. Although the two may not have shared experiences in their backgrounds, the counselor must be able to address issues that involve groups other than the counselor's own. Leong (1996) pointed out that using only the Universal dimension to understand people is severely limited due to the importance of group differences such as cultural differences. Indeed, Leong and Brown (1995) have proposed that when problems occur in establishing the cultural validity of a construct or model, culturally specific variables (often referred to as "indigenous" variables in cross-cultural psychology circles) can add greatly to our understanding of human behavior. It is important to note here that human behavior always occurs within a specific cultural context. In other words, the integrative combination of the Universal and Group dimensions of human personality provides a richer model with which to understand human beings. This in turn requires us to examine issues of both cultural validity and cultural specificity in the advancement of career development theories.

Finally, there is the Individual component of human personality within Leong's (1996) integrative model. While it is true that we all share some commonalities, as reflected by the Universal component, no two persons are identical in every way. Kluckhohn and Murray (1950) said "Each individual's modes of perceiving, feeling, needing, and behaving have characteristic patterns which are not precisely duplicated by those of any other individual" (p. 37). Kluckhohn and Murray seem to be referring to an idea akin to the concept of the "psychological environment" (Lewin, 1951), which referred to the idea that although two people may share the same physical space, they may not share the same psychological space. To neglect the Individual component would be to run the danger of stereotyping persons from various cultural groups due to overgeneralizations from the Group dimension. The Individual component of human personality is equally as important as the Universal or Group components, but it will not be dealt with directly in the current chapter because we are concerned primarily with the issues of cultural validity and cultural specificity.

The integrative model of cross-cultural counseling proposed by Leong (1996) has as one of its fundamental bases the notion that the individual client must exist at three levels—the Universal, the Group, and the Individual. The problem with much of the past research in the field of cross-cultural counseling is that the focus has been on only one of the three levels, ignoring the influence of the other levels in the counseling situation. Leong's (1996) integrative model includes all three dimensions of personality as well as their dynamic interactions, and thus will have better incremental validity than any model that only focuses on only one of the three levels. The integrative model for cross-cultural counseling and psychotherapy was conceived to provide a more complex and dynamic conception of human beings.

Cross-cultural career counseling that is based on Leong's (1996) integrative model would be an eccletic approach that seeks to apply knowledge from all three dimensions in order to understand and assist clients in their career problems and developmental tasks. For example, career counselors using this model would recognize that work is universal but that its meaning is embedded in a cultural context that shapes and colors it's nature and experience. Instead of mindlessly applying Western-based models of career counseling to all clients coming through their doors, career counselors using the integrative model would carefully select theories and models from both the universalist (mainstream psychology) and the cross-cultural and racial-ethnic minority psychology literature to guide their counseling with culturally different students. At the same time, these counselors also realize that theories and models from the universal and group dimensions will never fully capture or represent the unique experiences of individuals. Instead, they will recognize the complexity of the individual and seek to integrate all three dimensions of knowledge to guide their work with students.

To illustrate how the integrative model of cross-cultural career counseling would work, we would like to use an example based on Super's (1957) model of career development. One important component of Super's model is the concept of career maturity. According to Super, an individual's level of career maturity will influence the individual's ability to handle career developmental tasks at the appropriate stage. Those with high levels of career maturity would progress smoothly in their career development while those with low levels of career maturity would experience considerable difficulties. In using this model, school counselors would actually be intervening at the universal dimension within the integrative model, assuming that career maturity is a universal concept and is therefore applicable to all clients including those who are culturally different. And yet, research is beginning to show that such an assumption may not be correct.

A school counselor who is trying to help a culturally different student by simply adopting Super's model and proceeds to assess the student's career maturity level with the Career Maturity Inventory (Crites, 1965) may actually be making an error if the counselor does not understand the cultural relativity inherent in the concept and measurement of career maturity. This is because the concept of the self varies significantly across cultures and the Group dimension within the integrative models needs to be taken into account. According to Markus and Kitayama (1991), Asian Americans, with more collectivistic values, may conceive of the self as interdependent, whereas persons from individualistic cultures may view the self as independent. According to this model, the independent self has the core need to strategically express or assert the internal attributes of the self while the interdependent construal formulates self in relation to others (Markus & Kitayama, 1991). Being unique is very critical to the independent self and fitting in is very important for the interdependent self. The basis of self-esteem for the independent self is the ability to express the self and to validate internal attributes. For the interdependent self, the basis of self-esteem is the ability to adjust, restrain self, and maintain harmony with social context (Markus & Kitayama, 1991). Such differences in self-conception may make career decision making a much more interpersonal process for collectivists than for individualists. For the latter, career decision making may be an individual matter based mainly on personal interests, values, and aspirations, while for the former, career decision making may be a familial matter based on group interests, values, and needs.

Some research has already begun to demonstrate the value of self-construal as a culture-specific variable in our analysis of the career psychology of Asian Americans. In a research project examining ethnic differences in career maturity between Asian Americans and White Americans, Leong (1991) found an interesting anomaly. Using Crites' (1978) measure of career maturity, Leong (1991) found that although Asian Americans showed less mature career choice attitudes than did their European American counterparts, the two groups did not differ in terms of vocational identity, as measured by Holland, Daiger, and Power's *My Vocational Situation* (1980). He concluded that these results indicated that Asian Americans and European Americans approached the career decision-making process differently, yet still arrived at similarly crystallized vocational identities. Based on these results, Leong (1991) introduced the concept of cultural relativity in the construct of career maturity. He suggested that, rather than automatically assuming that Asian Americans actually have lower career maturity, researchers and counselors needed to carefully investigate possible ways in which cultural differences moderate the meaning of career maturity.

One such cultural difference may be the concept of independence. Crites' (1965) theory of career maturity, based on Super's (1957) theory of vocational development and the basis of the CMI, includes independence in career decision making as a crucial component of career mature attitudes, along with compromise, decisiveness, involvement, and orientation. Here, compromise is the extent to which one is willing to compromise wishes and reality. Decisiveness refers to how certain one is about a career choice. Involvement is the degree to which an individual is actively participating in the career choice process. Orientation is, "the extent to which an individual is familiar with and relates self to the decisional process" (Savickas, personal communication, 2/21/00). Independence in career decision making is defined as the "extent to which [an] individual relies upon others in the choice of an occupation" (Crites & Savickas, 1995, p. 9). More decisiveness, involvement, and independence in career decision making, a greater self-orientation, and more willingness to compromise one's desires with reality are all considered more career mature.

However, this emphasis on independence, to the exclusion of other alternatives such as interdependence, may underlie the aforementioned cultural differences discussed between Asian and European Americans in their approaches to the career decision-making process. To investigate this possibility, Hardin, Leong, and Osipow (2001) administered several instruments, including the Crites Career Maturity (CMI; Crites, 1978) and the Self-Construal Scale (SCS; Singelis, 1994) to 235 self-identified non-Hispanic, white European American and 182 self-identified Asian American college students. Consistent with previous research (Leong, 1991; Luzzo, 1992), the Asian American participants exhibited less mature career choice attitudes, as measured by the CMI, than their European American counterparts.

However, these results were moderated by self-construal. Specifically, interdependence, not independence, was found to be most associated with career choice attitudes. Those participants who had high interdependent self-construals, regardless of the level of their independent self-construals, had less mature career choice attitudes, as measured by the CMI, than did those participants who had lower interdependent self-construals. No differences in maturity of career choice attitudes were observed based on level of independence. Further, the three subscales on which the Asian Americans were found to exhibit less mature career choice attitudes than the European Americans (compromise, independence, and involvement) were also the three subscales found to be most related to interdependence. Specifically, those participants who were high in interdependence had lower scores on these subscales than participants who were low in interdependence.

In view of these findings, a counselor who applies only the universal dimension and administers a career maturity scale to Asian American clients without attending to the group dimension may actually be committing a diagnostic error. As shown by the research studies cited, current measures of career maturity are biased against an interdependent (collectivistic) construal of the self and therefore favors independent self-construal, which is dominant in Western societies. Using such measures without modifications may inappropriately diagnose Asian American clients as "career immature" when in actuality they are not. It is the recognition and attention to both the universal and group dimensions and their complex interactions within a unique individual that makes for a cross-culturally competent counselor.

DISCUSSION QUESTIONS

Culturally Different Students

1. Why is the counseling of culturally different students from ethnic and racial minority groups receiving more attention these days?

2. What are some problems that school counselors may face in counseling culturally diverse students?

3. What impact does the American School Counselor Association's position statement have on cross-cultural counseling in the schools?

4. Discuss the measures that can be taken to improve student development in the multicultural environment of our schools.

Why Do We Need Cross-Cultural Career Counseling?

5. Why is there a need for cross-cultural career counseling?

6. What problems are associated with existing career development theories and career counseling models?

7. According to Koss-Chioino and Vargas (1992), what are the three important social environmental factors in students' psychosocial development?

8. Discuss how social environmental factors can affect the psychosocial development of racial and ethnic minority students.

Problems with Western Models of Career Counseling

9. What are the major criticisms of Western-based career choice theories?

10. Name the assumptions made by most theories of career choice, as listed by Leong and Brown (1995).

11. Existing career development theories can be examined under two dimensions. Discuss these dimensions.

12. According to Leong and Brown (1995), what are the possible areas of research on the use of Western-based models of career counseling and career development with culturally different clients?

Culturally Appropriate Models of Career Counseling

13. What are some of the ways in which researchers attempt to address problems associated with Western-based models of career counseling to culturally different students?

14. Name the three recently developed models of cross-cultural career counseling.

15. Describe the Culturally Appropriate Career Counseling Model.

16. Describe the Career-Development Assessment and Counseling Model.

Toward an Integrative Model

17. Describe Kluckhohn and Murray's (1950) tripartite framework of human personality and identity.

18. Discuss the theoretical framework for Leong's (1996) Integrative and Multidimensional Model of Career Counseling.

19. Discuss the key aspects of Leong's (1996) integrative model of cross-cultural counseling.

20. In what ways has Leong's (1996) integrative model sought to overcome the problems faced by past research of cross-cultural counseling?

REFERENCES

American School Counselor Association. (1988). Position statement: Cross/multicultural counseling. Alexandria, VA: Author.

Aponte, J. F. & Crouch, R. T. (2000). The changing ethnic profile of the United States in the twenty-first century. In J. F. Aponte & J. Wohl (Eds.), *Psychological Intervention and Cultural Diversity* (2nd ed., pp. 1–17). Boston: Allyn & Bacon.

Betz, N. E. & Fitzgerald, L. F. (1995). Career assessment and intervention with racial and ethnic minorities. In F. T. L. Leong (Ed.), *Career Development and Vocational Behavior of Racial and Ethnic Minorities* (pp. 263–279). Mahwah, NJ: Erlbaum.

Bingham, R. P. & Ward, C. M. (1996). Practical applications of career counseling with ethnic minority women. In M. L. Savickas & W. B.

Walsh (Eds.), *Handbook of career counseling theory and practice* (pp. 291–314). Palo Alto, CA: Davies-Black.

Bingham, R. P. & Ward, C. M. (1997). Theory into assessment: A model for women of color. *Journal of Career Assessment, 5,* 403–418.

Bowman, S. (1993). Career intervention strategies for ethnic minorities. *Career Development Quarterly, 42,* 14–25.

Brooks, I. (1990). Recent developments in theory building. In D. Brown, L. Brooks, and Associates, *Career choice and development* (2nd ed., pp. 364–394). San Francisco: Jossey-Bass Publishers.

Carey, J. C., Reinat, M., & Fontes, L. (1990). School counselors' perceptions of training needs in multicultural counseling. *Counselor Education and Supervision, 29,* 155–169.

Crites, J. O. (1965). Measurement of vocational maturity in adolescence. I. Attitude test of the Vocational Development Inventory. *Psychological Monographs, 79*(2), (Whole No. 595).

Crites, J. O. (1978). *Theory and research handbook: Career Maturity Inventory.* Monterey, CA: McGraw-Hill.

Fitzgerald, L. F. & Betz, N. E. (1994). Career development in cultural context: The role of gender, race, class, and sexual orientation. In M. L. Savickas & R. W. Lent (Eds.), *Convergence in career development theories: Implications for science and practice* (pp. 103–117). Palo Alto, CA: Consulting Psychologists Press.

Fouad, N. A. (1995). Career behavior of Hispanics: Assessment and career intervention. In F. T. L. Leong (Ed.), *Career development and vocational behavior of racial and ethnic minorities* (pp. 165–191). Mahwah, NJ: Erlbaum.

Fouad, N. A. & Bingham, R. P. (1995). Career counseling with racial and ethnic minorities. In W. B. Walsh & S. H. Osipow (Eds.), *Handbook of vocational psychology: Theory, research, and practice* (2nd ed., pp. 331–365).

Frank, J. D. (1961). *Persuasion and Healing.* Baltimore, MD: Johns Hopkins University Press.

Hardin, E. E., Leong, F. T. L., & Osipow, S. H. (2001). Cultural relativity in the conceptualization of career maturity. *Journal of Vocational Behavior, 58,* 36–52.

Hartung, P. J., Vandiver, B. J., Leong, F. T. L., Pope, M., Niles, S. G., & Farrow, B. (1998). Appraising cultural identity in career-development assessment and counseling. *Career Development Quarterly, 46,* 276–293.

Hodgkinson, H. L. (1985). The changing face of tomorrow's student. *Change, 17,* 38–39.

Holland, J. L. (1985). *Making vocational choices: A theory of vocational personalities and work environments* (2nd ed.). Englewood Cliffs, NJ: Prentice-Hall.

Hughes, M. & Hertel, B. R. (1990). The significance of color remains: A study of life choices, mate selection, and ethnic consciousness among Black Americans. *Social Forces, 68,* 1105–1120.

Jackson, J. (1987). *Straight from the heart.* Philadelphia, PA: Fortress Press.

Jackson, S. E. & Associates (1992). *Diversity in the workplace: Human resources initiatives.* New York: Guilford Press.

Johnson & Packer. (1987). Workforce 2000. Indianapolis, IN: Hudson Institute.

Keith, V. M., & Herring, C. (1991). Skin tone and stratification in the Black community. *American Journal of Sociology, 97,* 760–778.

Kluckhohn, C. & Murray, H. A. (1950). Personality formation: The determinants. In C. Kluckhohn & H. A. Murray (Eds.), *Personality in nature, society and culture* (pp. 35–48). New York: Alfred A. Knopf.

Koss-Chioino, J. D. & Vargas, L. A. (1992). Through the cultural looking glass: A model for understanding culturally responsive psychotherapies. In L. A. Vargas & D. J. Koss-Chioino (Eds.), *Working with culture: Psychotherapeutic interventions with ethnic minority children and adolescents.* San Francisco, CA: Jossey-Bass.

Lee, C. C. (1989). Multicultural counselling: New directions for counselling professionals. *Virginia Counselors Journal, 17,* 3–8.

Lee, C. C. (1991). Cultural dynamics: Their importance in multicultural counseling. In C. C. Lee & B. L. Richardson (Eds.), *Multicultural issues in counseling: New approaches to diversity.* Alexandria, VA: American Association for Counseling and Development.

Lee, C. C. (1995a). *Counseling for diversity: A guide for school counselors and related professionals.* Boston: Allyn & Bacon.

Lee, C. C. (1995b). School counselling and cultural diversity: A framework for effective practice. In C. C. Lee (Ed.), *Counseling for diversity: A guide for school counselors and related professionals.* Boston: Allyn & Bacon.

Leong, F. T. L. (1991). Career development attributes and occupational values of Asian-American and European-American American college students. *Career Development Quarterly, 39*(3), 221–230.

Leong, F. T. L. (1993). The career counseling process with racial/ethnic minorities: The case of Asian Americans. *Career Development Quarterly, 42,* 26–40.

Leong, F. T. L. (1995). *Career development and vocational behavior of racial and ethnic minorities.* Hillsdale, NJ: Lawrence Erlbaum Associates.

Leong, F. T. L. (1996). Toward an integrative model for cross-cultural counseling and psychotherapy. *Applied & Preventive Psychology, 5,* 189–209.

Leong, F. T. L. & Brown, M. T. (1995). Theoretical issues in cross-cultural career development: Cultural validity and cultural specificity. In W. B. Walsh & S. H. Osipow (Eds.), *Handbook of vocational psychology: Theory, research, and practice* (2nd ed., pp. 143–180). Mahwah, NJ: Lawrence Erlbaum Associates.

Leong, F. T. L. & Hartung, P. J. (1997). Career assessment with culturally-different clients: Proposing an integrative-sequential conceptual framework for cross-cultural career counseling research and practice. *Journal of Career Assessment, 5,* 183–202.

Lewin, K. (1951). *Field theory in social science*. New York: Harper & Row.

Markus, H. R. & Kitayama, S. (1991). Culture and the self: Implications for cognition, emotion, and motivation. *Psychological Review, 98*, 224–253.

Myrick, R. D. (1987). *Developmental guidance counseling: A practical approach*. Minneapolis, MN: Educational Media Corp.

Omizo, M. M. & D'andrea, M. J. (1995). Multicultural classroom guidance. In C. C. Lee (Ed.), *Counseling for diversity: A guide for school counselors and related professionals*. Boston: Allyn & Bacon.

Osipow, S. H. & Littlejohn, E. M. (1995). Toward a Multicultural Theory of career development: Prospects and dilemmas. In F. T. L. Leong (Ed.), *Career development and vocational behavior of racial and ethnic minorities*. Mahwah, NJ: Lawrence Erlbaum Associates.

Pinderhughes, C. A. (1973). Racism and psychotherapy. In C. V. Willie, B. M. Kramer, & B. S. Brown (Eds.), *Racism and mental health*. Pittsburgh, PA: University of Pittsburgh Press.

Piaget, J. (1929). *The child's conception of the world*. New York: Harcourt Brace.

Ponterotto, J. G. & Casas, J. M. (1987). In search of multicultural competence within counselor education programs. *Journal of Counseling and Development, 65*, 430–434.

Savickas, M. L. (1995a). Current theoretical issues in vocational psychology: Convergence, divergence, and schism. In W. B. Walsh & S. H. Osipow (Eds.), *Handbook of vocational psychology: Theory, research, and practice* (2nd ed., pp. 1–34). Mahwah, NJ: Lawrence Erlbaum Associates.

Savickas, M. L. (1995b). Constructivist counseling for career indecision. *Career Development Quarterly, 43*, 363–373.

Singelis, T. M. (1994). The measurement of independent and interdependent self-construals. *Personality and Social Psychology Bulletin, 20*, 580–591.

Smith, E. J. (1983). Issues in racial minorities' career behvior. In W. B. Walsh & S. A. Osipow (Eds.), *Handbook of vocational psychology Vol. 1 Foundations*. Hillsdale, NJ: Erlbaum.

Subich, L. M. (1996). Addressing diversity in the process of career assessment. In M. L. Savickas & W. B. Walsh (Eds.), *Handbook of career counsel-*

ing theory and practice (pp. 277–289). Palo Alto, CA: Davies-Black.

Sue, D. W. & Sue, D. (1990). *Counseling the culturally different: Theory and practice* (2nd ed.). New York: John Wiley & Sons.

Super, D. E. (1957). *The psychology of careers*. New York: Harper.

Super, D. E. (1983). Assessment in career guidance: Toward truly developmental counseling. *Personnel and Guidance Journal, 61*, 555–562.

Super, D. E., Savickas, M. L., & Super, C. M. (1996). The life-span, life-space approach to careers. In D. Brown & L. Brooks (Eds.), *Career choice and development: Applying contemporary theories to practice* (3rd ed., pp. 121–178). San Francisco: Jossey-Bass.

Triandis, H. C. (1994). Cross-cultural industrial and organizational psychology. In H. C. Triandis, M. D. Dunnette, & L. M. Hough (Eds.), *Handbook of industrial and organizational psychology* (2nd ed., pp. 102–172). Palo Alto, CA: Consulting Psychological Press.

Triandis, H. C., Kurowski, L. L., & Gelfand, M. J. (1994). Workplace diversity. In H. C. Triandis, M. D. Dunnette, & L. M. Hough (Eds.), *Handbook of industrial and organizational psychology* (Vol. 4, 2nd ed., pp. 769–827). Palo Alto, CA: Consulting Psychologists Press.

U.S. Bureau of Census (2000). Population Estimates Program, Population Division, Washington, DC. http://www.census.gov/population/estimates/nation

Ward, C. M. & Bingham, R. P. (1993). Career assessment of ethnic minority women. *Journal of Career Assessment, 1*, 246–257.

Western Interstate Commission for Higher Education and the College Board (1988). The road to college: Educational progress by race and ethnicity. Boulder, CO.

Young, R. A., Valach, L., & Collin, A. (1996). A contextual explanation of career. In D. Brown, L. Brooks, & Associates (Eds.), *Career choice and development* (3rd ed., pp. 477–512). San Francisco: Jossey-Bass.

Zunker, V. G. (1990). *Career counseling: Applied concepts of life planning*. Pacific Cove, CA: Brooks/Cole.a

AUTHORS' NOTES

Frederick Leong is a professor of psychology at Ohio State University. He obtained his Ph.D. from the University of Maryland with a double specialty in Counseling and

Industrial/Organizational Psychology. He has authored or coauthored over 75 publications in various counseling and psychology journals and 40 book chapters. His latest book is an edited volume entitled *Contemporary Models in Vocational Psychology: A Volume in Honor of Samuel H. Osipow* (2001) (with Azy Barak) published by Lawrence Erlbaum Associates. Dr. Leong is a fellow of the American Psychological Association (Divisions 2, 17, 45, and 52) and the recipient of the 1998 Distinguished Contributions Award from the Asian American Psychological Association and the 1999 John Holland Award from the APA Division of Counseling Psychology. His major research interests are in vocational psychology (career development of ethnic minorities), cross-cultural psychology (particularly culture and mental health and cross-cultural psychotherapy), and organizational behavior.

Vicky L. M. Tan is an assistant professor in the Department of Social Work and Psychology, National University of Singapore. Dr. Tan graduated summa cum laude and received her training in Counseling Psychology from the University of Minnesota. She obtained her Ph.D. from the University of London with a focus on Health Psychology. Currently she teaches counseling and social psychology at the National University of Singapore and has coauthored books on the personality profiles of managers, marriage, and parenting. She is a life member of the Singapore Association for Counseling and a member of the British Psychological Society and the Singapore Psychological Society. Dr. Tan has conducted training sessions on group work, counseling, and family life. Her current research interests include the effects of stress and adaptation and counseling in health care settings.

PART FOUR

Special Problems of Multicultural School Counseling

The three chapters of Part Four identify some of the many specific problems facing multicultural counseling in schools. By now the reader can no doubt identify many additional problem areas beyond these three examples. The multicultural perspective of school counseling promises to complicate your life. Therefore, it is important to remember that complexity is your friend, not your enemy. There are no simple answers to complex problems. Simplistic solutions prove to be extremely dangerous in their long-term consequences. It is important to identify the opportunities for learning presented by each problem encountered and to build on our failures as well as our successes in dealing with these problems.

An important theme in Part Four is that of "special interest." In Chapter 13 by Boscardin, Brown-Chidsey, and González-Martínez, a special interest group is defined by disabilities that function in ways similar to those of other culturally defined groups in the broad definition of culture used in this book. The problems of over- and under-identification are discussed as well as the range of within-group differences for persons stereotyped as "disabled." This chapter provides a model for redefining many special interest groups in the school community as cultural groups. Specific cases are presented and questions are raised to help the reader become more sensitive. The special complications of persons from different ethnic, language, or nationality groups also having a disability are also addressed.

A second theme in Part Four is that of "accountability." Chapter 14 by Carey and Boscardin describes the ways to assess effectiveness of the school and how to deal with organizational constraints. Definitions of "effectiveness" in schools are described and evaluated. The attempts to legislate effectiveness are also evaluated along with the consequences of doing so. A bottom-up approach is preferred to a top-down alternative because of the many problems such an approach causes. However, the many complicated difficulties of a bottom-up approach are also acknowledged. Various forms of assessment are presented and discussed and specific case examples are presented. The importance of the "school culture" as an organization is highlighted. Chapter 15 by Colbert and Magouirk Colbert continues along the same theme by looking at educational reform, collaboration, and culture-centered approaches. The goal of this chapter is to present a model of how school counseling can facilitate collaboration both within the school and between the school and the community. A triadic consultation model between the student, the teacher, and the school/district is provided as an example for how school counseling can become more accountable.

13 Counseling Approaches to Working with Students with Disabilities from Diverse Backgrounds

MARY LYNN BOSCARDIN
University of Massachusetts, Amherst

RACHEL BROWN-CHIDSEY
University of Southern Maine

JULIO C. GONZÁLEZ-MARTÍNEZ
University of Massachusetts, Amherst

OBJECTIVES

1. To define and describe major areas of concern regarding the placement of students from diverse backgrounds in special education, including the over- and under-representation of students from specific racial, ethnic, linguistic, and socioeconomic groups
2. To offer a framework for understanding the relationship between sociocultural diversity and special education needs, as well as the differences between linguistic diversity and disability
3. To provide recommendations for assessment of students with disabilities from diverse backgrounds
4. To present strategies for working with families of students with special needs from diverse backgrounds
5. To offer recommendations for preservice and inservice counselor training, including specific questions counselors can use to guide their practices for working with students with disabilities from diverse backgrounds and their families

Counseling approaches that contribute to the accuracy of identification of students with disabilities from diverse backgrounds will be explored in this chapter. With U.S. schools becoming increasingly diverse, and the percentage of students with special needs on the rise (18th Annual Report to Congress, 1996), it is important that those involved with providing guidance and counseling have the appropriate background, knowledge, and skills to work with a diverse population of students.

School counselors are asked to wear many hats throughout their careers. One of those hats includes participation in decision making about the eligibility of students for special education services who are from diverse backgrounds. There are many variables counselors must consider when participating in eligibility decisions about special education services: how disability interacts with issues of over-identification, problems with under-identification, sociocultural diversity, linguistic diversity, assessment, collaboration with families, and preservice and inservice training. The impact of each of these issues on practice will be discussed in this chapter.

Issues with Over-Identification

Minorities are no more at risk of having a disability than are other groups of people, but are more likely to be in poverty which is a significant risk factor for disability (Fujura & Yamaki, 2000). Indeed, the risk for disability associated with racial or ethnic status increases when poverty and single parent households are factors (Asbury, Walker, Maholmes, Rackley, & White, 1991; Fujura & Yamaki, 2000). How data are collected and interpreted affects accurate understanding of the incidence of over-identification. As noted by MacMillan and Reschly (1998) and Harry (1994), special education statistics can be reported either as percentage of students within a disability category/program by minority group or percentage of minority group in disability category/program. Both sets of data reporting methods are important because one indicates the overall representation of minorities in special education and the other indicates the distribution of minorities among categories of disability. It is well documented that students from majority backgrounds are more likely to be identified as having learning disabilities whereas students from minority backgrounds are more likely to be identified as having behavior problems (Luft, 1995). This is illustrated in the following example below:

Case Study #1

Marcus is an African American student. In seventh grade, Marcus was placed in a substantially separate program for students with behavior problems. In this program, Marcus received individualized assistance with all instruction and assignments. Reports from Marcus's teachers indicated that he was able to make good progress when "motivated" but that his school performance was influenced by a lack of motivation and energy. The teachers also pointed out that his written work was disorganized and lacked a basic structure with a beginning, middle, and end. Several of Marcus's middle school teachers reported that he would often put his head on his desk and want to sleep or just stare out the window.

Marcus's situation has several features that suggest that he was inappropriately placed and would be better served by a different educational program. His inappropriate placement may have been the result of a misinterpretation of his learning difficulties as motivational problems, in this case oppositional behavior. Marcus's difficulties with written expression and apparent withdrawal from engagement in assignments are more suggestive of a learning disability than a behavior problem.

This is indicative of the disproportionate representation of any given minority group in a specific category that is so problematic today. Indeed, some scholars have suggested that there is a dearth of empirically validated and rigorous research on the incidence of disabilities among minority students (Artiles, Trent, & Kuan, 1997). In the absence of data, would-be service providers are left only with misperceptions about the validity of the identification practices used in their schools and districts. The importance of establishing a local database on the numbers of students from diverse backgrounds with special needs and the special education programs in which they are enrolled is paramount to creating valid identification protocols.

Problems with Under-Identification

Under-identification can occur in two instances: for gifted programs and for special education programs. While over-identification is a problem with students from diverse backgrounds in special education programs, the converse is also true when considering students for gifted and talented programs. There are few minority students in gifted and talented programs (Ford, 1998) because of the following reasons: biased instrumentation, reputation of sending schools, and lack of teacher training in gifted education. In particular, definitions of ethnicity and ability, as well as knowledge of exceptionalities, have impeded referrals of minority students to gifted and talented programs. Many minority students may be overlooked for participation in gifted and talented programs because of language bias; students for whom English is not a first language may score lower on traditional methods of assessment for gifted programs. Minority students also may not receive full consideration for gifted and talented programs if the reputation of their sending school is not well regarded. In addition, teacher training has focused on identification of learning problems instead of student strengths related to giftedness contributing to the under-identification of students from diverse backgrounds being identified for gifted and talented programs, and compromising access to gifted and talented programs can potentially gain limit future access to postsecondary opportunities for minority students.

In some cases students from minority backgrounds may be under-referred for special education programs because of concerns with accusations of potential charges of discrimination or misidentification, as well as fear of lawsuits. In certain urban districts there is a fear of legal action, as well as the realization that assessment procedures for students of diverse backgrounds may not be valid. This has led to a tendency towards under-referral of these students for special support services (Gersten & Woodward, 1994). The outcome is limited education and career opportunities when these students reach adulthood.

Sociocultural Diversity

Notions of disability and difference are confused with minority status (Artiles, 1998; Kauffman, Hallahan, & Ford, 1998). As noted by Artiles (1998), "minority people have been historically seen as different" (p. 32). This assumption rests on a cultural bias regarding the social-cultural norm; individuals see differentness according to their own experience. Those who work in schools must acknowledge their own cultural biases in order to be sensitive to the cultural experiences of the students with whom they work. The following example illustrates our point.

Case Study #2

Marla is a high school counselor who grew up and attended the Happy Valley public schools. After graduating she attended the state university, eventually receiving a master's in school counseling. She was then hired by the same school district she had attended as an elementary and secondary student and was assigned to Happy Valley High School (HVHS). Since the time she graduated, HVHS has experienced an influx of Eastern European refugees, changing the social-educational context of the school. Marla is expecting HVHS to have changed very little since she left, not realizing there has been a dramatic shift in population, accompanied by changes in the core values of the student body.

Arriving at conclusions about students based on stereotypes or discriminatory generalizations leads to inappropriate evaluation of academic abilities. Obiakor (1999) notes the importance of intraindividual and interindividual differences and the dangers in assuming that all members of a group share all characteristics. This mistake could easily occur in Marla's situation because the student body is White as are the Eastern European refugees. There is the potential for school counselors in certain settings, such as urban, suburban, and rural school districts, to erroneously assume that their schools have homogenous student populations. By making this assumption, school counselors are likely to undervalue the specific needs of their student population.

Given the example, Marla needs to be sensitive to the difference between her experience as a student at HVHS and that of the school's students today. In working with the HVHS students, Marla will need to be aware of their life experiences, language and cultural differences, religious affiliations, and gender roles. Although these students fit the category of refugee, Marla needs to learn about the students' hopes, desires, and aspirations for themselves and how these are related to the new environment in which they find themselves. Differences in definitions, perceptions, and understanding will affect how students from other countries are perceived by those who work with them. This creates the potential for interference with identification of students' actual instructional needs. These factors must be taken into consideration prior to making evaluations about the students' potential educational needs.

Linguistic Diversity

As noted by Fradd and Bermudez (1991), language skills and learning ability should not be confused. Students' academic competencies are often measured through their use of language because language forms the basis for all subject areas of instruction. Educators need to determine whether it is language, cultural background, disability, or some combination thereof that is hindering students' abilities to learn in school. These types of qualitative decisions will present counselors with one of their greatest challenges when trying to provide support to students and their families. Victoria's case demonstrates this point.

Case Study #3

Victoria is an Hispanic second-grade student who learned both English and Spanish as a child. Victoria lives at home with her mother and grandmother who speak mostly

Spanish. Victoria's fourth-grade class is required to make daily entries in a journal. Her teacher noticed that she has been using incorrect verb tenses and not developing complete sentences. For example, her entries include repetitive use of the same vocabulary words and tend to focus on one or two ideas. In comparison, other students in her class often write longer sentences and use a wider variety of words. Her teacher is concerned because Victoria appears to be able to interact well in informal conversations with her peers, but her written language is not commensurate.

Often a referral for counseling may be initiated by a teacher who is concerned about a student's progress. It will be the responsibility of the counselor and other support personnel (e.g., school psychologist, special educator, speech and language pathologist) to help the teacher discern whether or not further evaluation for a disability is needed by considering all the demographic variables discussed earlier. By consideration of those variables and of other potential reasons for delayed progress, such as congenital or developmental factors, a more accurate evaluation of the student is likely to be obtained.

Assessment

Assessments may be biased against students from diverse backgrounds because very often the criteria are established based on paradigms and the performance of students from majority backgrounds. The assumption of many traditional forms of assessment is that all students can be expected to learn and interact in similar ways despite evidence that educational practices and expectations vary within and between SES, racial, cultural, and linguistic groups (MacMillan & Reschley, 1998; Obiakor, 1999). Still, assessment of student skills is needed and counselors can help identify potential bias in tests.

For example, curriculum-based assessment (CBA) is potentially very useful for students from different SES, racial, cultural, and linguistic backgrounds because it measures progress according to the student's rate of change, rather than in comparison to external standards. In addition, it utilizes items from the actual curriculum of instruction and can help teachers determine whether the instructional materials are too advanced or too easy for a given student. One type of curriculum-based assessment, curriculum-based measurement (CBM) utilizes the number of words that a student can read in one minute as an indicator of reading skill (Shinn, 1989; 1998). Instruction in reading material appropriate to the student's current reading level is provided and progress toward reading more words per minute is measured weekly. While these seem like objective and quantifiable measures, if the readability of a given text includes material that is culturally bound, a student's performance on the one-minute reading sample could underestimate true reading ability. This is an opportunity for the school counselor to develop a process for helping families and school staff identify factors (e.g., level of acculturation, exposure to mainstream culture) in the assessment process that may contribute to a cultural bias and result in erroneous identification of a student in need of special education services. In general this process would involve a critical review of all the indicators used to make decisions about students. Individuals participating in such a review might include, but not be limited to, community members, family members, teachers, counselors, special educators, and administrators.

Another type of assessment, functional assessment of behavior (FAB), can help determine the reasons for specific behaviors and guide teachers' responses in ways that are appropriate and sensitive to the cause(s) of the problem(s) (O'Neill et al., 1997). The antecedents and consequences of a student's behavior are carefully recorded by a trained observer. These data are then evaluated to learn what events or conditions (antecedents) predict a certain behavior and what consequences follow the behavior. These patterns are used to develop hypotheses about the reason for a student's behavior. For example, observation of a student who frequently gets up during instruction could reveal that the student is avoiding the completion of math problems the student does not know how to do. If the two behaviors had not been linked as inappropriate, the consequence could be that the student is sent to the office, thereby effectively avoiding the math exercises. In another example, the student who gets up and moves about the class during math may be exhibiting a typical pattern of interaction for work completion in the student's community of origin. Sending the student out of the room as punishment could send the message that the student is not part of the classroom community and not welcome there. Accurate and nonbiased forms of assessment are a crucial element in addressing the over- and under-identification of students from diverse backgrounds. Counselors have an important role to play in assessment because they are the ones who most likely will have had frequent contact with families and may best understand families' unique cultural experiences.

Collaborating with Families

The families of students from minority backgrounds are often perceived as not being invested in their child's education (Harry, 1992). The work demands on immigrant and refugee families often are barriers to involvement in their children's education contributing to others' misperception of the parents "not caring." According to Harry, Rueda and Kalyanpur (1999), when working with families, provision of services should be informed by two principles. First, professionals need to work in a collaborative manner with families; those working with the student must take a broader perspective that focuses on the social-cultural dimensions rather than individual behaviors. Second, it is important to actively include the family in the process of determining what measures will be used to identify, assess, place, and monitor student progress. Furthermore, Serna, Forness, and Nielson (1998), propose that school personnel should invest energy and resources in early detection, primary interventions, and prereferral procedures in order to guard against the misidentification and misplacement of children from ethnically diverse backgrounds.

Collaboration with families is critical because it affects the ability of the family to relate to school culture (Artiles, Aguirre-Munoz, & Abedi, 1998; Luft, 1995). For example, families who have a higher degree of acculturation to U.S. practices are likely to have a better understanding of the culture of schools. In contrast, families with little experience with the larger U.S. culture are less likely to experience optimal family–school interaction. One approach to successful collaboration would be to incorporate the following questions adapted from the framework proposed by Bailey et al., 1998). These questions are organized into two categories: the family's experience and the impact of services provided. The questions are designed to strengthen the collaborative efforts between the families and school personnel.

Experience Questions

- Does the family see the proposed collaboration as appropriate in making a difference in the child's life?
- Does the family see the proposed collaboration as appropriate in making a difference in the family's life?
- Does the family have a positive view of counselors and others involved in the special service system?

Impact Questions

- Did the collaboration enable the family to help the child grow, learn, and develop?
- Did the collaboration enhance the family's perceived ability to work with the professionals and advocate for services?
- Did the collaboration assist the family in building a strong support system?
- Did the collaboration help engender an optimistic view of the future?
- Did the collaboration enhance the family's perceived quality of life?

It is important that counselors provide support in ways that are helpful to specific family needs rather than give out generic advice that will impede access to services (Bailey, Skinner, Rodriguez, Gut, & Correa, 1999). Some families are more aware of available services, and others may benefit from information that counselors can provide (Reyes-Blanes, Correa, & Bailey, 1999). One approach to collaboration is to understand the family's experience and the words the family uses to describe it (Skinner, Bailey, Correa, & Rodriguez, 1999). Parents' experiences will shape how they understand the nature of their children's disabilities and needs. One way parents develop this understanding is through the use of words and their associated meanings. If the meaning the family has attached to words does not match the meaning attached to words by school professionals, this can lead to an improper identification and placement (Harry, 1992). At this point the potential for parents being effective collaborators is lost, contributing to over-, under-, and misidentification of students for special education services. The following example depicts a possible scenario.

Case Study #4

Manolo is a three-and-a-half-year-old boy from a Central American country living in the United States. At his daycare, Manolo was characterized by his teachers and caregivers as being an active toddler when he first arrived a year ago. They expressed that Manolo tried to communicate with his caregivers and other children and most of the time succeeded in conveying his messages and needs. His teacher explained that Manolo is able to follow simple directions and that he responds well to clearly stated instructions. Recently, Manolo's head teacher expressed that Manolo was increasingly becoming more socially withdrawn and that he was choosing to do activities by himself on a regular basis while having very limited interactions with his caregivers and the other seven children in his daycare. At this time, Manolo's teacher is systematically making observations and gathering the necessary information to begin with the prereferal process.

It is evident that Manolo's teachers are taking the necessary steps to ensure that Manolo's needs are met by setting the stage for collaboration with his family. At the same time it is important for the school counselor to work closely with the family to enlist their help and support to determine whether the recent changes in Manolo's behavior are disability related. Using the experience and impact questions listed, a counselor might begin to inquire about Manolo's family situation. For example, it might be helpful to find out about the family constellation, the language spoken at home, job situations, who cares for Manolo once he arrives home from school, and any major transitions the family has undergone during the past year. The counselor might want to ask the family about recent changes in Manolo's behavior and language.

Just as it is important for families to collaborate with school personnel regarding the needs of their children, school counselors should take time to invest energy in building relationships with the families with whom they work. Traditionally, once a child has been referred, and the special education process is set in motion, it is often difficult to interrupt and change its course. A mutual understanding of the educational goals of each student is key to the child's achievement. Jordan, Reyes-Blanes, Peel, Peel, and Lane (1998) have suggested that effective family–school meetings will be facilitated when school personnel pay attention to cultural differences. Counselors who are aware of personal beliefs, values, and expectations, are more able to engage further in developing cultural competence. Counselors who build trust with parents of different cultures will learn about their customs and traditions and be more likely to prevent the over- and under-identification of students from diverse backgrounds (Jordan et al., 1998).

Preservice and Inservice Counselor Training

The preservice training that counselors receive plays an important role in how prepared they are to support students from diverse backgrounds. Supervised practice of the application of skills related to the needs of students with diverse backgrounds is a critical component to developing multicultural counseling competencies. These competencies need to extend beyond the basic use of interpreters and translation of documents (Lutz, 1995). Just as the student's family is working to develop cultural competency within the community in which they have chosen to live, counselors must work to develop competencies working within the culture of students' families that inhabit the community. Valles (1998, p. 53) recommends that pre-service training be expanded to, but not limited to, include "general language development, issues related to the acquisition of a second language, and strategies that foster acquisition." Skill acquisition is enhanced through self-reflection, flexibility, and a focus on understanding the cultural relativity of our own experiences (Harry et al., 1999). Harry et al. point out that "This kind of program will look quite different from a program that offers lists of characteristics of 'other' groups" (p. 133). In addition, pre-service training of counselors should include competencies in the identification of and intervention with students with disabilities from diverse backgrounds and the role counseling can play to produce efficacious results.

Ideally, it would be optimal to recruit counselors who possess the necessary competencies to work with students from diverse backgrounds with special needs, but this is not always possible. There are entire cohorts of school counselors who began their careers during a time when cultural assimilation was the expectation and individuals with disabilities were educated in substantially separate settings. For these resons, ongoing training to work with the ever-changing population of students in schools is needed so counselors will have the support, resources, and feedback they need to be effective. With in-service counselors it is even more important to incorporate "perceived needs, concerns, and values of the program participants" so institutional and personal biases concerning culture and disability can be addressed (Gallagher, Molone, Cleghorne, & Helms, 1997, p. 28).

In-service training that is related to culturally influenced behaviors among minority groups and that identifies distinct social behaviors which have been identified with Hispanic American, African American, Native American, and Asian American cultural groups increases counselor responsiveness (Delgado-Rivera & Rogers-Adkinson, 1997). Counselor in-service training in identifying these behaviors should help discriminate between typical behavior and disability. Such training helps separate individual expectations from cultural practices. In particular, counselors can play a vital role in helping teachers and other school personnel (e.g., principal, bus drivers, cafeteria staff, secretaries) get to "know" their students (Kea & Utley, 1998). Such professional development needs to extend well beyond typical in-service workshop models used to train teachers. Clinical supervision models include the indepth and ongoing support and consultation between counselors and other school personnel needed to fully integrate cultural considerations into daily practice.

Implications for Practice

Obiakor (1999) suggested a series of questions that school personnel can ask themselves when considering how best to prevent the over- and under-identification of students. These questions are designed to assist counselors as they work with students who are at risk of misidentification, misassessment, misplacement, and misinstruction (Obiakor, 1999). Based on Obiakor's suggestions, we have adapted the questions for use by school counselors.

1. Does the student's language affect my expectations of him or her?
2. What attributes do I bring to counseling and how do they foster achievement of students from diverse backgrounds?
3. Do I present positive models that enhance student development regardless of cultural background?
4. Do I establish appropriate expectations for minority members (i.e., students, parents, and colleagues) in school programs?
5. Is my assessment of individual behaviors appropriate and free from cultural bias?
6. Does my interpretation take into consideration linguistic and cultural differences as I work with students and families?

To illustrate how a counselor might use these six questions, we present the following case.

Case Study #5

Phan and her family immigrated to the United States from Cambodia when she was five years old. Phan was enrolled in English as a Second Language (ESL) programs through fifth grade. In the sixth grade, Phan's English skills were determined to be strong enough that she did not need additional ESL instruction and her academic performance was at grade level. For seventh grade, Phan enrolled at the regional middle school. Her first report cards were a surprise to her family because they indicated that she was struggling to complete assignments and having difficulty interacting with her peers. At the end of the second marking period, Phan's middle school house leader contacted the school guidance counselor and Phan's family to request a meeting to discuss Phan's progress. Phan's parents invited a family friend with strong English skills and familiarity with U.S. schools to attend the meeting to help them understand Phan's situation. At the meeting, the middle school teachers reported that Phan was not turning in most homework assignments and that when teachers asked if she needed help, she said she was all right.

Bill, the school counselor, has been at O'Leary Middle School for twenty years. His initial impression of Phan's situation is that she was not trying hard enough. Bill's orientation to school counseling was shaped in part by his family legacy of immigrating from Ireland. This legacy included the cultural belief that if you worked hard you would succeed. Bill is regarded as fitting in well at O'Leary because many of the students there share his background.

As Bill prepares to help Phan, he should reflect on the experiences and attributes that he brings to the counseling environment and how they might foster Phan's achievement. Next, Bill might want to contact Phan's former ESL teacher to investigate whether he and the teachers are setting appropriate expectations free from cultural and linguistic bias for Phan. If necessary Bill would want to facilitate an evaluation of Phan's academic skills which differentiates any discrepancies between her native language and English. Such an assessment would need to include assessment in both Cambodian and English in order to provide a rough estimate of Phan's current language competencies in both languages. It is important to keep in mind that Phan's native language skills may have evolved into a variation of Cambodian due to different experiences. It is essential to recognize that Phan's current language skills in both languages may be underdeveloped due to her unique experiences and this should not be misconstrued as a learning disability. In addition, Bill might want to talk with Phan's family directly to assess further the impact of socio-linguistic factors in Phan's school success and to learn about any other variables affecting her achievement.

Conclusion

Students from diverse backgrounds may be referred for special education services more often than their peers. As noted at the beginning of this chapter, however, students from diverse racial, cultural, and linguistic backgrounds are no more at risk of having a disability than other students. As a result, it is critical that school counselors recognize the unique experiences of students from different racial, cultural, and linguistic backgrounds as part of an overall process of determining the nature of a student's learning needs.

The so-called problem of over- and under-identification of students from diverse backgrounds as having disabilities is rooted in sociocultural practices. In addition, a student's linguistic skills may require more sensitive and careful assessment to determine if a disability actually exists or if school difficulties are the result of the process of language acquisition and adaptation. School counselors are poised to play a vital role in helping students from diverse backgrounds receive the educational assistance they need by facilitating the use of accurate and nonbiased forms of assessment. To help prevent the over- and under-identification of students from diverse backgrounds, it is imperative that school counselors collaborate closely with the families of students, take advantage of ongoing training opportunities, and implement demonstrated best practices. School counselors have a unique opportunity to ensure that all students, regardless of background, are provided with an appropriate education.

DISCUSSION QUESTIONS

1. What is meant by the terms over- and under-identification of students for special education services?

2. Why is it difficult to document the occurrence of over-identification of students from diverse backgrounds?

3. How might a counselor's personal sociocultural identity influence her interactions with students?

4. In what ways does linguistic, racial, and ethnic diversity present a special challenge when evaluating students' special learning needs?

5. How do traditional forms of assessment overlook the needs of students with disabilities from diverse backgrounds?

6. What types of assessment practices are most likely to provide helpful information regarding the specific needs of students with disabilities from diverse backgrounds?

7. What factors should counselors consider when working with families of students with disabilities from diverse backgrounds?

8. How does learning more about a child's family influence the approach to counseling?

9. What types of pre-service training do counselors need to enable effective provision of service for students from diverse backgrounds?

10. What steps should a counselor take to promote the use of culturally sensitive practices in schools for students with disabilities from diverse backgrounds?

REFERENCES

Artiles, A. J. (1998). The dilemma of difference: Enriching the disproportionality discourse with theory and context. *The Journal of Special Education, 32*(1), 32–36.

Artiles, A. J., Aguirre-Munoz, Z., & Abedi, J. (1998). Predicting placement in learning disabilities programs: Do predictors vary by ethnic group? *Exceptional Children, 64*(4), 543–559.

Artiles, A. J., Trent, S. C., & Kuan, L. (1997). Learning disabilities empirical research on ethnic minority students: An analysis of 22 years of studies published in selected refereed journals. *Learning Disabilities Research and Practice, 12*(2), 82–91.

Asbury, C. A., Walker, S., Maholmes, V., Rackley, R., & White, S. (1991). Disability prevalence and demographic association among race/ethnic minority populations in the United States: Implications for the 21st century. Washington DC: Howard University Research and Training Center for Access to Rehabilitation and Economic Opportunity.

Bailey, D. B., Jr., McWilliam, R. A., Darkes, L. A., Hebbeler, K., Simeonsson, R. J., Spiker, D., & Wagner, M. (1998). Family outcomes in early interventions: A framework for program evaluation and efficacy research. *Exceptional Children, 64*(3), 313–328.

Bailey, D. B., Jr., Skinner, D., Rodriguez, P., Gut, D., & Correa, V. (1999). Awareness, use, and satisfaction with services for Latino parents of young children with disabilities. *Exceptional Children, 65*(3), 367–381.

Delgado-Rivera, B. & Rogers-Adkinson, D. (1997). Culturally sensitive interventions: Social skills training with children and parents from culturally and linguistically diverse backgrounds. *Intervention in School and Clinic, 33*(2), 75–80.

Ford, D. Y. (1998). The underrepresentation of minority students in gifted education: Problems and promises in recruitment and retention. *The Journal of Special Education, 32*(1), 4–14.

Fradd, S. H. & Bermudez, A. B. (1991). POWER: A process for meeting the instructional needs of handicapped language-minority students. *eacher Education and Special Education, 14*(1), 19–24.

Fujiura, G. T. & Yamaki, K. (2000). Trends in demography of childhood poverty and disability. *Exceptional Children, 66*(2), 187–199.

Gallagher, P., Malone, D. M., Cleghorns, M., & Helms, K. A. (1997). Perceived inservice training needs for early intervention personnel. *Exceptional Children, 64*(1), 19–30.

Gersten, R. & Woodward, J. (1994). The language-minority students and special education. *Exceptional Children, 60*, 310–322.

Harry, B. (1994). The disproportionate representation of minority students in special education: Theories and recommendations. Alexandria, VA: National Association of State Directors of Special Education.

Harry, B. (1992). Making sense of disability: Low-income, Puerto Rican parents' theories of the problem. *Exceptional Children, 59*(1), 27–41.

Harry, B., Rueda, R., & Kalyanpur, M. (1999). Cultural reciprocity in sociocultural perspective: Adapting the normalization principle for family collaboration. *Exceptional Children, 66*(1), 123–136.

Jordan, L., Reyes-Blanes, M. E., Peel, B. B., Peel, H. A., & Lane, H. B. (1998). Developing teacher–parent partnerships across cultures: Effective parent conferences. *Intervention in School and Clinic, 33*(3), 141–147.

Kauffman, J. M., Hallahan, D. P., & Ford, D. Y. (1998). Introduction to the special section. *The Journal of Special Education, 32*(1), 3.

Kea, C. D. & Utley, C. A. (1998). To teach me is to know me. *The Journal of Special Education, 32*(1), 44–47.

Luft, P. (1995). Addressing minority overrepresentation in special education: Cultural barriers to effective collaboration. Paper presented at the Annual International Convention of the Council for Exceptional Children.

MacMillan, D. L. & Reschly, D. J. (1998). Overrepresentation of minority students: The case for greater specificity or reconsideration of the variables examined. *The Journal of Special Education, 32*(1), 15–24.

Obiakor, F. E. (1999). Teacher expectations of minority exceptional learners: Impact of "accuracy" of self-concepts. *Exceptional Children, 66*(1), 39–53.

O'Neill, R. E., Horner, R. H., Albin, R. W., Sprague, J. R., Storey, K., & Newton, J. S. (1997). *Functional assessment and program development for problem behavior: A practical handbook.* Pacific Grove, CA: Brooks/Cole Publishing Company.

Reyes-Blanes, M. E., Correa, V. I., & Bailey, D. B., Jr. (1999). Perceived needs of and support for Puerto Rican mothers of young children with disabilities. *Teaching Early Childhood Special Education, 19*(1), 54–63.

Serna, L. A., Forness, S. R., & Nielson, M. E. (1998). Intervention versus affirmation: Proposed solutions to the problem of disproportionate minority representation in special education. *The Journal of Special Education, 32*(1), 48–51.

Shinn, M. R. (Ed.) (1998). *Advanced applications of curriculum-based measurement.* New York: Guilford.

Shinn, M. R. (Ed.) (1989). *Curriculum-based measurement: Assessing special children.* New York: Guilford.

Skinner, D., Bailey, D. B., Jr., Correa, V., & Rodriguez, P. (1999). Narrating self and disability: Latino mothers' construction of identified vis-à-vis their child with special needs. *Exceptional Children, 65*(4), 481–495.

U.S. Department of Education. (1996). Eighteenth annual report to Congress on the implementation of the individuals with disabilities education act. Washington, DC: U.S. Government Printing Office.

Valles, E. C. (1998). The disproportionate representation of minority students in special education. *The Journal of Special Education, 32*(1), 52–54.

AUTHORS' NOTES

Mary Lynn Boscardin (University of Illinois at Urbana-Champaign, 1984) is director of the Special Education Leadership Training Project, a federally funded project through the U.S. Department of Education, dedicated to training graduate students to assume leadership roles in Special Education Administration, and editor of the *Journal of Special Education Leadership*, a journal of the Council for Exceptional Children's Division of the Council of Administrators of Special Education. She is also an ASHA-CCC, SP/L, certified speech and language pathologist. Dr. Boscardin's research interests include special education finance, provision of special education services to students attending Charter Schools, service delivery models for students with disabilities from diverse backgrounds, and curriculum access issues for students with disabilities in inclusive settings as they affect the development and implementation of special education policies. Dr. Boscardin is the author of several research articles, monographs, and book chapters which are the focus of the aforementioned topics. Most recently, Dr. Boscardin has coauthored an edited book, entitled *Learning Disabilities and Life Stories* (2001, Allyn & Bacon). The book is an anthology of stories written by college students who share interesting and poignant autobiographies of what it was like for their parents and them to navigate the educational system with a learning disability paired with scholarly essays by prominent researchers in the fields of learning disabilities, adolescent development, counseling, and diversity.

Rachel Brown-Chidsey, Whitman College, B.A., 1987; University of Massachusetts, Amherst, M.A., 1989; Smith College, M.A.T., 1991; University of Massachusetts, Amherst, Ph.D., 2000. Assistant Professor Brown-Chidsey teaches Abnormal Psychology, the Physical Bases of Behavior, Cognitive and Psycho-Educational Assessment, Psychological Foundations of Learning, and Seminar in School Psychology. She is the author of several book chapters on assessment of school-age children and has written articles on the use of computers in special education, and instructional strategies for students with learning disabilities. Her current research interests are the assessment of reading comprehension and intervention strategies for students with learning and behavior problems. Dr. Brown-Chidsey's service activities include consultation with Maine school districts regarding assessment and participation on the Maine Advisory Board for School Psychological Service Providers.

Julio C. González Martínez, is a visiting faculty member in the Psychology and Education Department, Mount Holyoke College, South Hadley, Massachusetts, and is a teaching associate in the Department of Human Development, University of Massachusetts, Amherst. Research interests are in the areas of culturally sensitive practices for working with children and families in early intervention and special education contexts. He is currently completing a doctoral degree in the Child and Family Studies Program at the University of Massachusetts, Amherst.

14

Improving the Multicultural Effectiveness of Your School in the Context of State Standards, Accountability Measures, and High-Stakes Assessment

JOHN C. CAREY

MARY LYNN BOSCARDIN
University of Massachusetts, Amherst

OBJECTIVES

1. To define and describe major concepts related to state standards, accountability, and high-stakes assessment
2. To offer a framework for understanding the relationship among multicultural issues, state standards, accountability measures, and high-stakes assessment
3. To provide recommendations for conducting effective assessments of students from racially, ethnically, linguistically, and socioeconomically diverse backgrounds
4. To present strategies that counselors can use for working with classroom teachers and other education personnel for ascertaining the multicultural effectiveness of a school using state standards, accountability measures, and high-stakes assessments
5. To offer recommendations for gathering information, including specific methods, for collecting data on student performance that will assess the multicultural effectiveness of a school within an academic context

The basic thesis of this chapter is that pupil personnel service professionals (school counselors, school psychologists, special education teachers, and related services professionals) can and should exert a positive influence on the culture of the school in which they work. We want you to learn how to do so. We want you to become an environmental engineer, student advocate, and social change agent. To this end, we will briefly review research that clearly describes the characteristics of schools that are effective in educating minority, at-risk students. We will identify the challenges associated with building effective schools in the current climate of accountability and high-stakes assessment. We will identify how your school can become more sensitive to and effective at serving the academic, linguistic, cultural, racial, and social needs of a diverse student body. We will illustrate how you can use assessment data for student advocacy. We will present a blueprint for a system to help you assess and influence your school's culture. Finally, within the context of state-wide curriculums and student testing programs we will suggest ways you can restructure your work to accomplish these tasks without burning yourself out.

What Are Effective Schools?

Some schools have reputations for being more effective than others but up until a few years ago such reputations were not supported by educational research. Traditional research, reflected most notably in the 1966 Coleman report, suggested that school-related factors have only minimal effects on students' academic performance and persistence. Socioeconomic factors and family conditions were identified as the primary determinants of academic achievement and socioemotional adjustment. Poor academic performance of low-income and minority children was attributed to poverty, low exposure to books, low need for achievement, and inadequate role models.

Research in the "effective schools" tradition has demonstrated that all schools do not do an equally good job educating at-risk children. The social environment of a school (which often characterizes the school's culture, ethos, or climate) has been linked to its ability to facilitate persistence and achievement. While a student's material circumstances and family conditions do exert a strong predisposing influence of the student's adaptation to school, student achievement is much more likely in some school cultures than in others. The social context of the school is an important determinant of whether or not children will bond to school and achieve.

Ethnic and racial minority students are at risk for underachievement, alienation, and dropping out. We know based on National Assessment of Educational Progress (NAEP) data that there is a large academic achievement gap between African American and Latino students and their White counterparts and that this gap is widening rather than narrowing (Education Trust, 1997). We also know that African Americans and Latinos are less likely to be placed in upper-level math courses than are their White or Asian counterparts (Education Trust, 1997). Likewise, ethnic and racial minority students are over-represented in special education placements, under-represented in gifted and talented programs, under-represented in advanced placement math and science, and over-represented in terms of school suspensions (Education Trust, 1997). At least part of the reason that minority students are at risk results from a basic mismatch between the students' cultures and the school's culture as well as a failure of the school culture to adapt to the students' culture. In order to improve the educational outcomes of at-risk children it will be necessary to address school-culture-related problems as well as social class and family-related issues.

In general there is great consensus on the characteristics of effective schools (see Bickel & Bickel, 1982; Cohen, 1982; Squires, Huitt, & Segars, 1983). Mackenzie (1983) has remarked, "The amount of agreement on the principal factors in school effectiveness is so striking that the question of what is important in school effectiveness may now be less significant than the results." Given the high level of agreement we will present illustrative seminal studies of effectiveness factors rather than present an exhaustive review.

In a seminal case study of four inner-city elementary schools which produced exceptional mastery of reading, Weber (1971) noted several salient commonalities. In these effective schools, school personnel had high expectations of students' capacity to learn, and the schools had an atmosphere of order. Teachers had a high level of concern for each student's learning and conducted frequent careful evaluations of student progress. Strong leadership from administrators was evident in terms of maintaining order and a focus on learning.

Edmonds (1979, 1982) also studied elementary schools serving inner-city, poor, primarily minority children. After controlling for the effects of eleven socioeconomic, community, and family factors, he found that some schools were still more effective than others. In comparison to the less effective schools, the social climate of the effective schools was characterized by: (1) high academic expectations by school personnel; (2) an orderly but nonoppressive atmosphere which is conducive to teaching and learning; (3) clear instructional priorities favoring the acquisition of basic skills; and (4) frequent monitoring of all students' progress. Edmonds also found that strong instructional leadership from (primarily) principals was essential to the creation and maintenance of an appropriate climate.

Rutter, Maugham, Mortimore, Ouston, and Smith's (1979) research on effective secondary schools in England suggests a similar pattern. Schools that were judged to be effective in terms of the highly intercorrelated outcome measures of high student achievement, high attendance rates, and low incidence of social problems were characterized by an "ethos" consisting of high teacher expectations, clear rules for student behavior, effective classroom management practices designed to increase student engagement, frequent success experiences, a genuine concern for student welfare as expressed by the staff's willingness to discuss student's personal problems, and staff consensus on the values and goals of the school.

Sammons (1998) found in an investigation of secondary schools' ability to promote academic achievement that pupil behavior and attendance were problematic in less effective schools. Blair (1999) in a review of United Kingdom effective schools literature found that effective schools were characterized by strong leadership, shared vision and goals, school organization, and high expectations for students. Central to the schools studied was treating students with dignity and respect.

In general, the effective school research suggests that school personnel's beliefs, attitudes, and behaviors interact to create a social environment—a culture—which has a strong influence on student academic achievement and personal adjustment. A poor environment can interact with predisposing conditions (e.g., linguistic and cultural difference, poverty) to produce student disaffection with school and accompanying self-concept and adjustment problems. Improving school culture/environment can lead to improved student bonding to school, increased sense of self-efficacy, increased academic comfort, increased persistence, and better academic performance.

The recipe for an effective school is not complicated. In an effective school, teachers, school counselors, school psychologists, special educators, related services personnel, and administrators believe that all children can learn. They believe in their own capacity to facilitate learning. In an effective school, school personnel structure learning so that all students have successful experiences. There are a few clear rules for student behavior which are fairly and consistently enforced and which are designed to create a good instructional environment. School personnel have achieved a consensus of school values, goals, and policy. School personnel communicate caring for students as people.

Few people would argue with the importance of these factors. Then why don't we have more effective schools? In our experience we do not find that schools are rendered ineffective by a conspiracy of malicious or inept individuals. Most often, schools are rendered ineffective because capable, well-meaning professionals perform their jobs in the context of some unexamined and false assumptions about the causes of underachievement and some unduly pessimistic estimations of the levels of competence of their students, their colleagues, their administrators, and themselves. Overly hierarchical administration and many routine school polices and procedures serve to disempower educational personnel. Even the Effective School Movement seems to buy into this by suggesting that a certain type of principal is necessary for school effectiveness.

We believe that most schools will never be blessed with a leader that is exceptional; but we also believe that top-down leadership is not absolutely necessary for the improvement of school effectiveness. In fact, we will argue that a grassroots movement within a school is more likely to lead to lasting positive change because the process of self-examination is more likely to be collaborative, safe, and empowering. We believe that school counselors must at least participate in this process and are in a good position to lead—because they serve a school-wide clientele and because they are in an excellent position to monitor the academic, social, and emotional development of children.

Finally, we believe that schools must be engaged in a re-examination of some of the basic assumptions that drive public education in the United States. Schools must become more competent in managing rather than minimizing cultural diversity. We believe that it's not sufficient for school personnel to have a consensus on school values if these values are based upon an outdated "melting pot" model of education. Effective schools will communicate respect for individual student differences and value a pluralistic view of education while simultaneously holding students to high standards. The climate of these schools will reflect a deep appreciation of the cultures of students and school personnel; diversity in culture will be seen as an educational resource. However, since the 1980s there has been a decline in research regarding effective schools and bottom-up educational reform. This literature has been replaced by an examination of student, teacher, and school accountability, and by the study of consequences associated with high-stakes assessment.

Environment of Accountability Based on Legislated Educational Reform

In the past ten years the majority of states have adopted rigorous state-wide student assessment systems based upon standard state curricula. The aggressive state-wide educational reform programs that states have implemented include mandated state curriculums, high-stakes educational testing for all students, and accountability reporting systems for students, teachers, and administrators. State policy makers believe that setting high standards of achievement and "raising the bar" will inspire greater effort on the part of students, teachers, and educational administrators and will result in more learning and higher achievement. Many of these state assessment systems are high stakes, meaning that if students fail to achieve there are serious consequences for students and educators. These various high-stakes testing applications are enacted by policymakers with the intention of improving public education. In some states, students are not eligible for their high school diploma unless they pass the state test. School districts can be placed in receivership based on district-wide assessment results. Principals and teachers' pay and continued employment decisions are contingent on their students' test scores. And because the assessment systems are based on state curriculum, schools have no choice but to conform to the prescribed curricular standards.

With any type of testing there is failure by a percentage of those tested. With the high levels of mastery required come high rates of failure. Because the tests are intended to communicate high expectations, all students in the state are required to pass the same tests at the same level of mastery. Few accommodations or modifications are made for students with disabilities or from linguistically diverse backgrounds. These high failure rates serve to marginalize those groups that are already culturally, racially, and linguistically disadvantaged. It is not unusual for middle and upper middle-class districts to do well and for districts with a high percentage of poor students and students from families who do not speak English, even as a second language, to do poorly. For example, it is not uncommon for 80 percent of students to fail a high-stakes high school exit test in the latter districts. In one study by Thurlow and Liu (2000), in 1998 16 percent of LEP students passed the graduation reading exam and 23 percent of LEP students passed the graduation math exam, whereas 68 percent of all students passed the graduation reading exam and 71 percent of all students passed the graduation math exam in Minnesota. Because high-stakes testing begins as early as the fourth grade, students begin to think of themselves as failures very early in their educational experience. Because students who experience failure early tend to drop out of school, the magnitude of the effects of students failing high-stakes assessments is unknown.

We have discussed an approach to improving education from the bottom up. These approaches to educational reform represent top-down efforts, which while well intentioned, may be contrary to grassroots reform efforts and may not be responsive to individual school and student characteristics that affect achievement. As yet, research has not determined how high-stakes assessment systems influence the climate of schools. However, our observations suggest that in many instances high failure rates and punitive measures influence student, parent, and teacher expectations negatively and impede the development of a positive school climate known to foster achievement. Similarly, in an attempt to create a rigorous and standardized curricula, policymakers have intruded into decisions that were once under the jurisdiction of local schools. This leaves administrators, teachers, and parents with the responsibility of determining how these standards will be achieved. A school district cannot opt for a multicultural curriculum unless that curriculum is consistent with the state standard curriculum upon which student promotion and graduation exams are based.

School Issues with Top-Down Reform

In July 2000, the American Educational Research Association adopted a policy statement regarding the use of high-stakes testing (www.aera.net/about/policy/stakes.htm). This position statement is based on the 1999 Standards for Educational and Psychological Testing. The statement is co-sponsored and co-endorsed by the American Psychological Association (APA) and the National Council on Measurement in Education (NCME). This statement is intended as a guide and a caution to policymakers, testing professionals, and test users involved in high-stakes testing programs. It is the position of the AERA that every high-stakes achievement testing program in education should meet a set of rigorous standards (see Box 14.1). The AERA standards clearly

---

BOX **14.1**

AERA Guidelines for High-Stakes Testing

Protection against High-Stakes Decisions Based on a Single Test
Decisions that affect individual students' life chances or educational opportunities should not be made on the basis of test scores alone. Other relevant information should be taken into account to enhance the overall validity of such decisions. As a minimum assurance of fairness, when tests are used as part of making high-stakes decisions for individual students such as promotion to the next grade or high school graduation, students must be afforded multiple opportunities to pass the test. More importantly, when there is credible evidence that a test score may not adequately reflect a student's true proficiency, alternative acceptable means should be provided by which students can demonstrate attainment of the tested standards.

(continued)

B O X **14.1**   *Continued*

Adequate Resources and Opportunity to Learn

When content standards and associated tests are introduced as a reform to change and thereby improve current practice, opportunities to access appropriate materials and re-training consistent with the intended changes should be provided before schools, teachers, or students are sanctioned for failing to meet the new standards. In particular, when testing is used for individual student accountability or certification, students must have had a meaningful opportunity to learn the tested content and cognitive processes. Thus, it must be shown that the tested content has been incorporated into the curriculum, materials, and instruction students are provided before high-stakes consequences are imposed for failing examination.

Validation for Each Separate Intended Use

Tests valid for one use may be invalid for another. Each separate use of a high-stakes test, for individual certification, for school evaluation, for curricular improvement, for increasing student motivation, or for other uses requires a separate evaluation of the strengths and limitations of both the testing program and the test itself.

Full Disclosure of Likely Negative Consequences of High-Stakes Testing Programs

Where credible scientific evidence suggests that a given type of testing program is likely to have negative side effects, test developers and users should make a serious effort to explain these possible effects to policymakers.

Alignment between the Test and the Curriculum

Both the content of the test and the cognitive processes engaged in taking the test should ad-equately represent the curriculum. High-stakes tests should not be limited to that portion of the relevant curriculum that is easiest to measure. When testing is for school accountability or to influence the curriculum, the test should be aligned with the curriculum as set forth in standards documents representing intended goals of instruction. Because high-stakes testing inevitably creates incentives for inappropriate methods of test preparation, multiple test forms should be used or new test forms should be introduced on a regular basis, to avoid a narrowing of the curriculum toward just the content sampled on a particular form.

Validity of Passing Scores and Achievement Levels

When testing programs use specific scores to determine "passing" or to define reporting cat-egories like "proficient," the validity of these specific scores must be established as should how successfully the scores represent test content. To begin with, the purpose and meaning of passing scores or achievement levels must be clearly stated. There is often confusion, for example, among minimum competency levels (traditionally required for grade-to-grade promotion), grade level (traditionally defined as a range of scores around the national aver-age on standardized tests), and "world-class" standards (set at the top of the distribution, any-where from the seventieth to the ninety-ninth percentile). Once the purpose is clearly established, sound and appropriate procedures must be followed in setting passing scores or proficiency levels. Finally, validity evidence must be gathered and reported, consistent with the stated purpose.

B O X **14.1**   *Continued*

Opportunities for Meaningful Remediation for Examinees Who Fail High-Stakes Tests

Examinees who fail a high-stakes test should be provided meaningful opportunities for remediation. Remediation should focus on the knowledge and skills the test is intended to address, not just the test performance itself. Students should have sufficient time before retaking the test to assure that they have studying time with which to remedy any weaknesses discovered.

Appropriate Attention to Language Differences among Examinees

If a student lacks mastery of the language in which a test is given, then that test becomes, in part, a test of language proficiency. Unless a primary purpose of a test is to evaluate language proficiency, it should not be used with students who cannot understand the instructions or the language of the test itself. If English language learners are tested in English, their performance should be interpreted in the light of their language proficiency. Special accommodations for English language learners may be necessary to obtain valid scores.

Appropriate Attention to Students with Disabilities

In testing individuals with disabilities, steps should be taken to ensure that the test score inferences accurately reflect the intended construct rather than any disabilities and their associated characteristics extraneous to the intent of the measurement.

Careful Adherence to Explicit Rules for Determining Which Students Are to be Tested

When schools, districts, or other administrative units are compared to one another or when changes in scores are tracked over time, there must be explicit policies specifying which students are to be tested and under what circumstances students may be exempted from testing. Such policies must be uniformly enforced to assure the validity of score comparisons. In addition, reporting of test score results should accurately portray the percentage of students exempted.

Sufficient Reliability for Each Intended Use

Reliability refers to the accuracy or precision of test scores. It must be shown that scores reported for individuals or for schools are sufficiently accurate to support each intended interpretation. Accuracy should be examined for the scores actually used. For example, information about the reliability of raw scores may not adequately describe the accuracy of percentiles; information about the reliability of school means may be insufficient if scores for subgroups are also used in reaching decisions about schools.

Ongoing Evaluation of Intended and Unintended Effects of High-Stakes Testing

With any high-stakes testing program, ongoing evaluation of both intended and unintended consequences is essential. In most cases, the governmental body that mandates the test should also provide resources for a continuing program of research and for dissemination of research findings concerning both the positive and the negative effects of the testing program.

describe the characteristics of appropriate high-stakes assessment systems. The standards also recognize that high-stakes assessment systems are likely to have unanticipated negative affects on students (e.g., increased dropout-ism, increased absenteeism, lower self-confidence, lower expectations for success) and that these unanticipated consequences must be documented at the state level. At the district and school level the results of assessments need to be used for instructional improvement and the negative effects of high-stakes assessment must be monitored and mitigated.

Many would argue that the development of state curriculums has resulted in fewer opportunities for input from various constituencies. While this is true, teachers still have an opportunity to customize a curriculum for which they have had little or no input in designing. This changes teachers' roles from that of content creators to customizers. Teachers need not abdicate responsibility for pedagogical content, simply becoming someone who delivers what is mandated. Although no known manuals exist that provide suggestions for curriculum modifications necessary to acknowledge cultural differences between schools, opportunities for curriculum adaptations abound. Teachers must be empowered and given the guidance they need to make the necessary curriculum modifications to accommodate the learning needs of all students from varying backgrounds. We suggest that state-wide curriculums are simply a foundation to which information can be added and innovative teaching strategies can be used to convey content.

Even though the curriculum is no longer under the complete control of local school boards, parents still have great opportunity to influence curricular decisions and advocate for culturally sensitive curriculum. Parents and teachers must now collaborate and assert their influence within the context of a prescribed curriculum. This requires a different set of skills for addressing diversity within the confines of a mandated curriculum because of related high-stakes outcome measures holding teachers and parents accountable for their decisions.

The advent of state-wide curriculums and student testing programs has ushered in a new era of accountability for students, teachers, and administrators. With these strides toward education reform, attempts have been made to identify why students are not learning. These reform efforts have asked all those in the learning process to assume responsibility. Students and their parents are responsible for making sure the material taught is learned, while teachers and administrators are responsible for the delivery of the material to be learned. Because of the introduction of accountability systems, it is imperative that each group find ways to make the curriculum material to be learned accessible. Not doing so invites failure for everyone involved. As mentioned in the preceding paragraphs, failure results in teachers and administrators risking loss of job, loss of merit pay, or demotion and in students risking receipt of their diplomas. In this high-risk environment that promotes competition rather than cooperation, it is imperative that all constituencies work together effectively. Paradoxically, this high-pressure environment can result in misplaced or inappropriate assignations of blame by all parties. School counselors have the opportunity to play a crucial role in helping all constituencies collaborate in creative ways to produce positive outcomes that will benefit all those invested in creating a multiculturally effective school environment.

Assessing the Multicultural Effectiveness of Your School

As was mentioned, there are many more filters besides high-stakes testing for gauging the effectiveness, particularly the multicultural effectiveness, of a school. In this section of the chapter we are going to shift your focus to other filters that can be used to assess all components of a school environment that contribute to student achievement in multicultural schools. When done correctly, this process results in data-based advocacy for students. The data are both quantitative and qualitative and reflects the practices, behaviors, expectations, and beliefs that make up the academic climate of multicultural schools.

Assessment as Intervention

We believe that an essential starting point in building a multiculturally effective school is the assessment of the school's present culture. We maintain that this assessment should be "proactive" and not be conducted in a "reactive" fashion. The assessment process itself should help to catalyze change. Assessment is not done before intervention but as a part of intervention.

Hart and Jacobi (1992) have identified the importance of counselors moving from a gatekeeper to a student advocate role. House and Martin (1998) have demonstrated the critical importance of using data to advocate for changes in educational programs. As a first step in this assessment process it is important to gather quantitative data on the academic achievement of different groups of children within your school to establish whether a gap in achievement exists and to provide a baseline against which achievement can be gauged. The Education Trust (2000) has produced a handbook, *The Education Trust Community Data Guide*, that presents a process for collecting data on student retention, dropout rate patterns, teacher preparation, assignments of homework, grades and test performance, absenteeism, special student placements (e.g., gifted, talented, special education, AP math and science placements, suspensions), college prep course enrollment, and standardized achievement test performance. These data are aggregated by ethnic and racial groups and socioeconomic status. The data represent the school's current ability to educate all students across several indicators. The differences between racial/ethnic or socioeconomic groups on any of these variables is a cause for concern and a focus for advocacy.

Once quantitative data are gathered, it is important to collect qualitative data that contribute to the explanation of the quantitative findings. For example, a school, by looking at numerical data, may discover it has a problem with absenteeism. The question then becomes why. Qualitative data will assist in answering such questions. In the following section we describe a qualitative approach to assessing schools' multicultural effectiveness that can be used to help you understand why your school is not educating all children effectively and to help you plan interventions targeted at improving your school.

Because we are presenting new notions about assessment, it would help to contrast them with a more traditional example. Ortiz (1988), for example, developed a checklist for evaluating a school or district's educational environment and its effectiveness for culturally diverse learners. In this procedure, respondents simply answer yes or no to twenty-five statements, such as "My school/district supports cultural pluralism." Checklists such as these are easy to complete and provide the assessor with some basic information. Unfortunately, the information provided does not tell us about the subtleties of what is being studied. We really don't know if different types of respondents (e.g., teachers and students) are approaching the checklist with very different implicit definitions of pluralism. More importantly, the assessment process may or may not help participants learn from each other. The process does not help people dialogue to develop more comprehensive and useful definitions of pluralism, and neither does it help participants develop respect, rapport, and understanding through cooperation on a common task. Assessment procedures that maximize dialogue and create opportunities for participants to learn from each other are more effective, efficient, and appropriate.

Focus of Assessment

There are a variety of ways school personnel can positively and negatively influence the academic and socioemotional development of students. Assessment can be targeted at the classroom, school, and/or district levels. At the most basic level, school personnel's attitudes toward a student's background and language, racial and ethnic attitudes, the nature of communication with students, expectations for student success, and the extent to which they value their students are all strong indicators to the future success of students. At the school-wide level we might also consider looking at the degree to which school personnel are aware of their own cultural background and the degree to which they are able to identify how common school policies, curriculum decisions, and choices about teaching methods are embedded in their own cultural heritage. At the school-wide level the following questions might be asked: Do teachers, administrators, and counselors talk about their own culture heritage? Can they trace how their educational practices are rooted in their heritage? What do they know about the language, world views, histories, values, and material circumstances of the students with which they work? Is the concept of "cultural difference" used in explaining problematic interactions? Can school personnel entertain the notion that students may fail because of cultural differences rather than cultural deficiencies?

Attitudes must then be translated into effective behaviors. Smith (1978) has shown that inquiries into effective multicultural educational programs should consider: (1) how students are praised and rewarded by both White and "minority" teachers; (2) the tone of the teachers' responses to students; (3) to whom teachers direct questions; (4) which students are the targets of teacher nondisapproving talk; (5) the average speaking time of students; and (6) whether curriculum focus exists.

If your state is also engaged in accountability-based, top-down reform, it is also important to assess how the effects of this reform are transmitted through the attitudes, beliefs, and behaviors of the school personnel at the classroom, school, and district levels. For example, it is not uncommon for achievement gaps to exist between the general school population and students from diverse backgrounds. It is important to understand how this achievement gap is understood, managed, and communicated. Every effort must be made to present these accountability discrepancies in a supportive, proactive manner in order to keep all constituencies engaged at each level and working toward the improvement and betterment of student learning outcomes. At the classroom level it is important to assess: (1) the extent to which teachers maintain and communicate to students and parents the high expectations for success in the face of contradictory information from state assessments; (2) the extent to which teachers can maintain a separation between student learning and test performance; and (3) the complexity of teachers' explanations for test-score gaps between their majority and minority children.

First, for example, a teacher may have a group of students from diverse backgrounds that has just failed the state test. Can the teacher communicate to students that they are capable of learning and acquiring the knowledge and skills that they need to eventually pass that test? Does the teacher ignore the results of the state assessment? Does the teacher attribute failure to deficiencies in students, parents, and the cultural group to which the students and parents are affiliated, lower expectations for students on the basis of the state test results, and communicate these lowered expectations in the classroom? Does the teacher understand the factors that contribute to achievement gaps?

Second, at the school level an additional degree of complexity is added. State departments of education and district administrators are responsible for communicating to teachers, counselors, special educators, school psychologists, and parents what is taught, how it is to be taught, and why it is taught. States with state-wide tests have communicated that high achievement on these tests is related to effective schools. Schools must be able to understand the reasons for the discrepancies between actual test performance and desired outcomes. Schools where these discrepancies exist are charged to mobilize the community to develop a plan and implement the steps necessary to improve test scores.

At the district level the focus of assessment is generally on broad-based policy issues and the extent to which community diversity is reflected in policy decisions. To evaluate cultural competence at the district level it would be helpful to know how policymakers ensure that the district's cultural groups are involved in decision making. Examples of these decisions include choices about curriculum (e.g., How shall American history be taught? Which types of career materials will be purchased for which schools?) and allocation of resources (e.g., Will an additional school counselor be hired for an overcrowded building?).

Lastly, how do districts promote characteristics that are unique to their population and simultaneously achieve the goals and objectives mandated by state curriculums and tests? Districts are in a position to ensure that parents are included in curriculum decisions despite the top-down approach to curriculum development and encourage their teachers to make innovative cultural adaptations within the mandated curriculum. For example, does the district have a mechanism by which parents are informed about state curriculum and understand where they can have input in supplementing and enriching the content?

Assessment Procedures

Early on in this chapter we provided you with qualitative methods with which to assess your school's culture and that could be built into your workload for the most part and not burn you out. In this section we will introduce to you a modified version of "multivocal synthesis." According to Ogawa and Malen (1991) a multivocal synthesis "enables [evaluators] to conduct [an] open-ended search for relevant information, identify major patterns associated with the phenomenon of interest, develop and adopt constructs that embrace the patterns, articulate tentative hypotheses about the meanings of the constructs and their relations, and refine questions and/or suggest conceptual perspectives that might serve as fruitful guides for subsequent investigations" (p. 271). Techniques used for conducting a multivocal synthesis include observations, interviews, and document reviews. We will now introduce you to focus groups, field notes and observations, interviews, and the collection of documents and other artifacts. First, we present a case example to which we will frequently refer in our discussion of qualitative methods.

Case Study #1

Marla is a White school counselor in Happy Valley Middle School. Happy Valley is one of three middle schools in Pleasantville—a town of 100,000. Pleasantville is in the midst of a cultural transition. Traditionally it was a White, Irish Catholic, blue collar, factory town. Most of the school personnel are White. In the past ten years there has been a gradual influx of Puerto Rican families. More recently, a small community of Cambodian immigrant families has moved into town.

The principal of Happy Valley Middle School is concerned about students' poor attitudes toward learning and a lack of cooperation from parents. At each grade level, the students are placed in one of four teams (A, B, C, and D). In general, teachers work only within their teams, referring problem students to counselors, with the expectation that counselors will "fix" the students. If students are suspected to need special education, classroom teachers refer them to the school psychologist and a special education teacher. Special education students spend as much time as possible in the classroom and receive services in the resource room only when necessary.

The district has a dropout rate of 70 percent. Three years ago the state implemented a mandated curriculum and assessment system with high stakes tests in fourth, eighth, and tenth grades. The district has performed poorly on the state test with over 75 percent of the children failing.

The school has been identified as "under performing," which means that unless there is marked improvement in test scores the district will be placed in receivership, with the principal being fired. The well-intentioned superintendent wonders why these minority students are having a difficult time adapting to American culture. He's interested in finding ways to help the students and keep his job.

The principal has asked Marla to perform an environmental scan to help him better understand the current school culture so he can work to improve the effectiveness of his school. Based upon data collected according to the *Education Trust Data*

Guide Procedures, Marla found that: (1) the student population is currently 80 percent Puerto Rican, 5 percent Cambodian, 5 percent African American, and 10 percent White; (2) student retention for grades 6, 7, and 8 was below 5 percent for all grades—however, students from linguistically, racially, and ethnically diverse backgrounds made up 87 percent of the 5 percent of the students retained; (3) the student dropout patterns for the middle school were negligible; (4) the number of students enrolling in college prep programs after eighth grade was 28 percent with the majority of students being White; (5) the percentage of teachers teaching out of their certified area and not having a minor in the subject area was 40 percent (math), 20 percent (science), 31 percent (English), and 18 percent (social studies); (6) more than 50 percent of the homework assignments did not meet the curriculum standards and only 25 percent of the teachers assign homework consistently; (7) 46 percent of the population is receiving As while 34 percent of the student population is receiving Ds or lower; (8) there is a 21 percent absenteeism rate on any given day with African Americans and Puerto Ricans making up the majority of those students absent from school; (9) 33 percent of African American, Cambodian, and Puerto Rican students are placed in AP math and science classes, whereas more than 40 percent were placed in special education classes or had been suspended; and (10) 23 percent of parents expect their children to attend college and of that percentage 75 percent are White.

Focus Groups. Focus groups are an efficient and effective way to begin an assessment of school culture. The recommended task sequence for the development of a focus group is: (1) formulate the initial task for the group; (2) select representative participants; (3) facilitate group activities; and (4) summarize and communicate the knowledge and understanding of the group. Many of the skills which you already have in small group leadership are applicable to focus groups.

In collaboration with other Happy Valley pupil personnel professionals and classroom teachers, Marla could form small groups to discuss environmental scan results and/or a specific piece of data that stands out as being significant. Group members would be selected to represent key players (e.g., parents, teachers, counselors, administrators, representatives of the business community, and students where appropriate) and perspectives that will need to be understood and respected. These focus groups could have the initial goal of understanding possible reasons for high failure rates on the eighth-grade state-wide assessment, high absenteeism among African American and Puerto Rican students, differences between minority and majority parental expectations for college, or the differences between minority and majority students placed in AP math and science courses and special education.

Marla should assume the leader role. With most groups, issues of trust will predominate early on. Marla would need to deal with this issue openly—briefly exploring the historical and contextual reasons for any mistrust and securing "good faith" agreements from participants to try to work together.

After the group members have learned to trust each other Marla can then take on the role of group facilitator, redirecting conversation when necessary, taking notes, and writing down observer comments (her interpretation of particular interactions or events). Marla can use these written accounts to organize the group's development of a formal summary of their work. After the initial goal is achieved (in this example the group has identified reasons why majority and minority parents differ on college expectations for their children), the focus group can disband or shift their agenda to what appears to be the next appropriate task (either exploring possible interventions to address college expectations or shifting to a different topic). At this point, the group needs to make a decision about whether or not to share their work with others and, if so, to whom and in what format. The group's next agenda item could be to develop possible explanations of high grade-retention rates based upon their conceptions of cultural differences.

Focus groups are a very efficient way to gather information because the perspectives of members of key groups are immediately present. The focus group is also an intervention; through cooperating in a focus group, participants establish trust and clear lines of communication with each other which will facilitate dealing with myriad issues as they arise in the future. Focus groups begin the process of building a network of people with common interests and a shared understanding of problems.

Field Notes and Observations.   It may seem strange to you to think of yourself as an educational anthropologist in your school. However, careful recording of your observations often leads to powerful new insights. Field notes and observations are very useful tools. They often highlight important characteristics of the environment that are easily overlooked.

For example, Marla could learn a great deal about what teachers believe about homework and why so much of the homework does not address state standards through the careful observation of school personnel interactions in the teachers' room, hallways, faculty meetings, and/or team meetings. Through notes about conversations in the school, Marla can capture how and when teachers assign homework and how teachers evaluate the homework once it is completed, and whether teachers consider the relevance of homework to the state prescribed curriculum.

We advocate that Marla assume the role of participant-observer as this role is more reactive and allows her to look at her own role in influencing school culture. This would mean that her field notes would also include descriptions of what happened after she intentionally introduced new ways of thinking or interacting. For example, it would be interesting to know what happened in the teacher's room after Marla began speaking about her own cultural heritage, how it relates to her expectations about education and work, or her frustration with the school and its district's poor academic achievement record. As she measures the school's culture she changes it. She can see first hand what happens to the system as it's perturbed. How does it resist change? This sort of information will be very valuable if and when more formal interventions are needed.

It is very easy to get overwhelmed by gathering too much information. It is also very easy to lose focus. One way to reduce your work is to have some specific ideas about what you're looking for—reminding yourself that the target is understanding how your school can be made to be more multiculturally effective. It pays to limit yourself, looking at one question at a time. For example, you might want to note anything that happens during your day that reflects what the school community believes are the causes of children's success and failure and the causes of the school's overall low performance. For example, do teachers blame students or do they take responsibility for identifying more effective educational practices?

It's best to record your field notes in a journal and to build a half hour into your day for doing so. Over several weeks you'll start noting patterns and themes. Marla, for example, might learn that many teachers have "given up" because they believe that the real roots of academic failure are in low student motivation and parent apathy. She might observe the operation of "self-fulfilling prophecies"—low teacher expectations contributing to low achievement (e.g., do teachers assign unchallenging homework assignments because they believe minority children cannot and will not do more?). She may also discover alternative explanations for low student achievement—for example, perhaps the school curriculum and homework instruction do not match the standards measured by the state-wide achievement exams. Marla will then be in a good position to alter her group's beliefs in a way that serves the children.

Interviews.   Another way Marla could gather information is through interviews with the key players in the lives of the multiculturally diverse students. Interviews should be free ranging and unstructured, permitting the continual clarification of terms, concepts, and perspectives expressed by the interviewee. As in counseling interviews, you need to be an active listener, and provide the key verbal prompts that will enable interviewees to share their thoughts. The skill in the interview rests in the setting of a comfortable tone, framing the questions openly, and providing adequate wait time for the interviewee to respond. Any desire to respond for the interviewee from your own perspective must be suppressed, yet must be balanced with knowing when and how to help the interviewee, thereby providing a comfort zone. It is often helpful to paraphrase what other interviewees had to say on a particular issue. This helps the interviewee compare perspectives and to "dialogue" with others. Again, assessment is intervention!

In the Happy Valley example, an administrator or teacher may tell Marla that minority parents are actively encouraged to participate in school functions. Marla can then ask the administrator or teacher what the definition of school functions is or what is meant by "actively participate." An administrator may say that school functions are PTA meetings, parent advisory council meetings, parent–teacher conferences, and open houses; whereas a teacher might list activities such as fundraisers, athletic events, and parent volunteer activities (tutoring, office support, library assistance). An administrator may explain to Marla that active support means notes in newsletters sent home, school board endorsements, the provision of organized school functions, and talking with parents when they drop off and pick up their children, whereas a teacher may talk about meeting parents out in the community or talking with them on the phone offering them verbal support, or sending written notes home. Marla may relay to the teachers and administrators that the "minority" parents she interviewed have very different views on how welcome they are at school functions and she may request help in understanding why this difference exists. The interview becomes a way of giving parents a voice that they might not otherwise have.

Artifact Collection.   Collecting educational artifacts is another useful method for learning about effective multicultural education practices. A review of relevant documents (e.g., instructional guidelines and curriculum frameworks from school districts, particularly districts with large numbers of English-language learners) is critical. Seating charts, student work, student records, teacher records, photos of bulletin boards, and sayings and cartoons posted throughout the school are just a few of the many items that will tell you something about how multicultural diversity is incorporated into the school culture.

Marla could collect artifacts for her own use or collect them as part of a group effort. Artifacts could be used as examples of things that promote cultural diversity while at the same time meet the educational goals of the school. Marla, together with the seventh-grade Team A in the Happy Valley Middle School, could review types of instructional strategies used, such as sheltered content area instruction, class-wide peer tutoring (Delquadri, Greenwood, Whorton, Carta, & Hall, 1986), the Stallings (1980) Effective Use of Time, the "tailoring of feedback" used for mathematical problem solving (Cardelle-Elawar, 1990), preteaching of vocabulary (Rousseau, Tam, & Ramnarian, 1993), building background knowledge (Saunders, O'Brien, Lennon, & McLean (1998), and the provision of focused and explicit instruction on math concepts (Henderson & Landesman, 1995).

Pulling It All Together

By using each of the methods discussed and synthesizing the resulting data, it is possible to discover a pattern or theme that could not have emerged otherwise. An example of multivocal synthesis follows: Marla observes a high frequency of oral-language engagement by the students in Team A, but a very low frequency of intellectual (cognitive) engagement. Team A has been using Instructional Conversation (Echevarria, 1995; Goldenberg, 1992–1993) and Cognitive Academic Learning Approach (CALLA; Chamot & O'Malley, 1996), both of which place a high emphasis on student dialogue. Each seventh-grade classroom in Team A appears to highly value oral-language acquisition because it enhances social interactions. However, Marla has reviewed the state-wide assessment achievement results of the students in Team A and notes an 80 percent failure rate. Marla takes the opportunity to meet with Team A. She learns after an in-depth discussion with the teachers that CALLA may have sacrificed academic engagement time in reading in favor of oral language development and self-monitoring activities that were essential to the program. At that point Team A can decide whether they want to deal with the issue knowing that it may have a significant impact on assessment outcomes. This observation may lead Team A to consider shifting the frequency with which students are intellectually engaged in the academic content driving the program.

In this example, Marla used observation, interviews through a modified focus group, and artifact collection to formulate her hypothesis about the assessment outcomes. Any of these methods on their own probably would not have led her to the same hypothesis. This illustrates the importance of synthesizing data obtained using multiple methods. Marla might also have enlisted another school professional, either in her own school or a neighboring school, to act as a peer debriefer. The debriefer would help Marla determine whether her interpretation of the data is valid and would assist Marla with hypotheses development based on her findings.

Conclusions

School culture affects students' academic learning. We know that a positive school culture is important to the socioemotional and academic development of "minority" children. The first steps in improving a school's culture are documenting present practices related to achievement and assessing its present culture. Quantitative methods yield information about a school's ability to effectively educate students from diverse backgrounds and provide a baseline against which improvement can be measured. Qualitative methods provide a richer description of a problem and begin to suggest what might be done. Qualitative methods for assessing multicultural effectiveness are designed to: (1) improve the school's culture through assessment process; (2) reveal contextually rich information; and (3) capitalize on those skills counselors already possess (e.g., interview skills). The methods which we've described can serve as an opportunity to bring people together to share perspectives and to work on common problems for the benefit of all students.

School counselors are in an ideal position to promote the development of effective schools. Counselors are in a position to assess the academic, social, and emotional development of children and have the school-wide perspective that is necessary to assess school culture and a school's multicultural effectiveness. By using quantitative and qualitative assessment procedures, counselors can document the information that is necessary for school improvement. By gathering this information in a participatory manner, counselors are instrumental advocates for change. Counselors have always been effective advocates for individual children. School climate and multicultural effectiveness requires school-level assessments. Counselors must now not only be prepared to advocate for children at the individual level but also must now be able to advocate for change at the school and district levels. This requires that counselors embrace the role as a school reform advocate and develop the additional skills necessary to facilitate that reform.

DISCUSSION QUESTIONS

1. What attributes are used to describe effective schools? What challenges are associated with identifying attributes associated with effective schools?

2. What is the achievement gap and why does it exist?

3. How can school counselors participate in "bottom-up" efforts to improve schools?

4. Identify the major components of educational reform legislation and how has each mandate contributed to outcomes used to measure school accountability?

5. Describe the testing, resource, validation, curriculum alignment, and other issues related to "top-down" reform efforts.

6. What other filters can be used to measure the components of a school environment that contribute to achievement in multicultural schools? Identify the advantages and disadvantages associated with each of these filters.

7. What are the five most important guidelines for using high-stakes assessment systems?

8. What quantitative indicator can be used to measure the multicultural effectiveness of a school?

9. What is multivocal synthesis and why is it important in assessment?

10. The chapter provided a case study and then described multiple methods for gathering data to assess the multicultural effectiveness of a school environment. Describe each of these methods and discuss the relative merits and disadvantages of each method.

11. Think about the school environment in which you are working. As a school counselor, what strategies might you use to develop a team of other school personnel, parents, and students invested in improving the multicultural effectiveness of academic programs?

12. Develop an assessment plan including quantitative and qualitative components for an elementary, middle, or high school.

13. How could you tell if the implementation of a high-stakes assessment system had a negative impact on school climate?

14. What does it mean to say that assessment is intervention?

15. What are the particular advantages of quantitative and qualitative approaches to evaluation of multicultural effectiveness?

REFERENCES

Bicker, W. E. & Bicker, D. D. (1986). Effective schools, and instruction: Implications for special education. *Exceptional Children, 52*, 489–500.

Blair, M. (1999). Successful strategies in multiethnic schools: A summary of recent research. *MCT—Multicultural Teaching, 17*(3), 18–21.

Cardelle-Elawar, M. (1990). Effects of feedback tailored to bilingual students' mathematics needs on verbal problem solving. *Elementary School Journal, 91*, 165–175.

Chamot, A. U. & O'Malley, J. M. (1996). The Cognitive Academic Learning Approach (CALLA): A model for linguistically diverse classrooms. *Elementary School Journal, 96*, 259–274.

Cohen, M. (1982). Effective schools: Accumulating research findings. *American Education, Jan.–Feb.*, 13–16.

Coleman, J. S., Campbell, E., Hobson, C., McPartland, J., Mood, A., Weinfeld, F., & York, R. (1966). *Equality of Educational Opportunity*. Washington, DC: U.S. Government Printing Office.

Delquadri, J., Greenwood, C. R., Whorton, D., Carta, J. J., & Hall, R. V. (1986). Classwide peer tutoring. *Exceptional Children, 52*, 535–542.

Echevarria, J. (1995). Interactive reading instruction: A comparison of proximal and distal effects of Instructional Conversations. *Exceptional Children, 61*, 536–552.

Edmonds, R. R. (1979). Effective schools for the urban poor. *Educational Leadership, 37*, 15–24.

Edmonds, R. R. (1982). Programs for school improvement: An overview. *Educational Leadership, 40*, 4–11.

Goldenberg, C. (1992–1993). Instructional conversations: Promoting comprehension through discussion. *The Reading Teacher, 46*, 316–326.

Hart, P. J. & Jacobi, M. (1992). *From gatekeeper to advocate: Transforming the role of the school counselor*. New York: College Examination Board.

Henderson, R. W. & Landesman, E. W. (1995). Effects of thematically integrated mathematics instruction on students of Mexican descent. *Journal of Educational Research, 88*(5), 290.

House, R. M. & Martin, P. J. (1998). Advocating for better futures for all students: A new vision for school counselors. *Education, 119*, 284–291.

Mackenzie, D. E. (1983). Research in school improvement: An appraisal of some recent trends. *Educational Researcher, 12*, 5–17.

Ogawa, R. T. & Malen, B. (1991). Towards rigor in reviews of multivocal literatures: Applying the exploratory case study method. *Review of Educational Research, 61*, 265–286.

Ortiz, A. A. (1988). Evaluating educational contexts in which language minority students are served. *Bilingual Special Education Newsletter, 7*, 3–4.

Rousseau, M. K., Tam, B. K. Y., & Ramnarian, R. (1993). Increasing reading proficiency of language-minority students with speech and language impairments. *Education and Treatment of Children, 16,* 254–271.

Rutter, M., Maughan, B., Mortimore, P., Ouston, J., & Smith, A. (1979). *Fifteen thousand hours: Secondary schools and their effects on children.* Cambridge, MA: Harvard University Press.

Sammons, P. (1998). Understanding differences in academic effectiveness: Practitioners' views. *School Effectiveness & Improvement, 9,* 286–309.

Saunders, W., O'Brien, G., Lennon, D., & McLean, J. (1998). Making the transition to English literacy successful: Effective strategies for studying literature with transition students. In R. Gersten & R. Jimenez (Eds.), *Effective strategies for teaching language minority students* (pp. 99–132). Belmont, CA: Wadsworth.

Smith, J. (1979). The education of Mexican Americans: Bilingual, bicognitive, or biased. *Teacher Education and Special Education, 2,* 37–48.

Squires, D. A., Huitt, W. C., & Segars, J. K. (1983). *Effective schools and classrooms: A research-based perspective.* Alexandria, VA: Association for Supervision and Curriculum Development.

Stallings, J. (1980). Allocated academic learning time revisited, or beyond time on task. *Educational Leadership, 9*(11), 11–16.

The Education Trust. (1996). *Education watch: The 1997 education trust state and national data book.* Washington, DC: The Education Trust.

The Education Trust. (2000). *The education trust community data guide.* Washington, DC: The Education Trust.

Weber, G. (1971). *Inner-city children can be taught to read: Four successful schools.* CBE Occasional Papers, N. 18. Washington, DC: Council for Basic Education.

AUTHORS' NOTES

John C. Carey is the associate dean for Academic Affairs and associate professor of School Counseling at the University of Massachusetts Amherst School of Education. He is strongly committed to reform in school counseling and school counselor education to ensure that all children in public schools have access to quality education. Carey's research interests are in the development, implementation, and continuous evaluation of effective systems of school counseling practice.

Mary Lynn Boscardin (University of Illinois at Urbana-Champaign, 1984) is director of the Special Education Leadership Training Project, a $620,000 federally funded project through the U.S. Department of Education, dedicated to training graduate students to assume leadership roles in Special Education Administration, and editor of the *Journal of Special Education Leadership*, a journal of the Council for Exceptional Children's Division of the Council of Administrators of Special Education. She is also an ASHA-CCC, SP/L, certified speech and language pathologist. Dr. Boscardin's research interests include special education finance, provision of special education services to students attending Charter Schools, service delivery models for students with disabilities from diverse backgrounds, and curriculum access issues for students with disabilities in inclusive settings as they affect the development and implementation of special education policies. Dr. Boscardin is the author of several research articles, monographs, and book chapters which are the focus of the aforementioned topics. Most recently, Dr. Boscardin has coauthored an edited book, entitled *Learning Disabilities and Life Stories* (2001, Allyn & Bacon). The book is an anthology of stories written by college students who share interesting and poignant autobiographies of what it was like for their parents and them to navigate the educational system with a learning disability paired with scholarly essays by prominent researchers in the fields of learning disabilities, adolescent development, counseling, and diversity.

15 Defining School Counselor Roles in Culture-Centered Education Reform Within the Context of Student Concern Collaboration Teams

ROBERT D. COLBERT
University of Connecticut

MARGE MAGOUIRK COLBERT
University of Massachusetts, Amherst

RUSS VERNON-JONES, LINDA GIANESIN, DEREK SHEA, NIAHSIN KUO, SUSAN KENNEDY MARX, AND ROBYN KONOVITCH
Amherst, Massachusetts Public School District

OBJECTIVES

1. To present a process for incorporating the school counselor education and practice model (presented in Chapter 1) into the ongoing collaborations between school counselors and other staff members

2. To provide a method for integrating single school-building-level activities with those of district-level culture-centered education reform goals, within the context of addressing students concerns

3. To provide a method for examining influences related to student concerns within a multisystemic perspective

4. To provide direction for transitioning from a school counseling program based on a responsive services strategies to one that is based primarily on proactive strategies

The conceptualization of school counselor involvement in culture-centered education reform provides theoretical grounding for the development of new school counselor roles (see Colbert & Magouirk Colbert, Chapter 1). The next step is to develop a more specific delineation of these new roles in a way that makes sense given the realities of school counseling practice. In order to do so, we engaged in a collaborative investigation as university researchers, practicing school counselors, and elementary school teachers, working together as research partners to construct knowledge about school counselor roles. This chapter describes our collective views about application of the framework in the context of day-to-day practice in schools.

The Collaboration

Drawing from concepts in action research (Lewin, 1946) and participatory action research (Freire, 1970), which bring all of the participants into the research and evaluation process from the beginning, school counselors and teachers from three elementary buildings in the Amherst district have been meeting regularly with graduate students and the first author, a school counselor educator. The group has been attempting to define, implement, and evaluate new school counselor roles that emerge from analysis of the schooling process model and frameworks. After several discussions, the group decided to focus on four questions: (1) what situations currently exist in school counselors' day-do-day work roles that are natural beginning points for the implementation of the schooling process model and associated framework?; (2) what would implementation of the model and frameworks look like at the building level?; (3) how do school counselors identify factors that enhance or hinder staff members' collaborative and individual efforts to meet reform goals?; and (4) what kinds of roles allow school counselors to facilitate and monitor aspects of culture-centered education reform? The group was faced with examining these questions in the context of the changes created by the school administrators' attempts to integrate culture-centered education reform within the day-to-day, routinized operation of each school building (see Colbert & Magouirk Colbert, Chapter 1). This chapter describes the groups' ideas and answers related to the first two questions.

Logical Starting Points

School counselors who are attempting change in their roles must do so in the context of their practice which is ongoing, time consuming, and complex. Few school counselors and teachers have the luxury of stopping what they are doing to create and try out something new. Because of this, the general consensus in the investigative group was that any kind of change should be incorporated into already existing situations, meetings, or roles. After identifying as many potential starting points as we could, the group decided to focus on ongoing weekly "Teacher Assistance Team" (TAT) meetings as the ideal, logical place to begin thinking about incorporating change.

For much of the past decade, in each elementary school building in the Amherst Public Schools, the school counselors, teachers, and other staff members have been participating in weekly TAT meetings to discuss and formulate strategies to address concerns about students. These meetings were initially set up by school counselors and other staff members to provide a problem-solving orientation to staff discussions about students and to develop interventions to meet student needs. For a few years, teachers and counselors were satisfied with these TAT meetings. However, as the district's student population changed, it became clear that these meetings were not meeting the full range of issues that students presented.

One original intent of the TAT meetings was to develop early interventions to avert the inappropriate funneling of students into special education. In recent years, some school counselors and teachers have expressed dissatisfaction with the process, stating that they feel it does not adequately address the concerns of many of the district's students of color and those who are from lower socioeconomic groups. In fact, they expressed feelings that the TAT meetings had become an initial referral step into special education for many students. Participants have also been troubled by school district data which document that a disproportionate number of students participating in special education are students of color and/or are from lower socioeconomic brackets.

Some of the counselors in the district still conduct TAT meetings; however, others discontinued them and searched for alternative ways to address student needs. The group of school counselors and teachers who participated in the work described in this chapter work in schools that have an operating TAT and all have noted the need for change in order to better address the increasingly complex needs of the district's diverse population. This identified need for change in the TAT meetings made them a prime place to begin planning, implementing, and researching different strategies. We also felt that the TAT meetings offered a special opportunity for school counselors to help all school staff think about students' needs from new perspectives.

In addition to leading the TAT meetings, school counselors participate in the district-level organizational team (SOT) and the building-level teams (SBT) that have been implemented in the Amherst district within the past two years (see Chapter 1). As part of the SOT, they work with a wide range of school community members to develop a districtwide set of reform goals and objectives. As part of their SBTs, they collaborate to develop, implement, and evaluate strategies for meeting the district reform goals and objectives in their respective schools. Redefinition of the TAT process fits within this larger reform context and could potentially inform the work of the other teams.

Designing Building Level Implementation

Once the group had identified a logical starting point, we began discussing and negotiating answers to our second question, What would implementation of the model and frameworks look like at the building level? We agreed that we needed to narrow the complex, seemingly overwhelming, ideas proposed by the schooling process model.

To do so, we decided to limit our focus to the process of the TAT meetings and work to define steps that could actually be carried out by school counselors and teachers in those meetings.

The group agreed to hold as its central focus two of the three necessary transitions for school counselors outlined in Chapter 1. We wanted to try to create a way for teachers and school counselors to make the shift from focus on service delivery to individual students, their families, or a small subgroup of students, to focus on whole-school concerns. Most often in the past decade of TAT meetings, the intervention strategies fell within the traditional frame of problems being primarily "in the student" with little or no focus on the possible contributions from the schooling process. In order to make the shift, the group felt that school counselors and other TAT members would need a method to determine the relationships between concerns about individual students and whole-school concerns.

The second transition for school counselors that we advocated was from a primarily responsive service orientation to school counseling partnerships that are proactive and developmental. The group felt that this would be a change that is hard to accomplish because responsive services have been, and might likely continue to be, a primary mode of intervention developed in the TAT meetings.

The group also felt, however, that specific methods could be developed to guide the transition from a responsive service strategy to one that is proactive. For example, if TAT members spent time identifying school practices and/or processes that might be contributing to a student's problems or difficulties, they then could develop interventions aimed at these practices. In this way, the TAT meetings could become more proactive by eliminating sources of potential problems for many students. Both transitions were consistent with the district's overall education reform plan. Our efforts were focused on developing a process that could be researched through action research, would facilitate the transitions identified above, and would be realistic to implement.

The Process

The process outlined in this section was designed primarily so that school counselors and others could address student concerns in a manner consistent with the district's education reform goals and strategies. Drawing on the information presented in Chapter 1 we knew that the process must incorporate a way to view student concerns from a multisystemic perspective, "one that applies systems principles to interactions among different levels of a system and across different systems" (Keys & Lockhart, 1999). We agreed that each component of a system has influence on, and is influenced by, other components of that system (Bochner & Eisenberg, 1987; Minuchin, 1974) and that all processes and events should be considered within the context of the entire system and its reciprocal interactions within the environment (Katz & Kahn, 1978). The group highlighted the importance of considering the interrelatedness of each component within the context of the total system, and across different systems.

Previously, the TAT meetings were primarily designed to focus on only the student or family—only one component in the total system. In reconceptualizing the process, we extended the focus to include teacher factors and school/district structures and operating processes. The group's challenge was to create a way to incorporate the two new components within the actual TAT meetings. A structured process emerged from our dialogues. The process consists of the following three stages: preview, analysis and strategy development, and review and follow-up.

Preview.   The preview stage begins the assessment phase of the TAT process and consists of information gathering, data collection, and reflection. The purpose of this stage is to clarify the TAT situation from the teacher and student's perspectives. Teachers who will be presenting student concerns at an upcoming TAT meeting first prepare by completing the following:

1. Describe what it is that you want the student to do that the student is not currently doing.
2. Describe this student's strengths.
3. Describe the parts of the educational program in which this student is not successful.
4. List any relevant background information and/or test scores.
5. Describe the interventions that have been tried.

Preparing for meetings in this manner helps teachers formulate their thoughts beforehand and serves to facilitate communication and discussion.

In a similar manner, the school counselor prepares for the TAT meeting by gathering information relevant to the question, How does this student see himself/herself as a learner? Each counselor addresses this question in a manner consistent with the counselor's own theoretical perspective(s). For example, one counselor in the group bases her work on Glasser's (1998) Choice Theory. According to Glasser, students must attempt to gain certain perceptions of school learning in order for learning to occur. This school counselor would strive to gain a clear understanding of the student's perception of herself or himself as a learner and a member of the school community. This counselor gathers information to assess the perceptual match between the student and teacher (Glasser, 1998), or looks at opportunities for choice in the student's educational life.

The preview steps were enhanced and emphasized in order to make the TAT meetings more time efficient. Teachers and school counselors using the preview process come prepared so that they can use the meetings to present the information they have gathered, which results in a more complete picture of the teacher's concerns. Once the TAT situation has been clarified, the discussion moves on to the second step of the process, which begins with the analysis of other possible influential components.

Analysis of Other Components.   The next stage of the process rests first on a more in-depth analysis of the TAT situation and its relationship to other components in the system. The group decided that Colbert's (1998) Triadic Consultation Analysis (TCA) would be a useful tool for this stage. The TCA was developed to provide direction for school counselors as they attempt to gather information and form a database in order to facilitate consultative interventions related to student educational development.

Using the TCA, the TAT members would examine student-related factors, teacher-related factors, and school- and district-related factors as outlined in Figure 15.1.

The team looks at information related to each of the three factors first in isolation, as if each were separate from the others, asking How is the information regarding this factor related to the TAT situation? Secondly, the team looks at the three factors combined, striving to determine how the various factors are related and how they are related to the TAT situation at hand.

Examining information in this way prepares a team to develop intervention strategies that go beyond individual child, responsive, and "Bandaid" interventions. Usually the teams brainstorm strategies first and then select those that seem to be the most appropriate starting points and most likely to succeed. They may decide to intervene at a first-order or second-order change level. The team may design interventions related to the student, the teacher, and the school/district level. As this model is more widely implemented in the district, we expect multifactor or multilevel interventions to become more common.

In strategy planning, it is very important that team members be clear and specific about who will do what by when. Once intervention strategies are planned and implemented, it is very important to collect data and reflect on the efficacy of the strategies. Implementers must keep data and notes on their intervention

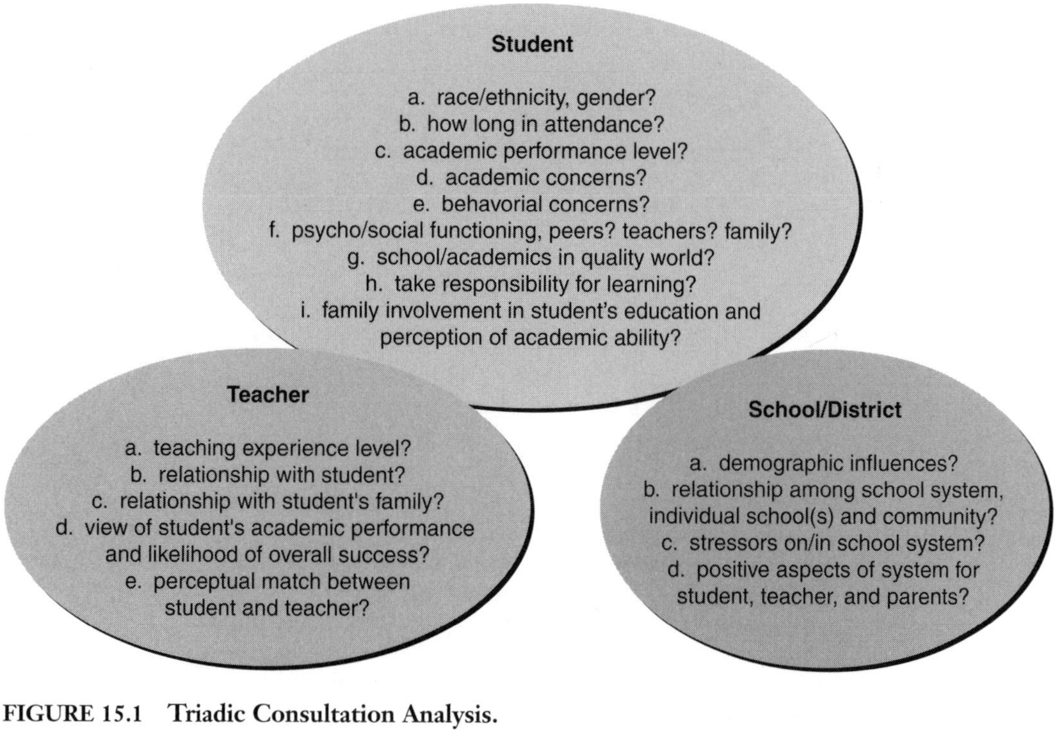

Student

a. race/ethnicity, gender?
b. how long in attendance?
c. academic performance level?
d. academic concerns?
e. behavorial concerns?
f. psycho/social functioning, peers? teachers? family?
g. school/academics in quality world?
h. take responsibility for learning?
i. family involvement in student's education and perception of academic ability?

Teacher

a. teaching experience level?
b. relationship with student?
c. relationship with student's family?
d. view of student's academic performance and likelihood of overall success?
e. perceptual match between student and teacher?

School/District

a. demographic influences?
b. relationship among school system, individual school(s) and community?
c. stressors on/in school system?
d. positive aspects of system for student, teacher, and parents?

FIGURE 15.1   Triadic Consultation Analysis.

attempts so that modifications can be made if necessary and to inform future strategy development.

Review and Follow-up. TAT members set aside time at each weekly meeting to get updates, review data, and reflect on the status of the intervention strategies being implemented. Such reflection can help the team decide whether or not their strategies are working, which need modification, and which need to be ended. Ongoing follow-ups are important so that changes can be maintained in the context of the district's changes due to education reform.

At first glance, carrying out this process may seem impossible or hard to envision. For that reason, the research group spent time applying the process to several current TAT cases that were being presented by teachers. One such case that illustrates how the process might look in a real situation is informative and is described in the next section.

Case Study #1
In this case study, a teacher presented information concerning a sixth-grade student in a TAT meeting. There were about nine weeks left in the school year.

Teacher's Preparation
1. Describe what it is that you want the student to do that s/he is not currently doing.
   a. "I want Sally to increase her academic performance effort."
   b. "I want Sally to stay more on task during her academic classroom assignments."
   c. "I want Sally to engage with friends for social purposes at appropriate times."
2. Describe this student's strengths.
   a. "I think that Sally's biggest strength is the amount of effort that she will put out for her academic assignments when she wants to."
   b. "Sally not only gets along well with the other students, I would say that she is very popular."
   c. "Sally is a very strong art student; her drawings are magnificent!"
   d. "Sally is a very engaging person; she can carry on an exceptionally mature conversation, both one-on-one and in groups."
3. Describe the parts of the educational program in which this student is not being successful.
   a. "Sally will sit and work on her classroom assignment for just a few minutes."
   b. "The biggest challenge now for Sally is how will she complete enough of her academic assignments to get back to the level she worked so hard to maintain for most of the school year."
4. List any relevant background information and/or test scores.
   a. "Sally is Latina."
   b. "The middle school and high school are attempting to open up more rigorous courses to minority students."
   c. "There is exceptional family support for Sally's education."
   d. "I have a very good relationship with Sally and her parents."
5. Describe the interventions that have been tried.
   a. "I have developed homework contracts with Sally, which have involved both parents and the school counselor."

b. "I moved Sally's desk up close to mine."
c. "I tried talking with her."

School Counselor's Preparation
1. How does this student see herself as a learner?
    a. "Sally stated that she likes to come to school; however, it appears that she constantly compares herself to other, 'smarter' students. In these comparisons, Sally does not fare well most of the time."

Analysis of the Three Education Reform-Related Factors
The TAT team proceeded with the notion that the concerns stated by the teacher do not reside solely in the individual student. First, they examined the three TCA focal areas, the student-related factors, the teacher factors, and school/district factors. They reflected on and discussed their perceptions, noted the themes and relationships that emerged from their analysis of each of the factors in isolation, began to develop hypotheses relative to the emergent themes, and modified their themes and hypotheses according to insights they gained as they moved from viewing the factors in isolation to discussing the interrelatedness of the factors and Sally's teacher's concerns.

Student's Perspective of Self as a Learner and other Student Factors
First, the team considered factors associated with the student (see Fig. 15.1). In this situation, Sally

a. was Latina/female;
b. had been attending the school for several years;
c. usually performed C-level work, but her academic performance had dropped off drastically;
d. was not completing assignments and might be at risk for failure during the next school year;
e. was having difficulty valuing various aspects of school academics as relevant to her and as meeting her needs (see Glasser's (1998) concept of "quality world");
f. was socializing with classmates when she was supposed to be working on assignments;
g. was experiencing strained relationships with her family and teachers; and
h. had very involved parents, who saw Sally as bright within the home environment and able to contribute to various problem-solving tasks within a team approach.

One primary theme that emerged was the apparent discrepancy between the home and school regarding learning. The fact that Sally was able to demonstrate academic type behaviors in the home environment indicated that she indeed had a view of herself as a learner. She did not, however, at the time of the TAT meeting, seem to be applying her ability to learn in the home environment to the school environment. Sally had been able to transfer her perceptions of learning to the school environment previously, therefore the TAT team hypothesized that there must be something within the school environment contributing to her current status. The team further hypothesized that the problem was related to the comparisons that Sally was making between herself and other students which usually did not end up putting her in a positive light.

Teacher Factors
Next, in considering the teacher factors (see Fig. 15.1), the team found that this teacher

a. had a Master's degree;
b. had ten years of teaching experience;
c. had a very good relationship with the student, although at that time, it was strained;
d. had a very good relationship with the student's family;
e. perceived the student as a very diligent worker, yet was very concerned that student was not maintaining her usual academic efforts and would be at risk for academic failure in middle school the following year; and
f. had different perceptions than the student regarding learning, in that the teacher was striving for all students to learn, while Sally was primarily seeking perceptions of friendship or belonging.

School/District Structures and Operating Process Factors
The final area for the team's analysis was that of the school/district (see Fig. 15.1). Factors pertaining to the school in this situation included

a. a wide range of families differing in socioeconomic status and race/ethnicity in the district/school;
b. the district had enjoyed a very positive relationship with the general community although that relationship was strained because of competing views for how all students should be educated;
c. the district had instituted the system-level "Becoming a Multicultural School System Initiative" to ensure that all students, inclusively, were educated equitably. This initiative became a stressor for many educators and parents in terms of how to meet these multicultural goals, particularly regarding the elimination of academic tracking in the secondary schools that placed disproportionate numbers of students of color and those from lower socioeconomic groups in basic and standard-level courses, compared to their middle-class counterparts who were placed primarily in advanced-level courses; and
d. in general (and on a surface level), teachers, parents, and students believed that the school climate was conducive to a high-quality education experience. The primary theme the team noted in this area was that the greater school district was involved in adjusting to the major transitions of school reform and changing demographics. The team was interested in understanding effects of the larger system's stress at the individual building level. Not only was the district trying to become a multicultural district, it was struggling to cope with the stress of the recent addition of the Massachusetts Comprehensive Assessment System (MCAS), a statewide, high-stakes test required for high school graduation. The team hypothesized that this combination of stressors was influencing the classroom environment and wondered if this was related to Sally's teacher's concerns.

Interrelationship of Factors
Given that the district was under scrutiny in terms of curriculum content, instructional pedagogy, student placement for academic tracking, and the like, the team knew that

many teachers felt as though their classroom instruction was being closely observed and questioned. The team believed that this scrutiny could lead to increased teacher stress, especially in cases where the teacher felt as though students in their classrooms were not learning, "as they should." The team hypothesized that, in this case example, the teacher felt slightly distressed about the changes in the student's behaviors, thus the TAT presentation of the case.

The most striking information for the team was that the teacher perceived the student to be a negative influence on her ability to be a good teacher. Drawing on choice theory (Glasser, 1998), the team hypothesized that some attention to how the teacher viewed teaching and sought satisfaction in it and how the student viewed learning and sought satisfaction in it was needed. They wondered how the team might help the teacher and student to interact from complementary perceptions regarding teaching, learning, and meeting their respective needs.

TAT Intervention Strategies

The TAT team hypotheses and data formed the basis for the intervention strategies that the team formulated. The strategies were developed within the context of a comprehensive developmental school counseling program. The intervention strategies included the following program component activities: (a) student assessment; (b) consultation; (c) classroom guidance; (d) home–school communications; and (e) placement and follow-up.

Student Assessment

The first point of intervention was further assessment with Sally by the school counselor for the purpose of gaining a sense of whether her psychological needs were being met within the context of school. Sally stated that she felt a strong sense of connecting with friends at school as well as outside of school. Also, Sally's perspective on other psychological needs assessed by the counselor was similar to the school counselor's first impressions presented in the TAT meeting.

Consultation

Secondly, the school counselor consulted with Sally's teacher regarding her perceptions of Sally's psychological needs. The teacher, while very supportive of students' psychological needs being met in school, was not aware of the importance of some of Sally's needs for power, freedom, and fun (Glasser, 1998). The teacher was aware of students' needs for belonging and worked to help all her students feel a sense of belonging in her classroom. The teacher and school counselor agreed that the notion of better meeting all students' psychological needs in school was critical to the overall success of the school's culture-centered reform agenda, and that further discussion with other TAT members might be helpful.

Home–School Communications

The next intervention strategy was that of consulting with Sally's parents. The school counselor, teacher, and Sally agreed that it was important for her parents to be informed of what was occurring at school on Sally's educational behalf. Thus, the school counselor met with both parents and shared the teacher's concerns raised at the TAT meeting as well as the school counseling program follow-up interventions.

The counselor engaged the parents in a discussion of how the school could better meet their daughter's needs. In sharing their knowledge about how Sally meets her psychological needs at home, the parents offered insight into how school staff might proceed to meet her needs within the context of school. For example, at home, Sally and other children often participate in decision making regarding meals, activities, and the like, all of which are related to the need for freedom. In regard to power, the parents stated that at home Sally gains a great deal of her sense of "I can" from problem-solving situations. For instance, in planning out a family trip, the parents include the children by posing questions regarding how much money they will need to budget for gasoline and food. Sally's parents shared that Sally is quite good at figuring out such problems, especially in the context of each person being assigned a specific role and task. The school counselor took this information back to the TAT team and teacher, and worked to incorporate some of the same responsibilities into the classroom for Sally.

Classroom Guidance

The developmental-guidance academic and career domains relevant to this case were Academic Development Standard A (Campbell & Dahir, 1997) with the related student competencies of improving academic self-concept, acquiring skills for improving learning, and achieving school success. In addition, the Career Development Standard A (Campbell & Dahir, 1997) with student competencies pertaining to the development of career awareness were implicated. The school counselor in collaboration with Sally's teacher decided that a classroom guidance unit on self-identity (Paisley & Hubbard, 1994) would provide Sally and other students with experiences that could improve their academic self-concepts.

In order to continue integrating intervention strategies, the school counselor and Sally's teacher agreed that the teacher be included in the classroom guidance unit. This allowed the teacher to learn about each of her students' academic self-concepts. The teacher then developed a complementary classroom cooperative learning unit that integrated aspects from each student's academic self-concept needs. Within this unit, Sally was given a decision-making and fact-finding role, which was consistent with what she did at home in meeting her needs. This resulted in Sally being able to draw upon her strengths in a new context, participate in a new way in academic lessons in school, and maintained her sense of belonging with friends in on-task ways.

In addition, school counselors at both elementary and middle school levels began work on implementing career development strategies for Standard A (Campbell & Dahir, 1997). By implementing these school counseling program strategies, students in elementary school would, early in their schooling, begin to make connections between schoolwork and career-related information. Specifically for Sally, her desire to become an athlete in college and professionally could become connected with academics so that her own motivation could be tapped, increasing the probability that she would succeed in more rigorous academic courses.

Review and Follow-up

The TAT members received follow-up reports from the school counselor and teacher regarding the efficacy of the strategies. During one of the follow-up TAT meetings, Sally's teacher stated that Sally had shared information that shed light on all three of the teacher's concerns. In particular, the concern that she might be at risk for academic failure in middle school was explained by Sally when she stated that she was afraid to go to middle school because she would hardly ever see her friends because most of them were White and they would be placed in "smart classes" and that she would be placed in the "dumb classes." The district was attempting to eliminate its academic tracking system; however, in most subjects, some tracking was still apparent and obviously known to the district's students.

The TAT team decided that they should look further into working with the middle school staff to help Sally with gaining more rigorous academic experiences after leaving elementary school. The members thought that they needed more evidence to present to their middle school colleagues, so they worked with the school counselor to conduct a survey of all sixth-grade students regarding their concerns about middle school. The results indicated that the overwhelming majority of sixth graders were concerned with whether they would remember their locker combinations, how to move from class to class, and about interactions with older kids. There was a small percentage of students who were also concerned about being placed in classes where they would feel dumb. Ninety-three percent of these respondents were students of color or students from lower socioeconomic level families.

The TAT members decided that the survey results should be shared with the school's culture-centered education reform team (SBT). The SBT saw the results as clearly critical to the school and district reform goals—particularly, a goal that related to all students, regardless of race or SES, achieving at high academic levels. The district had set an objective for meeting this goal which was to create "bridges" between elementary, middle, and high school in order to establish and maintain high academic achievement for all students. It was decided that the survey information should be shared with the district-level culture-centered education reform team (SOT).

At the SOT meeting, representatives from all schools and levels were in attendance, including at least one school counselor. Upon hearing the survey results, the SOT developed strategies for attending to these concerns. First, the team decided to work toward structural change in the middle school related to the selection and to offering rigorous academic courses to all students and secondly, to provide staff development and other learning experiences for school personnel so that all will perceive that all students are capable of meeting rigorous academic challenges.

Discussion

This chapter describes one aspect of a "work in progress," the ongoing work of our research group. We are currently involved in the implementation of these ideas in the Amherst school district, conducting action research, and refining and modifying our approach, ideas, hypotheses, and processes. While much research needs to be done, our work so far has shown us that identifiable aspects of school counselors' day-to-day work roles provide logical starting points for beginning change.

While this particular school district chose the TAT process, other districts might focus on different, already existing operating structures, meetings, or forums. In most schools there are numerous routine situations where school counselors collaborate with other staff members. School counselors can tap these collaborative groups to begin developing ideas about how culture-centered education reform might look in their unique school situation. Our account of the direction our work took may be helpful to others who are beginning work with a similar focus.

In response to our second question—What would implementation of the model look like in reality?—the research group tackled implementation by focusing on one subcontext in each building and by defining a process. The group continues working to make the process more efficient through applying it in TAT meetings. We are learning many important lessons. For example, our beginning implementation alerted us to the fact that it is very important to ensure that all people who are involved in the process are trained so that they become cognizant of and take responsibility for incorporating the expanded focal factors into the process.

We found out that the TAT members need to learn about the schooling process model and frameworks and how they tie into the larger district's culture-centered education reform goals (see Chapter 1, Colbert & Magouirk Colbert). They need to understand the necessary concepts, how to use the TCA as a tool, and the school counselor's theoretical perspective. Such training allows for the school counselor to step out of a sole leadership role in the TAT meetings and creates the opportunity for shared leadership.

The process we have developed holds promise for providing school counselors and others a structured way to make the necessary transitions from a student-only focus to a whole-school-concerns focus, and increase school counselors' ability to implement proactive strategies in the context of their ongoing work. The TAT process demonstrated how school counselors, in collaboration with others, can intervene in ways that might initially fall into the program component of responsive services (i.e., the teacher's concerns with Sally) and proceed in a fashion that leads to proactive strategy implementation. This bridging between responsive service activities to proactive strategies occurred at the individual classroom, individual building, and districtwide levels.

We anticipate that our experiences and research will provide future direction for other educators who are attempting to implement complex changes in school counselor roles. In addition, we encourage others to take risks, experiment with the model and frameworks, develop their own processes, conduct action research, document, and share what is learned. In the end, our combined efforts can serve to enhance educational experiences for all students.

DISCUSSION QUESTIONS

1. If you could interview anyone at any level in a school district that is trying to eliminate the academic achievement gap among student groups, what questions would you ask and why?

2. Choose any aspect of culture-centered education reform as defined in Chapter 1 and define a set of goals and a rationale for making it a districtwide policy.

3. Identify at least three reasons that school personnel might give to explain why the district should not implement the culture-centered education reform goals stated in question #2.

4. Let's further imagine that you're a school counselor in the district that has to implement the goals you identified in question #2 and that the district has a central and building-level committee like the

one discussed in Chapter 1. Develop a rationale as to why implementing the kind of TAT process (discussed in this chapter) would be helpful.

5. Discuss the importance of culture-centered education reform goals being reflected in the daily routine activities of school staff members.

6. Based on your experience in any particular school district, discuss what you think would happen were the goals that you identified in question #2 mandated to be integrated into the daily roles of staff members at the single building level. What might teachers, counselors, principals. and parents say, think, feel, etc.?

7. Observe a student concern-focused meeting (ideally pertaining to a minority student) and make note of the perspective(s) taken for defining the problem. Pretend that you are one of the team members that you observed, and borrowing from the TAT process presented in this chapter, discuss what you might add to the meeting.

8. Interview school staff members about a student concern and gather information pertaining to the information in the three concentric circles in Figure 15.1. (Student information area "g" and teacher area "d" are based on Choice Theory. When using a different theoretical perspective, please develop information consistent with that particular theory.)

9. Apply the modified TAT process described in this chapter and assess the student concern presented in question #8.

10. Based on your assessment (question #8), identify a school counseling program intervention that could be developed and implemented to address the student concern.

11. Explain whether the intervention identified in question #10 would be first- and/or second-order change.

12. For each intervention identified in question #10, discuss steps that could be taken to transition to a proactive strategy. What could you do to prevent the problem from reoccurring?

REFERENCES

Bochner, A. & Eisenberg, E. (1987). Family process: System perspectives. In C. Berger & S. Chaffee (Eds.), *Handbook of communication science* (pp. 540–563). Newberry Park, CA: Sage.

Campbell, C. A. & Dahir, C. A. (1997). *The national standards for school counseling programs*. Alexandria, VA: American School Counseling Association.

Colbert, R. D. (1998). The triadic consultation analysis: School counselors promoting educational development. *The Journal for the Professional Counselor, 13*(1), 7–17.

Colbert, R. D. & Magouirk Colbert, M. (2002). Defining school counselor roles in culture-centered education reform within the context of student concern collaboration teams. In P. Pedersen & J. Carey (Eds.), *Multicultural counseling in schools: A Practical handbook* (2nd ed.). Boston, MA: Allyn & Bacon.

Freire, P. (1970). *Pedagogy of the oppressed*. New York: Continuum.

Glasser, W. (1998). *Choice theory: A new psychology of personal freedom*. New York: Harper Perennial.

Katz, D. & Kahn, R. L. (1978). *The social psychology of organization*. New York: Wiley.

Keys, S. G. & Lockhart, E. J. (1999). The school counselor's role in facilitating multisystemic change. *Professional School Counseling, 3*(2), 101–107.

Lewin, K. (1946). Action research and minority problems. *Journal of Social Issues, 2*, 34–46.

Minuchin, S. (1974). *Families and family therapy*. Cambridge, MA: Harvard University Press.

Paisley, P. O. & Hubbard, G. T. (1994). *Developmental school counseling programs: From theory to practice*. Alexandria, VA: American Counseling Association.

AUTHORS' NOTES

Our deepest and most sincere appreciation goes to the teachers in the Amherst Public Schools for allowing us the opportunity to observe and study their Teacher Assistance Team meetings. We would also like to thank the School Counseling graduate students at the University of Massachusetts, Amherst, for being open minded and adventuresome, for without their sustained efforts in this new area, many of the ideas in this chapter would not have emerged. In particular, we would like to thank graduate students Kelynne Bisbee, Michael Smith, and Jennifer Stavely for assisting with the presentation of many of the ideas expressed in this chapter before a national audience.

Robert D. Colbert is an assistant professor at the University of Connecticut, Neag School of Education, Department of Educational Psychology, and Counseling Psychology Program. Colbert's primary scholarly interests are research-based school counselor practice in culture-centered education reform and the application of an ecological perspective to the consultation process. Colbert is an active member of state and national counseling associations. He recently served on the Governing Board of the Massachusetts School Counselor Association, the Professionalization Committee of the American Counseling Association, and the Editorial Board of *Professional School Counseling*.

Marge Magouirk Colbert teaches in the Department of Teacher Education and Curriculum Studies at the University of Massachusetts at Amherst. Her work focuses on education reform models and the redesign of teacher and counselor education programs. Current research involves case studies of fourteen school districts that are restructuring around Career Pathways models and the development of alternative supervision models for teacher education.

INDEX